T0259672

# Samsung ARTIK Reference

## The Definitive Developers Guide

Cliff Wootton

Apress®

*Samsung ARTIK Reference*

Cliff Wootton
Crowborough, East sussex, United kingdom

ISBN-13 (pbk): 978-1-4842-2321-5        ISBN-13 (electronic): 978-1-4842-2322-2
DOI 10.1007/978-1-4842-2322-2

Library of Congress Control Number: 2016956942

Managing Director: Welmoed Spahr
Lead Editor: Jonathan Gennick
Technical Reviewer: Fred Patton
Editorial Board: Steve Anglin, Pramila Balan, Laura Berendson, Aaron Black, Louise Corrigan, Jonathan Gennick, Todd Green, Robert Hutchinson, Celestin Suresh John, Nikhil Karkal, James Markham, Susan McDermott, Matthew Moodie, Natalie Pao, Gwenan Spearing
Coordinating Editor: Jill Balzano
Copy Editor: Mary Behr
Compositor: SPi Global
Indexer: SPi Global
Artist: SPi Global

Distributed to the book trade worldwide by Springer Science+Business Media New York, 233 Spring Street, 6th Floor, New York, NY 10013. Phone 1-800-SPRINGER, fax (201) 348-4505, e-mail orders-ny@springer-sbm.com, or visit www.springer.com. Apress Media, LLC is a California LLC and the sole member (owner) is Springer Science + Business Media Finance Inc (SSBM Finance Inc). SSBM Finance Inc is a **Delaware** corporation.

For information on translations, please e-mail rights@apress.com, or visit www.apress.com.

Apress and friends of ED books may be purchased in bulk for academic, corporate, or promotional use. eBook versions and licenses are also available for most titles. For more information, reference our Special Bulk Sales–eBook Licensing web page at www.apress.com/bulk-sales.

Any source code or other supplementary materials referenced by the author in this text are available to readers at www.apress.com. For detailed information about how to locate your book's source code, go to www.apress.com/source-code/. Readers can also access source code at SpringerLink in the Supplementary Material section for each chapter.

Printed on acid-free paper

*To Annie Parker*
*Mum, you have always inspired me to do my best.*

# Contents at a Glance

# Contents

# About the Author

**Cliff Wootton** is an award-winning former Interactive TV systems architect at the BBC, specializing in Interactive TV, content management systems and digital video playout with commodity hardware. Previously invited as a guest speaker on pre-processing for video compression at the Apple WWDC developer conference, he has also taught about the IoT, real-world computing with Arduino, video compression, metadata, and how to build multimedia art installations in an MA course at the University of the Arts, London. Cliff now concentrates on research and development projects; building digital media tools for creating audiovisual content; multimedia; electronic book publishing; writing; teaching; and playing the bass guitar.

# Acknowledgments

Huge thanks are due to the following people who created resources online and contributed ideas and practical help while I was writing this book. Their assistance was truly invaluable and is gratefully acknowledged.

- Jill Balzano and Jonathan Gennick at Apress for two projects in one year! Amazing. Great times, as always.

- Glenn Cameron at Samsung, who provided prototype hardware and technical resources.

- Fred Patton at Samsung for his excellent photographic contributions once again, for wrangling the ARTIK blogs, and for helping out with the technical review process.

- Kevin Sharp for his helpful contributions to the ARTIK blog.

- Robert Nelson for contributing extremely helpful online advice on how to build a new OS for ARTIK modules.

- All the artik.io Forum posters whose questions inspired me to cover interesting topics.

- Gaynor Bromley at Panasonic Electric Works UK Ltd for the AXT connector images.

# Introduction

You are no longer a beginner in the Samsung ARTIK community. It is time to flex your coding muscles and extend your skills by trying out more advanced techniques.

The companion book, *Beginning Samsung ARTIK - A Guide for Developers*, focused on getting you started. That book concentrated on helping you get your development systems up and running, and showing you how to use the tools.

This reference book builds on what you learned earlier and takes you deeper into the ARTIK world. The narrative is not designed to be a linear reading experience. Reference books need to help you find things in a random fashion when you need them.

A lot of material in here was gathered by inspection and reverse engineering, coupled with the analysis of the schematic diagrams for the developer reference boards. I have presented this information in tables that are designed to help you as you design and build your own products. The coverage on the Samsung developer web site is an excellent introduction; if you read that information first, this book builds on what you find there and describes the foundations that underpin that material. The online sources of reference that I found are also described here for you to study.

The posts in the discussion forum suggested topics that readers would like to know more about. These posts inspired both books. The fruits of my own forensic research for *Beginning Samsung ARTIK* and further experimentation are distilled into this book to help you find what you need and quickly move on to more advanced things.

Things do not stand still for very long in the Samsung ARTIK world, and just as I was drawing things to a close, more new developer resources were released. I have incorporated as much of that new material as I can. Keep a close watch on the Samsung developer web site for more new material because there are still many new and exciting things to come.

*—Cliff Wootton*
*Crowborough UK*
*Summer 2016*

# CHAPTER 1

■ ■■ ■

# Learning More About ARTIK

It is time to start stage two of your ARTIK journey. By now, you should have a working ARTIK development system up and running, and you should have explored the hardware and software. You are ready to move on to more complex challenges and develop a totally awesome and amazing project. If you don't have your system up and running yet, take a look at the companion book, *Beginning Samsung ARTIK*, for help in getting started.

This reference book uses the ARTIK command line environment and the GCC compiler to illustrate coding examples. Your terminal emulator should be set up and your serial connection working so you can interact with your ARTIK module. If you have access across your Local Area Network (LAN), you can use `telnet`. Experienced UNIX developers will feel at home in this environment. The command line environment is a powerful tool and it can seem daunting at first. It has a varied and useful collection of small tools and utilities. Each command does one thing very well. You can learn about them one by one. They are all easy to understand when looked at individually. The power comes from the way you combine the commands together to create processing workflows. The learning process is much easier than you might think.

To fully understand your ARTIK, you must be conversant with the developer reference board circuit schematics, U-Boot, the kernel, and operating system internals. Then you can begin to work with the peripheral interfaces such as GPIO and I2C. To get the whole picture, aggregate the knowledge from all of these resources with what you see by inspection. This is not a trivial task but if you tackle it step by step, it is possible to learn things quickly and it can be enjoyable as you become more adept.

## Change and Evolution

The Samsung Developer Conference 2016 (SDC) introduced a lot of useful new technologies to help you with your ARTIK projects. There are more new things to come. Keeping up with the changes is a challenge in itself.

**Model numbers** that describe each different type of ARTIK have changed to accommodate potential future additions to the range. For now, the Commercial Beta of the ARTIK 5 is a Model 520 and the ARTIK 10 is a Model 1020. Updated versions of the ARTIK modules will use variations of that naming convention. The ARTIK modules are usually described as an ARTIK 5 or ARTIK 10 to distinguish between the two currently available products unless it makes sense to describe version-specific details.

**ARTIK Cloud** is the new name for the SAMI infrastructure that was documented in *Beginning Samsung ARTIK*. Because this forms such a crucial part of the IoT ecosystem, it has been adopted as part of the ARTIK product family. If you are using the first edition of *Beginning Samsung ARTIK* to help you get started, where you see SAMI mentioned, do a global search-and-replace in your mind to convert that to ARTIK Cloud. Read about developing for ARTIK Cloud at the Samsung developer web site at `https://developer.artik.cloud/`.

---

**Electronic supplementary material**  The online version of this chapter (doi:10.1007/978-1-4842-2322-2_1) contains supplementary material, which is available to authorized users.

The **ARTIK IDE** is a specially designed development environment for creating and debugging applications for your ARTIK. It is based on the Eclipse CHE platform and it supports local and remote debugging. Consider the ARTIK IDE as an alternative to installing Eclipse and a cross-compiling toolchain as it might offer some advantages. Samsung will release more documentation for it as it becomes ready for deployment. Read about the CHE tools at the Eclipse web site at www.eclipse.org/che/artik/.

**IoTivity** is an IoT open source integration platform maintained by the Linux Foundation as a library to download and use in your own projects. It is designed to help you communicate from device to device. Find out more at the IoTivity web site at www.iotivity.org/.

The **Resin•io** system provides tools for updating your IoT systems remotely over the air. This can be a challenging problem to solve if you have to develop your own solution. Find out more at the Resin•io web site at https://resin.io/.

The SDC 2016 developer presentations and tutorials will all be made available on the developer web site in due course. There is also a YouTube channel that represents the developer support services. Reach the samsung_dev home page to access the video resources via one of these routes:

www.youtube.com/results?search_query=samsung_dev
www.youtube.com/user/SMInnov8

More recently, the ARTIK OS source code has been released under an open source license. There are also new, up-to-date, and complete data sheets for the ARTIK model 520 and 1020 modules that describe all of the hardware characteristics.

The open source components used in the ARTIK operating system will change. These all contribute to a gradual evolution and improvement of the ARTIK. These changes often happen without any fanfare. They are only discovered when they affect the development process or when something breaks as a consequence. Table 1-1 summarizes the potential areas you should expect to change and the possible consequences for technologies aside from the development work that the Samsung engineering team is working on.

***Table 1-1.*** *Changes and Consequences*

| Component | Consequences |
|---|---|
| Kernel | The kernel is maintained independently of the OS. There is a lot of work being done on the inside plumbing. Expect changes to sysfs, procfs, runfs, and udevfs as various driver items are moved around. Where appropriate, any expected changes are mentioned in this book when they may affect what you do. There are many components of the kernel that are maintained as separate projects. The IIO interface for analog inputs is a typical example. |
| Fedora OS | Fedora has been upgraded from version 20 in the Alpha ARTIK modules to version 22 in the Commercial Beta modules. The current developer open source code version of Fedora is somewhat more advanced than that. One of the later revisions will become the dominant version when the ARTIK OS is upgraded. |
| yum vs. dnf | One consequence of the latest upgrade is that the yum installer in the ARTIK module has been completely replaced by a new command called dnf. The yum command is no longer available. The dnf command is upwards compatible with yum but adds many new features. This was covered in *Beginning Samsung ARTIK* but to clarify things further, dnf is now always used inside the ARTIK module for installing packages directly there. On your development workstation, the installer depends on the version and revision of Linux. Your installer there may be dnf, yum, rpm, or apt_get. Be sure that you distinguish between commands you execute on the ARTIK command line and others that are only appropriate on your developer workstation command line. |
| Yocto | Changes to Yocto are generally benign and are concerned with making the OS build easier to manage. |

*(continued)*

***Table 1-1.*** *(continued)*

| Component | Consequences |
| --- | --- |
| U-Boot | U-Boot has been stable for a long time; fundamental changes to how it works are rare. |
| ALSA | The audio tools revolve around the ALSA project and the mPlayer application. These are likely to be stable until the industry develops new technologies for audio systems. The I2S support for digital audio is very mature and not prone to changes. |
| Video4Linux | The video processing uses Video4Linux, which is moving forward as new TV formats are deployed to the broadcast industry. Most new work is with 4K video; on the horizon, 8K video may start to become popular from 2020 onwards. Video coding has used the H.264 standard for some years. That is well-supported by the ffmpeg tool, which is actively maintained as an open source project. The newer HEVC codecs will be more useful as the 4K video format is taken up by the industry. Upgrades to the MIPI standards will affect the V4L source code as they are incorporated. |

Topics that were addressed in *Beginning Samsung ARTIK* are covered in more detail in this book. For example, hardware debugging with the JTAG port driven from a Segger J-Link was suggested as a way forward in *Beginning Samsung ARTIK*. In Chapter 14, that topic is revisited in much more depth to cover scan chains and recommended configurations of the debugger for diagnosing applications running in multiple cores. It is also possible to run several debug sessions simultaneously when you have factored your application into several separate processes.

Peripheral devices are dealt with in much greater detail and all the inner workings are discussed for GPIO, I2C, I2S, IIO, and SPI. Each interface has a chapter devoted entirely to the inner workings.

# Your Journey Through This Book

The programming examples in this book are more sophisticated than the ones in *Beginning Samsung ARTIK*. They are designed to help you build and maintain reusable code libraries of your own to avoid reinventing the wheel every time you start a new project. Where *Beginning Samsung ARTIK* was designed to be a coherent narrative that took you step by step through the setup process, this reference guide is designed for random access to in-depth coverage of the topics. However, if you do want to read the whole book, the content is organized in a logical way, and each chapter builds on the earlier ones.

The first few chapters talk about the platform internals to help you construct a robust mental map of where everything is. It is essential to get to know the territory before you go on a quest for individual API components. Some of the topics that were addressed more simplistically in *Beginning Samsung ARTIK* are expanded in this book.

Understanding how the kernel builds the virtual file systems and maps the hardware devices to them is valuable knowledge. You can then choose the right approach for developing an application to interface with GPIO pins or I2C-driven sensors.

Topics dealt with in this book are occasionally quite deep and complex. I have tried to break them down into small and easily digested pieces. This makes it easier to assimilate the knowledge. As you read through the chapters, new concepts are revealed one by one.

Please do not be daunted by the complexity and scope of the technology inside the ARTIK. The development process becomes easier as you become more familiar with the technology, and the time devoted to understanding the internals of your ARTIK is well spent.

# Samsung Developer Resources

Following SDC 2016, the previously available developer documentation has been updated with new material, and the Downloads page has new items added from time to time. June 2016 saw the release of the source code for the ARTIK OS and the ARTIK 10 modules via a Git repository. New firmware for the OS in the ARTIK 5 and 10 arrived also, and the developer documentation was updated with a lot of new material for users interested in using audio and video on their ARTIK projects.

The Samsung developer resources are organized into several categories. The documentation takes you through a straightforward getting-started process. This is useful if you are using a Windows workstation; there is some useful material for Linux users, too. For Linux and the Apple Macintosh development workstations, consult the companion book *Beginning Samsung ARTIK* for additional material.

The online developer guide provides some basic instruction on accessing GPIO pins. This is backed up here with code examples. Chapter 17 illustrates the GPIO internals in some detail. Check out the Samsung developer support channel on YouTube for video tutorials and presentations. Third-party material is available at the hackster•io web site or on the Instructables blog. Access more resources via these links:

```
https://developer.artik.io/overview
https://developer.artik.io/documentation/
https://developer.artik.io/documentation/getting-started-beta/
https://developer.artik.io/documentation/developer-guide/
https://developer.artik.io/documentation/tutorials/
https://developer.artik.io/documentation/tutorials/color-mqtt-client.html
www.hackster.io/
www.instructables.com/
www.youtube.com/channel/UC4rolvSm8ikmnymdbbznNJw
```

# Samsung Developer Downloads

Check the Samsung developer downloads page from time to time. Useful resources to help your development process are added when the Samsung engineers release new features. Look out for new firmware downloads to install. Installing new firmware wipes out anything that you previously installed in your ARTIK module, including any configuration or experimental applications you might have written and compiled there. Make sure that anything important to you is documented and backed up before installing new firmware. The following is the link to the Downloads page. Sign in with your Samsung developer account to reach it.

```
https://developer.artik.io/downloads
```

Getting copies of everything on the Downloads page should be a routine activity; once a month you should check to see if there is anything new. Collect an archive of older versions to track the evolution of the ARTIK family and to be able to revert back to an earlier configuration if necessary. Download these items and read them for useful coverage of your ARTIK internals:

- Developer board schematics (Type 5 and Type 10)

- Data sheets (ARTIK models 520 and 1020)

- Software developers guide (not yet released as of July 2016)

# ARTIK OS Source Code

Now that the Commercial Beta ARTIK 1020 has been released, the new downloadable developer resources also include Git repositories where the source code for the ARTIK OS is maintained. Check this web page regularly to see if new components have been introduced at the head of the Samsung ARTIK code repository: https://github.com/SamsungARTIK. Table 1-2 describes the items that have been released.

*Table 1-2. ARTIK Git Source Code Repositories*

| Component | Description |
| --- | --- |
| build-artik | This code helps to create an ARTIK SD Fuse image. This is loaded onto a micro SD card to install new software into the eMMC memory of your ARTIK. Due to the long build time of a Fedora operating system image, the root file system is provided by a pre-built binary. Download it from the server during the build process. The binary image of the Fedora OS is built as a separate process. |
| fedora-spin-kickstarts | Creates an ARTIK Fedora root file system. The ARTIK Fedora OS is based on Fedora 22 ARM version and is customized for ARTIK 5 and 10 modules. |
| initrd-artik | Initial boot time RAM disk source for ARTIK 5 and 10. It recovers the eMMC partitions from the micro SD card Fuse image. |
| linux-artik | Linux kernel source for ARTIK 5 and 10. The base kernel version of ARTIK is Linux version 3.10.93 and is conditionally compiled as the Samsung Exynos kernel. |
| u-boot-artik | This is the U-Boot source for ARTIK 5 and 10. It is based on the Samsung Exynos U-Boot variant. |
| slate | The Slate API documents generator helps you create beautiful, intelligent, responsive API documentation. |
| artik-discourse | Discourse is a discussion platform built for the next decade of the Internet. It works as a mailing list, discussion forum, or a long-form chat room. |
| heroku-buildpack-nodejs-grunt | This is a slightly modified version of the official Heroku buildpack for Node.js applications with added support for the Grunt notification system. |
| nginx-buildpack | Runs the NGINX web delivery platform on your application server that runs Heroku. |
| heroku-buildpack-webpack | This is a Heroku buildpack for web applications that use webpack. |
| heroku-buildpack-php | The official PHP buildpack for Heroku. |

The following are the links for the repositories containing ARTIK OS components that have already been released. Put them into your Git client tools to map them into your workspace and replicate the repository into your developer workstation to have a copy of the source code to work on:

```
https://github.com/SamsungARTIK/build-artik
https://github.com/SamsungARTIK/fedora-spin-kickstarts
https://github.com/SamsungARTIK/initrd-artik
https://github.com/SamsungARTIK/linux-artik
https://github.com/SamsungARTIK/u-boot-artik
```

The following repositories contain useful utilities to help you manage your development process; they are not part of the canonical ARTIK OS source kit:

```
https://github.com/SamsungARTIK/slate
https://github.com/SamsungARTIK/artik-discourse
```

The following repositories are part of the Heroku cloud platform support and are versions that are compatible with the ARTIK OS. Use them to enhance your ARTIK when you are experimenting with cloud based architectural designs:

```
https://github.com/SamsungARTIK/heroku-buildpack-nodejs-grunt
https://github.com/SamsungARTIK/nginx-buildpack
https://github.com/SamsungARTIK/heroku-buildpack-webpack
https://github.com/SamsungARTIK/heroku-buildpack-php
```

# Samsung Developer Blog

Keep current with the new technical information that Samsung publishes on the Samsung Developer Blog. All of the Samsung ARTIK developer blog articles have been reorganized. The ARTIK Cloud, ARTIK Module, and ARTIK Generic materials are all sensibly gathered together in one place. Each category is color coded to help you navigate the collection. These blogs include press releases, partner profiles, 101 tutorials, and example projects. Many offer useful links to other helpful resources. This is a magnificent job and it is well managed by Fred Patton and the ARTIK team at the Samsung Strategy and Innovation Centre.

Sign up to receive the newsletter mailings, which alert you to important announcements. It may be useful to capture a PDF copy of the blog articles to read offline but bear in mind that the copy is not updated automatically if something changes. Read the Samsung ARTIK developer blog at www.artik.io/blog/.

# Samsung Developer Forums

There is a lot of useful help at the Samsung Developer Forum. If there is a problem that many users trip over, it is very likely that another developer will have posted a question on the forum. If they haven't, post one yourself. There is a great community spirit; people are ready to help when fellow developers run into difficulties.

Some questions do not have a definitive answer, such as ones about technology that is not yet implemented. I found it helpful to survey the Samsung ARTIK Developer Forum for questions that ARTIK developers wanted help with because I knew that those questions would make great topics for inclusion in these Apress books. Check out the Samsung ARTIK developer forum at https://developer.artik.io/forums/.

# Get Your Samsung Developer Account Now

The developer resources for the ARTIK hardware and the ARTIK Cloud data exchange are only accessible to you when you are logged on with a developer account, so sign up for one! Then start developing code for your ARTIK module right away. The sign up process is straightforward and easy to follow. Go to www.artik. io/developer/users/auth/samsung.

Once you have signed up, log in with your new ARTIK developer account and explore the resources that Samsung prepared for you. Having a developer account is not the same as having a Samsung user account registered for use with your smartphone. Register for both kinds of account. Use a different password for each one and do not use those passwords for anything else to protect yourself against identity theft. Join a wider Samsung developers group by signing up for a Samsung developer account at http://developer. samsung.com/signup.

This gives you access to SDK libraries for a range of Samsung technologies, including the ARTIK family. See http://developer.samsung.com/sdk-and-tools.

# An Even Quicker Start

In *Beginning Samsung ARTIK*, the **Quick Start** example got things going right away. Assuming you now have your system up and running, try the following example, which introduces you to the file system inside your ARTIK. If your system is not yet up and running, put this book to one side, work through the steps in *Beginning Samsung ARTIK*, and then come back here when it is all working.

1. Open a new session with your terminal emulator, connect to the ARTIK, and log in when it has booted.

2. Go to the temporary files directory.

    cd /tmp

3. Use the vi editor to create a file called file_reader.c:

    vi file_reader.c

4. Switch to insert mode by pressing the upper case letter [**I**] key and type this code into the editor:

```
#include <stdio.h>

int main()
{
  FILE *fp;
  char str[60];

  /* open a file for reading */
  fp = fopen("/etc/fedora-release" , "r");

  if(fp == NULL)
  {
    perror("Error opening file");
    return(-1);
  }
  if( fgets (str, 60, fp)!= NULL )
  {
    /* write the file content to stdout */
    puts(str);
  }
  fclose(fp);

  return(0);
}
```

5. Type these keystrokes to exit from vi and save the changes to disk:

    [**Escape**] [**:**] [**w**] [**q**] [**Return**]

6. Now compile the source code with GCC:

    gcc -Wall file_reader.c -o file_reader

7. Run your compiled program with this command:

   `./file_reader`

8. The text "`Fedora release 22 (Twenty Two)`" should be echoed on the screen. If your ARTIK operating system has been updated, a different version number will be displayed.

Congratulations! You just built and ran a native application in your ARTIK module. Your application interacted with the file system to read the operating system version.

# CHAPTER 2

# Hardware

The ARTIK module family spans a huge range of capabilities. The ARTIK 1020 is a hugely powerful, media-processing–capable, eight-core computer with a lot of onboard capabilities and many interfacing possibilities due to the range of I/O processors integrated with the CPU. For less challenging computational needs, the ARTIK 520 has media processing playback capabilities but also has a generous complement of inputs and outputs. Many features are engineered and implemented in a similar way on each of the ARTIK modules. This helps you develop code that you can reuse on multiple projects running on different hardware.

## The ARTIK Family

The Samsung ARTIK is all about versatility. Samsung describes it as "The Ultimate Platform Solution for IoT." Providing the computing power of a UNIX workstation in a form factor as compact as the ARTIK modules will revolutionize the way that smartness is engineered into products. With computing power delivered as a commodity, the ARTIK can make everything smarter.

The Samsung ARTIK platform is designed to jump-start your development of products that exploit the diverse potential of what is becoming known as the Internet of Things (IoT). This is a structured way for all kinds of devices from tiny wearable items to entire homes and factories to communicate with each other and adjust their behavior to accommodate real-time changes in their interactions with humans and other systems.

The ARTIK modules are only possible due to the prior success of mobile phone technology. As phones have become smarter and smaller, the integration of memory and computing power into ever-smaller packages can be leveraged to create a general-purpose computer in a very compact form. The further reduction in device sizes results in technologies such as the ARTIK modules. As these modules become increasingly popular, the economies of scale reduce the unit cost and they can be deployed everywhere.

The following are the key differentiating features of the ARTIK modules, taken from the Samsung promotional literature:

- Complete module lineup

    - Pre-certified modules with processors, memory, connectivity, and sensors

    - Best power, form factor, and performance

    - Software compatibility across the family

- Leveraging Samsung economies of scale in quality manufacturing

    - Samsung chips, memory, and processors

    - Unique ePoP packaging

    - Exploits Samsung's manufacturing expertise and branding

© Cliff Wootton 2016
C. Wootton, *Samsung ARTIK Reference*, DOI 10.1007/978-1-4842-2322-2_2

- Best-in-class end-to-end security and privacy
  - Advanced security
  - Embedded hardware-based secure element
  - Trusted Execution Environment (TEE)
  - True random number generator
  - Crypto accelerator
  - Secure memory for keys
- Hybrid cloud solution
  - Local and distributed open cloud intelligence
  - Data storage
  - Analytics
- Ecosystem
  - Strong developer community
  - Best-in-class partners across the value chain
- Production-ready hardware
- Broad range of connectivity
- Advanced software support
  - Open source
  - Software development kits
  - Increased developer productivity

# Provenance

This book is based on the Commercial Beta revision of the ARTIK hardware. If you are still working with prototype Alpha or Early Beta hardware, upgrading to the latest available production model ARTIK module is a good idea. Doing so will ensure a trouble-free development process going forward, and any future software upgrades are more likely to be compatible with your prototyping system. Table 2-1 summarizes the versions of the ARTIK already released to the public.

***Table 2-1.*** *ARTIK Version Number History*

| Version | Description |
|---------|-------------|
| 0.1.0 | Pioneer edition available in limited numbers when ARTIK was first announced |
| 0.2.0 | Alpha development prototypes |
| 0.3.0 | Early Beta development prototypes |
| 0.3.1 | Updated Beta development prototypes |
| 0.3.2 | Updated Beta development prototypes |
| 0.5.0 | Commercial Beta prototypes. At launch, ARTIK 520 and 1020 modules are this version. |

The currently shipping model is an ARTIK 520 or 1020 module at version 0.5.0. This is what Samsung describe as a Commercial Beta product. The Samsung ARTIK is still at an early phase of its product lifecycle. Many aspects will evolve and change over the next few years. Table 2-2 describes the features of the Commercial Beta ARTIK 520 and 1020 modules based on the current developer documentation. Basic video support is present in the June 2016 operating system upgrades running on the ARTIK 1020.

***Table 2-2.*** *Commercial Beta Features*

| Beta Features | ARTIK 520 | ARTIK 1020 |
|---------------|-----------|------------|
| Ethernet | External SPI | External USB |
| Bluetooth | √ | √ |
| Bluetooth LE | √ | √ |
| ZigBee | √ | √ |
| USB device mode | 2.0 | 2.0/3.0 |
| USB host mode | n/a | 2.0/3.0 |
| SD card | √ | √ |
| Speaker/microphone | √ | √ |
| Video output | n/a | HDMI |
| Video input | n/a | MIPI |
| GPIO analog read | 2 Channels | 6 Channels |
| GPIO analog write | √ | √ |
| GPIO digital read | √ | √ |
| GPIO digital write | √ | √ |

■ **Note** If you are still working with pre 0.5.0 Commercial Beta development systems, be aware of some differences from the developer boards that were released to early adopters. The PWM0 and PWM1 have been exchanged so the pin numbers are different. Also the hardware I/O headers have moved to better accommodate Arduino shields. On very early development systems, the HIGH and LOW values on GPIO pins were reversed.

# Choose the Right Model

Choose an appropriate ARTIK module based on what you are trying to accomplish. Samsung has alternative configurations with different feature sets and computing power. The ARTIK modules run embedded UNIX operating systems and accept a variety of input/output sensors and controls to operate other equipment or systems. Remote operation is possible because the ARTIK modules are equipped with wireless communications so they can collaborate with one another or via a secure cloud connected ecosystem. The ARTIK modules in Figure 2-1 are shown at the same scale to compare the sizes. The internal layout of the ARTIK 520 module is visible because the protective outer shielding has been removed.

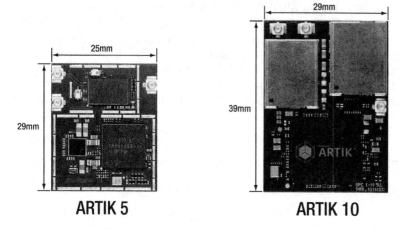

**ARTIK 5**     **ARTIK 10**

*Figure 2-1.* *Comparing the ARTIK modules*

# Introducing the ARTIK 520

The smaller module is called the ARTIK model 520 (as of July 2016). This module has dual ARM CPU cores. This is powerful enough to create a home media player attached directly to a video monitor. This creates opportunities to build digital signage systems that can talk to one another and potentially alter their behavior when somebody approaches while wearing a compatible device. An ARTIK 520 could take over significant responsibilities in running a wired home or a manufacturing process with the status display being generated onboard and presented on a view screen.

The ARTIK 520 has fast and capable CPU cores. The module is carefully screened against radio frequency interference (RFI) to avoid interfering with nearby equipment. There are several wireless connection options, plus support for the ZigBee protocol, which is gaining popularity in wired home installations.

The 25mm x 29mm form factor is a significant achievement when you consider the capabilities that Samsung has accommodated in this device. It has a versatile array of multimedia support, analog and digital input/output, and peripheral interconnect buses.

The ARTIK 520 module also supports the Samsung Secure Element protocols that afford robust protection against hacking at the module level. Integrate your distributed systems so they can collaborate by connecting them together via the ARTIK Cloud-based protocols.

The ARTIK module shown in Figure 2-2 can decode a variety of video playback formats through its integral hardware codecs and present the output directly on an attached video monitor. The ARTIK 520 is well suited for building smart home hubs, high-end smart watches, drone flight controllers, and embedded IP-based camera management systems.

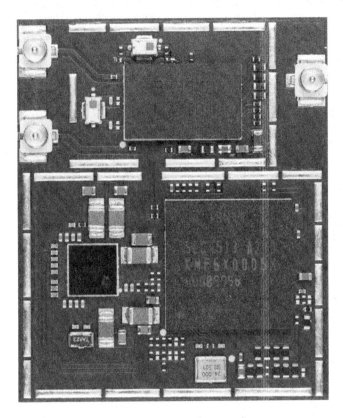

**Figure 2-2.** *The ARTIK 520 module (top view)*

Find out more about the ARTIK 520 from the Samsung developer documentation. Read the data sheet for the ARTIK model 520 and examine the Type 5 developer reference board schematics. Together, they will answer many of your questions about how the ARTIK works; see `www.artik.io/modules/overview/artik-5/` for more details.

# General Arrangement

Figure 2-3 shows a layout of the components on an ARTIK 520. The three Panasonic AXT connectors are on the underside of the module but their position is shown in this top view. Use this image file as a starting point for adding some layout markup to the screen-printed artwork for your own circuit boards. Do not take measurements from this diagram because it was rotoscoped from a photograph and any positions of items are merely for guidance.

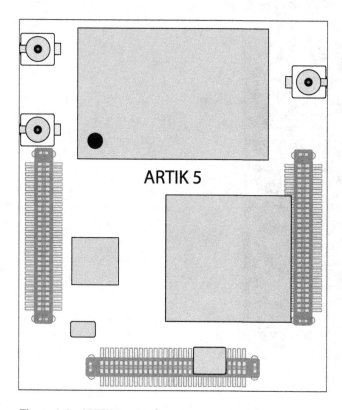

***Figure 2-3.*** *ARTIK 5 general arrangement*

# Functional Organization

A simplified functional breakdown of the ARTIK 5 module is shown in Figure 2-4. This diagram shows the important subsystems inside an ARTIK 5.

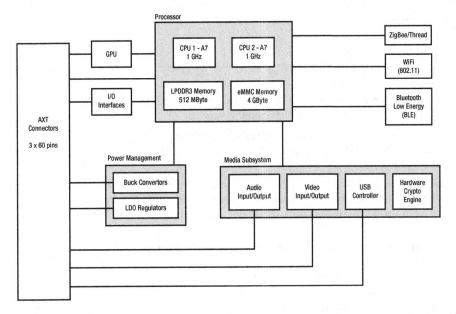

***Figure 2-4.*** *The ARTIK 520 module block diagram*

The various connectivity and interfacing technologies are covered in detail in later chapters and are summarized in Table 2-3.

***Table 2-3.*** *ARTIK 520 Connectivity Cross-Reference*

| Topic | See also |
| --- | --- |
| Panasonic AXT connectors | Chapter 13 describes the pinouts for the ARTIK 520 connectors (J3, J4, and J7) |
| GPIO | Digital switching and sensing is managed via the GPIO interface. Refer to Chapter 17 for more details. |
| I2C | Some sensor devices are connected via I2C bus interfaces. These are described in Chapter 20. |
| Analog input | The analog input circuits and their ADC conversion to a digital value are covered in Chapter 18. |
| PWM output | The pseudo analog PWM outputs are described in Chapter 19 |
| SPI | The SPI interface is only partially implemented at present. Details of how it works are covered in Chapter 21. |
| Audio | The audio capabilities are covered in Chapter 22. |
| Video | The Video4Linux support is not yet complete. Examine the online resources and the connectors in the schematic diagrams to understand how it works. See Chapter 23 for more details. |
| USB | The ARTIK 520 supports USB 2.0 connections in device mode. |

## Known Firmware Versions

Table 2-4 lists the publicly available firmware versions that have been released for the ARTIK 520 via the Samsung Developer Downloads page. Only download new firmware from a trustworthy source such as the Samsung Developer Downloads page to ensure you have an authoritative copy. You must be signed on with your developer account to reach the Downloads page and access the resources at `www.artik.io/developer/downloads`.

***Table 2-4.*** *ARTIK 5 Firmware Release History*

| Date | Notes |
| --- | --- |
| 2015-10-17 | Only use this on Alpha boards. It's Alpha firmware built with Yocto from Fedora 20. Ethernet driver support is unavailable on this version. |
| 2015-11-09 | Only use this on 0.3 version (Beta) boards. It's Beta firmware built with Yocto from Fedora 22. It adds support for Ethernet interface, analog write, and I2C device access. The Temboo library is not available on this version. |
| 2015-12-09 | This is the image delivered on the ARTIK 520 modules shipped with the Version 0.5 (Commercial Beta) developer boards. It is based on Fedora 22. This image may be flashed to Ver. 3.2 (early Beta) boards. Do not use this image with Ver. 3.0 or 3.1 (early Beta) boards. |
| 2016-01-21 | Revised firmware released for the ARTIK 520 as the ARTIK 1020 Commercial Beta units start to ship. |

# Introducing the ARTIK 1020

The most capable module is called the ARTIK model 1020 (as of July 2016). This has significantly more compute capacity with a pair of quad ARM CPU cores and assistive hardware co-processors for video coding/decoding, graphics rendering, and a very large number of versatile input/output connections. This could operate as a centralized server or high-powered media ingest engine.

The ARTIK 1020 shown in Figure 2-5 is the most capable and powerful of all the modules in this family. It has more of everything compared with the ARTIK 520. In terms of computing capacity it has eight CPU cores in all. There are many more connector outputs and it can handle a higher quality HD video output or encoding throughput. This would make a very capable starting point for building TV set-top boxes with interactive TV capabilities. It is probably powerful enough to create a home Intranet server or media hub for a digital entertainment system. If you delegate more of the hard work to a centralized ARTIK 1020, use ARTIK 520 modules in your client players instead of deploying more ARTIK 1020 modules. If you construct a home Intranet around an ARTIK 1020, it could also provide a personal cloud integration for all the devices around the home and then gateway access to the Internet via a single interface. If an ARTIK 5 is not powerful enough for your needs, an ARTIK 1020 is certainly up to the task of managing the throughput for all kinds of smart machines.

The 29mm x 39mm form factor is astonishing when you consider this is a fully featured UNIX computer with high-definition video encode/decode capabilities integrated into the ARTIK module. This ARTIK can decode a variety of video playback formats and present the output directly on an attached video monitor.

This module is powerful enough to live encode incoming video for onward delivery to a media storage system. This opens up possibilities for use in security monitoring and personal video recorder products. It could also find applications in the broadcast industry for building master control and file-based edit/storage systems.

The ARTIK 1020 module also supports the Samsung Secure Element protocols that afford robust protection against hacking at the module level. Integrate your distributed systems via the ARTIK Cloud-based protocols.

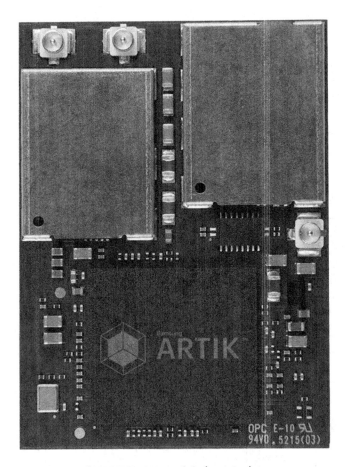

*Figure 2-5.* *The ARTIK 1020 module (top view)*

Find out more about the ARTIK 1020 from the Samsung developer documentation. Read the data sheet for the ARTIK model 1020 and examine the Type 10 developer reference board schematics. Together, they answer many of your questions about how the ARTIK works; see www.artik.io/modules/overview/artik-10/ and http://developer.samsung.com/sdk-and-tools.

# General Arrangement

Figure 2-6 shows the layout of the ARTIK 1020 module components. The four Panasonic AXT connectors are on the underside of the module but their position is shown as viewed from the top. Use this image file as a starting point for adding some layout markup to the screen-printed artwork for your own circuit boards. Do not take measurements from this diagram because it was rotoscoped from a photograph and any positions of items are merely for guidance.

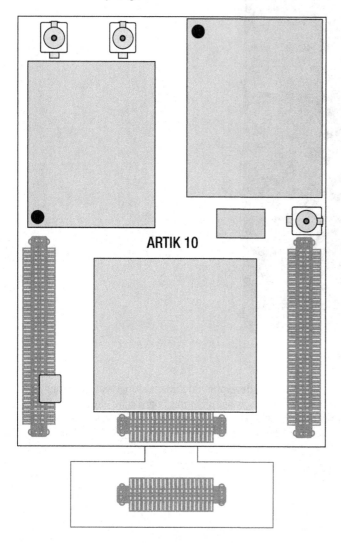

***Figure 2-6.*** *ARTIK 10 general arrangement*

---

▪ **Note** Two 40-pin debug connectors are shown in this illustration. The ARTIK 1020 modules can be used without the second auxiliary debug connector. The version shipped with the Type 10 developer reference board has the additional connector fitted. It is plugged into the developer reference board to support JTAG hardware debugging. Chapter 13 describes these AXT connectors in detail and also describes the additional debugging connector.

---

# Functional Organization

The functional breakdown of the ARTIK 1020 module is shown in Figure 2-7. This diagram shows the main internal subsystems in an ARTIK 1020.

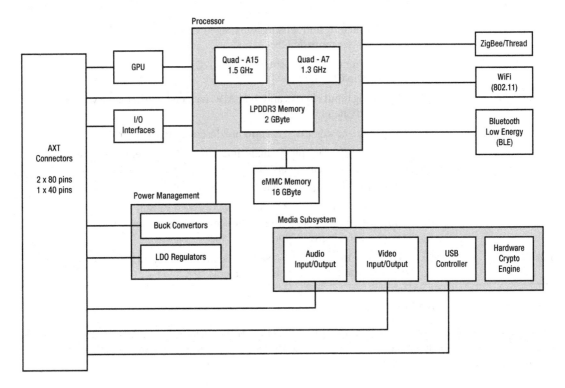

***Figure 2-7.*** *The ARTIK 1020 module block diagram*

The various connectivity and interfacing technologies are covered in detail in later chapters and are summarized in Table 2-5.

*Table 2-5.* *ARTIK 10 Connectivity Cross-Reference*

| Topic | See also |
|---|---|
| Panasonic AXT connectors | Chapter 13 describes the pinouts for the ARTIK 1020 connectors (J1, J2, J3, and J4) |
| GPIO | Digital switching and sensing is managed via the GPIO interface. Refer to Chapter 17 for more details. |
| I2C | Some sensor devices are connected via I2C bus interfaces. These are described in Chapter 20. |
| Analog input | The analog input circuits and their ADC conversion to a digital value are covered in Chapter 18. |
| PWM output | The pseudo analog PWM outputs are described in Chapter 19 |
| SPI | The SPI interface is only partially implemented at present. Details of how it works are covered in Chapter 21. |
| Audio | The audio capabilities are covered in Chapter 22. |
| Video | The Video4Linux support is incomplete as yet. Examine the online resources and the connectors in the schematic diagrams to understand how it works. See Chapter 23 for more details. |
| USB | The ARTIK 1020 supports USB connections in host and device modes running with version 2.0 or 3.0 protocols. |

# Known Firmware Versions

Table 2-6 lists the publicly available firmware versions that have been released for the ARTIK 1020 via the Samsung developer downloads page. Sign on with your developer account to reach the Downloads page at www.artik.io/developer/downloads.

*Table 2-6.* *ARTIK 1020 Firmware Release History*

| Date | Notes |
|---|---|
| 2015-10-07 | Only use this on Alpha boards. It is Alpha firmware built with Yocto from Fedora 20. |
| 2015-11-09 | Only use this on 0.3 version (Beta) boards. It is Beta firmware built with Yocto from Fedora 22. It adds USB camera support via the Linux UVC driver, analog write, and I2C device access. The Temboo library is not available on this version. |
| 2015-12-17 | A firmware image for the ARTIK 10 Ver. 3.2 (early Beta) boards, it is based on Fedora 22. Do not use this image with Ver. 3.0 or 3.1 boards. |
| 2016-06-21 | This is revised firmware released as the ARTIK 10 Commercial Beta devices become available to purchase. |

# ARTIK Module Connections

The connections are all brought out of the ARTIK modules via Panasonic AXT multi-pin headers soldered to the underside of the ARTIK. The ARTIK stands off from the board where the connectors are fitted. You must use matching sockets like the one shown in Figure 2-8 on your own main circuit board inside the product you want to empower with an ARTIK module.

***Figure 2-8.*** *Panasonic AXT socket (Courtesy of Panasonic Electric Works)*

There are several different variants of these sockets. Choose different heights of mating connectors to allow more space underneath the ARTIK. This might be helpful for ventilation. Trade this off against the overall height of your base circuit board plus the height of the ARTIK module. You can clearly see this if you look at your developer reference board with its ARTIK module mounted on top.

The accuracy of positioning the sockets on your baseboard during manufacture is absolutely critical to avoid damaging your ARTIK. If you have to force the ARTIK into misaligned AXT sockets, it puts excessive strain on the ARTIK module printed circuit board and could damage it as a result.

These connectors are described in more detail in Chapter 13 where the individual pinouts are listed. The following are the signals that are brought out through these connectors on ARTIK 5 and 10 modules:

- General Purpose Input/Output (GPIO)
- Pulse Width Modulated (PWM) outputs
- Analog inputs (ADC) and IIO kernel support
- UART serial I/O
- I2C bus for sensor devices
- Serial Peripheral Interconnect (SPI) for driving video displays
- I2S bus for audio applications and the ALSA library
- USB 2.0 and 3.0 bus running in device and host mode (module dependent)
- MMC memory support
- MIPI DSI display interfaces
- MIPI CSI camera interfaces
- Clock outputs
- Auxiliary power to peripherals
- Video output
- Accessing the Power Management Integrated Control (PMIC) devices

# Physical Dimensions

The ARTIK modules are very small when viewed from the top. The height of the module when it is plugged into the AXT socket determines the size of the product you intend to deploy. The choice of low or high profile AXT connectors affects the minimum internal size for these products. Figure 2-9 is a cross-section view showing the important dimensions for your ARTIK modules. The minimum internal space inside your product is the sum of the height of the mated connector plus the thickness of your PCB and the stand-off height of any surface mounted ARTIK components. Allowing a little extra space to insulate the ARTIK from the outer casing and the miniature co-axial connectors for Wi-Fi adds to the overall height. Ensure there is adequate airflow to allow the ARTIK to remain cool if it needs to carry out compute-intensive tasks. Because of the density of connections, a multi-layer board may be required. This is slightly thicker than a single or dual layer PCB. Allowing 1mm for the baseboard thickness should be sufficient space. Allow clearance above the top of the Wi-Fi antenna miniature co-axial connectors so they are not subjected to vibration; they should also not come into contact with any conductive surfaces to avoid the risk of short circuits. Underneath the base printed circuit board there may be some soldered tags protruding through the board. These must have clearance and very likely some insulating material to prevent more short circuits. The minimum internal height may be bigger than you first thought. Surface mounting your components on your base printed circuit board may alleviate the need to solder through to the back of the board and would reduce the height a little.

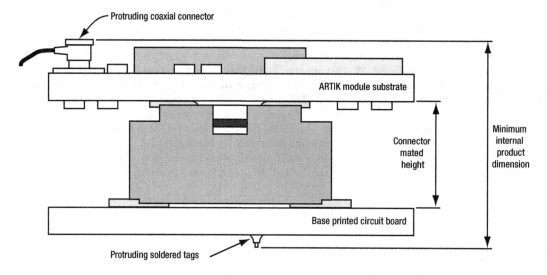

***Figure 2-9.*** *Cross-sectional view*

When you connect a cable to a miniature co-axial socket, the top of the plug stands off from the substrate of the ARTIK module a little higher than most other components. The height of these connectors without an antenna cable plugged in is 1.25mm. Allow a little more space for the plug body. Calculate the overall dimensions of the ARTIK when plugged into its AXT socket and add the height of the miniature co-axial connectors with their cables plugged in. Refer to this URL for data sheets with production dimensions to plan enough space for these connectors inside your product design:

www.digikey.com/product-detail/en/hirose-electric-co-ltd/U.FL-R-SMT(10)/H9161CT-ND/2135256.

Refer to the Samsung data sheets for the ARTIK modules for additional details regarding the physical characteristics of the AXT implementation replicated in your own product designs. Table 2-7 summarizes the key dimensions and tolerances.

*Table 2-7.* *Key Dimensions and Tolerances*

| ARTIK | Dimension | Value | Tolerance |
|-------|-----------|-------|-----------|
| 5 | Width | 25.00mm | ± 0.5mm |
| 5 | Length | 29.00mm | ± 0.5mm |
| 5 | Center line of AXT connector axis | See data sheets | ± 0.2mm |
| 5 | Middle of AXT connector | See data sheets | ± 0.3mm |
| 5 | Base PCB thickness | 0.72mm | ± 0.1mm |
| 5 | Maximum stand-off height of top components (not including the plugged in miniature co-axial connectors) | 1.50mm | ± 0.2mm |
| 5 | Maximum stand-off height of bottom components (not including AXT headers) | 1.24mm | ± 0.2mm |
| 5 | Connector mated height (low profile) | 1.50mm | n/a |
| 5 | Connector mated height (high profile) | 2.50mm | n/a |
| 10 | Width | 29.00mm | ± 0.5mm |
| 10 | Length (without auxiliary debug connector) | 39.00mm | ± 0.5mm |
| 10 | Length (with auxiliary debug connector) | 47.00mm | ± 0.5mm |
| 10 | Center line of AXT connector axis | See data sheets | ± 0.2mm |
| 10 | Middle of AXT connector | See data sheets | ± 0.2mm |
| 10 | Base PCB thickness | 1.10mm | ± 0.12mm |
| 10 | Maximum stand-off height of top components (not including the plugged in miniature co-axial connectors) | 1.60mm | ± 0.2mm |
| 10 | Maximum stand-off height of bottom components (not including AXT headers) | 1.24mm | ± 0.2mm |
| 10 | Connector mated height (low profile) | 1.50mm | n/a |
| 10 | Connector mated height (high profile) | 2.50mm | n/a |

# Buy an ARTIK Development System Now

The ARTIK 520 Commercial Beta development systems went on sale as the Mobile World Conference got underway in Barcelona in February 2016. The ARTIK 1020 Commercial Beta modules joined them in June 2016. The ARTIK 1020 modules are a little bit more expensive than the ARTIK 520 modules but they are capable of so much more. The primary supplier is Digi-Key. Go their web site and search using the keyword "ARTIK" to find all the Samsung ARTIK-related products available. Digi-Key has international representation. Use the correct version of their site to order and pay for products in your local currency. The international territories are listed at the bottom of the web page.

## Component Suppliers

There are many suppliers that offer add-on components. Samsung has chosen Digi-Key as a central place to distribute their recommended accessories and ARTIK-compatible components. Useful components are also available from Adafruit, Sparkfun, Oomlout, and many other companies worldwide. There is a useful list of suppliers at the Arduino web site and a few others are listed here:

```
http://playground.arduino.cc/Main/Resources
www.adafruit.com
www.sparkfun.com
www.radioshack.com
http://oomlout.co.uk
http://uk.farnell.com
www.hobbytronics.co.uk
www.coolcomponents.co.uk
www.bitsbox.co.uk
www.maplin.co.uk
www.tandyonline.co.uk
http://hobbycomponents.com
www.rs-components.com
```

## Summary

Getting to know the ARTIK modules and how the different models compare and contrast helps you to choose the right one for your product design. If your product does not merit the power of an ARTIK 10, the ARTIK 5 solution is more cost effective. If you are a developer who experiments with prototyping a range of ideas, having ARTIK 5 might constrain what you can do, and the ARTIK 10 is a better choice for general purpose research and development work. Although the specific model numbers are currently the ARTIK 520 and 1020, the rest of this book will refer to them simply as an ARTIK 5 and 10 unless it is necessary to draw your attention to features that are specific to the 520 and 1020 module versions. These model numbers will change when new versions start to ship.

# CHAPTER 3

# Developer Reference Boards

The best way to start learning how the ARTIK modules work is to connect the developer reference board to your development workstation. This board conveniently extends the connectivity of the ARTIK out to Arduino-compatible header pins. The developer reference board also provides hardware debugging facilities via a JTAG connector. The developer reference board is designed to safely mount your ARTIK to work on your product design without needing to directly handle the module. This protects it from undue wear and tear and the risk of electrostatic discharge (ESD) damage. Always make sure you have grounded yourself and the equipment you are handling before touching it in order to dissipate any gradual build-up of static charges. Avoid handling your ARTIK modules directly because they are small and easily damaged.

If your ARTIK module has shaken loose from its socket during shipment, watch the following YouTube video provided by the Samsung support team. It shows you where to carefully apply pressure without damaging the ARTIK when reseating the module onto the developer reference board:

```
http://www.youtube.com/watch?v=FxWXYONLmzY.
```

---

**Note**    The ARTIK modules are static-sensitive devices. Make sure you ground yourself and observe the proper safeguards to avoid electrostatic discharge when handling modules and development boards.

---

## A Little History

Each kind of ARTIK module has a developer reference board specifically designed for it. The developer boards and the ARTIK modules are marked with version numbers to identify their provenance. Early examples are lacking a leading zero so the version number looks like 3.1 when it should be 0.3.1. The ARTIK 520 Commercial Beta version (0.5.0) began shipping in March 2016. Table 3-1 summarizes the different version numbers and release dates to help you identify the vintages. The Type 5 and 10 developer reference boards are sometimes referred to as Type V and Type X in the developer documentation.

***Table 3-1.*** *Developer Reference Board and ARTIK Version Numbers*

| Prototype | Type | Version | Revision date | Description |
|---|---|---|---|---|
| Pioneer | 2 | 0.1.0 | 2015-05-06 | Demonstrated on the Cybercode Twins video |
| Alpha | 2 | 0.2.0 | 2015-04-20 | Universal developer board, compatible with ARTIK 10. With the addition of a small mezzanine board, the ARTIK 5 can be mounted on the same board. |
| Alpha | 2 | 0.2.1 | Mid 2015 | Revised prototype |
| Alpha | 2 | 0.2.2 | Mid 2015 | GPIO circuits are incorrectly set to active **LOW**. Later models are correct with GPIO active **HIGH**. |
| Beta | 5/10 | 0.3.0 | Late 2015 | Development prototype |
| Beta | 5/10 | 0.3.1 | 2015-09-02 | Compatible with Beta ARTIK modules |
| Beta | 5/10 | 0.3.2 | 2015-10-22 | Compatible with Beta ARTIK modules |
| Beta | 5/10 | 0.3.3 | Late 2015 | Compatible with Beta ARTIK modules |
| Commercial Beta | 5 | 0.5.0 | 2015-12-23 | At launch, ARTIK 520 modules are this version. |
| Commercial Beta | 10 | 0.5.0 | 2015-12-23 | Pre-launch ARTIK 10 modules |
| Commercial Beta | 10 | 0.5.0 | 2016-02-12 | At launch, ARTIK 1020 modules are this version. |

■ **Note**   Because Samsung is still developing the ARTIK platform, the developer reference board, version numbers, ARTIK module features, and the model number designations may change from what is documented here.

# Connecting External Devices

The developer reference boards provide connectivity for a variety of external hardware. There are camera connections directly on the ARTIK modules for delivering video. These are brought out to Molex connectors on the developer reference board. At present, the video support for these boards is still being developed. This will change as more developers try things out and publish their results. Plug additional hardware into the USB connector and install suitable drivers for it. Optionally, write new drivers or recompile the existing ones to be compatible with the ARM CPUs. The USB port provides a way to add large amounts of external storage for surveillance and video related products such as media servers or video recorder applications. On the ARTIK 10, the USB connector is also a means of adding a camera. Consult the schematic diagrams for pinout details of the various connectors on the developer reference board and where they enter the ARTIK module through the Panasonic AXT multi-pin connectors.

Controlling those external devices requires programming of GPIO, I2C, I2S, IIO, and SPI interfaces. Libraries that make it easier to interact with them support a few of these interfaces, and more libraries will be developed in future, and some interfaces are managed via the kernel. Because of the open standards nature of the ARTIK, finding out how to control these interfaces is not particularly difficult. Some guidance is included in later chapters.

# Schematic Diagrams

Samsung released schematic diagrams for the developer reference boards. Get a copy of them from the Developer Downloads page. You must be logged in with your developer account to access them. These schematic diagrams help you design and build a basic breakout board for your ARTIK modules. To reduce your manufacturing costs, construct a much simpler board with only the support needed by your application.

The developer board schematic diagrams are particularly helpful because they show you the pin numbers on the connectors underneath the ARTIK module. These are the Panasonic AXT multi-pin connectors to incorporate into your product when you eventually go into production. The RF circuits on the antenna connectors are also shown on these schematics. Also, you can find out what the jumper pins and test points are for. Very often there are small tables of helpful information beside the jumper pins on the schematic diagrams.

Carefully examining the schematic diagrams can fill in a lot of blanks in your knowledge about how the ARTIK works. Study the source code in the ARTIK OS repositories and in the Exynos version of the Linux kernel. Combining this with recursive listings of the file system living under the /sys directory helps you grasp the details of the hardware subsystems your application needs to talk to. The circuit schematics show the pin numbers for wiring JTAG test harnesses to connect hardware debuggers.

Table 3-2 lists the schematic diagrams that have been published. The Type 5 and 10 boards are the most relevant to the Commercial Beta ARTIK modules but there might be some informative comments and useful example supporting circuits on the earlier Type 2 developer board schematic for Alpha prototype ARTIK 5 and 10 modules even though the board is now discontinued. Download the schematic diagrams for the Type 5 and 10 developer reference boards from

https://developer.artik.io/downloads.

***Table 3-2.*** *Schematic Diagram Releases*

| Type | Version | Date | Description |
|------|---------|------|-------------|
| 2 | 0.2.0 | 2015-04-14 | Early Alpha prototype ARTIK 10 devices shipped on this Type 2 developer reference board. Some ARTIK 5 modules shipped with a small mezzanine board to match them to the ARTIK 10 AXT connector pinouts. |
| 5 | 0.1.0 | 2015-01-14 | First version; hardware not publicly available. |
| 5 | 0.2.0 | 2015-04-14 | Second version; Alpha prototypes. |
| 5 | 0.3.0 | 2015-07-28 | Third version; Early Beta prototype. |
| 5 | 0.3.1 | 2015-08-26 | Minor revision to Beta design |
| 5 | 0.3.2 | 2015-09-14 | Z-Wave, LPWA, RJ45, and other pinout changes |
| 5 | 0.3.3 | 2015-10-06 | Minor revision |
| 5 | 0.5.0 | 2015-11-05 | Commercial Beta goes into production for early adopters to buy. |
| 5 | 0.5.0 | 2015-11-18 | Added some test points (current) |
| 10 | 0.1.0 | 2015-01-14 | First version; hardware not publicly available. |
| 10 | 0.2.0 | 2015-04-14 | Second version; Alpha prototypes. |
| 10 | 0.3.0 | 2015-07-12 | Third version; Early Beta prototype. |
| 10 | 0.5.0 | 2015-11-02 | Commercial Beta goes into production for early adopters to buy. |
| 10 | 0.5.0 | 2015-11-19 | Added some test points (current version) |
| 10 | 0.5.0 | 2015-12-23 | Released to developers |

# Reading the Schematic Diagrams

Learning how to read schematics is a worthwhile skill to acquire, especially as IoT projects involve a mix of hardware and software design. The Samsung developer board schematics tell you all about the pinouts of the various connectors and components. The schematics and data sheets are the most authoritative information on those connector pinouts. Each page of the schematics is designed to cover part of the developer reference board functionality. If you have a large format printer, the diagrams are easier to read if you print them out on A3 sized paper. Look for the special notes and tables on these diagrams, which reveal useful information about jumper connections and their purpose.

Figure 3-1 illustrates how the schematics route connections to other pages. Trace these connections to see how the AXT connector pins on the ARTIK module are routed to the hardware header I/O connectors. These schematics and the product data sheets were used as the source material to develop the AXT connector reference tables in Chapter 13.

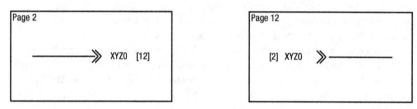

*Figure 3-1.* *Schematic diagram page jump*

The connector component types are denoted near the pinout diagram. Figure 3-2 shows the J35 connector on an ARTIK 10 module. This connector is for the 3L2 Camera interface. All the surrounding circuits are omitted to keep the illustration simple. The J35 label helps you find this connector on the developer reference board.

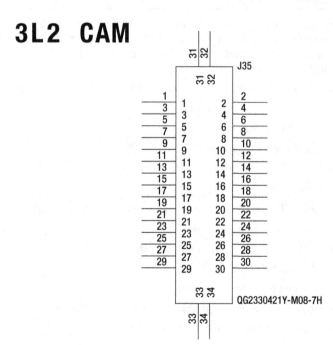

*Figure 3-2.* *Interface connector for 3L2 camera (J35)*

Note the legend underneath. Searching for that component part number online reveals a lot of suppliers and data sheets that you need to acquire. Switching to an online image search sometimes helps to find the component you are looking for. Compare the pictures with the board in front of you. Once you have a description of the component, look for a local supplier or find one online such as Digi-Key, Sparkfun, or Adafruit. If they do not stock the component you need, try the larger component supplier companies such as Farnell or RS components.

The same approach can be used to find out the technical specifications for other devices such as the connectors for the SD cards. The voltage level convertor chips for the Arduino connectors and other hardware devices that are connected to the I2C bus for power management, Ethernet, audio, and video can also be searched for. Gather the data sheets for those and other I2C devices to interact with the correct registers when you call the I2C read and write functions. These data sheets are the only place to find this information. This is why it is important to become familiar with the circuit schematics.

# Type 5 - Version 0.5.0

The Type 5 developer reference board has evolved from the earlier models but now that it is shipping, the version 0.5.0 product is currently the definitive Type 5 board. Table 3-3 summarizes the release history of the Type 5 developer reference board for ARTIK 5 modules. Table 3-4 summarizes the various connectors on the developer board and their purpose.

*Table 3-3.* *Type 5 Developer Reference Board Revisions*

| Board revision | Release date | Description |
|---|---|---|
| Alpha 0.2.0 - 0.2.2 | Mid 2015 | This board is now obsolete. The GPIO circuitry uses an active level that is the inverse of later boards. |
| Early Beta 0.3.0 - 0.3.3 | Late 2015 | To help you identify the board, all antenna connectors run along the top edge and left side. This system shipped with Fedora OS version 20. |
| Commercial Beta 0.5.0 | Feb 2016 | This hardware has a fully functional feature set although there may still be some software drivers added later. The Wi-Fi antenna connector moves to the bottom edge. This system ships with Fedora OS version 22. |

A photograph of the Type 5 Commercial Beta developer reference board for the ARTIK 5 is shown in Figure 3-3.

***Figure 3-3.*** *Commercial Beta developer reference board Type 5*

*Table 3-4.* *Developer Reference Board Type 5 Connectors*

| Connector | Description |
| --- | --- |
| Arduino pins | It offers a full complement of Arduino-compatible pins positioned to accommodate Arduino shields. |
| GPIO pins | The Arduino-compatible pins can be driven directly as General Purpose Input/Outputs (GPIO) connections. Chapter 17 discusses GPIO interfacing in detail. |
| I2S, I2C, and other I/O pins | Chapter 14 discusses the developer reference board header I/O pinouts. |
| Debug USB | This is a standard USB port with a built-in serial adapter for your development workstation to connect to it via a serial terminal application. |
| USB | A USB interface for connection to auxiliary devices. |
| Ethernet | The RJ45 Ethernet connector provides for wired networking connections. |
| 5V power port | Connect your power supply here. |
| 3.5mm audio jack socket | This is a standard audio output. Audio capabilities of the ARTIK modules are discussed in Chapter 22 where the ALSA tools are also described. |
| Analog audio inputs | The ARTIK 5 supports 2-channel analog audio input. This is covered in Chapter 18. |
| Display (J17) | The Type 5 developer reference board has a Molex ribbon connector socket to attach a video display. Chapter 23 provides some supporting material on video related topics. |
| Camera (6B2) | The Type 5 developer reference board has a Molex ribbon connector socket to attach a model 6B2 video camera for video input. |
| JTAG | The JTAG connector on the ARTIK 5 and 10 is specially designed for debugging ARM processors. |
| Jumpers | The main source for details about the jumpers is the developer reference board schematic diagrams that Samsung releases to the developers. |
| Antenna connections | Chapter 15 describes the antenna connectors on the ARTIK modules and the developer reference boards. |
| SD card holder | This is used for loading software into your ARTIK or installing operating system upgrades. |

Inspect the screen-printed component labels on your developer board to locate the various connectors. Some of the developer board connectors are not labeled with their J number on the screen-printed artwork. Study the circuit schematics for the developer reference boards to figure this out. The schematics also carry useful identifying part numbers for the connectors. Purchase matching components for use in your own projects. Table 3-5 summarizes the various connectors on a Type 5 developer reference board listed with their identifying label.

*Table 3-5. Type 5 Connectors Listed by Board Label*

| Label | Description |
|-------|-------------|
| BAT1 | Coin cell battery backup (**MS621F** battery available from Digi-Key) |
| CON3 | Auxiliary battery supply connector (type **12505WS-02A00**) |
| CON4 | USB serial adapter for connection to the development workstation (Type **HI05-AG0250**) |
| CON5 | USB accessories connector |
| J3 | Panasonic AXT connector to the ARTIK 5 module |
| J4 | Panasonic AXT connector to the ARTIK 5 module |
| J5 | 3.5mm Stereo audio output jack socket |
| J7 | Panasonic AXT connector to the ARTIK 5 module |
| J8 | Labeled SD CARD on the board artwork. Receptacle for installing micro SD cards (Type **DM3AT-SF-PEJ**). |
| J9 | 5-volt power port |
| J10 | Molex ribbon connector for attaching a **6B2** video camera |
| J12 | JTAG hardware debugging connector |
| J13 | Ethernet RJ45 connector |
| J15 | SMA-F antenna connector for LPWA wireless communications |
| J16 | SMA-F antenna connector for Z-Wave wireless communications |
| J17 | Molex ribbon connector for **EH400WV-25A** video display and touch panel connection |
| J21 | SMA-F antenna connector for wireless communications. Linked to J22, which carries a coaxial connection from the ARTIK 5 module. |
| J22 | Miniature coaxial connector to the ARTIK 5 module |
| J23 | SMA-F antenna connector for wireless communications. Linked to J32, which carries a coaxial connection from the ARTIK 5 module. |
| J24 | Analog input pins |
| J25 | Power supply, ground, and reset lines |
| J26 | Arduino pins (A) |
| J27 | Arduino pins (B) |
| J28 | SMA-F antenna connector for ZigBee wireless communications. Linked to J29, which carries a coaxial connection from the ARTIK 5 module. There is a J6 label adjacent to this socket on the Commercial Beta developer reference board. |
| J29 | Miniature coaxial connector to the ARTIK 5 module |
| J32 | Miniature coaxial connector to the ARTIK 5 module |
| J510 | ADC interface |
| J511 | SPI, UART, I2C, and I2S interfaces |
| J512 | GPM and interrupt lines |
| J513 | PWM and clock output |

Table 3-6 summarizes the jumper pins on the Type 5 developer reference board. These jumpers are factory configured to the correct settings, so unless you are doing very advanced development they do not need to be altered.

*Table 3-6. Type 5 Developer Reference Board Configuration Jumpers*

| Label | Description |
|-------|-------------|
| J6 | ZigBee DN configuration header (ZIGBEE DN TOOL). The board labeling is very ambiguous regarding this and the J28 antenna connector. |
| J11 | Z-Wave configuration |
| J14 | ZigBee 2.8 volt power supply isolator |
| J20 | Controls the selection of power supply from MAIN_BAT vs. battery backup from coin cell |
| J28 | ZigBee DN tool |
| J30 | Connect a switch across the two pins on this jumper to control the 5-volt supply to pin J25-8 (VIN). This connector is one of the hardware I/O headers. |
| J31 | ARTIK 5 power isolation of J3 power input pins from MAIN_BAT power rail. Functional equivalent to J17 on a Type 10 board. |
| J33 | Controls the selection of power supply from MAIN_BAT vs. CON3 battery backup from coin cell |
| J508 | Bus type setting configuration (a.k.a. J8 in the table on page 11 of the schematics) |
| J509 | Bus type setting configuration (a.k.a. J9 in the table on page 11 of the schematics) |

# Type 10 - Version 0.5.0

The Type 10 developer reference board has evolved from the earlier models on a parallel path with the Type 5 board. There are a few subtle differences: some components have moved to different locations when you compare the two side by side. Aside from the need for functional differences due to the more advanced feature set of an ARTIK 10, the major connectors, switches, and support circuits are much the same. Now that the Commercial Beta ARTIK is shipping from Digi-Key, the version 0.5.0 product is currently the definitive Type 10 board. Table 3-7 summarizes the release history of the Type 10 developer reference board for ARTIK 10 modules.

*Table 3-7. Type 10 Developer Reference Board Revisions*

| Board revision | Release date | Description |
|----------------|--------------|-------------|
| Early Beta 0.3.0 | Mid 2015 | Development prototype. This board is now obsolete. |
| Beta 0.3.1 | September 2015 | Compatible with Beta ARTIK 10. This board is now obsolete. |
| Commercial Beta 0.5.0 | June 2016 | This hardware has a fully functional feature set although there may still be some software drivers added later. This system ships with Fedora OS version 22 |
| Pre-launch Beta 0.5 | December 2015 | Pre-launch ARTIK 10 modules. Engineering design is completed. |
| Commercial Beta 0.5 | June 2016 | The Commercial Beta units when the ARTIK 10 first went on sale to the public. |

Figure 3-4 shows the Type 10 Commercial Beta developer reference board for the ARTIK 10.

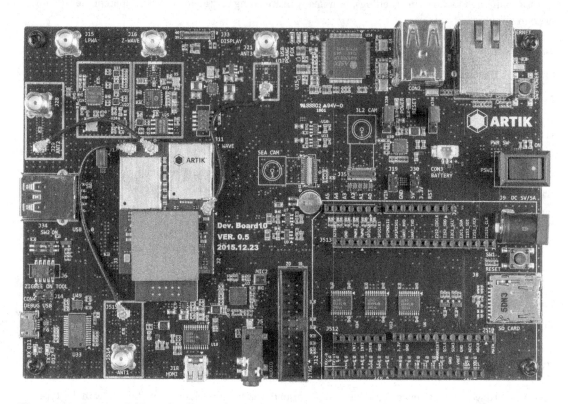

***Figure 3-4.*** *Commercial Beta developer reference board Type 10*

___

■ **Note** The currently shipping Commercial Beta boards are dated 2016-02-12 but are otherwise identical to the one in the photograph.

___

Table 3-8 summarizes the various connectors on the developer board and their purpose. There are some slight differences from the Type 5. On this board, there is an additional camera interface and neither camera is the same kind as the one on the Type 5 developer boards.

*Table 3-8.* *Developer Reference Board Type 10 Connectors*

| Connector | Description |
| --- | --- |
| Arduino pins | It offers a full complement of Arduino-compatible pins positioned to accommodate Arduino shields. |
| GPIO pins | The Arduino-compatible pins can be driven directly as General Purpose Input/Outputs (GPIO) connections. Chapter 17 discusses GPIO interfacing in detail. |
| I2S, I2C, and other I/O pins | Chapter 14 discusses the developer reference board header I/O pinouts. |
| Debug USB | This is a standard USB port with a built-in serial adapter for your development workstation to connect to it via a serial terminal application. |
| USB | USB interface for connection to auxiliary devices. |
| Ethernet | The RJ45 Ethernet connector provides for wired networking connections. |
| 5V power port | Connect your power supply here. |
| 3.5mm audio jack socket | Standard audio output. Audio capabilities of the ARTIK modules are discussed in Chapter 22. |
| Analog audio inputs | The ARTIK 10 supports multi-channel analog audio input. This is covered in Chapter 18. |
| Display (J17) | The Type 10 developer reference board has a Molex ribbon connector socket to attach a video display. Chapter 23 provides the supporting material on video topics. |
| Camera (5EA) | The Type 10 developer reference board has a Molex ribbon connector socket to attach a model 5EA video camera for video input. |
| Camera (3L2) | The multi-pin J35 connector is for attaching a model 3L2 camera. |
| JTAG | The JTAG connector on the ARTIK 10 is specially designed for debugging ARM processors. This connector is similar to the JTAG connector on the Type 5 developer reference board. |
| Jumpers | The main source for details about the jumpers is the developer reference board schematic diagrams that Samsung releases to the developers. |
| Antenna connections | Chapter 15 describes the antenna connectors on the ARTIK modules and the developer reference boards. |
| SD card holder | This is used for loading software into your ARTIK or installing operating system upgrades. |

Inspect the screen-printed component labels on your developer board to locate the various connectors. Some of the developer board connectors are not labeled with their J number on the screen-printed artwork. Study the circuit schematics for the developer reference boards to figure this out. The schematics also carry useful identifying part numbers for the connectors. Purchase matching components for use in your own projects. Table 3-9 summarizes the various connectors on a Type 10 developer reference board listed with their identifying label.

***Table 3-9.*** *Connectors Listed by Board Label*

| Label | Description |
| --- | --- |
| BAT1 | Coin cell battery backup |
| CON2 | USB accessories connector |
| CON3 | Auxiliary battery supply connector |
| CON4 | USB serial adapter for connection to the development workstation (Type **HI05-AG0250**) |
| J1 | Panasonic AXT connector to the ARTIK 10 module |
| J2 | Panasonic AXT connector to the ARTIK 10 module |
| J3 | Panasonic AXT connector to the ARTIK 10 module |
| J4 | Panasonic AXT connector to the ARTIK 10 module |
| J5 | 3.5mm stereo audio output jack socket |
| J8 | Socket labeled as SD CARD for installing SD cards (type **DM3AT-SF-PEJ**) |
| J9 | 5 -volt power port |
| J10 | Molex ribbon connector for attaching a **5EA** video camera. Note this connector is unlabeled on the Commercial Beta boards. |
| J12 | JTAG hardware debugging connector |
| J13 | Ethernet RJ45 connector |
| J15 | SMA-F antenna connector for LPWA wireless communications |
| J16 | SMA-F antenna connector for Z-Wave wireless communications |
| J18 | HDMI video output |
| J21 | SMA-F antenna connector for wireless communications. Linked to J22, which carries a coaxial connection from the ARTIK 10 module. |
| J22 | Miniature coaxial connector to the ARTIK 10 module |
| J24 | Analog input pins |
| J25 | Power supply, ground, and reset lines |
| J26 | Arduino pins (A) |
| J27 | Arduino pins (B) |
| J28 | SMA-F antenna connector for ZigBee wireless communications. Linked to J29, which carries a coaxial connection from the ARTIK 10 module. |
| J29 | Miniature coaxial connector to the ARTIK 10 module |
| J33 | Kyocera multi-pin connector for LCD video display output |
| J34 | USB 3.0 accessories connector |
| J35 | Multi-pin connector for attaching a **3L2** video camera |
| J510 | ADC interface |
| J511 | SPI, UART, I2C, and I2S interfaces |
| J512 | GPM and interrupt lines |
| J513 | PWM and clock output |

(*continued*)

***Table 3-9.*** (*continued*)

| Label | Description |
|-------|-------------|
| J514 | SMA-F antenna connector for wireless communications. Linked to J515, which carries a coaxial connection from the ARTIK 10 module. |
| J515 | Miniature coaxial connector to the ARTIK 10 module |

Table 3-10 summarizes the jumper pins on the Type 10 developer reference board. These jumpers are factory configured to the correct settings, so unless you are doing very advanced development they do not need to be altered.

***Table 3-10.*** *Type 10 Developer Reference Board Configuration Jumpers*

| Label | Description |
|-------|-------------|
| J6 | ZigBee DN tool |
| J11 | Z-Wave configuration |
| J14 | ZigBee 2.8 volt power supply isolator |
| J17 | ARTIK 10 power isolation of J1 power input pins from MAIN_BAT power rail. Functional equivalent to J31 on a Type 5 board. |
| J19 | Isolates the DC 5-volt power supply input from the VDD_5VB rail |
| J20 | Controls the selection of power supply from MAIN_BAT vs. battery backup from coin cell |
| J30 | Connects a switch across the two pins on this jumper to control the 5-volt supply to pin J25-8 (VIN). This connector is one of the hardware I/O headers. |
| J36 | Controls the selection of power supply from MAIN_BAT vs. CON3 battery backup from coin cell |

# Test Points

The developer reference boards have several test points to probe what is going on in the ARTIK and its surrounding support hardware. Examine the circuit schematics for your developer reference boards to locate these test points and then find them on your hardware. They are very small circular pads about 0.5mm in diameter. Tables 3-11 and 3-12 list the test points for each type of developer reference board.

***Table 3-11.*** *Developer Reference Board Test Points (Type 5)*

| TP | Description |
|-----|-------------|
| TP1 | **AK4953** audio codec. Speaker output - positive (SPP). |
| TP2 | **AK4953** audio codec. Speaker output - negative (SPN). |
| TP5 | Port B pin 4 (SPI) on the **ATA8520** chip, which manages the SIGFOX RF transceiver. This indicates the power on status of the chip. |
| TP11 | Z-Wave memory write protect status |
| TP13 | Fuel gauge quick start pin |
| TP14 | Indicates the buffer enable state of the J510 I2C signals controlled by SW2-2 |
| TP15 | Power key value |
| TP16 | Current power status |

*Table 3-12.* *Developer Reference Board Test Points (Type 10)*

| TP | Description |
|---|---|
| TP1 | **AK4953** audio codec. Speaker output - positive (SPP). |
| TP2 | **AK4953** audio codec. Speaker output - negative (SPN). |
| TP3 | **AX88760** - USB downstream port 1 |
| TP4 | **AX88760** - USB downstream port 1 |
| TP5 | Port C pin 2 on the **ATA8520** chip, which manages the SIGFOX RF transceiver |
| TP11 | Z-Wave memory write protect status |
| TP13 | Fuel gauge quick start pin |
| TP15 | Camera type when **5EA** camera is attached |
| TP17 | Camera flash when **5EA** camera is attached |
| TP18 | Indicates the buffer enable state of the J510 I2C signals controlled by SW2-2 |
| TP19 | Power key state |
| TP20 | Current power status |
| TP21 | Switch 2 boot mode setting. Indicates whether SD or eMMC boot is selected. |
| TP22 | Battery connection status |

Tables 3-13 and 3-14 summarize the test point connections available on the AXT connectors underneath your ARTIK module. The connections for the ARTIK 5 and 10 are each shown in their own tables. Refer to the data sheets for more information about voltage levels and other detailed specifications regarding these pins.

*Table 3-13.* *ARTIK 5 Test Point AXT Pinouts*

| Connector | Name | Function |
|---|---|---|
| J4-53 | Xi2c3_SCL | Bus I2C-3 SCL |
| J4-55 | Xi2c3_SDA | Bus I2C-3 SDA |
| J5-4 | GPM3_1 | Not used |
| J5-6 | GPM3_0 | Not used |
| J5-22 | 32768HZ | 32 kHz clock |
| J5-32 | XspiCLK1 | Bus SPI-1 CLK |
| J5-34 | XspiCSn1 | Bus SPI-1 CSn |
| J5-36 | XspiMISO1 | Bus SPI-1 MISO |
| J5-38 | XspiMOSI1 | Bus SPI-1 MOSI |

*Table 3-14.* *ARTIK 10 Test Point AXT Pinouts*

| Connector | Name | Function |
|---|---|---|
| J1-71 | Xi2c0_SCL | Bus I2C-0 SCL |
| J1-73 | Xi2c0_SDA | Bus I2C-0 SDA |
| J4-23 | 32768HZ | 32 kHz clock |
| J1-59 | XspiCLK1 | Bus SPI-1 CLK |
| J1-61 | XspiCSn1 | Bus SPI-1 CSn |
| J1-63 | XspiMISO1 | Bus SPI-1 MISO |
| J1-65 | XspiMOSI1 | Bus SPI-1 MOSI |

■ **Note**    The test points for the ARTIK 10 are not listed in the current version of the data sheet. This table of information describes the AXT pins on the ARTIK 10 that correspond to similar test points listed for the ARTIK 5.

# Interesting Chip Data Sheets

Consult the developer reference board schematics and the data sheets for your ARTIK module to identify the large-scale integrated components. If you plan to build a product based on the reference board, consider using the same chips as Samsung built into the developer reference boards because the ARTIK is already configured to interact with them. Some of these chips are controlled via GPIO/I2S/SPI/I2C and other means. Gather details of how they are programmed, their addressing characteristics, and details of their internal registers. This information is all readily available online in their data sheets. Just use the component identifying part number to search for a PDF file to download and read. Some other interesting devices emerged during the preparation of this book and provided helpful insights even though they are not used in the ARTIK product. They may be useful for your own projects; see Table 3-15.

*Table 3-15.* *Important Chips and Device Identifying Part Numbers*

| Chip | Function |
|---|---|
| **AD5206** | Digital potentiometer (controlled by SPI) |
| **AK4953A** | Stereo codec chip |
| **AT93C56B** | Three-wire serial eeprom |
| **ATA8520** | SigFox transmitter |
| **AX88760** | USB and Ethernet controller used in ARTIK 10 |
| **AX88796C** | Ethernet controller used in ARTIK 5 |
| **BCM4354** | Broadcom Bluetooth and Wi-Fi |
| **BQ2429x** | Battery charger |
| **Cortex-A15** | ARM CPU used in the ARTIK 10 |
| **Cortex-A7** | ARM CPU used in the ARTIK 5 and 10 |
| **CW2015** | Fuel gauge |

*(continued)*

*Table 3-15.* (*continued*)

| Chip | Function |
| --- | --- |
| **EM3587** | ZigBee/80 2.15.4 |
| **Exynos 3250** | ARTIK 5 module core |
| **Exynos 5433** | ARTIK 10 module core |
| **FDV301N** | Digital FET used for enhancing configuration switches |
| **FT232RL** | Future Technologies serial interface UART |
| **FXMA108** | Voltage level shifter |
| **ICMEF112P900MFR** | Common mode ESD filter |
| **KLMAG2GEAC-B002** | 16GB eMMC flash memory |
| **M25PE10** | Serial flash memory |
| **MALI** | ARM MALI graphics processor unit (GPU) |
| **MMA8452Q** | Accelerometer |
| **MOE-C110T42-K1** | Solid-state microphone |
| **NLSX4014** | Configurable dual-supply level translator |
| **PCA9306** | I2C bus level convertor/enable switch |
| **S2ABB01** | Buck convertor chip for power regulation |
| **S2MPS11** | ARTIK 10 Power Management IC driver (PMIC) |
| **S2MPS14** | ARTIK 5 Power Management IC driver (PMIC) |
| **S3FV5RP** | Secure element crypto co-processor |
| **SC300** | Secure CPU |
| **SCP1000** | Barometric pressure sensor (controlled by SPI) |
| **SD3503** | Z-Wave serial interface |
| **SE2432L** | ZigBee front end |
| **TPD12S016** | HDMI companion chip |
| **TPS65632** | Display driver |
| **TXS0108E** | Voltage convertor for buffering Arduino pins |
| **XC6220** | LDO voltage regulator |
| **XR20M1172** | Two channel I2C/SPI UART |
| **74 series** | The Texas Instruments 74 series is a world standard in digital logic components. You can choose a variety of voltages and types to suit all kind of designs. They are the glue that integrates complex hardware systems together and makes incompatible devices compatible. |

# Summary

Now that you have looked at the basic hardware layout, the next few chapters will examine the software architecture inside the ARTIK. Hardware topics must be visited again later to examine all the connectors that the ARTIK provides but this can wait until the operating system software has been explored.

# CHAPTER 4

■ ■ ■

# About the Operating Systems

The ARTIK 5 and 10 modules run a version of the Linux kernel with the Fedora operating system loaded on top. To make the best use of this, you should become familiar with UNIX commands, scripts, and how the file system works. It helps to know about regular expressions and how to pipe the output of one command into another. There are many other books available to teach you about the UNIX command line shells.

## Comparing the ARTIK Operating Systems

The ARTIK 5 and 10 modules both use a Yocto configured version of the Fedora Linux operating system. This is a General Purpose Operating System (GPOS) and it works somewhat differently than the Real Time Operating Systems (RTOS) normally used in embedded applications. The Yocto process pares down the Fedora operating system image to remove unnecessary components so it can be embedded into a small device. The Fedora operating system used as a basis for this process is a full Linux implementation and runs on the Exynos variant of the Linux kernel.

## About Fedora OS

The latest Fedora documentation covers the currently-in-progress version upgrade that the Fedora community is working on. The Fedora web site also has documentation about many previous versions of Fedora, including the one used to create the ARTIK OS; see `https://docs.fedoraproject.org/en-US/index.html` and `https://fedoraproject.org/wiki/Overview`.

The documentation includes advice on installation, booting, networking, and system administrator responsibilities. This link takes you directly to the Fedora 22 system administrator's guide: `https://docs.fedoraproject.org/en-US/Fedora/22/html/System_Administrators_Guide/index.html`.

Table 4-1 lists the version of Fedora shipping with different vintages of the ARTIK modules as of Spring 2016. Fedora is upgraded from time to time as new releases are developed. The production revision of the ARTIK modules may be running a later version.

*Table 4-1. Fedora Operating System Versions*

| Fedora version | ARTIK revision |
| --- | --- |
| 20 | Alpha prototype |
| 22 | Beta prototype and launch version of the ARTIK 5 |
| 23 | Current live version of Fedora. Not yet released for ARTIK. |
| 24 | Planned to be ready for integration mid 2016 |
| 25 | Planned to be ready for integration late 2016 |

© Cliff Wootton 2016
C. Wootton, *Samsung ARTIK Reference*, DOI 10.1007/978-1-4842-2322-2_4

Fedora focuses on rapid release life cycles with new features added often. Releases arrive approximately every six months. It is used as the basis of the Red Hat Linux distribution that powers many corporate systems. CentOS is a community-supported derivative used in many virtual private servers that power the World Wide Web. Because of this relationship, the Fedora base operating system is well supported by a large community and there are many resources to support your development activity. The version history is well documented on the Fedora Wikipedia page at `https://en.wikipedia.org/wiki/Fedora_(operating_system)`.

Fedora is greatly appreciated by developers because of its stability. Without getting into arguments about the relative merits of one Linux distribution over another, a developer needs this stability because trying to develop code on a system that is not robust and stable is very difficult. The Fedora source code receives a lot of support from the developer community, which ensures that new features, bug fixes, and security improvements feed through all the time. Fedora is updated frequently with new features and patches to existing code.

---

■ **Note** Interestingly, Linus Torvalds chose Fedora as the operating system of choice for his own workstations. This is an encouraging endorsement of its reliability as a development foundation.

---

# But What Is Yocto?

Samsung uses Yocto to configure and build the embedded version of Fedora, which is installed as the default operating system on the ARTIK 5 and 10 modules.

Yocto is a free, community-driven, open-source embedded Linux development environment complete with tools, metadata, and documentation. The tools are easy to start using even if you have never built an embedded OS before. Yocto includes emulation environments, debuggers, an Application Toolkit Generator, and other useful utilities. The Yocto project tools carry your design changes forward from prototype to production without losing optimizations and design choices made during the early phases of the project.

The Yocto Project provides resources based on the OpenEmbedded project. Each platform is based on a Board Support Package (BSP) layer designed around a standard format. Each hardware platform then creates a compatible BSP, which is then bound into the chosen operating system source code as Yocto builds an embeddable image. Yocto also provides an Eclipse IDE plug-in and a graphical user interface to the Hob build system.

Given the complexity and range of technologies, it is not surprising that confusion can arise when solutions are chosen for projects such as the Samsung ARTIK modules. It is easy to confuse Yocto with Linux in general and assume that the ARTIK is running a Yocto operating system, which is not the case.

The Yocto project is not an operating system itself but a template for taking an existing Linux distribution and paring it down to be embedded onto a single board computer. The ARTIK modules use the Fedora Linux distribution as a basis for the Yocto embedding process. There are alternatives to Yocto but they must all accomplish the same goals of building a coherent boot loader, kernel, and application building toolkits, which are cross-compiled, to run on the target hardware.

Here is the home page for the Yocto project: `www.yoctoproject.org/about`. It is a good place to start searching for resources. The Wikipedia page also provides some useful background and links to other resources: `https://en.wikipedia.org/wiki/Yocto_Project`.

Yocto is useful for creating embedded versions of the source operating system for the ARM architectures (among others). The Yocto build system is constructed on top of the OpenEmbedded architecture: `https://en.wikipedia.org/wiki/OpenEmbedded`.

Yocto also facilitates the building of cross-compiling toolchains, SDKs, and plug-in integration with the Eclipse IDE. It does a lot more than just cut down the Fedora OS to fit it into a small space.

# Other Operating System Choices

Although there are already several alternative operating systems that have been proven to run on the ARTIK hardware, you are not limited just to using one of them. You really can implement anything you want to; it just depends how much effort you want to expend. It is always good practice to check whether someone has already invented the wheel you are about to make. If they have not, you have an opportunity to amaze the world with your creativity, knowledge, skill, and all-around coolness. Bringing up a new operating system on an unfamiliar platform is at the very least a big challenge and the risk of failure may deter many developers from attempting this. For the few brave souls who dare to try, great kudos can be had. Take each step very carefully and always have a means to back up and undo each step. Experiment first with restoring the firmware on your ARTIK. Then you know that you have a good chance of recovery when things go wrong. Table 4-2 summarizes some of the alternatives already deployed onto the ARTIK hardware.

***Table 4-2.*** *Alternative Operating Systems*

| OS | Description |
| --- | --- |
| Snappy Ubuntu Core | This is designed to prove that a transactional-based operating system can be deployed on the ARTIK. The Canonical group that made this possible would have worked very closely with the Samsung ARTIK engineering team to get this working. |
| Tizen | Samsung use Tizen to drive a range of interactive TV set-top boxes. It is also embedded in consumer TV receivers. One of the long-term goals of Samsung for the ARTIK is to be able to use it in all manner of consumer products to save having to re-engineer a controller from scratch when every new product starts its development lifecycle. This proves that ARTIK is viable for use in TV products. There is some evidence of Tizen startup support in the U-Boot environment variables of a Commercial Beta ARTIK 5 module. |
| SE Linux | This is a special, secure version of Linux. There is some evidence of this in the Commercial Beta systems and more will come to light as the Samsung engineering team delivers the Trusted Execution Environment (TEE) and the Embedded Secure Element (ESE) support via the Crypto hardware. |
| Fedora 20 | This version of Fedora shipped on early Alpha and Beta prototype ARTIK 5 and 10 modules. |
| Fedora 22 | This is the current version of Fedora being shipped on the Commercial Beta hardware available from Digi-Key. |
| Android | There is evidence in the U-Boot environment variables indicating that an ARTIK might be booted as an Android-compatible device. There is no official documentation about how it can be used at the moment but it is interesting to discover it. |

# Tizen Secrets

The Tizen operating system has been demonstrated running on the Samsung ARTIK hardware at various consumer electronics conferences. This operating system is designed for creating interactive TV receivers and could be incorporated into a TV or a set-top box. Some time before the ARTIK OS source code was published, the Tizen project published their own source code and developers started to explore it and experiment with it.

Tizen works on the same hardware and is an open source project. Some of that source code is informative and may have some useful comments that provide insights into how the ARTIK OS source code works, but it is a distinctly different system.

Some developer questions can be answered by inspecting the virtual file systems created by the kernel. Other deductions can be made by seeing what the Tizen OS project is doing on the same ARTIK hardware. The Tizen source files provide useful clues about power management and system configuration. Now that Samsung has released the source code for the ARTIK OS, these alternative operating system resources can provide supplementary help.

The device tree source code in the Tizen project is particularly interesting to read. Comparing it with the source code of the Exynos version of the Linux kernel yields insights into the boot process.

Getting a developer account for the Samsung Tizen operating system project is helpful. There are unique resources in the Tizen developer documentation that describe ARTIK internals. This knowledge is a useful cross-reference to help you understand the ARTIK OS source code better. Go to the Tizen project home page to access the Tizen resources or register an account.

```
www.tizen.org
https://en.wikipedia.org/wiki/Device_file
https://wiki.tizen.org/wiki/ARTIK_5_for_Tizen_3.0
https://wiki.tizen.org/wiki/ARTIK_10_for_Tizen_3.0
```

# Summary

Early on in the ARTIK development process, it was clear that developers were keen to embrace the ARTIK and even replace its operating system with one of their own choice. That has been proven to be quite possible, with several alternative operating systems already working. This should present opportunities to build any kind of system you want to because there is no barrier to implementing exactly the OS you want. It might not be easy. In fact, it might be very challenging, but it is possible.

# CHAPTER 5

■ ■ ■

# Operating System Internals

As an IoT and ARTIK developer, you need to be capable in many areas. Hardware design is necessary to put together the electronics that your ARTIK will control and you need to be skilled in that. Your hardware will not do anything unless your software can control it properly. To do so, you must understand the internals of the operating system (OS). Knowing about the OS capabilities will also save you wasting time reinventing something the ARTIK already does for you. Understanding the hardware and software equips you to balance the trade-off between whether to code something or add a hardware chip to accomplish the same goal.

## Under the Hood

The OS keeps everything running efficiently and provides services that your applications can exploit to get their work done. The OS protects you from inadvertently damaging something important and also protects your system from intrusion by unauthorized parties. Although things are kept under tight control, your application can gain access when needed if it has the right credentials and uses the correct API calls.

Source code to use for modifying the operating system internals is publicly available for the Fedora implementation that is used in the ARTIK 5 and 10 modules. Samsung also released source code to support developers who want to rebuild the OS installation kit. To alter the way something works, download the source code for it, modify it, and recompile just that component. Being able to look at the source can teach you a lot about how the operating system works. Acquire some knowledge of the following internals to help you understand the operating system and write better applications as a consequence:

- The kernel
- Input/output processes
- Memory and storage
- File systems
- Startup and shutdown behavior
- Code libraries
- UNIX command line
- The alternative API options available

The operating system manages the hardware and maintains the information you store in files on the local storage. As the computer starts up, the file system organizes everything for you and the scheduler starts various processes running. Then the operating system manages your secure login so you can run application programs.

© Cliff Wootton 2016
C. Wootton, *Samsung ARTIK Reference*, DOI 10.1007/978-1-4842-2322-2_5

One of the most useful things that the kernel does for you is to create a series of virtual file systems that make kernel internals available to your applications running in a publicly accessible user space. There are several of these virtual file systems to learn about:

- /dev is a directory containing references to devices. These are higher-level abstractions of the hardware mapped to individual drivers.

- /sys is a file system that has regular files that the kernel creates to reflect hardware interfaces that it manages into user space where your application can access them.

- /proc contains a directory for each running process with internal structures reflected as regular files.

- /run is a file system maintained while the system is running. It contains volatile items that may change from one boot to another.

# The Component Parts of the ARTIK OS

An operating system is composed of many parts and the OS in the ARTIK 5 and 10 comes from a variety of open source projects. Samsung integrates them to create the system. Because it is open source, you can potentially alter or replace any part of it. This is now practical because Samsung released the source code for developers to download and use to modify the ARTIK-specific parts of the OS. Other components must be obtained from their open source project web sites to complete the build process. You must very careful if you are delving into this kind of operating system modification because if you break something, your ARTIK might not boot and recovery may be problematic depending on what you just broke. If the boot loader is still intact, reinstall the operating system from the standard, Samsung-provided, downloadable firmware. If you damage the U-Boot code, recovery becomes very difficult without the kind of resources that Samsung has in the factory. The main parts of the main component of the ARTIK OS are

- U-Boot loader
- Device tree
- Kernel
- Kernel configuration
- Fedora distribution
- Yocto build manager
- Yocto Board Support Packages (BCPs)
- Additional software

## U-Boot Loader

The U-Boot startup code is described as the boot loader. This is equivalent to the BIOS in a PC or the EFI firmware in the Apple Macintosh systems. It locates the bootable kernel within the OS, creates a file system, and mounts the kernel and then starts it. You have an opportunity to modify the instructions that U-Boot gives to the kernel if you are prepared to interrupt the normal start up and modify the U-Boot environment variables. Here are some useful links for the U-Boot project web site and Wikipedia pages:

www.denx.de/wiki/U-Boot
https://en.wikipedia.org/wiki/Das_U-Boot

> ■ **Note** Do not alter anything in the U-Boot environment unless you are very clear about what you are changing and why. Ensure that you can undo any changes that you make so the system can be restored to normal operation if you break something.

## Device Tree

The U-Boot start-up process passes a compiled binary device tree to the kernel so it can build its initial device virtual file system that loads the drivers for the various hardware components in the ARTIK. The official Linux kernel source repository has been updated recently with a device tree source file for the ARTIK 5; see
https://github.com/torvalds/linux/blob/4a5219edcdae52bfb5eea0dfc2a7bd575961dad7/arch/arm/
boot/dts/exynos3250-artik5.dtsi.

## Kernel

The kernel of the Linux operating system in your ARTIK is the piece of software developed by Linus Torvalds. This kernel defines the Linux operating system. Everything else is built on top of it.

The kernel is a core part of the operating system that creates an infrastructure for the device drivers to live in. The initial device driver tree is constructed in the /dev virtual file system. Other devices are added to this directory by loadable kernel modules. You might introduce drivers for your own proprietary hardware by creating a loadable module of your own. Here are some useful links to kernel related resources:

www.kernel.org/
https://en.wikipedia.org/wiki/Linux_kernel
https://github.com/torvalds/linux
www.kroah.com/lkn/

## Fedora Distribution

The Fedora software is maintained by the Red Hat Linux organization. Early ARTIK prototypes were running a Fedora 20-based operating system but the Commercial Beta ARTIK modules are now on Fedora version 22. There are later versions of that Linux distribution, and future OS upgrades from Samsung will track the progress of the Fedora project. Fedora is released every few months and the oldest versions of the OS are deprecated as the new ones are introduced. This does not mean your ARTIK will stop working. However, when your OS is a dozen releases behind, getting updates for bug fixes and security exploits will become increasingly more difficult.

The Fedora source code is easy to access and there is a great deal of useful documentation about it if you want to learn about system administration and configuring your system. Having the source code may allow you to rebuild portions of the OS to update some of the tools but always be careful to have a back-out plan to restore the original code in case your changes do not work.

https://getfedora.org/
https://en.wikipedia.org/wiki/Fedora_(operating_system)
https://fedoraproject.org/wiki/Fedora_Project_Wiki

## Yocto Build Manager

The Yocto project is designed to help migrate an operating system that would normally be used in a desktop system into a form that works in an embedded scenario. Embedded operating systems run with less memory and with all of the unnecessary code stripped away. The drivers map onto the hardware in the embedded system by way of a Board Support Package. Yocto uses that BSP with a configuration file to build the Fedora operating system from its source code and cross-compile the output to run on the ARM processors in the ARTIK. Some forum postings have indicated dismay at using Yocto but it is not an operating system in its own right. It is a configuration tool for deploying Fedora. You are not running Yocto in the ARTIK; you are running Fedora combined with the code in the Yocto BSP. The ARTIK BSP source code is not yet available to the developer community. You cannot build a complete replacement for the Fedora operating system with Yocto for the time being. The documentation in the Samsung source code repositories suggests other ways to build the OS binary image to create the SD Fuse package for installation.

```
www.yoctoproject.org/
https://en.wikipedia.org/wiki/Yocto_Project
```

## Additional Software

Once you have a viable operating system, add useful tools to it such as language compilers, interpreters, and SDK developer libraries. Apache web servers, Node.js, Python, GCC, dnf/yum, rpm, curl, and wget fall under this category although some of these tools are already bound into the Fedora distribution. Add other tools if necessary, but be aware that you are working within a limited memory space. A deployable image that does not contain development tools helps to defeat the nefarious hacker community in their attempts to penetrate your system.

# Looking Inside the Kernel

The kernel is the lowest level and most foundational part of an operating system. It maps the hardware to all the higher layers of the operating system. If you are bring up a new computer system from scratch, this is where your engineers will spend a lot of time writing software that interacts directly with your hardware. The hardware in each kind of computer platform can be radically different but the kernel presents a uniform API to the rest of the operating system so it can be coded in a more generic way. Read about the kernel on Wikipedia at https://en.wikipedia.org/wiki/Linux_kernel.

The kernel manages the devices, maps the hardware to the virtual file system, keeps track of processes and memory allocation, and manages file storage. The code that runs inside the kernel space is highly privileged and the operating system needs to provide sufficient access to it so that users can run applications that exploit it but without giving them the "keys to the kingdom." Security and permissions control are critical here because if a user can gain unauthorized access to the kernel, they can completely subvert the machine. The continual vigilance of the system administrator and the kernel's own security countermeasures are the primary protections against unwanted intrusion.

Sitting above the kernel is the user space. The security privileges here depend on the owning account that manages the files and running processes. Files can be owned by an account, which can prohibit them from being seen by other accounts. You can see your own files but you cannot see the ones belonging to someone else. Likewise, the kernel protects your memory space from being accessed by other processes but allows your process to access all the assets it owns.

The kernel exposes the privileged parts of its inner workings to the user applications via the virtual file systems it constructs. These access points behave like an application programming interface (API), which your applications can access either as regular files or via libraries of function calls. There are four principal file system trees to learn about. Historically, a few items have migrated from one file system to another and although the organization is stable and logical, there are a few places where they overlap. Some device information and system API interfaces are located in multiple places within the /proc file system and the /dev and /sys file systems.

- /dev: Devices owned by the kernel and managed with drivers
- /proc: Process-related statistics and controls
- /run: Runtime temporary storage for applications
- /sys: System controls and interfaces to hardware

## Kernel Versions

The Commercial Beta version of the ARTIK 5 ships with a Yocto-configured Fedora 22 operating system running on top of the version 3.10 Linux kernel. The kernel versions are well documented on Wikipedia at https://en.wikipedia.org/wiki/Linux_kernel.

Check your kernel version with these commands after you log in to your ARTIK:

```
uname -a
cat /proc/version
```

It is very rare for shipping products to be using the very latest version of the kernels and operating system code. This is because of the extended lead-time required for the engineers to port the operating system source to the platform hardware and release it through to production and then on to end users.

Read the available resources and do further research on some topics to find out if there are important changes. The release notes for each major revision of the Linux kernel are available and provide insights into its inner workings. Decide whether the features you need for your application development are available or not. Each documented feature has links to useful supporting documentation:

```
http://kernelnewbies.org/LinuxVersions
```

This gradual forward progress of kernel development incurs risks when migrating your kernel to a later version in case something breaks. The cautious approach would leave the kernel well alone and not do any upgrades. If you have a truly compelling reason to upgrade the kernel, version 3.19 may have moderate risks associated with it. Run a 3.19 kernel and build Fedora 22 on top of it as a test install on a spare computer before risking the installation on your ARTIK.

Version 4 of the kernel is not a major new evolution but merely a reset of the version-numbering scheme. The release notes describe this as an arbitrary version change. Going to a version 4.5 kernel from a 3.10 kernel might work without any problems but there are increased risks because of new or modified API calls that the Fedora OS relies on. The more versions you skip, the greater your risk of breakage due to the compounded changes.

If you jump forward a long way, you might consider upgrading the Fedora OS at the same time. The Samsung engineering team needs to release the Yocto BSPs in addition to the OS source code. Then the developers can create an updated Fedora installer running on top of a new kernel.

## Interacting with the Kernel

The security of the kernel needs to be maintained at all times. If it is too secure, your applications cannot talk to it and your options for building useful applications become very limited.

The kernel exposes those of its own internal structures and values that are safe for users to access via the /sys and /proc virtual file systems. The /dev virtual file system is also managed by the kernel and some interaction can take place through it.

49

The kernel creates these virtual file systems and constructs a tree of directories in them, which represent various components within the kernel as if they were objects. The properties of those objects are then implemented as regular files with protection managed using the usual file system permissions.

Reading from one of those files passes information out of the kernel and allows your application to see it. To change the value for an internal property within the kernel or one of its modules, you would write the new value to one of these regular files.

The kernel only publishes interfaces for things that it wants to allow you to see or change and the file permissions control whether you are allowed to do anything at all. It is a rather neat solution to giving user space applications access to kernel internals.

If you are writing extensions to the kernel or making your own installable kernel modules, use this mechanism to export parameters to allow other applications to communicate with your kernel extension.

Refer to Chapter 10 for a discussion about the /proc virtual file system (procfs). The /sys virtual file system (sysfs) is discussed in Chapter 8.

## Using the Kernel debugfs Filesystem

The computing industry is getting crowded with technologies to the extent that names and acronyms can mean several things. The term debugfs describes a virtual file system for examining the internals of the kernel if it has previously been compiled to include the necessary support. Confusingly, there is also an unrelated debugfs command line tool, which you can use to debug file systems in general and even use to recover deleted files.

The debugfs virtual file system is already mounted for you at /sys/kernel/debug. This mount point is only accessible to the root user account. Read the following advice on accessing your kernel and access some links to useful resources for debugging:

```
https://en.wikipedia.org/wiki/Debugfs
www.kernel.org/doc/Documentation/filesystems/debugfs.txt
```

Listing 5-1 shows you the different kinds of debugging reports that are created by the kernel as it manages the devices and drivers for the OS.

***Listing 5-1.*** Kernel Debug Reports

```
ls /sys/kernel/debug
```

```
12480000.usb  dma_buf    iommu      mmc1     regmap          suspend_stats
asoc          extfrag    ion        mmc2     regulator       suspend_time
bdi           gpio       iovmm      pd_gpio  s2mps14         sync
bluetooth     hid        mali       pinctrl  s3c-fb          sysmmu
clk           ieee80211  memblock   pm_qos   sched_features  tracing
dhd           iio        mmc0       pwm      shrinker        wakeup_sources
```

# Standard Input/Output Devices

Every process has three important input and output streams associated with it. Sometimes processes share them; at other times they each maintain their own private I/O channels. It depends how the process was created. When you log in to your user account, your command line shell has the three file streams summarized in Table 5-1 opened automatically for you.

**Table 5-1.** *Standard Input/Output Streams*

| File | Purpose | Path |
|------|---------|------|
| Standard input | Incoming data arrives through this file, usually from the keyboard but can be redirected from another process. | /dev/stdin |
| Standard output | When your applications write output with a shell echo command or a C language printf() function, the characters are sent to this file. | /dev/stdout |
| Standard error | When something goes wrong, the error messages are delivered to this file to keep them separate from the genuine output stream. | /dev/stderr |

If you have several network connected sessions open at once, their standard input/output devices each point at different /dev/tty files when you follow the chain of symbolic links to their end point. This ensures that the output from a command typed in one session does not show up on the screen of another. It makes sense for it to work in this manner. If you log in with a second session, perhaps via a telnet or ssh command, that command line shell will have its own separate standard I/O steams connected to different files.

Back in your original session, when you type a command or run a shell script, it inherits the standard I/O channels from its parent or calling process. The relationship between parent and child processes is obvious when you type the ps -ef command.

Examining this mapping with an ls command can only get you so far because the ls command itself is running as a child process. When it lists a Process ID number, it is not the PID for your shell command line but the PID for the child process running the ls command. Getting an instinctive feel for child processes and how they affect what is happening pays big dividends later when you are trying to debug your applications. You can waste a lot of time trying to deduce why something did not get altered in process space for your application without realizing you are looking at the process space for a completely different application.

Figure 5-1 shows how the standard I/O channels are mapped to files in the current (self) process space and how these are then mapped to the serial device that you logged in from. This is all accomplished by symbolic links in the kernel managed virtual file systems.

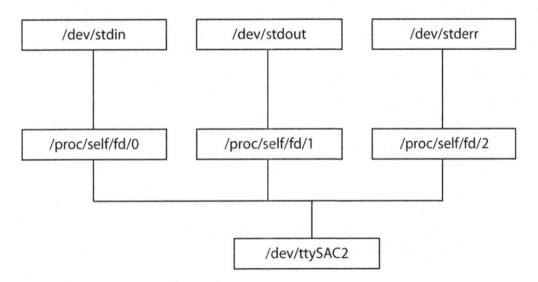

**Figure 5-1.** *Standard I/O redirections*

Early on in the boot process, the kernel creates the /dev/ttySAC device. If you are connected via a serial interface, your session uses this as its base driver. It represents the console where all keystrokes are expected to come from and where all output is directed. If you log on with a network session, it would be a different device but things would work the same.

As your command line shell process is started, the /proc virtual file system is populated with details of your process that are reflected from the kernel into the user space. The standard I/O in a command line shell needs somewhere to send normal output and error messages and somewhere to receive input. The very first file buffer that is opened is used to get keystrokes from your console. The second one is used to manage normal application output. The third is reserved to keep errors and warning messages separate from normal output. This makes it very easy to turn them off to declutter the console output. These first three files are taken from your process resources and reduce the number of available file buffers accordingly. This explains why you may have a few less file descriptors than you expected if you exhaust the supply.

Finally, the symbolic devices for standard input, output, and error are connected to the corresponding file descriptors. Now you are equipped to manage the redirection of your standard I/O from the command line. Standard input can be taken from an alternative place by constructing a pipe or using < meta-characters in the shell to take input from a **here** file. Standard output and standard error can be directed to other files to spool them into a permanent file or they can be redirected to /dev/null and discarded with the > shell meta-characters. They can also be redirected by piping commands from one command to another.

While this redirection takes place, the three nodes in the /proc/self directory remain intact so the standard I/O can be redirected back to its default targets. Listing 5-2 illustrates the results of exploring these from an ARTIK command line.

*Listing 5-2.* Standard I/O Exploration

```
ls -la /dev/stdin

lrwxrwxrwx 1 root root 15 Apr  8  2014 /dev/stdin -> /proc/self/fd/0

ls -la /dev/stdout

lrwxrwxrwx 1 root root 15 Apr  8  2014 /dev/stdout -> /proc/self/fd/1

ls -la /dev/stderr

lrwxrwxrwx 1 root root 15 Apr  8  2014 /dev/stderr -> /proc/self/fd/2

ls -la /proc/self/fd

lrwx------ 1 root root 64 Feb 16 20:18 0 -> /dev/ttySAC2
lrwx------ 1 root root 64 Feb 16 20:18 1 -> /dev/ttySAC2
lrwx------ 1 root root 64 Feb 16 20:18 2 -> /dev/ttySAC2
lr-x------ 1 root root 64 Feb 16 20:18 3 -> /proc/2665/fd

ls -la /proc/self

ls -la > /tmp/xxx.txt 2> /dev/null
```

Note how node 3 points back at the directory belonging to the process running the ls command when you list the contents of the /proc/self/fd directory.

The /proc/self virtual file points at an entry in the /proc directory for a PID that no longer exists because the ls command process has completed and exited. That PID number is not recycled again until the system is rebooted. The /proc/self entry always points at properties for the currently running process. Because the command line shell readily spawns sub processes, this is more useful to you as a C Language programmer.

The last command shows how to redirect standard output to a file and standard error to /dev/null to discard error messages. The symbolic links change correspondingly. Figure 5-2 shows how those streams are remapped.

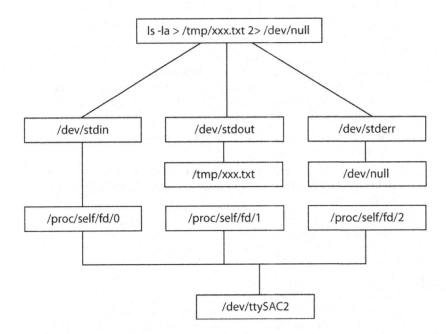

*Figure 5-2.* *Redirecting standard I/O*

# Peripheral Interfaces

The ARTIK 5 and ARTIK 10 modules support a variety of programmable signal pins. Some of these are implemented as General Purpose Input/Output (GPIO) digital pins, while others are dedicated to specific jobs such as analog input, pulse-width-modulated output, and serial communications. A few are used for controlling peripherals such as sensors using I2C or SPI interfaces.

There are several kinds of interfaces to access from an application running on your ARTIK module. These interfaces are provided to interact with or control external and internal peripherals. Table 5-2 summarizes the available interfaces.

*Table 5-2.* *Available Peripheral Interfaces*

| Interface | Purpose |
| --- | --- |
| GPIO | These general purpose input and output via pins on the developer reverence board are useful for reading digital switch inputs or controlling external devices via a hardware pin. See Chapter 17 for more details. |
| I2C | This interface is used for controlling hardware devices within the ARTIK such as the UARTs for serial communication. It's also available for connecting external sensors. See Chapter 20 for more details. |
| SPI | This hardware bus is used for driving display outputs. It's not yet fully supported as a user space programmable interface. There is a functional description in Chapter 21 with some practical help based on using the Arduino IDE. Refer also to Chapter 23, which describes video toolkits, cameras, displays, and connectivity that will be enhanced further in a later release of the ARTIK OS. |
| I2S | This bus is used for managing audio input/output and is accessed via the ALSA library. See Chapter 22. |
| IIO | This kernel subsystem is a new interface standard for reading analog inputs. It's accessed most easily through the sysfs virtual file system. See Chapter 18. |
| PWM | The PWM output is part of the GPIO subsystem and managed via sysfs files. See Chapter 19 for more details. |

# Programmable I/O Pins

The ARTIK modules are designed to be a flexible solution to be used as a starting point for controller design in a wide variety of products. From TV set-top boxes to fridges and other appliances, the ARTIK modules will sense and control many external devices. Consider a simple fridge-freezer, which needs to have sensors for temperature in each compartment and also in other parts of the refrigeration hardware. You might detect leaks by adding a pressure sensor or reservoir level detector to sense the coolant. The pump motor needs feedback so the controller knows it is running. Door switches can be sensed and timers set up when a door opens so an audible warning can be generated if the door is left open. The pump motor and interior lights can be turned on and off as necessary and some kind of indicator display needs to show you the temperature. You might also need some mode control buttons.

Table 5-3 summarizes these items and indicates whether they are sensors or controls and which interface you might use to connect them to your ARTIK module.

***Table 5-3.*** *Fridge Freezer Sensors and Controls*

| Peripheral device | Type | Interface |
|---|---|---|
| Fridge door open | Switch | GPIO in |
| Freezer door open | Switch | GPIO in |
| Fridge compartment temperature | Temperature sensor | Analog input pin |
| Freezer compartment temperature | Temperature sensor | Analog input pin |
| Coolant temperature | Temperature sensor | Analog input pin |
| Coolant pressure | Pressure sensor | Analog input pin |
| Coolant level | Switch | GPIO in |
| Pump running | Pulse train via a sample-hold circuit | GPIO in |
| Pump motor control | Power transistor driver or relay | GPIO out |
| Fridge compartment light | Lamp driver | GPIO out |
| LCD display | Video or LCD feed | SPI or I2C |
| Mode button | Switch | GPIO in |
| Setting button (+) | Switch | GPIO in |
| Setting button (-) | Switch | GPIO in |
| Audible warning output | A/V | ALSA driven I2S |

This project concept requires more analog inputs than an ARTIK 5 could support. More temperature sensors could be added to the external I2C bus. An ARTIK 10 would have more than enough analog inputs without needing those extra sensors but is much too powerful a module for this job. In terms of compute capacity, an Arduino might even be sufficient as a front-end processor to manage the sensors.

# Accessing the Peripherals

The peripherals are mapped into the ARTIK file system so your application can operate on them as if they were simple regular files. Just open the relevant virtual file to get a file descriptor. Read or write the value and close the file. This uses the virtual file system installed as the /sys directory. This is the head of the sysfs virtual file system. Earlier blog articles and example code generated by the early prototype ARTIK support in Temboo illustrate how to use the files in the hierarchy to control the GPIO pins and switch LED indicators on and off.

There are some simple rules about how to access the contents of the /sys directory hierarchy; they are merely the normal access controls on a regular file that allow your user space application the necessary permissions to open the file. There are future plans to change some of the organization of this tree structure. Keep current with the changes so you can be ready to alter your application source code if that happens as a consequence of an ARTIK OS upgrade later.

# Summary

Now that the OS internals are becoming clearer, it is time to look at the OS start up process. This involves a boot loader priming the kernel and giving it instructions about how to start things up. The next chapter examines that booting process and also looks at power management support.

# CHAPTER 6

■ ■ ■

# Startup, Sleep, and Shutdown

Your ARTIK does a lot of work behind the scenes as it starts up. Your design may not need to use all of those facilities but before you start turning things off, you need to know what they are. Introducing new startup code of your own might be necessary if you are building something more ambitious as a project. Being able to spot a warning or error message during the startup is only possible if you are already comfortable with what happens by default. Read this chapter to learn about the startup message, the boot loader, and power management. It also covers sleep/wake cycles and shutdown issues.

## The System Administrator Console

When your ARTIK starts up, it displays status messages on the system administrator's console about each process or utility as they are initiated. This console output is presented on your terminal emulator screen if you are connected through the USB serial interface. Start your terminal emulator application first and connect to the serial port before starting up your ARTIK. Capture the U-Boot startup message stream to a text file and inspect it. Some messages are a little opaque but with practice you will be able to recognize if there are any problems with your configuration when you start altering it. Sometimes, the messages convey a useful identifier for use later when you use the command line to interact with a process.

## Power and Reset Buttons

The developer reference board has a toggling main power switch. This needs to be turned on before you start up your ARTIK. This switch is labeled **PWR SW** on the screen-printed developer reference board artwork.

Nearby is a momentary action push-button switch labeled **SW3 POWER**. This is somewhat confusing because when describing a power switch it is easy to confuse the two. In this book, I try to be consistent and describe them as the main power switch and the power (boot) button to distinguish the two similarly named items.

Adjacent to the power inlet socket is a [**Reset**] button labeled **SW1 RESET**. This is connected to the master reset line on the ARTIK module via the multi-pin AXT connector.

The power (boot) button restarts the ARTIK when you have just powered it on with the main power switch. Press and hold the power (boot) button for about half a second. At this time the [**Reset**] button does nothing; later it becomes active when the ARTIK is running. The ARTIK continues the normal boot process until it presents the login prompt.

© Cliff Wootton 2016
C. Wootton, *Samsung ARTIK Reference*, DOI 10.1007/978-1-4842-2322-2_6

If the system is in a suspended state after executing a `systemctl suspend` command, pressing the power (boot) button instantly wakes it up using the previously saved memory contents. If you pressed the [**Reset**] button in the meantime, the ARTIK reboots from scratch and without using the saved memory state. Table 6-1 summarizes the behavior of the ARTIK when the various buttons are pressed.

***Table 6-1.*** *Power and Reset Button Actions*

| State | Power (boot) button | [Reset] button |
|---|---|---|
| Just powered on with main power switch | Performs a cold boot | Does nothing |
| At login prompt | Ignored | Forced reset followed by a cold boot |
| After login | Ignored | Forced reset followed by a cold boot |
| `systemctl suspend` | Resumes instantly | Flushes saved state forcing power (boot) button to cold boot |
| `echo freeze > /sys/power/state` | Resumes instantly | Flushes saved state forcing power (boot) button to cold boot |
| `echo mem > /sys/power/state` | Resumes instantly | Flushes saved state forcing power (boot) button to cold boot |
| `systemctl suspend` followed by [**Reset**] button | Performs a cold boot | No further observable effect although this invokes an internal interrupt handler |
| `echo freeze > /sys/power/state` followed by [**Reset**] button | Performs a cold boot | No further observable effect although this invokes an internal interrupt handler |
| `echo mem > /sys/power/state` followed by [**Reset**] button | Performs a cold boot | No further observable effect although this invokes an internal interrupt handler |

Be sparing in your use of the [**Reset**] button while the ARTIK is running. It forces the ARTIK to halt and restart but it has no chance to clean up any temporary files. If a file was in the middle of write operation, the file could be left in a corrupted state. Your application might want to make note of when it is writing to create a flag to indicate that it was halted abnormally.

If your ARTIK is seized up as a result of a deadlock or crashed application, shell command, or launch service, then a forced reset is the only way to recover without power cycling the system.

# Setting the Boot Mode Switches

Alter the way your ARTIK boots when it is running on the developer reference board by setting the boot mode switches. They are located in different places on the Type 5 and 10 developer reference boards. Figure 6-1 shows where **SW2** is positioned on a Type 5 board—very close to the micro SD card receptacle.

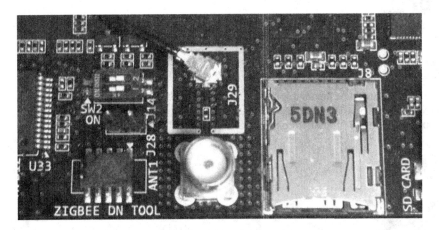

*Figure 6-1.* Boot mode switches on a Type 5 developer board

The corresponding **SW2** switch on a Type 10 developer reference board is on the left edge adjacent to the USB 3.0 connector. See Figure 6-2.

*Figure 6-2.* Boot mode switches on a Type 10 developer board

The functionality of these switches has changed from the original design. The developer documentation states that both switches should be in the **OFF** position as shown in Figure 6-3 if you want to boot the internal firmware stored in the eMMC memory inside your ARTIK module. The boot loader looks for an EMMC memory image that contains a viable and bootable operating system kernel.

***Figure 6-3.*** *Boot mode configured for eMMC*

To boot from a microSD card with a new installable operating system on it, both switches should be set to the **ON** position, as shown in Figure 6-4. The boot loader looks for an installed microSD card containing a Fuse installer image and runs the firmware update from there.

***Figure 6-4.*** *Boot mode configured for microSD*

If you try to boot an ARTIK with an empty SD card while the boot switches are set to microSD mode, even the most basic parts of the boot process cannot work. Make sure you install an SD card with a genuinely bootable image if you set the switches to boot from it.

The data sheets mention that the boot loader falls back to booting from a secondary device (which is always the USB interface) if it cannot find a bootable image where it has been told to look. It can only do this if you have a viable USB device plugged in with a bootable OS stored on it.

---

■ **Note** The ARTIK 5 data sheet describes pins J3-35 (XOM2) and J3-37 (XOM3) on the AXT connector of an ARTIK 5 module as the boot mode control pins. Earlier documentation shows only one of the switches being **ON** at a time while the other is **OFF**. The circuit schematic diagrams have a small table showing that setting XOM2 **HIGH** and XOM3 **LOW** boots from the SD card while setting XOM2 **LOW** and XOM3 **HIGH** boots from eMMC. The circuit schematic suggests all of that boot selector logic is controlled from SW2-1 with the complementary states on XOM2 and XOM3 being managed via a digital FET. SW2-2 appears to be an enable control for I2C signals on the J510 connector and has nothing to do with controlling boot modes. This may be where the confusion over switch settings has arisen in the older documentation.

---

# Cold vs. Warm Boots

There are two fundamentally different kinds of startup: cold boots or warm boots. A cold boot is when the ARTIK starts by running the U-Boot firmware, followed by the autoloader and the kernel. A warm boot is when the system comes back from a suspended or hibernated state. The uptime value would be reset for a cold boot but should remain intact for a suspended or hibernated warm boot.

There may be some scenarios where a hardware reset is required and just restarting is not sufficient; you may need to power cycle the ARTIK. The different types of boot are listed in Table 6-2.

***Table 6-2.*** *Boot Types*

| Boot type | Description |
| --- | --- |
| Power cycle | Complete power off and on again with the main power switch. Removing the power cable is not necessary as this switch should completely isolate the main power supply. A small coin cell battery provides some backup power while this switch is turned off or the power cable is unplugged. |
| Cold boot | Called by a [**Reset**] button or shutdown reboot command. Some hardware may not be reinitialized if the power is not cycled. |
| Warm boot | Restarting the ARTIK without going all the way back to a complete cold boot. Perhaps by reloading the memory contents from a cache. Sleep or hibernate are examples of warm boots. |
| Sleep/wake | Using the systemctl suspend command stores the processor memory and CPU state in a battery backed cache to be recalled instantly. |
| Hibernate/wake | Using the systemctl hibernate command stores the processor memory and CPU state in a persistent offline cache to be reloaded. This is not currently fully working in the Commercial Beta ARTIK modules. |
| Forced halt and reboot | Crash and burn followed by a cold boot. There is some risk of data loss if this happens. This can be triggered by pressing the [**Reset**] button or halting without an orderly shutdown. |
| Network boot | Download the boot image from a networked server. This might be useful for multi-processor grids and clusters. Alter the U-Boot defaults to call the appropriate command and define a server to load it from. You also need the network up and running first for this to work. There are a variety of different protocols available to choose from when you call down the boot image. Refer to the U-Boot command summary for details. |

Read the module reset descriptions in the ARTIK data sheets for more information about sleep states and wakeup/reset scenarios.

# Starting Up the ARTIK

Watching the startup messages when you are getting to know the ARTIK can appear very confusing at first. A long list of messages is presented as individual processes are started. Some of this verbose messaging can be turned off but since it is only presented on the serial console, leave it as it is. In a development context, it is useful to see what is running at boot time. Customize this startup process to turn off unwanted services or add new ones to the boot sequence. The onscreen feedback shows you whether that configuration worked correctly. Useful and important values are revealed for use in your ARTIK applications. Learn how this part of the process works to spot unusual behavior as soon as it happens. The booting sequence of an ARTIK is described in the data sheets available from the Samsung developer web site.

# The Boot Loader

The U-Boot subsystem exists to configure the way your ARTIK boots up. There are some diagnostic tools to debug things during that process or inspect and modify memory locations that control things.

Interfering with the U-Boot kernel startup procedure is an advanced technique. Because it is somewhat risk-prone, you must be completely confident of what you are doing in the U-Boot environment. The U-Boot environment is not the same as the command line shell you see when you log in to the root account on your ARTIK. Inexperienced users may not realize that they should have halted the auto boot process and should be interacting with the U-Boot command line instead of the ARTIK command line.

Also be aware that some U-Boot parameters may have a limited number of times that they can ever be set. If you set one of these incorrectly, you cannot alter it and your system is "toast" unless you have the capabilities to re-flash the U-Boot software. This can only be done at the Samsung factory, so your ARTIK module is now broken. Does this frighten you? It should! Altering U-Boot settings needs to be done very carefully and only after you have found out exactly what they affect.

Now that Samsung has released the source code for the U-Boot support in your ARTIK, download it from the Git repository and inspect it to better understand the internals of the boot loader.

# U-Boot Commands

The U-Boot command line comes with important health and safety warnings. Reading values from the embedded memory is reasonably safe. Writing changes is very dangerous if you do not know what you are doing. Changing anything in the configuration of your U-Boot environment should be avoided unless you get detailed instructions from Samsung about what to do. Developers always like to explore new possibilities and alter things as an experiment. Just be careful.

Table 6-3 lists the available U-Boot commands. Read the online U-Boot documentation to learn more about them before starting to use them. Not all of these commands are supported in the ARTIK U-Boot image even though the help command lists them.

*Table 6-3.* *U-Boot Commands*

| Command | Description |
|---|---|
| ? | An alias for the help command |
| base | Displays or sets the address offset. By default the base address is set to 0x00000000. |
| bdinfo | Displays the board info structure |
| boot | Calls for a default boot (i.e., run the bootcmd) |
| bootd | An alias for calling the default boot to action |
| bootm | Calls a boot application image from memory |
| bootp | Calls a boot image via a network connection using **BOOTP/TFTP** protocol |
| cmp | Compares memory location contents |
| coninfo | Displays the console devices and information |
| cp | Copies memory locations |
| crc32 | Calculates a checksum |
| date | Displays, sets, or resets the date and time |
| echo | Displays the arguments on the console |
| editenv | Edits an environment variable |
| erase | Erases the FLASH memory. This is obviously **VERY** dangerous. |
| ext2load | Loads a binary file from an Ext2 filesystem |
| ext2ls | Lists the files in a directory (by default from the root directory at /) |
| fatinfo | Displays information about the filesystem |
| fatload | Loads a binary file from a DOS filesystem |
| fatls | Lists the files in a DOS directory (default /) |
| fdt | Utility commands for managing a flattened device tree |
| flinfo | Displays the FLASH memory information |
| go | Starts running an application at the address passed as a parameter |
| help | Displays a description of the available commands and usage |
| iminfo | Displays the header information for an application image |
| imls | Lists all the application images found in the flash memory |
| imxtract | Extracts a part from a multi-image file |
| itest | Compares two integer values and returns true or false |
| loadb | Loads a binary file over the serial line using **KERMIT** mode. **KERMIT** is a legacy file transfer protocol that predates the Internet. |
| loads | Loads an S-Record file over the serial line |
| loady | Loads a binary file over the serial line using **YMODEM** mode for the transfer. **YMODEM** is a file transfer protocol that was invented in 1985. |
| loop | Runs an infinite loop on an address range |
| md | Displays the contents of the memory |

*(continued)*

63

***Table 6-3.*** (*continued*)

| Command | Description |
| --- | --- |
| mm | Modifies the contents of some memory (auto-incrementing the address each time) |
| mmc | Accesses the MMC sub system |
| mmcinfo | Displays information about the MMC sub system |
| mtest | A simple read/write RAM test |
| mw | Fills the memory by writing a block of data to it |
| nfs | Calls up a boot image via a network connection using the **NFS** protocol |
| nm | Modifies a memory location (keeping a constant address instead of auto incrementing each time) |
| Ping | Sends an **ICMP ECHO_REQUEST** to a remote network host to test that you can reach it. Configure your networking support within U-Boot for this work. |
| Printenv | Displays the whole collection of environment variables |
| protect | Enables or disables the write protection on the FLASH memory |
| rarpboot | Calls up a boot image via a network connection using the **RARP/TFTP** protocol |
| reset | Performs a hard **RESET** of the CPU |
| run | Runs the commands contained in an environment variable |
| setenv | Sets the value of environment variables |
| sf | Interacts with the SPI flash subsystem |
| sleep | Delays the execution for some time |
| source | Runs a stored script from memory |
| sspi | Utility commands for the SPI sub system |
| tftpboot | Calls up a boot image via a network using the **TFTP** protocol |
| version | Displays the version of the U-Boot command line monitor application |

The version request output for a Commercial Beta ARTIK 5 is shown in Listing 6-1.

***Listing 6-1.*** U-Boot Version Command Output

version

```
U-Boot 2012.07-00020-g5430e19 (Dec 09 2015 - 11:31:37) for ARTIK5
arm-linux-gnueabihf-gcc (Linaro GCC 4.9-2015.01-3) 4.9.3 20150113 (prerelease)
GNU ld (GNU Binutils) Linaro 2014.11-3-git 2.24.0.20141017
```

By the time your ARTIK has started and is running its own kernel and command line, you cannot easily access the U-Boot environment to inspect the ARTIK internals. Interrupt the auto boot to start up the kernel manually with your own custom instructions and parameters. Listing the environment variables and inspecting things without changing them can tell you a lot about how your ARTIK works. Read more about the U-Boot commands at the following links:

```
https://en.wikipedia.org/wiki/Das_U-Boot
www.wiki.xilinx.com/U-boot
www.denx.de/wiki/U-Boot
```

https://compulab.co.il/workspace/mediawiki/index.php5/U-Boot_quick_reference
www.denx.de/wiki/U-Boot/Documentation
www.denx.de/wiki/DULG/Manual

---

■ **Note**    Be wary of modifying anything in the U-Boot command line without understanding it first. Unless your needs are very advanced and you know exactly what you are doing, leave the U-Boot environment settings unchanged.

---

# Boot Loader Console Messages

These messages are generated by the initialization code when the U-Boot Universal Boot Loader runs. This U-Boot software presents a description of the hardware and CPU model. In a PC, the equivalent would be the BIOS; in a Macintosh, it would be the EFI Firmware. This brings up the hardware to a point where it can look for an operating system kernel and start that running. Press any key to halt the automatic loading of the operating system and interact with U-Boot to explore your ARTIK hardware. Listing 6-2 shows what happens when you boot a Beta revision ARTIK 5 module.

If you press any key at this point, the automatic booting process stops. Interact with the U-Boot command line provided you are confident and know what you are doing. The U-Boot environment is an advanced topic and there is nothing to do in there from the perspective of a beginner. Leave it alone to start the kernel automatically. Listing 6-2 illustrates the U-Boot startup messages.

*Listing 6-2.* U-Boot Startup Messages

```
U-Boot 2012.07-00020-g5430e19 (Dec 09 2015 - 11:31:37) for ARTIK5

CPU: Exynos3250 [Samsung SOC on SMP Platform Base on ARM CortexA7]
APLL = 700MHz, MPLL = 800MHz

Board: ARTIK5
DRAM:   504 MiB
WARNING: Caches not enabled

TrustZone Enabled BSP
BL1 version: 20140203

Checking Boot Mode ... EMMC4.41
MMC:    S5P_MSHC0: 0, S5P_MSHC2: 1
MMC Device 0: 3.6 GiB
MMC Device 1: [ERROR] response error : 00000006 cmd 8
[ERROR] response error : 00000006 cmd 55
[ERROR] response error : 00000006 cmd 2
In:     serial
Out:    serial
Err:    serial
rst_stat : 0x10000
Net:    AX88796C_SPI
Hit any key to stop autoboot:
```

Now that Samsung has released the source code, you can see how it works by studying the code. The [ERROR] messages are because U-Boot is attempting to access a non-existent microSD card. If you insert an empty one into the receptacle, the [ERROR] messages are replaced by the contents of Listing 6-3. U-Boot is then able to look for a third MMC device, which it did not previously attempt because it bailed out when the [ERROR] happened.

*Listing 6-3.* MMC Device Detected

```
MMC Device 1: there are pending interrupts 0x00000001
15.4 GiB
MMC Device 2: MMC Device 2 not found
```

The I/O is then configured to communicate via the serial interface. The **AX88796C** Ethernet Controller chip is detected on an SPI bus during the startup. Even without fully booting the ARTIK, it is starting to give up its secrets. Search online for a device data sheet to understand how the Ethernet controller works.

# Passing Arguments to the Kernel

Some parameters are compiled into the kernel and others may be loaded from a file that lives in the boot partition. Pass parameters to the kernel to alter the default behavior at boot time as it starts up. The U-Boot loader passes parameters to the kernel by combining the values in various environment variables into a boot command. Before altering any of the environment variables that affect the booting process, look at what is already there. Document the current value. Then you can restore things back to the default state again. Listing 6-4 shows the output for a Commercial Beta ARTIK 5 module when you type the printenv command. Your device may display slightly different values.

*Listing 6-4.* U-Boot Environment Variables

```
printenv

android_boot=setenv bootargs ${console} root=/dev/ram0 ${opts};run boot_cmd_initrd

android_format=gpt write mmc 0 $partitions_android;setenv bootcmd run android_boot;saveenv;
mmc rescan; fastboot

baudrate=115200

boot_cmd=fatload mmc 0:1 $kernel_addr $kernel_file;fatload mmc 0:1 $fdtaddr $fdtfile;bootz
$kernel_addr - $fdtaddr

boot_cmd_initrd=fatload mmc 0:1 $kernel_addr $kernel_file;fatload mmc 0:1 $fdtaddr
$fdtfile;fatload mmc 0:1 $initrd_addr $initrd_file;bootz $kernel_addr $initrd_addr $fdtaddr

bootcmd=run ramfsboot

bootdelay=3

bootpart=1

console=console=ttySAC2,115200n8

consoleoff=set console=ram; saveenv; reset
```

consoleon=set console=console=ttySAC2,115200n8

emmc_dev=0

ethact=AX88796C_SPI

factory_load=factory_info load mmc ${emmc_dev} 0x80 0x8

factory_save=factory_info save mmc ${emmc_dev} 0x80 0x8

fdtaddr=40800000

fdtfile=exynos3250-artik5.dtb

initrd_addr=43000000

initrd_file=uInitrd

kernel_addr=40008000

kernel_file=zImage

mmcboot=setenv bootargs ${console} root=/dev/mmcblk${rootdev}p${rootpart} ${root_rw} rootfstype=ext4 ${opts};run boot_cmd

opts=loglevel=4

partitions=uuid_disk=${uuid_gpt_disk};name=boot,start=1MiB,size=32MiB,uuid=${uuid_gpt_boot}; name=modules,size=32MiB,uuid=${uuid_gpt_module};name=rootfs,size=-,uuid=${uuid_gpt_rootfs}

partitions_android=uuid_disk=${uuid_gpt_disk};name=boot,start=1MiB,size=32MiB,uuid=${uuid_gpt_boot};name=system,size=1024MiB,uuid=${uuid_gpt_system};name=cache,size=128MiB,uuid=${uuid_gpt_cache};name=userdata,size=-,uuid=${uuid_gpt_userdata}

partitions_tizen=uuid_disk=${uuid_gpt_disk};name=boot,start=1MiB,size=32MiB,uuid=${uuid_gpt_boot};name=modules,size=32MiB,uuid=${uuid_gpt_module};name=rootfs,size=2048MiB,uuid=${uuid_gpt_rootfs};name=system-data,size=256MiB,uuid=${uuid_gpt_system_data};name=user,size=-,uuid=${uuid_gpt_user}

ramfsboot=run factory_load; setenv bootargs ${console} root=/dev/mmcblk${rootdev} p${rootpart} ${root_rw} rootfstype=ext4 ${opts} ${recoverymode} asix.macaddr=${ethaddr} bd_addr=${bd_addr};run boot_cmd_initrd

recoveryboot=run sdrecovery; setenv recoverymode recovery;run ramfsboot

root_rw=rw

rootdev=0

rootfslen=100000

rootpart=3

```
sdrecovery=sdfuse format; sdfuse flashall 3
```

```
stderr=serial
```

```
stdin=serial
```

```
stdout=serial
```

```
tizen_format=gpt write mmc 0 $partitions_tizen;mmc rescan; fastboot
```

```
Environment size: 2353/16380 bytes
```

> ■ **Note** Changing any of the U-Boot environment variables carries the risk of stopping the ARTIK from booting correctly if you make a mistake. Do not risk compromising your ARTIK unless you completely understand what you are doing.

This web page discusses the boot arguments in more detail. Study similar systems to the ARTIK and synthesize your solution by understanding how things work on other implementations and then transfer that knowledge carefully step-by-step to the ARTIK world. Go to www.denx.de/wiki/view/DULG/LinuxKernelArgs.

Studying the environment variables reveals the details of the serial communications on the console. This line specifies the serial communications speed:

```
baudrate=115200
```

This line describes the format of the serial communications (8-bit, no parity):

```
console=console=ttySAC2,115200n8
```

The compiled device tree that the kernel uses as it starts up is defined by this line:

```
fdtfile=exynos3250-artik5.dtb
```

The fdtfile variable contains the name of a file to locate with the bash command line after logging in. Reading these values as a learning exercise is safe enough but altering them is most definitely not a good idea unless you fully understand what you are doing.

# Kernel Boot Options

Observe the boot options that the U-Boot loader used when it initially started the kernel by inspecting the /proc/cmdline virtual file with this command. Listing 6-5 shows the results for a Commercial Beta ARTIK 5. Trace back through the U-Boot environment variables to see which one constructed this set of options in the bootargs definition. The values are described in Table 6-4.

*Listing 6-5.* Kernel Command Line Options From U-Boot (Reformatted for Readability)

```
cat /proc/cmdline
```

```
console=ttySAC2,115200n8
root=/dev/mmcblk0p3 rw
```

```
rootfstype=ext4
loglevel=4
asix.macaddr=
bd_addr=F8:04:2E:EC:D8:A1
```

**Table 6-4.** *Kernel Boot Parameters*

| Property | Description |
|---|---|
| console | The console serial port is configured for 115200 baud, 8-bit data with no parity. |
| root | The root file system uses the eMMC partition labeled mmcblk0p3, which is mounted at the / location to create the head of the filesystem tree. It has the additional flag rw to control the modes of access. |
| rootfstype | The root file system type is described as ext4. |
| loglevel | The diagnostic message logging level is set to 4. Altering this value in the boot arguments string may be a way to silence debugging messages when you create a deployable product. |
| asix.macaddr | This value is currently empty. Define the network mac address for this device using this parameter. |
| bd_addr | This is the Bluetooth device address. |

# Device Tree

The Device Tree Blob is created by compiling a .dts source file, installing it onto the boot partition, and then making sure that the U-Boot environment variables describe the correct file name. The source code for the .dts file used by an ARTIK is now included in the source code for the Exynos version of the Linux kernel. Refer to these pages for other sample Device Tree Source files for the ARTIK 5 and 10 modules. At runtime, the current device tree is reflected by the kernel into the /proc/device-tree directory for access from user space applications. If you download these source files for inspection, be sure to also look at the files they include during compilation. Some features are described generically in files that are shared by several device tree builders. Go to the following links:

```
https://github.com/torvalds/linux/blob/master/arch/arm/boot/dts/exynos3250.dtsi
https://github.com/torvalds/linux/blob/master/arch/arm/boot/dts/exynos3250-artik5.dtsi
https://en.wikipedia.org/wiki/Device_tree
http://elinux.org/Device_Tree
http://devicetree.org/
www.kernel.org/doc/Documentation/devicetree/bindings/gpio/gpio.txt
```

# Starting Up the Kernel

The following online article describes the booting process for ARM Linux. Although it is not describing an ARTIK, the process is very similar. Go to www.simtec.co.uk/products/SWLINUX/files/booting_article.html.

If the boot loader was not halted by a keystroke, the OS kernel is started up automatically for you. If you interrupted the auto boot and now want to start the kernel manually, type the boot command into the U-Boot command line. The ARTIK only takes a few seconds to boot up to the login prompt. During this booting process, the autoloader needs to locate some secure file systems containing bootable code. Then it can look for a viable kernel and start it up. Listing 6-6 illustrates the sequence of messages during a Commercial Beta ARTIK 5 startup.

*Listing 6-6.* Starting the OS Kernel

```
boot

reading zImage
4375376 bytes read in 22484 ms (189.5 KiB/s)
reading exynos3250-artik5.dtb
38601 bytes read in 23426 ms (1000 Bytes/s)
reading uInitrd
1353683 bytes read in 24402 ms (53.7 KiB/s)
## Loading init Ramdisk from Legacy Image at 43000000 ...
   Image Name:   uInitrd
   Image Type:   ARM Linux RAMDisk Image (uncompressed)
   Data Size:    1353619 Bytes = 1.3 MiB
   Load Address: 00000000
   Entry Point:  00000000
## Flattened Device Tree blob at 40800000
   Booting using the fdt blob at 0x40800000
   Loading Ramdisk to 43eb5000, end 43fff793 ... OK
   Loading Device Tree to 43ea8000, end 43eb46c8 ... OK

Starting kernel ...
```

This process accesses the secure boot images stored in the ARTIK memory by the OS installer. One of the important files it needs is the compiled device tree. The source for this has been incorporated into the official sources for the Exynos version of the Linux kernel. The compiled binary device tree file describes the initial device configuration in a predigested form that the kernel can use as it starts up. These boot time partitions are only visible after booting because they are mounted as virtual file systems by the kernel. Having found and mounted all the resources it needs, the autoloader then runs the kernel.

# Kernel Startup Messages

As the kernel starts up, it reads the configuration details and builds various other virtual file systems. These are well documented in the Linux Filesystem Hierarchy Standard. Listing 6-7 is an example kernel start up message log recorded from a Commercial Beta model ARTIK 5 as it starts up. First, the hardware is prepared and then it locates the Fedora OS and starts that running. There are more references to hardware chips. Search online to find their data sheets. Because some processes are starting asynchronously, some of these lines may display later on in the boot process in amongst the Fedora booting messages.

*Listing 6-7.* Kernel Startup Message Output

```
Starting kernel ...

[0.059284] /cpus/cpu@0 missing clock-frequency property
[0.059312] /cpus/cpu@1 missing clock-frequency property
[0.212586] bq2429x_charger 1-006b: Failed in reading register 0x0a
[0.282180] cw201x 1-0062: get cw_capacity error; cw_capacity = 255
[0.606924] (unregistered net_device): timeout waiting for reset completion
[0.653910] jpeg-hx2 11830000.jpeg: failed to get parent1 clk
[0.764548] exynos-adc 126c0000.adc: operating without regulator vdd[-19]
[3.817001] s5p-decon-display 11c00000.fimd_fb: wait for vsync timeout
[4.911975] dhd_wlan_set_carddetect: notify_func=c041bb74, mmc_host_dev=d8df9810, val=1
```

# Fedora Startup Messages

Once the kernel is running, it locates the operating system (Fedora in this case) and the startup scripts are executed to bring up the system in an orderly fashion. The Fedora startup messages from a Commercial Beta ARTIK 5 are shown in Listing 6-8. This is completed when it presents the login prompt. Study the boot listing on your own ARTIK and inspect the messages about these services as they start.

***Listing 6-8.*** Fedora Operating System Startup Messages

```
Loading, please wait...

Welcome to Fedora 22 (Twenty Two)!

[OK] Created slice Root Slice.
[OK] Listening on udev Kernel Socket.
[OK] Created slice User and Session Slice.
[OK] Listening on Journal Socket (/dev/log).
[OK] Listening on Journal Socket.
[OK] Reached target Paths.
[OK] Listening on udev Control Socket.
[OK] Reached target Encrypted Volumes.
[OK] Created slice System Slice.
     Starting Load Kernel Modules...
     Mounting Debug File System...
     Mounting NFSD configuration filesystem...
[OK] Created slice system-getty.slice.
[OK] Reached target Slices.
     Mounting Temporary Directory...
     Starting Create list of required st... nodes for the current kernel...
[OK] Created slice system-serial\x2dgetty.slice.
[OK] Listening on /dev/initctl Compatibility Named Pipe.
[OK] Reached target Swap.
     Starting Journal Service...
     Starting Remount Root and Kernel File Systems...
[OK] Listening on Delayed Shutdown Socket.
[OK] Mounted NFSD configuration filesystem.
[OK] Mounted Debug File System.
[OK] Mounted Temporary Directory.
[OK] Started Create list of required sta...ce nodes for the current kernel.
[OK] Started Remount Root and Kernel File Systems.
     Starting Configure read-only root support...
     Starting udev Coldplug all Devices...
     Starting Create Static Device Nodes in /dev...
[OK] Started Create Static Device Nodes in /dev.
     Starting udev Kernel Device Manager...
[OK] Reached target Local File Systems (Pre).
[OK] Started Journal Service.
     Starting Flush Journal to Persistent Storage...
[OK] Started Configure read-only root support.
[OK] Started udev Kernel Device Manager.
     Starting Load/Save Random Seed...
```

```
[OK] Started Flush Journal to Persistent Storage.
[OK] Started udev Coldplug all Devices.
[OK] Started Load/Save Random Seed.
[OK] Found device /dev/ttySAC2.
[OK] Found device /dev/mmcblk0p1.
     Mounting /boot...
[OK] Mounted /boot.
[OK] Reached target Local File Systems.
     Starting Preprocess NFS configuration...
     Starting Create Volatile Files and Directories...
[OK] Started Preprocess NFS configuration.
[OK] Started Create Volatile Files and Directories.
     Starting Update UTMP about System Boot/Shutdown...
     Mounting RPC Pipe File System...
     Starting Network Time Synchronization...
[OK] Mounted RPC Pipe File System.
[OK] Started Update UTMP about System Boot/Shutdown.
[OK] Started Load Kernel Modules.
[OK] Started Network Time Synchronization.
[OK] Created slice system-systemd\x2drfkill.slice.
     Starting Load/Save RF Kill Switch Status of rfkill1...
     Starting Load/Save RF Kill Switch Status of rfkill2...
[OK] Reached target System Time Synchronized.
     Mounting Configuration File System...
     Starting Apply Kernel Variables...
[OK] Reached target Sound Card.
[OK] Mounted Configuration File System.
[OK] Started Load/Save RF Kill Switch Status of rfkill1.
[OK] Started Apply Kernel Variables.
[OK] Started Load/Save RF Kill Switch Status of rfkill2.
     Starting Load/Save RF Kill Switch Status of rfkill0...
[OK] Started Load/Save RF Kill Switch Status of rfkill0.
[OK] Reached target System Initialization.
[OK] Listening on RPCbind Server Activation Socket.
[OK] Listening on D-Bus System Message Bus Socket.
[OK] Listening on Avahi mDNS/DNS-SD Stack Activation Socket.
[OK] Reached target Sockets.
[OK] Started Manage Sound Card State (restore and store).
     Starting Manage Sound Card State (restore and store)...
[OK] Reached target Timers.
[OK] Reached target Basic System.
     Starting RFKill-Unblock All Devices...
     Starting GSSAPI Proxy Daemon...
     Starting Login Service...
     Starting BCM4354 Bluetooth firmware service...
     Starting Avahi mDNS/DNS-SD Stack...
     Starting Network Manager...
[OK] Started D-Bus System Message Bus.
[OK] Started Avahi mDNS/DNS-SD Stack.
     Starting D-Bus System Message Bus...
[OK] Started pulseaudio service.
     Starting pulseaudio service...
```

```
[OK] Started RFKill-Unblock All Devices.
[OK] Started GSSAPI Proxy Daemon.
[OK] Started Login Service.
[OK] Started BCM4354 Bluetooth firmware service.
[OK] Reached target NFS client services.
[OK] Reached target Remote File Systems (Pre).
[OK] Reached target Remote File Systems.
     Starting Permit User Sessions...
[OK] Started Network Manager.
[OK] Reached target Network.
     Starting Network Name Resolution...
[OK] Started OpenSSH server daemon.
     Starting OpenSSH server daemon...
     Starting Notify NFS peers of a restart...
[OK] Started Permit User Sessions.
[OK] Started Serial Getty on ttySAC2.
     Starting Serial Getty on ttySAC2...
[OK] Reached target Login Prompts.
[OK] Started Command Scheduler.
     Starting Command Scheduler...
[OK] Started Network Name Resolution.
[OK] Started Notify NFS peers of a restart.
     Starting WPA Supplicant daemon...
     Starting Authorization Manager...
[OK] Reached target Multi-User System.
     Starting Update UTMP about System Runlevel Changes...
[OK] Started WPA Supplicant daemon.
[OK] Started Update UTMP about System Runlevel Changes.
     Starting Bluetooth service...
[OK] Started Bluetooth service.
[OK] Started Authorization Manager.

Fedora release 22 (Twenty Two)
Kernel 3.10.9-00008-g48685d2 on an armv7l (ttySAC2)

localhost login:
```

Inspecting this listing reveals more useful information about the ARTIK internals. The Broadcom **BCM4354** Bluetooth firmware is loaded. Search online for technical information about this chip to understand how it works. Interaction with the Bluetooth networking is managed via the built-in libraries but reading the data sheets for the hardware in your ARTIK is helpful. Based on Listing 6-7, the Fedora boot carries out these steps as it starts up:

- Prepares the hardware

- Locates the operating system image to be booted

- Runs the OS startup scripts

- Encrypted volumes are located

- Memory swap space is set up

- Memory is configured into privileged space and user space

- Journal logging is started

- File system is set up and volumes are mounted

- Serial TTY is set up

- NFS file system is created for remote file system mounts

- Device virtual file system is created

- Random number seed is initialized

- MMC memory device is located

- Boot file system is mounted

- Sound card is located

- Kernel extension modules are loaded

- Remote Procedure Call support is initialized

- Time synchronizer is started

- Hardware timers are configured

- DNS bind is set up

- D-Bus is set up

- Avahi mDNS is started

- Login service is established

- GSS Proxy daemon is started

- PWM audio services are started

- Bluetooth firmware is initialized

- Network manager is started

- OpenSSH server is started

- NFS peers are notified that a restart has happened

- Presents the login prompt to the user

Now login and explore your ARTIK from the command line.

# Reconfiguring the Startup

Reconfigure the startup of your operating system by altering the way that the `systemd` logic initializes various processes. You would not normally inhibit any processes from being started. You may introduce some of your own startup instructions in addition to what is already happening.

In the past, adding your own startup instructions was done via the `/etc/rc` configuration files but these are now deprecated and have been replaced by `systemctl` commands and the configuration files in the `/etc/systemd/system/` and `/lib/systemd/` directories. Read all about `systemctl` and how it works before randomly altering things. Consult the following Red Hat guide for details about this subsystem and read the command line manual pages with the `man` command: `https://access.redhat.com/documentation/en-US/Red_Hat_Enterprise_Linux/7/html/System_Administrators_Guide/sect-Managing_Services_with_systemd-Targets.html` and `man systemd.special`.

■ **Note**    You might accidentally compromise your ARTIK if you type the wrong command and render it unbootable. Reinstall the operating system to enable it to boot again.

# The /boot Directory

This is the boot partition that your U-Boot loader found and used to start the system with. The /boot directory contains the boot loader files used by the U-Boot firmware. This directory is mounted by the kernel as the ARTIK is started up. Table 6-5 describes the contents of this directory.

***Table 6-5.***  *Contents of the /boot Directory*

| Filename | Description |
|----------|-------------|
| exynos3250-artik5.dtb | Boot time device tree blob for the kernel to use when it starts up drivers during the boot process. This was compiled from a .dts source file. |
| uInitrd | U-Boot Initial Ram Disk. See the Initrd page in Wikipedia for more details. The source code for this is available in the Samsung open source Git repository. |
| zImage | A compressed image file containing a version of the kernel in object code format that might be useful for debugging kernel extensions. See the Wikipedia page describing vmlinux for more details. |

Find out more about this directory at the following links. The leading slash character (/) on the topic name may confuse some web browsers. In that case, access this page via the Filesystem Hierarchy Standard page.

```
https://en.wikipedia.org/wiki//boot/
https://en.wikipedia.org/wiki/Filesystem_Hierarchy_Standard
https://en.wikipedia.org/wiki/Initrd
https://en.wikipedia.org/wiki/Vmlinux
www.informit.com/articles/article.aspx?p=1647051&seqNum=5
```

■ **Note**    **Do not remove this directory** or your ARTIK will not be able to boot because U-Boot will be unable to find the kernel.

# Login Credentials

The system administrator of a UNIX system is described as the "root" user. This user has sufficient permission and privileges to completely destroy the operating system and render the ARTIK unbootable. You must always be very careful when you are logged in as the root user. Always think carefully about what you are about to type at the command line. The initial login credentials are listed in Table 6-6.

*Table 6-6.* *Default Login Credentials*

| Account | Password | Description |
|---------|----------|-------------|
| root | Root | Summer 2015 pioneer edition ARTIK modules onwards |
| root | f@s)P!A$RTNER | Early firmware Alpha prototype ARTIK modules |

Earlier prototype versions of the ARTIK firmware have a different initial root account password. This indicates that you have older firmware, which should be updated. Now that the Commercial Beta ARTIK 5 and 10 modules are available, it is time to retire those older Alpha and Early Beta hardware prototypes.

For security reasons, change this administrator password if your ARTIK is likely to be accessible to the general public. It is a very important step when you go into production with your new design that has an ARTIK embedded within it. Be sure to carefully note the new password because if you lock out the root account, gaining access to the system again is difficult. Reinstalling the operating system from scratch may be necessary.

Use the passwd command on the ARTIK command line to alter the root account password. Enter your password carefully twice to confirm that you typed it correctly. The ARTIK operating system suggests that any passwords shorter than eight characters are bad. Remember to note this in a safe place or use one that is easy to remember. Make sure you change the password before shipping a product to end-users or they will deduce your root account credentials.

# Shutdown Commands

If you are reconfiguring your ARTIK or building applications and services to be reconnected at boot time, shut down the ARTIK and reboot it to test your changes. Be careful not to accidentally shut down your development workstation instead of your ARTIK module. Power-cycling an ARTIK would also work but it is never a good idea to just remove the power from a running UNIX system. It is much better to shut it down in an orderly way. This gives the OS an opportunity to record important information about the system and restore it again when it restarts. While you are logged into a command line on your ARTIK module, use the shutdown command with options to modify its behavior.

```
shutdown {control options} {time value} {warning message}
```

The most useful command line options are listed in Table 6-7. Use the man shutdown command to see all the descriptive help pages.

*Table 6-7.* *Optional Arguments for the shutdown Command*

| Option | Description |
|--------|-------------|
| --help | Displays a brief help message |
| -H | Halts the ARTIK |
| -P | Powers off the ARTIK. Restart it again by pressing the power (boot) button. |
| -r | Shuts down and reboots the ARTIK from the U-Boot as if the power (boot) button has been pressed |
| -c | Cancels a pending deferred shutdown command |

The time values can be specified as a specific hh:mm time in 24-hour format. Use the keyword now to indicate the shutdown must happen right away. Alternatively, use the +{minutes} format to indicate a delay measured in minutes before the shutdown happens. Without a time value, the shutdown command assumes a +1 value by default and waits 60 seconds before shutting down. When you indicate a delay, the operating system inhibits new logins 5 minutes prior to the shutdown. That happens immediately if you indicate a time that is less than 5 minutes in the future. Table 6-8 illustrates a few example shutdown command variations.

*Table 6-8.* *Example shutdown Commands*

| Command | Description |
|---|---|
| shutdown -r now | Shuts down gracefully right away and automatically runs the Universal boot loader again to restart the ARTIK |
| shutdown -P now | Shuts down gracefully right away and returns the ARTIK to the initial powered on but not yet booted state. Press the power (boot) button to reboot. |
| shutdown -r +5 | Reboots the ARTIK in 5 minutes. |
| shutdown -r 11:55 | Reboots the ARTIK just before midday. This would be tomorrow if the command is typed in the afternoon. |
| shutdown -c | Cancels a pending shutdown. |
| shutdown --help | Displays the list of commands. |

Modern Linux systems can use the systemctl utility to set the run level to a target that shuts down, powers off, or reboots the ARTIK. Refer to this Red Hat document for details of the different ways to shut down or sleep your system: https://access.redhat.com/documentation/en-US/Red_Hat_Enterprise_Linux/7/html/System_Administrators_Guide/sect-Managing_Services_with_systemd-Power.html.

Table 6-9 summarizes the systemctl commands for shutting down the ARTIK. They must all be executed in the root account.

*Table 6-9.* *Example systemctl Commands*

| Command | Description |
|---|---|
| systemctl halt | Brings the system to a halt without powering it off. Press the [**Reset**] button and then press the power (boot) button. The ARTIK will reboot. It will not respond to the power (boot) button alone without the [**Reset**] button. |
| systemctl poweroff | Shuts down and powers off the system. Pressing the power (boot) button beside the main power switch reboots the ARTIK. |
| systemctl reboot | Reboots the system as if it had just been powered on. |

# Shutdown Console Messages

When you tell the ARTIK to shut down without specifying a time delay, the default timeout is assumed and the default message shown in Listing 6-9 appears on the console display.

*Listing 6-9.* Default Shutdown Warning Message

```
Shutdown scheduled for Tue 2016-06-28 07:00:49 EDT, use 'shutdown -c' to cancel.
Broadcast message from root@localhost (Tue 2016-06-28 06:59:49 EDT):
The system is going down for power-off at Tue 2016-06-28 07:00:49 EDT!
```

Override this message with your own to inform your users about what is happening. Adding a message for your users makes sense in the context of a delayed shutdown. The warning message is sent to all currently logged in user sessions. When you add a message, you must specify a time value to avoid the message being misinterpreted as command line options.

If you are shutting down now, your users will not have time to take any action, although the message may still be helpful. At least tell them why the system is shutting down right away and when it will be up again.

Use the shutdown -c command to cancel a shutdown. Listing 6-10 shows you the shutdown cancellation message.

***Listing 6-10.*** Shutdown Cancelled Warning Message

```
Broadcast message from root@localhost (Tue 2016-06-28 07:00:38 EDT):
The system shutdown has been cancelled at Tue 2016-06-28 07:01:38 EDT!
```

The operating system displays a log of what is happening as it closes down processes and returns to a quiescent state. Execute this command to shut down and see the messages on your console screen as the operating system tears down all the processes that it started when the system was booted:

```
shutdown -P now
```

It may be tempting to power off or disconnect your ARTIK without closing your terminal window first. Shutting down in an orderly manner is always the recommended approach to avoid corrupting your ARTIK operating system files. Randomly disconnecting a running ARTIK from your development workstation without an orderly shutdown is also a bad idea. Once the ARTIK has shut down, exit from your terminal session and quit out of your terminal emulator application in an orderly manner.

---

■ **Note**  **Be very careful!** I observed on my **macOS** development system that detaching USB serial interface hardware from a running serial driver can trigger a kernel panic in the Macintosh workstation. It is extremely bad if this happens because you may have other applications running that are writing to the hard disk. There is a risk that this might completely blow away a disk partition. In a worst-case scenario, you might lose all your files if you did not make backups. Make sure you shut down the ARTIK in an orderly way, exit the serial communications session, and quit out of the terminal emulator before unplugging or powering off the ARTIK.

---

# About Power Management

Contemplate the different ways that the ARTIK modules are going to be applied. Power management is relevant as your design becomes more mobile. Energy conservation needs may impact many parts of your design. Running the CPU unnecessarily when there is no work for it to do wastes precious energy. The design of your code also can consume unnecessary energy reserves. Continuously polling means your CPU is busy spending most of its time waiting. Setting up some kind of interrupt mechanism that triggers an event that calls your application to action is more energy efficient. Allowing the CPU to nap or sleeping the ARTIK altogether via the suspend mechanisms is also good. Slowing the CPU clock speed may be helpful in extreme situations. Pay careful attention to the power drain by your sensors and other hardware attached to the ARTIK.

When an ARTIK is embedded into a permanently powered chassis, this becomes less important, but good design makes good ecological decisions on how it consumes resources regardless of the amount of power available.

If you are using Arduino-style coding, then it has a built-in power saving mode. Manage power usage at the operating system level with the `systemctl` command. Access the power management circuits in the ARTIK via the I2C bus and turn off various subsystems. If you intend to shut down parts of your ARTIK via the PMIC chips, you must make sure you restore the correct values to the Low Drop Out (LDO) regulators and the Buck voltage convertors. The documentation for these values in the context of an ARTIK 5 or 10 module is the Device Tree Source code in the Exynos version of the Linux kernel.

Read the ARTIK 5 and 10 data sheets from the Samsung developer resources web site. These documents contain a lot of very useful information about power management.

## Power Management Integrated Circuit (PMIC)

Power consumption is reduced to a very low level by incorporating the same embedded power management controller in all ARTIK modules. This maintains a steady power source for all the chips on the board and the voltages being supplied to externally connected devices.

The PMIC is a critically important part of the power management that extends the life of the battery that provides power to your ARTIK module. The buck convertors step down the incoming power supply to the correct regulated voltage to deliver power to the onboard processor and other components. The Low-Dropout (LDO) circuits maintain the supply when the battery runs down.

The PMIC support in the ARTIK 10 has more buck convertors and LDOs for regulating the power supply than the ARTIK 5. It has a more complex architecture to control for the extra circuits. Learn more about PMIC concepts here and study the data sheet for your ARTIK module, which describes the power management in great detail. See `https://en.wikipedia.org/wiki/Low-dropout_regulator`.

## Monitoring Power Consumption

The ARTIK community continues to thrive and publish useful material that all developers can benefit from. Kevin Sharp has posted a couple of very informative blog articles on the ARTIK developer blog. Check these articles for insights into how to measure the current drain on your battery with a Hall Effect sensor:

`www.artik.io/2016/03/iot-201-power-management-part-1/`
`www.artik.io/2016/03/iot-201-power-management-part-2/`

In part 2, Kevin makes some valuable suggestions about how to eke out your precious energy resources:

- Measure and log a typical day or week or longer period of power consumption and plat that on a graph against what you were doing with the device. This indicates where your power is being used the most.

- Slow your code down and do not waste effort being busy waiting. Take the measurements less often.

- Do not use wireless communication unless you are communicating something meaningful. Wireless devices expend a lot of energy searching for networks they can connect to. Turn off auto detection processes to conserve energy.

- Make sure your antenna design is efficient. Poor antenna designs consume much more energy.

- Consider using directional antennas to focus the energy towards the receiver.

- Delegate power consuming computation tasks to the ecosystem (or cloud servers) so the minimum of work needs to be done inside the ARTIK.

If you come up with other good suggestions during your development process, please share them with the rest of the community either with a blog article or a posting on the developer forums. The data sheets contain a lot of useful information about the power consumption of the various internal subsystems within the ARTIK.

## Arduino Power-Saving Mode

If you are writing your applications as Arduino sketches inside the Arduino IDE, use the built-in power management that the Arduino supports natively. Control whether your CPU is running in power save or performance mode with these two function calls:

```
goPowerSave();
goPerformance();
```

Track the power-saving state by storing a flag value inside the application. Switch these states based on the flag value and manage that flag value according to the needs of your application. Define the data type of the powersave variable to get an unambiguous Boolean test. A fragment of example code is shown in Listing 6-11.

*Listing 6-11.* Example Powersave Programming

```
// Test this variable later on in your application code with a conditional branch
Binary powersave = TRUE;

... more code here ...

if(powersave)
{
  goPowerSave();
}
else
{
  goPerformance();
}
```

## Power Management with systemctl

The systemctl utility can be used to carry out simple power management tasks in your ARTIK. Refer to this Red Hat document for details of the different ways to hibernate or sleep your system: https://access. redhat.com/documentation/en-US/Red_Hat_Enterprise_Linux/7/html/System_Administrators_Guide/ sect-Managing_Services_with_systemd-Power.html.

This article also has some useful guidance on power management commands for hibernating and suspending the operating system to conserve energy. Table 6-10 summarizes the systemctl commands that are useful in this context. They must all be executed in the root account. The shutdown command provides some additional mechanisms for controlling the ARTIK.

*Table 6-10.* *Power Management With systemctl*

| Command | Description |
| --- | --- |
| systemctl poweroff | Shuts down and powers off the system. Pressing the power (boot) button beside the main power switch reboots your ARTIK module. |
| systemctl suspend | Suspends the system and saves the current state in RAM. Peripheral devices are powered off to save power. Provided the RAM is backed up by a battery, starting the machine should be much quicker than a normal cold boot from a halted or powered off state. Pressing the power (boot) button restarts the ARTIK instantly. |
| systemctl hibernate | Hibernates the system in a way similar to the suspend action. Instead of saving to RAM, the hibernation saves the current system state onto hard disk. This is more resilient and does not require a battery backup but it is not as instantaneous when the system wakes. |
| systemctl hybrid-sleep | Hibernates and suspends the system |

■ **Note** The systemctl hibernate and systemctl hybrid-sleep commands both throw an error message due to a problem with dependencies in its target configurations. This may be due to a missing state value ('disk') in the /sys/power/state implementation. This may be corrected in a later OS build. Diagnose the problem with a journalctl -xe command to see the error log. You may attempt to fix the dependency by modifying and rebuilding the kernel but the problem will regress back again after an OS upgrade unless it is fixed in the master build of the OS.

# /sys/power

The sysfs file system collects the power management control together in the /sys/power directory. This directory provides a unified interface to the power management subsystem. This is described in detail in the kernel documentation. The foundations and architectural design of power management are described in great detail in the ACPI specification, which is the basis on which power management is architected. The ACPI specification is available from the specifications page at the UEFI web site. Consult the following links for more information:

```
www.kernel.org/doc/Documentation/power/interface.txt
www.kernel.org/doc/Documentation/ABI/testing/sysfs-power
www.kernel.org/doc/Documentation/power/states.txt
www.kernel.org/doc/Documentation/ABI/testing/sysfs-class-regulator
www.kernel.org/doc/Documentation/power/basic-pm-debugging.txt
http://uefi.org/specifications
```

Table 6-11 lists the items that live in the /sys/power directory and what they do. Although you could potentially write to these files from a C language application, the systemctl and shutdown commands are probably easier to use from bash.

***Table 6-11.*** *Power Management Controls Via /sys/power*

| Property | Description |
|---|---|
| Autosleep | This file can be written with one of the strings used by /sys/power/state. When this happens, it triggers a transition to the requested sleep state. |
| pm_freeze_timeout | Maximum time in milliseconds to freeze all user space processes or all freezable kernel threads |
| wake_lock | Provides user space control of wakeup requests and activates them on demand |
| wakeup_count | Allows user space to put the system to sleep while managing potential wakeup events |
| pm_async | Controls whether user space can enable or disable asynchronous suspend and resume of devices |
| state | Controls system sleep states. Reading from this file returns the available sleep state labels. Writing one of these strings to this file causes the system to transition into the corresponding state, if it is available. ARTIK supports the "freeze" and "mem" states. |
| wake_unlock | This file allows user space to deactivate wakeup requests created by wake_lock. |

When you read the /sys/power/state file, it returns the available states that your ARTIK can be set into. A Commercial Beta ARTIK 5 returns just two options out of the full set that are available. Others may be added at later revisions of the operating system. Writing one of these values to the file sets the ARTIK into that state, which gives you a simple way to access this behavior from a C language application. The systemctl commands are easier to use from bash scripts. Table 6-12 lists the different state values and indicates the two that the ARTIK currently supports. The ACPI state labels are commonly used conventions in PC systems.

***Table 6-12.*** *Available Low-Power States*

| ACPI | State | Supported | Description |
|---|---|---|---|
| S0 | freeze | √ | Suspend-to-Idle. A lightweight system sleep state, which can be woken by asserting a **HIGH** value on the power pin (J3-10 on an ARTIK 5 and J1-16 on an ARTIK 10). Some peripherals are powered down and the CPU is able to take short naps. |
| S1 | standby | | Power-On Suspend. Not currently supported on the ARTIK. |
| S3 | mem | √ | Suspend-to-RAM. The current run state of the CPU is preserved in battery backed-up memory and everything goes into low-power mode. |
| S4 | disk | | Suspend-to-Disk. This is not currently supported in the ARTIK, which may explain why systemctl hibernate does not work. |

# Wake Locks

Wake locks are a feature inherited from the Android operating system for keeping the system awake when it is attempting to go into a suspended state. They are called wake locks because they lock the device into an "awake" condition and prevent it going to the S3 low-power state. They can lead to increased power consumption if you use them inappropriately.

The kernel debug file system maintains a log of the wakeup sources to inspect. Display the /sys/ kernel/debug/wakeup_sources file with a cat command. The wakeup sources it lists correspond to devices, GPIO pins, and networking events, which inhibit the sleep state. Table 6-13 lists the available wake locks.

***Table 6-13.*** *Wake Locks*

| | |
|---|---|
| BT_bt_wake | mmc1_detect |
| BT_host_wake | mmc0_detect |
| wlan_wd_wake | s2m-rtc |
| wlan_ctrl_wake | s3c-hsotg |
| wlan_rx_wake | alarmtimer |
| wlan_wake | rk-ac |
| gpio_keys.5 | rk-bat |
| 11c00000.fimd_fb | autosleep |
| mmc2_detect | |

## Relevant Power Management AXT Connections

Tables 6-14 and 6-15 summarize the power- and reset-related connections available on the AXT connectors underneath your ARTIK module. The connections for the ARTIK 5 and 10 are each shown in their own tables. Refer to the data sheets for more information about voltage levels and other detailed specifications regarding these pins.

***Table 6-14.*** *ARTIK 5 Power and Reset AXT Pinouts*

| Connector | Name | Function |
|---|---|---|
| J3-10 | PWR_KEY | PMIC power on key, active **HIGH** |
| J3-31 | V_ADP_SENSE | AC power detect |
| J3-35 | XOM2 | Boot from SD when this pin is **HIGH** |
| J3-37 | XOM3 | Boot from eMMC when this pin is **HIGH** |
| J3-15 | XEINT_17 | Charge status interrupt (CHG_IRQ) |
| J3-25 | XEINT_25 | Fuel gauge interrupt |
| J4-49 | COIN_BAT | Auxiliary backup coin battery 3-volt input |
| J4-51 | AP_NRESET | Cold ARTIK 520 Module reset by PMIC. RST signal on connector J25-3 and J510-7 (a.k.a. RST/MRNRESET) |
| J4-48 | AP_NWRESET | Warm reset from PMIC (for development purposes) |
| J7-18 | XjTRSTn | JTAG debug reset line |
| J7-56 | ZB_RSTn | JTAG debug reset line |
| J4-15 | Xi2c1_SCL | Bus I2C-1 used by FUEL subsystem (PMIC) |
| J4-17 | Xi2c1_SDA | Bus I2C-1 used by FUEL subsystem (PMIC) |
| J3-34 | XGPIO17/XT_INT163 | Power management external IC interrupt (a.k.a. XT_INT163) |
| J3-23 | XEINT_24 | Turn device on |

*Table 6-15.* *ARTIK 10 Power and Reset AXT Pinouts*

| Connector | Name | Function |
| --- | --- | --- |
| J1-16 | PWR_KEY | PMIC power on key, active **HIGH** |
| J1-39 | V_ADP_SENSE | AC power detect |
| J1-43 | XOM2 | Boot from SD when this pin is **HIGH** |
| J1-45 | XOM3 | Boot from eMMC when this pin is **HIGH** |
| J1-23 | XEINT_17 | Charge status interrupt (CHG_IRQ) |
| J1-33 | XEINT_25 | Fuel gauge interrupt |
| J2-53 | COIN_BAT | Auxiliary backup coin battery 3-volt input |
| J2-43 | AP_NRESET | Cold ARTIK 1020 Module reset by PMIC. RST signal on connector J25-3 and J510-7 (a.k.a. RST/MRNRESET) |
| J2-47 | AP_NWRESET | Warm reset from PMIC (for development purposes) |
| J4-13 | XjTRSTn | JTAG debug reset line |
| J4-16 | ZB_RSTn | JTAG debug reset line |
| J1-71 | Xi2c0_SCL | Bus I2C-0 used by FUEL subsystem (PMIC) |
| J1-73 | Xi2c0_SDA | Bus I2C-0 used by FUEL subsystem (PMIC) |
| J2-46 | GPIOC40 | Power management external IC interrupt |
| J2-63 | CHG_SDA_1.8V | Change I2C SDA lines to 1V8 signaling |
| J2-65 | CHG_SCL_1.8V | Change I2C SCL lines to 1V8 signaling |

# /sys/class/power_supply

A generic approach to monitoring the power supplies is to access the /sys/class/power_supply/rk-ac directory for power adapter details and the /sys/class/power_supply/rk-bat directory for properties of the battery. Some useful paths are summarized in Table 6-16.

**Table 6-16.** *Useful Power Supply Status Values*

| Path | Description |
|------|-------------|
| /sys/class/power_supply/rk-ac/ type | Indicates that the rk-ac power supply is a "Mains" device |
| /sys/class/power_supply/rk-ac/ uevent | Power supply properties list including name and online status. This value is writable and forwards changes to the kernel when you want to control the power supply. |
| /sys/class/power_supply/rk-bat/ capacity | Battery charge capacity |
| /sys/class/power_supply/rk-bat/ health | Battery health status |
| /sys/class/power_supply/rk-bat/ power | Wake up controls |
| /sys/class/power_supply/rk-bat/ present | Returns the value 1 if the battery is plugged in |
| /sys/class/power_supply/rk-bat/ status | Indicates the charging status. Will display the message "Not charging" when the battery capacity is 100%. |
| /sys/class/power_supply/rk-bat/ technology | Describes the kind of battery that is attached |
| /sys/class/power_supply/rk-bat/ time_to_empty_now | How long the battery will last (measured in seconds). This value should remain constant while the ARTIK is attached to a mains power supply. |
| /sys/class/power_supply/rk-bat/ type | Indicates that the rk-bat power supply is a "Battery" device |
| /sys/class/power_supply/rk-bat/ voltage_now | Current battery power supply voltage measured in microVolts |
| /sys/class/power_supply/rk-bat/ uevent | Power supply properties list. This value is writable and it forwards changes to the kernel when you want to control the power supply delivered by the battery. |

# Power Management Devices

Explore the sysfs file system for details of power management-related components to interact with if you want to explore specific devices rather than use the generic approach. The /sys/bus/i2c/drivers directory contains the devices connected to the I2C bus, several of which are used for power management tasks. The power supply requirements are described in the data sheets, which are available from the developer's Downloads page. The Commercial Beta ARTIK 5 reveals the device drivers listed in Table 6-17, although not all of these devices are used for power management.

*Table 6-17. ARTIK 5 Power Management I2C Devices*

| Device | Bus | Address | Description |
|---|---|---|---|
| ak4953 | I2C-1 | 0x13 | Stereo audio codec |
| bq2429x_charger | I2C-1 | 0x6B | Battery charger |
| cw201x | I2C-1 | 0x62 | Battery level fuel gauge |
| dummy | I2C-0 | 0x06 | Used to map devices that respond to multiple addresses such as storage devices |
| sec_pmic | I2C-0 | 0x66 | Power management Integrated Circuit. The device drivers reveal that this is a **S2MPS14-PMIC** chip. Use a search engine to locate useful resources about it. Read the kernel power regulator documentation that describes it. |

## BQ2429 - Battery Charger Chip

The battery charger is listed as a device driver but is not instantiated as an I2C node so it has no address. This may be because at the time this listing was created, there was no battery charger attached. Deduce the address by inspecting the contents of the /sys/bus/i2c/devices directory.

Check out the following URL on the Digi-Key web site for technical information about the **BQ2429** chip. Download the data sheet to get the I2C register descriptions to interact with the PMIC battery charger controller directly from your application. Go to www.digikey.com/product-detail/en/texas-instruments/ BQ24296RGET/296-39592-1-ND/.

On the Type 5 developer reference board schematics, this is shown on the power and reset items page. This page describes it as chip number U30. Find the chip on the developer reference board between the battery connector and the coin cell backup battery.

## CW2015 - Battery Fuel Gauge Chip

The **CW2015** monitors the state and condition of an attached Lithium-ion or other battery types. The general state of charge and condition of the battery is monitored and accessible over the I2C bus. The data sheet for the CellWise 2015 fuel gauge chip is available from this URL. The data sheet contains the I2C register details for applications to interact with it.

```
http://www.lean-chip.com/mc-download.html?id=154
```

This code illustrates how to access the **CW2015** chip from your own C language application. Go to the following link: https://github.com/SamsungARTIK/linux-artik/blob/artik-exynos/v3.10.x/drivers/ power/cw2015_battery.c.

The following is a useful tutorial article hosted by Digi-Key. It describes how an I2C bus connected fuel gauge chip can work better than sensing values through the generic ADC interface. Go to www.digikey.com/ en/articles/techzone/2014/jan/fuel-gauge-ics-simplify-li-ion-cell-charge-monitoring.

Inspect the properties of the CW201x fuel gauge device with this command:

```
ls -la /sys/bus/i2c/drivers/cw201x
```

If you trace the symbolic link to its target, it leads you to the device, which also tells you the base address of the driver:

```
ls -la /sys/devices/13870000.i2c/i2c-1/1-0062
```

The following bash command displays the battery charge status. Wrap the access to this readable file in a C language function and then parse the result to integrate it with your application. Although there is no battery connected, the charger status still presents some output.

```
cat /sys/devices/13870000.i2c/i2c-1/1-0062/charger_status
online(0), change(0), vol(4996815), cap(100) tte(8191)
```

According to the kernel documentation here, these voltage values are in microVolts ($\mu$V). Take this into account and scale accordingly when you parse the results. This kernel documentation is very informative regarding power management through the kernel-supported mechanisms: www.kernel.org/doc/Documentation/power/power_supply_class.txt.

On the Type 5 developer reference board schematics, this component is chip number U49 and positioned next to the battery connector if you want to locate the physical device.

## The sec_pmic (S2MPS14-PMIC) Chip

The fully integrated PMIC support uses Samsung **S2MPS14** chips. Examining the /sys/bus/i2c/drivers/sec_pmic directory for this device reveals a symbolic link to a device which includes the device base address. This is not enough on its own because the I2C registers inside the device are used to configure it. The bindings for this device in the official Linux kernel sources have some helpful information about interfacing via the I2C bus. Go to https://github.com/torvalds/linux/blob/master/Documentation/devicetree/bindings/mfd/samsung,sec-core.txt.

Useful voltage values can be inferred from the device tree source file in the Linux kernel. The ARTIK 5 device tree source has recently been added to the official kernel Git repository:

```
https://github.com/torvalds/linux/blob/master/arch/arm/boot/dts/exynos3250.dtsi
https://github.com/torvalds/linux/blob/master/arch/arm/boot/dts/exynos3250-artik5.dtsi
```

If you inspect the sysfs file system for this device, eventually you arrive at this directory:

```
/sys/devices/13860000.i2c/i2c-0/0-0066/s2mps14-pmic/regulator/
```

On a Commercial Beta ARTIK 5, there are 16 subdirectories in this tree, one for each power regulator. An ARTIK 10 would have more. Inspect them to find out the current power settings. There are also properties that describe the state of each regulator in its normal running condition and when the system is in a suspended state. Read these regular file from the bash shell or from a C language application. Figure 6-5 illustrates the internal structure of the directory tree for this I2C device.

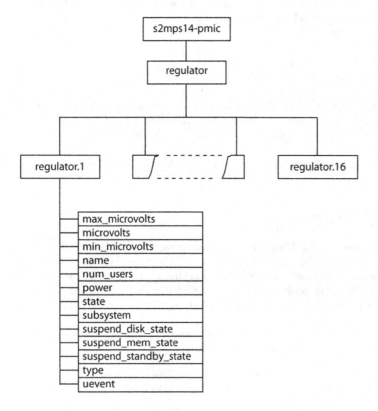

***Figure 6-5.*** *PMIC regulator objects*

The properties belonging to these regulators are intended for read only access. Changing their values from your application is not feasible because you might set the wrong voltages and damage something inside the ARTIK. You cannot possibly second-guess the Samsung engineers and work out more efficient power saving strategies. It may be helpful read the values and present them in a power management monitoring UI for your users. Checking the microvolts property may indicate a fault in the ARTIK module so they are helpful for diagnosing power supply problems. Table 6-18 lists the properties of the regulator object and explains what they are for.

*Table 6-18.* *Regulator.1 Object Properties*

| Property | Description |
|---|---|
| device | Symbolic link to the device that manages this regulator |
| exynos3250-devfreq-mif-vdd_mif | Symbolic link to the Dynamic Voltage and Frequency Scaling (DVFS) for memory controller and peripheral buses as defined in the device tree loaded by the kernel at boot time |
| max_microvolts | The maximum safe working regulator output voltage setting for this domain measured in microVolts |
| microvolts | The regulator output voltage setting measured in microVolts for regulators that control voltage. This value is not the current voltage value, just a configuration for when the regulator is enabled. |
| min_microvolts | The minimum safe working regulator output voltage setting for this domain measured in microVolts |
| name | A string that identifies the regulator for display and debugging purposes |
| num_users | The number of consumer devices that have called the regulator_ enable() function on this regulator |
| power | A directory containing parameters related to the suspend behavior of this regulator |
| state | Indicates the current state of the regulator: enabled, disabled, or unknown. |
| subsystem | A symbolic link to the sysfs subsystem that this regulator is categorized under |
| suspend_disk_state | The voltage value to be used when the power state is set to "disk" |
| suspend_mem_state | The voltage value to be used when the power state is set to "mem" |
| suspend_standby_state | The voltage value to be used when the power state is set to "standby" |
| type | Indicates what type of regulation is employed: voltage, current, or unknown. |
| uevent | Generic kernel device messaging support |

When regulators are used to control current, the voltage-related properties are replaced by current related properties whose names are based on the string "amps" instead of "volts." Table 6-19 lists the configurations contained in the voltage regulator directories. In this example, several regulators are present but unused.

*Table 6-19. Voltage Regulator Configurations*

| Index | Name | Max microVolts | Current microVolts | Min microVolts | Num users | State |
|---|---|---|---|---|---|---|
| 1 | vdd_mif | 1600000 | 800000 | 600000 | 0 | enabled |
| 2 | vdd_arm | 1600000 | 850000 | 600000 | 0 | enabled |
| 3 | vdd_int | 1600000 | 850000 | 600000 | 0 | enabled |
| 4 | vdd_zb_2.8 | 2400000 | 2400000 | 2400000 | 1 | enabled |
| 5 | vdd_lcd_3.3 | 3375000 | 3300000 | 1800000 | 1 | enabled |
| 6 | vcc_peri_device_2.8 | 3375000 | 2800000 | 1800000 | 1 | enabled |
| 7 | vcc_avdd_1.8 | 2375000 | 1800000 | 800000 | 1 | enabled |
| 8 | vcc_peri_device_1.8 | 2375000 | 1800000 | 800000 | 0 | disabled |
| 9 | zbcore_1.25 | 1250000 | 1250000 | 1250000 | 1 | enabled |
| 10 | vcc_peri_1.8 | 2375000 | 1800000 | 800000 | 0 | enabled |
| 11 | VDD_USB_AP_1.0V | 1000000 | 1000000 | 1000000 | 0 | enabled |
| 12 | VDD_UOTG_AP_3.3V | 3000000 | 3000000 | 3000000 | 1 | enabled |
| 13 | LDO2 | 0 | 1200000 | 0 | 0 | enabled |
| 14 | LDO4 | 0 | 1800000 | 0 | 0 | enabled |
| 15 | LDO5 | 0 | 1000000 | 0 | 0 | enabled |
| 16 | LDO7 | 0 | 1800000 | 0 | 0 | enabled |

These regulators are all managing a voltage value. This is indicated in their type property. Each maintains a min and max microvolt value and a current (nominal) value. These values are defined in the device tree source, which is passed to the kernel by U-Boot. The values here differ somewhat from the examples in the device tree source file that has just been embedded in the Linux master kernel sources. Be very careful if you are altering the voltage values based on any of the online sources. The values in Table 6-17 were detected on a running ARTIK 5. The state property indicates whether the regulator is enabled or disabled. In the suspended state, the regulators are all set into a disabled state. Read the kernel documentation that describes these values at the following links:

```
www.kernel.org/doc/Documentation/power/regulator/overview.txt
www.kernel.org/doc/Documentation/ABI/testing/sysfs-class-regulator
```

---

■ **Note**  All of the available registered regulators are also listed in the /sys/class/regulator directory. You can use that as an alternative path to reach them if you need to operate on the regulators from your application.

---

## Saving Power by Slowing Things Down

One helpful approach to conserving power is to run the CPU more slowly. Your end users may not even notice you have done this because the CPU probably spends a lot of time waiting for user input. Each CPU has the same internal structure but only one is described here. Inspect the /sys/devices/system/cpu/cpu0/ cpufreq/ directory where there are properties available to tell you about the current processor performance. Several scaling properties are writable from your user-space application. These are described as **governors** in the kernel documentation. This terminology is derived from the hardware used on ancient steam engines to control the operating speed of the engine. Altering the values in these files will communicate with the kernel and request that it adjusts the CPU speed. The /sys/devices/system/cpu/cpu0/cpuidle/ directory is also worthy of some attention. Inspect the /sys/class/devfreq directory contents for controls you can operate on the Exynos devices that manage internal clocks and power regulators (bucks). User space applications can directly control the CPU and bus frequencies through these interfaces to save power. Refer to these articles for more ideas about power conservation:

```
https://access.redhat.com/documentation/en-US/Red_Hat_Enterprise_Linux/6/html/Power_
Management_Guide/cpufreq_governors.html
www.kernel.org/doc/Documentation/cpu-freq/user-guide.txt
www.kernel.org/doc/Documentation/cpu-freq/governors.txt
https://wiki.archlinux.org/index.php/CPU_frequency_scaling
www.pantz.org/software/cpufreq/usingcpufreqonlinux.html
www.ibm.com/developerworks/library/l-cpufreq-1/
https://lwn.net/Articles/384146/
www.kernel.org/doc/Documentation/cpuidle/sysfs.txt
www.ibm.com/support/knowledgecenter/linuxonibm/liaat/liaattunproctop.htm
```

# Summary

As you explore more of the ARTIK internals, it gives you a solid foundation on which to learn new things. Now that the power management, booting, startup, and shutdown procedures are covered, the next chapter starts to delve more deeply into the OS internals. First, the file system needs to be explored at a high level. Then a more detailed examination of the kernel managed virtual file systems is possible.

# CHAPTER 7

# File Systems

The file system organizes all the components of the operating system and provides a sensible context for your applications to live in. Without the file system, you would never be able to find anything or access the peripheral interfaces by talking to the kernel and driver collection. This chapter introduces the basic file system components but you also need to read about the virtual file systems in the following few chapters.

## About the File System

The file system is the scaffolding around which your ARTIK operating system is constructed. It provides a predictable way to organize and find all the various components. The file system provides an environment where applications can coexist with the rest of the operating system components. Managing collections of files in directories and allowing those directories to be nested within one another, the file system builds a tree of locations that can be navigated very easily. Well-known locations are reserved for storing configuration files, and other things that are needed during the ARTIK start-up are placed where they can be found easily.

The file system concept has been extended to include ephemeral or virtual files. These files look like regular files to be opened for reading and writing but they are hooks for mechanisms inside the kernel. The kernel uses virtual file systems (VFS) to reflect the internal objects that it manages into user space so your application can access their properties. The virtual file systems are each covered in their own chapters.

Think of the file system as one facet of the API your ARTIK makes available to your applications. Knowing the important locations within the file system enables you to build more sophisticated and efficient applications without reinventing wheels that are already provided for you.

## Filesystem Hierarchy Standard (FHS)

Modern Linux file systems conform to a common Filesystem Hierarchy Standard (FHS). This describes how the file system should be organized and helps developers write portable software that is more likely to work across a range of different platforms. The current version of FHS is 3.0 and it has the most up-to-date descriptions of the standardized directories in the ARTIK module. There are a few additional directories that are discussed separately in their own chapters. The UNIX FHS explains a lot of the fine detail about the organization of your ARTIK module directory structure and is available for downloading at http://refspecs.linuxfoundation.org/FHS_3.0/fhs-3.0.pdf. Read the Wikipedia page to see the background and history behind FHS at https://en.wikipedia.org/wiki/Filesystem_Hierarchy_Standard.

## File System Inodes

The file system has some metadata that controls its limits and scope. Two important properties are compiled into your operating system kernel. They describe the maximum number of files that can be open within a single process and the total number of inodes that can be created on a single storage partition. When the number of files being stored exhausts the total number of inodes, the partition reports an error saying it is full. This can happen when it still has 50% or more of its blocks free. The number of available inodes must be tuned to suit what you plan to store on a partition. If you expect to store video clips, you will probably run out of disk blocks before your inodes are all used up. If your plan to store lots of very small parameter files, you might consume all your inodes first.

Each file is associated with an inode within the filesystem. This inode maintains all the metadata that describes the file, such as the filename and extension, the access controls, and the details of the directory to which it belongs. The inode can be manipulated independently of the file contents, although the way it is presented to the user, they can appear to be one single integrated entity.

Conceptually speaking, all of the inodes in a file system are stored in a table. A directory is a collection of inodes, which are attached by linking them to an item in the table. Figure 7-1 illustrates this concept.

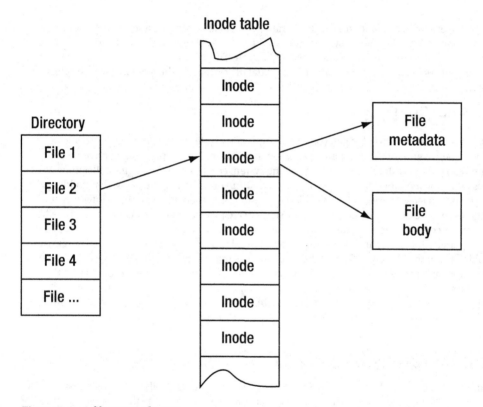

**Figure 7-1.** *A file system element*

A directory is implemented as a virtual file so it can grow to accommodate more inodes. Putting a file into a directory attaches an inode to that directory. The ls command lists the files attached via their inodes.

Because inodes are just links, they can be referred to by multiple directory entries. If you make a hard link to a file, it creates a directory reference to an inode that may already be in use elsewhere. Deleting one of those directory references merely unlinks the inode from the directory but keeps the file intact via its alternative link. Removing all the links effectively deletes the file but the space it occupied and the inode persist for a while until the operating system needs it. You have a small window of opportunity to undelete files because their inode structures are still intact.

Collections of inodes are gathered together into a directory which itself may be implemented as a file on the disk. These directories are presented as folders in a GUI desktop environment and lists of files in the command line shell. The terms "directory" and "folder" are generally interchangeable but there may be some differences in what you can do with them in the two environments. In the command line shell we call them directories rather than folders.

The files are contained within directories and directories can be contained within other directories. This creates a tree structure where the file system has a single root inode at the top. Figure 7-2 shows a nested directory tree structure.

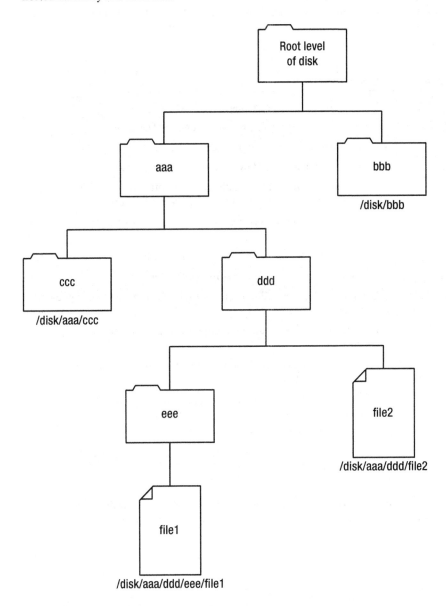

*Figure 7-2.* *Nested directory tree*

# File System Types

The file system type describes how the contents of a partition are organized. A partition may live on physical media or it may be created on a temporary basis. Most of the temporary file systems are created and managed by the kernel but few might be managed by applications that create disk images. Each kind of file system is designed for a different purpose. They each have different characteristics and limitations. Some data loss is possible when moving files from one file system type to another. If you move a file whose name is spelled with uppercase and lowercase letters to a file system that does not preserve case in its file names, moving that file back might effectively rename it. File name lengths can also be accidentally truncated in the same way. Table 7-1 summarizes the different types of file systems used inside the ARTIK module.

*Table 7-1.* *File System Types*

| Type | Existence | Description |
| --- | --- | --- |
| cgroup | Virtual | Process control groups managed in a hierarchy |
| configfs | Virtual | Configuration filesystem where user-created kernel objects live |
| debugfs | Virtual | Kernel internals presented in a debuggable form |
| devpts | Virtual | Pseudo terminals created by ssh and telnet connections |
| devtmpfs | Virtual | A dynamically created device directory maintained by the kernel and available for modification from user-space applications |
| ext4 | Real | Linux extended file system version 4. Based on the earlier ext3 file system. |
| nfsd | Real | A Network File System shared from a remote file server |
| proc | Virtual | Linux kernel process spaces mapped into a file system |
| rpc_pipefs | Virtual | Used by the Network File System to resolve IP addresses to shared file systems |
| sysfs | Virtual | Provided by the kernel for interacting with kernel objects from user space |
| tmpfs | Virtual | A temporary file system discarded when the system shuts down. Similar to a RAM disk. |
| vfat | Real | A Virtual File Allocation Table originally introduced by Windows 95 to support long file names on top of the 8•3 notation supported by the underlying FAT file system |

# File Types

The ls command lists the files contained in each directory. The extreme left column of the file listing describes the access permissions for the file or directory. The first character is called a mode flag and shows you what kind of entity it is. These are listed in Table 7-2.

**Table 7-2.** *File System Entity Object Types*

| Type | Mode | Description |
| --- | --- | --- |
| Regular file | - | When these are listed, they have a dash character in the mode field. Open these files for reading and writing. The files may be character streams or binary files. UNIX treats both file types the same. Use appropriate techniques for accessing them from your application. |
| Directory | d | This is a list of inodes with each one describing a file and where it is stored. |
| Symbolic link | l | This is a reference to a real file. It contains no information itself other than a pointer to a target file. The file protections are always set to 777 (rwxrwxrwx) because the access control of the target file is used to control whether a user can open the file. |
| Named pipe | p | Used for interprocess communication where the output of one process is piped to the input of another. This is sometimes called FIFO (First In, First Out). Two complementary pipes are necessary for bidirectional communication between processes. |
| Socket | s | A bidirectional duplex connection used for interprocess communication within the same host. The connection behaves like a network socket connection with a client and server exchanging data via a request and response. |
| Device file (character) | c | Character devices such as a TTY are used for unbuffered I/O access in variable sized units. Although it is an interface to the hardware, your application can treat it as if it were a normal file. |
| Device file (block) | b | Blocks access devices such as a disk drive. These files are accessed using fixed length read and write operations to access an entire block at a time. |
| Optimized data file | C | A high-performance data file optimized by using contiguous storage blocks. |
| Unknown | ? | A setting for some other kind of file. |

This gives rise to two fundamentally different kinds of files that your applications can operate on: character files that you can read and write one line at a time and binary files that you might read or write a block at a time or in one single operation. Character (or text) files sometimes have some transformation required to clean up control characters, escape sequences, and line breaks whereas binary files are accessed as raw data.

The UNIX operating system determines the purpose of a file by its file extension. This is usually a three or four letter suffix following a single full stop (period) character. Although this appears to be distinct from the file name, as far as UNIX is concerned, the filename and extension are both considered to be the identifying text and the file extension is also stored in the directory as part of the filename description. Some file systems store the file type as a distinctly separate property. A UNIX file type is based on the file name extension. This is a convention rather than a characteristic of the filesystem.

# File Access Control

There are two main ways to control access to file system entities. The simplest way is to use the properties belonging to the inode that represents the file or directory. These permission values are shown in a full `ls -la` listing. Following the mode descriptor character, there are three groups of three characters. Figure 7-3 shows how these map to individual file access controls.

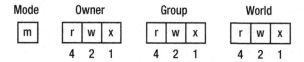

***Figure 7-3.*** *Simple access permission flags*

The access control flags are grouped into three triads. The first triad controls what the file owner can do. The second controls what a group member can do. The file needs to be a member of a group and the users who can access it using group permissions must also be members of that group. The third triad controls what everyone else in the world can do to the file. The permission character is either a letter to describe the kind of access allowed or a dash if no access is permitted.

Each triad can control read access and write access independently of one another. A file can legitimately be writable but not readable. There are files like this in the `sysfs` virtual file system that reflect kernel object properties. In each triad, it is also legal for a file to have no access although there should be some access allowed that the root user can still use to manage the file. The third character controls the execution disposition. This is irrelevant for data files but command line shell scripts cannot run unless this value is set, nor can compiled binary executable applications. The executable flag can be set on the same owner/group/world basis.

The executable flag can also carry other values to fine-tune the way in which it can be executed. A lowercase letter `s` or `t` indicates that an executable can inherit the user ID or group ID of the file owner when it is run. A capital letter `S` or `T` applies the same logic to non-executable data files when they are opened. Other characters indicate whether extended attributes are available.

The permission flags are set with the `chmod` command. Use the related `chown` command to set the file owner and the `chgrp` command to set the group ownership. Individual flags can be set by adding command line options. Use a numeric value to define a binary bit mask to set multiple permissions with a single `chmod` command. The bit weights are indicated underneath each triad in Figure 7-3. Table 7-3 shows how those bit masks map to the symbolic permission flag values.

*Table 7-3. Symbolic and Numeric Notation for Access Permission Flags*

| Symbolic | Numeric | Description |
|---|---|---|
| ---------- | 0000 | No permissions |
| -rwx------ | 0700 | Read, write, and execute only for owner |
| -rwxrwx--- | 0770 | Read, write, and execute for owner and group |
| -rwxrwxrwx | 0777 | Read, write, and execute for owner, group, and others |
| ---x--x—x | 0111 | Execute |
| --w--w--w- | 0222 | Write |
| --wx-wx-wx | 0333 | Write and execute |
| -r--r--r-- | 0444 | Read |
| -r-xr-xr-x | 0555 | Read and execute |
| -rw-rw-rw- | 0666 | Read and write |
| -rwxr----- | 0740 | User can read, write, and execute; group can only read; others have no permissions. |

The alternative to the file permission attributes on an inode is to add an Access Control List (ACL) to the files. These are much more complex to set up but can provide a more flexible arrangement. ACL implemented **owner** like permissions can be granted to multiple individual user accounts without them needing to be **group** members. Rules for allowing and denying can be defined and the permissions can be propagated to child directories lower down in the tree. Read more about UNIX file permissions at the following links:

```
https://en.wikipedia.org/wiki/File_system_permissions
https://en.wikipedia.org/wiki/Access_control_list
https://linux.die.net/man/1/chmod
https://linux.die.net/man/1/chown
https://linux.die.net/man/1/chgrp
```

# File System Trees

Now that you are logged in to a working command line, inspect the OS internals to get to know your ARTIK better. There are many interesting places to start looking. Knowing what the top-level directories contain helps you to find things inside your ARTIK module from the command line. These file system paths are used to access files and devices from inside your application source code. Table 7-4 describes the important directories starting at the head of various file systems within your ARTIK module.

**Table 7-4.** *Important Directories*

| Directory | Content |
| --- | --- |
| / | Primary hierarchy root and root directory of the entire file system hierarchy |
| /bin | OS command line tools (symbolic link to /usr/bin). These are essential command line tools, which must be available for all user accounts. These commands must also be available when the system is booted into single user mode. |
| /boot | Support for the boot process. The static files for the boot loader, kernel, and initial device tree live here. This is mounted during the auto boot process. |
| /dev | A virtual file system that mirrors the logical devices. These devices are considered essential and include things like /dev/null, which is used as a sink for unwanted data. This is managed with the udev tools. |
| /etc | Host-specific, system-wide configuration files |
| /home | Home directories for user accounts |
| /lib | Libraries of code and kernel extensions (symbolic link to /usr/lib). Libraries essential to the /bin and /sbin executables must live here. |
| /lost+found | Files or sometimes only fragments of them recovered by a disk repair |
| /media | Removable media mount points for CD-ROMs, etc. |
| /mnt | Temporary file systems and devices mount point. These might be file systems on external hard drives or network file systems. |
| /opt | Optional add-on software not part of the default OS |
| /proc | A virtual file system that mirrors the content of running processes and kernel information, presented as files. One directory is created dynamically for each process as it is spawned. The directories are destroyed automatically as processes close down when they quit. The top level contains some useful runtime information about the system. |
| /root | System administrator home directory |
| /run | A virtual file system containing information about the running system since it was last booted. |
| /sbin | System administrator tools (symbolic link to /usr/sbin) |
| /srv | A virtual file system containing site-specific, service-related data |
| /sys | A virtual file system that mirrors the system hardware via the kernel. In the context of an ARTIK, this is where your user space applications can access the hardware in an API-like format that the kernel understands. |
| /sys/ kernel/ debug | A debugging virtual file system that reveals many interesting aspects of the kernel's internal structure |
| /tmp | Temporary working data purged at shutdown/reboot. Only remove the items you created. There may be severe constraints on how much data you can store here. This will be a symbolic link to /run/tmp when the planned kernel changes are applied to a later version of the OS but you can safely continue to use /tmp. |
| /usr | User-provided binaries, data, and applications. This is also where tools and applications live when they are only needed in multi-user mode. |
| /var | System-related variable data storage. Things here are expected to change during the normal operation of the system. |

# File System Mapped Properties

Inside your ARTIK module, the Linux operating system does some very smart things to help you interact with your system. During the startup, the bootstrap loader helps the kernel reflect its internal objects and properties out to the user space through virtual file systems that are constructed as the ARTIK boots. This makes it much easier to find and read various operating properties of the system and the processes running in it. Things that were hard to do before are easier now because you can access them like regular files subject to the permissions imposed by the file system. The running processes are mirrored into the /proc virtual file system tree. The /sys and /dev virtual file system trees also provide information about the operating system and its devices. There has not been very much published information about this aspect of the ARTIK operating system. The knowledge needs to be reverse engineered from various public sources by a process of inspection and then assembled forensically. Then it can be proven experimentally by writing a small application. Read the online documentation and then explore.

---

■ **Note** At first, make sure you only read things from the file system and be careful not to write data to places you do not understand. The following is a good proverb to keep in mind: "Take only photos. Leave nothing but footprints. "

---

Table 7-5 lists the virtual file systems created and mounted by default in your ARTIK 5 module. This was found in a Commercial Beta model and may change in the future.

***Table 7-5.*** *Virtual File Systems in the ARTIK OS*

| Type | Mount point | Description |
|---|---|---|
| udev | /dev | All the logical devices and the drivers for physical devices are gathered together in one place here. The VFS type is sometimes called udevfs or devfs in some documentation resources. |
| procfs | /proc | Each running process has a directory here where its internals are mirrored. This is useful for interprocess communication but needs to be maintained securely. You can only see the internals of processes for which you have permission. Some items live here which might be better located in the /run file system. |
| tmpfs | /run | Runtime data for the system is maintained here. Some files look similar to configuration files in the /etc directory but they are live copies of the data, which may have been modified by subsequent commands. This is often called a runfs file system. |
| sysfs | /sys | The sysfs manages the hardware API via the kernel. This is a gateway that the kernel creates to access each individual endpoint as if it were a simple file. This is most often called a sysfs file system. |
| debugfs | /sys/kernel/debug | This file system is normally mounted at /sys/kernel/debug and is used for debugging kernel code. This is present in the Commercial Beta version of the ARTIK 5 but it may not always be there in future releases. |
| tmpfs | /dev/shm | Used for sharing memory between processes |
| tmpfs | /sys/fs/cgroup | Part of the control group management that aggregates several processes and devices under the same security regime |
| tmpfs | /tmp | Temporary storage that is cleared when rebooting the ARTIK module |
| tmpfs | /run/user/0 | Temporary storage for processes running under the logged in account |

The major VFS file systems are dealt with separately in their own chapters because they are functionally different to one another and used for different purposes.

# Summary

Now that you have a firm grasp of how the file systems work, it is time to look at the kernel managed virtual file systems. They are dealt with one by one in their own chapters. Understanding them is an important step because later on when the peripheral buses (I2C, I2S, SPI, etc.) are explored, they will use these virtual file systems to interact with the hardware via the kernel. If you have not yet grasped these virtual file systems, getting your peripheral interfaces to work will be much more challenging.

# CHAPTER 8

■ ■ ■

# The /sys Virtual File System

The kernel manages the internals of the operating system and prevents unauthorized access to its internal structures. Some user space applications need to access and communicate with those internal objects but the kernel must protect itself from unwanted intrusions. It does this by reflecting its internal objects out to the user space as regular files and gathers them together in a virtual file system which it mounts as the /sys directory. This is not the only virtual file system but it is very important that you understand it very well because it is used as the main interface from your application to all of the peripheral interfaces.

## About sysfs

The /sys virtual filesystem is created by the kernel to export its internal values out to the user space. Your applications can then interact with the contents of the /sys file system. Because the kernel can see all file accesses to this directory tree, it can intercept what your application would see as simple file opens and read/write operations to regular files. Because it knows that those are virtual files, it can take the values you write and convert them into changes to its internals. When your application requests data via a read, the kernel can vend back the contents of one of its internal registers or object properties in a compatible format that your application can understand. Some files contain formatted versions and lists of internal structures within the kernel. They can be used to construct dynamic behavior in your application to avoid hard coding configurations that would only run on a single version of the ARTIK OS installed in a specific model.

The sysfs file system in the /sys directory greatly simplifies access to the peripheral hardware devices in a Linux-driven system such as the ARTIK 5 and 10 modules without sacrificing secure access control. The mapping of kernel internals to user-space–accessible entities is shown in Table 8-1.

***Table 8-1.*** *Mapping of Kernel Internals to User Space*

| Kernel internal item | External user space entity |
| --- | --- |
| Kernel object | Directory |
| Object properties | Regular files |
| Object relationships | Symbolic links |
| Kernel register | Regular file |

This mapping is very easy to grasp. To access an object property, locate the directory that represents that kernel object, find the file that describes the property you want to access, and then open that regular file. This provides you with a file descriptor that you can use to assign a new value to a property. If you read from the file descriptor, the kernel transfers the value from the hardware and provides it as a result. Reading and writing files is very easy to do within your application.

© Cliff Wootton 2016
C. Wootton, *Samsung ARTIK Reference*, DOI 10.1007/978-1-4842-2322-2_8

Where kernel objects are related to one another, a symbolic link provides the reference that describes the relationship. Resolve that symbolic link back to a concrete directory reference to locate the target object.

There are some important locations within the sysfs file system. There is not enough space in this book to cover every single one of them. Explore the contents of the /sys directory tree with the ls command to view the contents of each kernel object directory and then use the cat command to view the readable files in there that represent the object properties. The relational symbolic links help you navigate the file system more conveniently. Download and read these resources to find out more about the sysfs file system:

www.kernel.org/pub/linux/kernel/people/mochel/doc/papers/ols-2005/mochel.pdf
https://en.wikipedia.org/wiki/Sysfs

## Inside sysfs

The sysfs tree of the virtual file system entities mounted as the /sys directory provides direct access to the system hardware and attached peripherals. Table 8-2 lists the major subsystems registered with sysfs.

*Table 8-2.* *Inside the /sys Virtual File System*

| Path | Description |
| --- | --- |
| /sys/block | Block structured devices such as disks and memory |
| /sys/bus | Registered hardware buses |
| /sys/class | Devices organized to classes |
| /sys/dev | Devices collated by type (block or character access) |
| /sys/devices | Devices known by the kernel |
| /sys/firmware | Embedded firmware images |
| /sys/fs | User accessible file systems |
| /sys/kernel | Mount points for other virtual file systems |
| /sys/module | Currently loaded kernel modules |
| /sys/power | Power management subsystem |

As the kernel starts up and parses the device tree, it discovers various kernel objects that it maps into this file system. If you plan to write applications that interact with the peripheral hardware in your ARTIK module, become familiar with the contents of this file system.

Document the locations within /sys that you use and check if they are still there after an operating system upgrade. It saves a lot of time if you have a list of things to check immediately after the upgrade, when things are expected to move. Then alter your application source code to point at the new locations and recompile it.

## Kernel Developers Roadmap

The kernel developers have a roadmap that they use to plan and manage the gradual evolution of their code. They know where they plan to take this technology and can advise how to avoid problems by coding appropriately. If you follow their guidance, your code is more likely to continue working as the kernel evolves and the /sys file system changes. These are the key recommendations from the kernel implementers:

- Do not use the deprecated support in libsysfs to access the /sys file system. This library has been obsoleted now.

- The kernel always provides access to the sysfs API at the /sys mount point automatically.

- Do not try to mount the sysfs virtual file system.

- Everything the kernel exports to user space is a simple device.

- Never try to fix apparently missing items within the /sys file system. If there is not already a symbolic link to a driver, there is no driver available.

- Eventually, all device directories will be implemented under the /sys/devices tree. This is the only future-proofed place to look for a specific device. Devices located in other places are likely to move.

- The organization of subsystems is likely to change. Beware if you use /sys/class, /sys/block, and /sys/bus.

- No hierarchy is preserved in the /sys/block structure. All devices are maintained in a flat list regardless of their mount points.

- Avoid using the device symbolic links if possible for interacting directly with devices. They are there for legacy support and will disappear later. Using them to detect whether devices exist or to determine where they are is relatively benign provided you understand the risks.

- The kernel is free to add devices to the tree in any order at any location and at any time. Use the subsystem paths to navigate to parent devices and then acquire their children.

- Do not rely on specific error codes as they are defined inside the kernel and may change.

- The format and contents of the property files should remain consistent from one version to another unless a change is mandated as a result of adding some functionality.

# /sys/devices

This /sys/devices directory contains the physical devices that the kernel knows about. They represent the hardware in the ARTIK. For memory-mapped devices, the name is formed from the location in memory and a symbolic device name. These memory locations can change if the kernel startup process or the device tree is disturbed. Use the symbolic name to locate the memory address to construct an API endpoint path. This is an authoritative list of devices. You may discover other devices by exploring the file system but if a device is not listed here, it is not active and is unavailable for use. Listing 8-1 provides an example. The base addresses are expected to change with each OS release and are different between the ARTIK 5 and ARTIK 10. This listing is from a Commercial Beta ARTIK 5 running Fedora version 22.

***Listing 8-1.*** The Contents of /sys/devices

```
ls /sys/devices
```

```
10000000.chipid          11e20000.sysmmu          13860000.i2c
10010000.sysreg_localout 120a0000.fimc_is_sensor  13870000.i2c
10023c00.pd-cam          12180000.fimc_is         13890000.i2c
10023c40.pd-mfc          12260000.sysmmu          138d0000.i2c
```

```
10023c60.pd-g3d              12270000.sysmmu          13920000.spi
10023c80.pd-lcd0             12280000.sysmmu          13970000.i2s
10023ca0.pd-isp              122a0000.sysmmu          139d0000.pwm
10030000.clock-controller    122b0000.sysmmu          205f000.firmware
10050000.mct                 122c0000.sysmmu          amba.0
10060000.watchdog            122d0000.sysmmu          artik_zb_power.7
10070000.rtc                 12480000.usb             bluetooth.4
100c0000.tmu                 12510000.dwmmc0          breakpoint
10481000.interrupt-controller 12520000.dwmmc1         gpio_keys.5
11000000.pinctrl             12530000.dwmmc2          ion.1
11400000.pinctrl             125b0000.usb2phy         mdev_output.2
11830000.jpeg                126c0000.adc             platform
11850000.gsc                 13000000.mali            software
11860000.gsc                 13400000.mfc             sound.6
11a20000.sysmmu              13620000.sysmmu          system
11a30000.sysmmu              13800000.serial          tracepoint
11a60000.sysmmu              13810000.serial          virtual
11c00000.fimd_fb             13820000.serial          wlan.3
11c90000.smies               13830000.serial
```

Each of these items is an object that behaves as a container with regular files inside. Those regular files represent properties or parameters of the objects that these items represent. Find out more about /sys/devices from the following technical article on the Linux Weekly News blog: https://lwn.net/Articles/646617/.

The /sys/dev/block and /sys/dev/char directories contain another set of symbolically linked references to the devices. They are organized into the two major types of device driver.

---

■ **Note**    Make sure you check the use of your symbolic links after an OS upgrade. The sysfs documentation recommends against using these symbolic links to open files from within your application because they may disappear in future releases. If you have documented the ones you use, check your list after an OS upgrade to confirm that they are still where you expect them to be. Preemptive bug fixing is always better than post deployment correction.

---

# Memory-Mapped Base Addresses

The kernel loads devices in an arbitrary order defined by its configuration files and also the placement of references within its source files. There are no guarantees that devices live at a specific memory address or that the address will remain the same if anything is altered. Modifications to the kernel source may affect which drivers are loaded. The configuration can turn drivers on and off and can dynamically load modules after booting. These configuration options move drivers around within the ARTIK memory. Fortunately, the kernel manages a table of base addresses. User space applications can obtain these values to dynamically load portions of the memory. Mapping them into an application provides access to parameters within the driver. This is how kernel-driven access to GPIO pins works. Figure 8-1 illustrates how the drivers are mapped into the ARTIK memory.

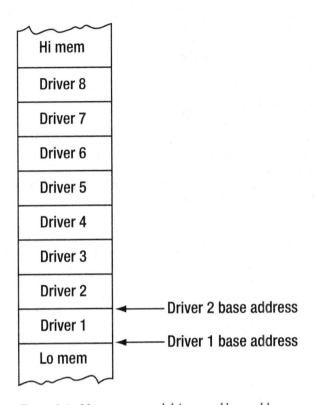

*Figure 8-1.* *Memory-mapped drivers and base addresses*

# Finding Base Addresses in bash

If you know the symbolic name of the device you want to find the base address for, automate the detection of that value and decouple your application from the changes that happen when you move code from an ARTIK 5 to an ARTIK 10 or perhaps when the operating system is upgraded. Type the commands at a shell prompt in your ARTIK to try out the examples. The ADC interface on an ARTIK 5 lives at a different base address to the ARTIK 10. The following command yields the name of the ADC virtual device and it works in an ARTIK 5 or 10:

```
ls /sys/devices | grep adc$
126c0000.adc
```

Use the grep command and append a dollar sign to the regular expression that matches the search key. The dollar sign ($) marks the string as the last three characters at the end of a line. The letters "adc" appearing anywhere else in the line will not match. You should see a single file listed in a Commercial Beta ARTIK 5. The base address can be isolated by refining the command to strip off the suffix automatically. Add a cut command to split every line that is passed to it using a period (.) character. This is not the only way to remove that trailing portion of the line but it is the least complicated way to do it. It extracts field 1 and discards the rest of the line. This command line delivers the base address by itself:

```
ls /sys/devices | grep adc$ | cut -d'.' -f1
126c0000
```

Call this command during the initialization of the application to detect the base address of the chosen device. You may prefer to add this to your login .profile configuration instead and perhaps even create an environment variable containing the value. An environment variable can be used from inside any process because it is inherited as child processes are created.

# Finding Base Addresses in the C Language

The same mechanism works well from the C language but you must wrap the call in a function for maximum reuse. Alternatively, build a small command line tool that returns the base address given a symbolic name. This code needs to be typed into a file in your ARTIK module and compiled there with the built-in GCC compiler. Use the /tmp directory so it is discarded and garbage collected at the next reboot. Create a source file called baseaddress.c with your vi editor and type in the code from Listing 8-2.

*Listing 8-2.* Base Address Extraction Tool

```c
#include <stdio.h>
#include <stdlib.h>

int main( int argc, char *argv[] )
{

  FILE *fp;
  char myResult[1035];
  char myCommand[64];

  // Manufacture a command line from the first argument
  sprintf(myCommand, "ls /sys/devices | grep %s$ | cut -d'.' -f1", argv[1]);

  // Open the command for reading
  fp = popen(myCommand, "r");

  if (fp == NULL)
  {
    printf("Failed to run command\n" );
    exit(1);
  }

  // Read and output the result
  while (fgets(myResult, sizeof(myResult)-1, fp) != NULL)
  {
    printf("%s", myResult);
  }

  // Close and quit
  pclose(fp);

  return 0;
}
```

Compile the source code with the gcc command. Then run the new tool you just created to see the base address of the ADC interface. Check that it works with a different symbolic name. In both cases, the base address is written out. Listing 8-3 illustrates the steps.

*Listing 8-3.* Running the Base Address Tool

```
gcc -Wall baseaddress.c -o baseaddress

./baseaddress adc
126c0000

./baseaddress usb
12480000
```

If you install this tool somewhere more permanent, you can then invoke it from within a shell script. Perhaps even enclose it in back ticks to substitute the result and assign it to a variable. By doing so, you decouple your shell script from any changes that Samsung makes to the base address of your devices because now you are accessing them symbolically.

In the UNIX/Linux world, it is traditional to make small powerful tools and use them in many places. By breaking your design down into components, you benefit by reusing the same code in many projects and reducing your maintenance overhead. Chaining small components together into larger workflows is very much the right approach.

In the Samsung developer documentation, it is suggested that you use a manifest constant to define the value according to which ARTIK module you are using. That approach works perfectly well, but because it is a static solution it must be hand edited if the base address ever changes. The dynamic auto-detecting approach requires less maintenance because it copes with the change automatically.

# Peripheral Interconnect Buses

The peripherals in a Linux computer system are managed as a collection of similar devices with interfaces organized as if they were on a bus system. A bus system transmits signals through a single channel that all devices are listening in on. When they identify a message that is for them, they act on it. They ignore all messages for other devices. The advantage is the reduced number of routing connections and decisions. The internal architecture is much simpler to maintain because the responsibility for reacting to a message is delegated to the target destination. Table 8-3 summarizes the peripheral interconnect buses in your ARTIK modules and their uses.

*Table 8-3.* *Peripheral Interconnect Bus Types*

| Bus type | Description |
| --- | --- |
| SPI | Not yet implemented for user space applications in the Commercial Beta versions of the ARTIK 5 and 10. See Chapter 21 for details of how SPI works so you can deploy it in the future. |
| I2C | If you add external sensors, they probably use this kind of interface. There is a lot of online knowledge, and many sensor devices are compatible with I2C. See Chapter 20. |
| I2S | See Chapter 22 for details of the ALSA-driven audio capabilities, which use this bus. |
| GPIO | See Chapter 17 for details of how to connect digital input/output devices for single pin digital controls. |
| IIO | Used for analog input. See Chapter 18 for more information. |

In Figure 8-2, the CPU, memory, and I/O devices are all shown connected together on a common bus system.

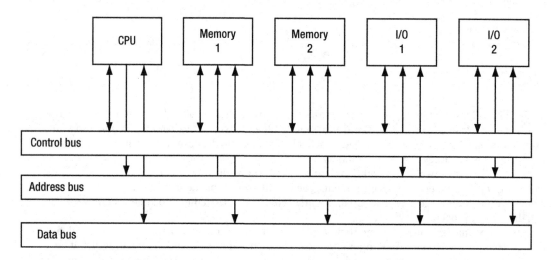

**Figure 8-2.** *Common bus arrangement*

The CPU or the I/O devices can assert a value onto the address bus that can be used to identify either a memory location or an I/O device. The CPU does not need an address. All devices can assert values on the control bus. The CPU might tell a memory location that it must write a value to storage. The memory might assert a value on the control bus to indicate that it is ready to be accessed. The I/O devices can indicate various status conditions about their readiness. All devices can read and write via the data bus.

A typical scenario is that the CPU tells the memory to store a value that it asserts onto the data bus in a location indicated by the value on the address bus. Or perhaps the CPU uses the address bus to select a slave I/O device that it then reads some data from.

# /sys/bus

The kernel manages the low-level bus structures via the drivers for each kind of peripheral component. It then maps a virtual file system into user space to interact with the different bus subsystems. In the command line of your ARTIK module, type this command to see the available buses that the kernel is managing for you:

```
ls -1 /sys/bus
```

Because the kernel is designed for general-purpose use, it may implement some buses that have no meaning or context inside an ARTIK. Others are named for legacy reasons even though their name makes no sense inside an ARTIK. The /sys/bus/scsi directory would be useful if you had a SCSI disk drive attached, but even if you don't, the interface is still there as a placeholder. Table 8-4 describes the uses of each bus.

*Table 8-4. /sys/bus Structures*

| Path to bus | Description |
| --- | --- |
| /sys/bus/amba | The ARM Advanced Microcontroller Bus Architecture (AMBA) is an open standard, on-chip interconnect specification for the connection and management of functional blocks in system-on-a-chip (SoC) designs. |
| /sys/bus/clocksource | Used for time keeping |
| /sys/bus/cpu | Properties of your CPU and its bus connections. Useful when writing systems applications. |
| /sys/bus/event_source | Used when building and using performance monitoring. Adds instrumentation to your application to generate statistics for measuring the performance. |
| /sys/bus/exynos-core | Details of the Exynos CPU cores in the ARTIK |
| /sys/bus/hid | Support for the human interface devices |
| /sys/bus/i2c | The I2C devices and their user-space–mapped interfaces are all managed under this file system tree. |
| /sys/bus/iio | The Industrial I/O core provides support for sensor devices and analog-to-digital Convertors (ADC). |
| /sys/bus/mdio_bus | Implementation of the physical layer (PHY) in the networking architecture |
| /sys/bus/media | Support for video media devices |
| /sys/bus/mmc | SD card management via the MMC driver is controlled via this sysfs entity. |
| /sys/bus/platform | This pseudo-bus is used to connect devices on buses with minimal infrastructure, like those used to integrate peripherals on many system-on-chip processors or some legacy PC interconnects, as opposed to large, formally specified ones like PCI or USB. |
| /sys/bus/scsi | Supports the addition of SCSI-compatible devices such as disks. There are none by default but the kernel support is there in case you want to add them to your hardware system. |
| /sys/bus/sdio | Part of the MMC memory support |
| /sys/bus/serio | Touch screen support and interfacing |
| /sys/bus/spi | The Serial Peripheral Interface (SPI) is a synchronous, four-wire serial link used to connect microcontrollers to sensors, memory, and peripherals. It is a simple, de facto standard, not complicated enough to acquire a standardization body. SPI uses a master/slave configuration. |
| /sys/bus/workqueue | Useful for kernel performance tuning and setting the CPU affinity for processes so they run in the correct CPU core. |

Read about I/O bus structures at the following link to better understand how they work: www.karbosguide.com/hardware/module2c1.htm.

# /sys/class

The kernel exports a list of devices organized into different categories or classes. This is a collection of symbolic links to the devices in the /dev virtual file system. Because they are organized according to their functional use, the devices are easier to find and more resilient to changes as the operating system is upgraded. This part of the sysfs file system is undergoing some changes and these items may migrate to the subsystems directory in a future OS upgrade. Table 8-5 summarizes the available device classes.

***Table 8-5.*** *Device Classes in sysfs*

| Class | Description |
| --- | --- |
| android_usb | Android-compatible USB debugging tools |
| backlight | Screen display backlight control |
| bdi | Backing device information |
| block | Block structured storage devices |
| bluetooth | Bluetooth comms support |
| bsg | Block structured scatter-gather storage management |
| devfreq | Speed control for Android debugging support |
| dma | Direct memory access |
| firmware | Firmware loading support |
| gpio | General Purpose Input/Output |
| graphics | Graphics frame buffer support |
| i2c-adapter | Each registered I2C adapter gets a number, counting from zero. Examine the /sys/class/i2c-dev/ directory to see what number corresponds to which adapter. |
| i2c-dev | Manages the I2C adapters. On the ARTIK 5, there are four of them. |
| ieee80211 | Wi-Fi support |
| input | Keyboard input via GPIO |
| ion_cma | Currently undocumented in the context of the ARTIK but suspected to be the Android ION memory allocator. Possibly part of the Android debugging support but also implicated as part of the video display support. |
| lcd | Display support |
| leds | System LED control |
| mdio_bus | Networking support |
| mem | Memory management support |
| misc | Miscellaneous devices |
| mmc_host | MMC memory support |
| net | Networking support |
| power_supply | Power management |
| pwm | PWM audio output |
| regulator | Power management voltage regulators |
| rfkill | Wi-Fi disable |

*(continued)*

*Table 8-5.* (*continued*)

| Class | Description |
|---|---|
| rtc | Real-time clock |
| scsi_device | SCSI device interface |
| scsi_disk | SCSI disk drives |
| scsi_generic | SCSI generic devices |
| scsi_host | SCSI host controller |
| sec | Power management |
| sound | Audio support for sound cards |
| spi_master | SPI interfaces |
| switch | Android switch class for ADBD |
| thermal | Thermal sensing and cooling device control |
| timed_output | Android vibrator support |
| tty | Serial terminal ports |
| udc | USB gadget device support |
| video4linux | Video support |
| watchdog | Watchdog interrupt mechanism |

■ **Note** This class-based structure is gradually being deprecated in favor of the /sys/devices/*/subsystem directories. It is useful for now but it might disappear in future OS upgrades. Make sure you check the use of your symbolic links after an OS upgrade. The sysfs documentation recommends against using these symbolic links from within your application because they may disappear in future releases.

# Summary

The sysfs virtual file system is integral to getting your peripheral interface buses to work correctly. A few of the bus interfaces can be driven via ioctl() function calls directly on the device driver but most of the easier interactions involve reading and writing to regular files in the sysfs file system.

■ ■ ■

# CHAPTER 9

# The /dev Virtual File System

Each unique hardware component needs a driver to manage it. Similar hardware components may be able to share a driver because they have a common interface. Adding your own new hardware may require that you create a driver for it. Where there are multiple hardware components of the same kind, the kernel will create an instance of the driver for each. Each driver instance and its associated hardware are called a device. The kernel collects all of its devices into the /dev directory, which it creates as the ARTIK is booted. Become familiar with this part of the kernel architecture because there are some hardware interfaces that can only be operated by talking directly to their device driver.

## About /dev

The kernel in your ARTIK constructs a virtual file system reflecting the device driver internals to the user space to access them subject to the normal file access permissions. Like everything else in UNIX-based operating systems, the end points are presented as files. This /dev hierarchy is constructed by the udev tools according to the rules in the udev configuration as the ARTIK is booted. Online resources sometimes describe it as the udevfs or the udev file system.

## Communicating With Devices

Although the contents of the /dev directory are represented as regular files, you are communicating with a low-level driver in the kernel and not with a physical file that is stored on your disk. Looking at each driver in context, some are only used for reading and others only for writing. The kernel driver then communicates with some hardware in the system or processes your input/output in other ways. There are several ways to interact with the device drivers. Table 9-1 lists the main techniques to use from your application.

© Cliff Wootton 2016
C. Wootton, *Samsung ARTIK Reference*, DOI 10.1007/978-1-4842-2322-2_9

*Table 9-1.* *Communicating With Device Drivers*

| Technique | Description |
| --- | --- |
| Open the device file and read | Treat the device as a regular file and read its contents. |
| Open the file and write | Pass instructions to the kernel via the regular file that it maps to the /dev file system. |
| fcntl() function calls | This configures currently open files and lets you operate on them in more sophisticated ways than reading or writing to them. Create non-blocking asynchronous I/O mechanisms with this function. |
| ioctl() function calls | The ioctl() function is also designed to communicate directly with the drivers. The ioctl() function is discussed in the context of SPI bus devices in Chapter 21. If you intend to do multiple, rapidly repeating ioctl() calls, you may find performance is much better with a memory-mapped approach. |
| Memory mapping | Map the kernel memory starting at the base address for the driver into your user space application's process memory and operate on it directly. This requires permissions for your application to be able to access the device memory. This is a very efficient way to transfer bulk data in and out of a device. See the coverage of GPIO pin control in Chapter 17 for an example of how to do this. |
| Special purpose system calls | These calls make it very easy to interact with the driver but are not often used because developers do not know that they exist. Having an enquiring approach to your ARTIK development reveals them if you search for them diligently. They do not exist for every case but they may provide a much simpler interface for your code to call. Knowing things like this greatly improves your developer skills. |
| Network sockets | Some devices can be used like network end points. These modes of access are interesting because they help you create stream-like behaviors. They can be set up as blocking synchronous connections, which stalls a thread or process until the operation is complete. Alternatively, use the select() functionality to call something to action and get a call back when it is done. |
| setsockopt() function calls | These calls manage socket connections and are helpful if you are using a networking or messaging interface to a driver. |
| Netlink | The Netlink mechanism behaves like a socket and is seen as a successor and replacement for the ioctl() function. |

Learn about the /proc and /sys file systems and observe how they interact with the /dev directory because they also access the same hardware or kernel but from a different context. The /sys directory is used to communicate with the kernel and the /proc directory relates to how a running application is working with devices. Some helpful resources also exist in the /run directory. They are each dealt with in their own chapters. The video and audio devices and their drivers are examined in more detail in Chapters 22 and 23 in order to gather the related material together more coherently. See the following online reference documentation for more details:

```
https://en.wikipedia.org/wiki/Ioctl
http://man7.org/linux/man-pages/man2/ioctl.2.html
https://en.wikipedia.org/wiki/Device_file
```

```
https://en.wikipedia.org/wiki/Udev
www.freedesktop.org/software/systemd/man/udev.html
https://en.wikipedia.org/wiki/Netlink
```

Modify the behavior of the kernel as it constructs the /dev file system by using udev rules. Because this is managed as an internal kernel-related task, you should not alter it unless you fully understand what you are doing. The following is a tutorial about how to write udev rules: www.reactivated.net/writing_udev_rules.html.

## Listing the Devices

List the devices your operating system supports in the /dev directory. Listing 9-1 shows an abridged extract of the resulting output.

*Listing 9-1.* Device Listing Extract

```
ls -la /dev

A          B C    D       E       F          G
crw-------  1 root root    251,  0 Apr  3  2014 iio:device0
lrwxrwxrwx  1 root root         25 Apr  3  2014 initctl -> /run/systemd/initctl/fifo
drwxr-xr-x  3 root root         80 Apr  3  2014 input
crw-------  1 root root     10, 63 Apr  3  2014 ion
crw-------  1 root root     10, 50 Apr  3  2014 kfc_freq_max
crw-------  1 root root     10, 51 Apr  3  2014 kfc_freq_min
crw-r-----  1 root kmem      1,  2 Apr  3  2014 kmem
crw-r--r--  1 root root      1, 11 Apr  3  2014 kmsg
lrwxrwxrwx  1 root root         28 Apr  3  2014 log -> /run/systemd/journal/dev-log
brw-rw----  1 root disk      7,  0 Apr  3  2014 loop0
brw-rw----  1 root disk      7,  1 Apr  3  2014 loop1
```

From this listing there are several useful deductions to make about the devices your ARTIK supports. At this early Commercial Beta stage of the ARTIK lifecycle, many of them are undocumented and some may not have complete implementations. Inspecting this list is a first step in reverse engineering your ARTIK module to understand it better. The columns are marked with letters in the heading of Listing 9-1 and are summarized in Table 9-2.

*Table 9-2.* Device Listing Details

| Column | Description |
| --- | --- |
| A | Device type and access permissions |
| B | Hard links to this device |
| C | Owning user account |
| D | Group membership |
| E | Device ID or file size |
| F | Modification date |
| G | Device name |

**Column A:** The first character on each line of the ls -la listing of the /dev directory indicates what kind of device is being described. The rest of the characters in this first column describe the access control permissions. Refer to Chapter 7 for a discussion on file access controls.

**Column B:** Indicates how many hard links point at this file. A number larger than one suggests the same device is available in multiple locations within the file system. This is usually necessary to support legacy software that might expect the devices to live in certain locations.

**Column C and D:** Lists the owner and group membership. This is part of the normal permissions control in UNIX. All of the devices in the /dev file system are owned by the root user because they are created and maintained by the kernel. The group membership subdivides them into functional categories and allows subprocesses running under different user accounts to access them. Your user account must be a member of a specific group before it is allowed to access the device, although the permissions may allow access under world (everyone else) flags. As a rule, you use libraries or possibly interact via the /sys virtual file system.

**Column E:** This is a pair of comma-separated values that describe the device number within the driver catalogue. These numbers are managed by a central registry. This information is important because a device is recognized primarily by its device number rather than its name. The name is useful for applications to use to open a file descriptor but the device numbers organize the devices into logical and meaningful categories. The block and character devices are two separate name spaces. A block device in the major number category 1 is not a member of the same set as the character devices in category 1.

**Column F:** The date value is meaningless when describing a device driver. It probably reflects the build date for the kernel instead of the modification date for a regular file.

**Column G:** The filename that forms a component of the device location within the file system. Constructing a fully qualified path to an end point is considered to be the device name. Refer to /dev/null rather than just null when describing the data sink.

This variant of the ls command makes a recursive listing and works down through the directory hierarchy to list all the end points in the /dev tree because some devices are collated together into sets and stored in a common directory:

```
ls -laR /dev
```

Obtain a list of loaded and active devices from the /proc/devices file. Listing 9-2 shows the contents of that file and has been wrapped into two columns to save space.

***Listing 9-2.*** The Contents of the /proc/devices Directory

```
cat /proc/devices
Character devices:          Block devices:
  1 mem                       1 ramdisk
  5 /dev/tty                 259 blkext
  5 /dev/console              7 loop
  5 /dev/ptmx                 8 sd
 10 misc                     65 sd
 13 input                    66 sd
 21 sg                       67 sd
 29 fb                       68 sd
 81 video4linux              69 sd
 89 i2c                      70 sd
116 alsa                     71 sd
128 ptm                     128 sd
136 pts                     129 sd
204 ttySAC                  130 sd
```

```
216 rfcomm              131 sd
248 ttySDIO             132 sd
249 ttyGS               133 sd
250 bsg                 134 sd
251 iio                 135 sd
252 watchdog            179 mmc
253 media               254 device-mapper
254 rtc
```

# About Device Numbers

The kernel recognizes and manages devices internally using their major and minor device numbers. The device names are convenient for application developers but meaningless to the kernel. The device number is constructed from two parts. The major and minor numbers group drivers into different categories to help you understand what they are used for. In earlier versions of UNIX, the major number identified a specific driver and the minor number denoted an instance of that driver so multiple devices could be driven by one device driver. This is no longer the case and the major number behaves more like a category with various special purpose drivers being mapped to the major:minor combination. The standard set of default device drivers are described by a registry that is maintained by the IANA. Access that registry and download the text file from www.kernel.org/doc/Documentation/devices.txt.

The IANA registry has not been updated for some time and there may be proprietary devices implemented on a Linux platform that are not listed there. So the IANA document may not be the definitive resource for Linux-oriented developers. A more useful document is maintained and updated often by the Linux kernel developers who have made many changes to the original IANA document; the latest definitive version is available on GitHub at https://github.com/torvalds/linux/blob/master/Documentation/devices.txt.

The published information should be current, aside from any pending device registrations that have not yet been incorporated. Their major device number should inform you about their purpose. You may contemplate registering a new device with IANA or the Linux kernel developers. Look at the sysfs and udev support first to see if you can accomplish your goal without needing a new device registration. Figure 9-1 illustrates how the device numbering maps to a kernel driver and then to a device.

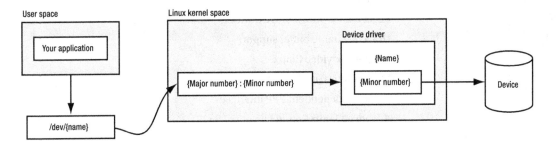

***Figure 9-1.*** *Device numbers mapped to kernel drivers*

The major categories found in a Commercial Beta ARTIK 5 module are summarized in Table 9-3. Note that the audio support is implemented by the **ALSA** project and the video support is implemented by the **Video4Linux** project. There is a lot of online documentation available to guide your experiments with the A/V capabilities of the ARTIK. Only the subset seen in the Commercial Beta ARTIK 5 module is listed here. Consult the registry at IANA for a complete listing. Sometimes you may encounter a device whose file name does not immediately tell you what it does. Checking the device number for that item and comparing it with the IANA lists can tell you what sort of device it is and from that you can figure out how to interact with it. Developing this skill for cross-referencing your knowledge of the ARTIK internals will speed up your development process.

***Table 9-3.*** *Device Number Categories*

| Type | Major number | Description |
| --- | --- | --- |
| Block | 1 | RAM disks |
| Block | 7 | Loopback devices |
| Block | 8 | Reserved for SD devices |
| Block | 65 to 71 | Reserved for SD devices |
| Block | 128 to 135 | Reserved for SD devices |
| Block | 179 | MMC block devices |
| Block | 254 | Device mapper |
| Block | 259 | Block extended device information. Used dynamically to hold additional partition minor numbers and allow large numbers of partitions per device. |
| Character | 1 | Memory devices |
| Character | 3 | Pseudo TTY slave devices |
| Character | 5 | Alternate TTY devices |
| Character | 10 | Non-serial mice, misc features. Obtain a list of these from the /proc/misc file. |
| Character | 13 | Input core |
| Character | 21 | Reserved for SCSI storage devices |
| Character | 29 | Universal frame buffer support |
| Character | 81 | Support for video4linux |
| Character | 89 | I2C bus interface |
| Character | 108 | Device-independent PPP interface |
| Character | 116 | Advanced Linux Sound Driver (ALSA) |
| Character | 128 | Pseudo terminal master devices (ptm) |
| Character | 136 | Pseudo terminal slave devices (pts) |
| Character | 204 | Low-density serial ports (ttySAC) |
| Character | 216 | Bluetooth interaction via rfcomm |
| Character | 248 | Pseudo terminal ttySDIO |
| Character | 249 | USB serial gadget driver ttyGS |

(*continued*)

*Table 9-3.* (*continued*)

| Type | Major number | Description |
|------|--------------|-------------|
| Character | 250 | Reserved for bsg SCSI storage devices |
| Character | 251 | iio devices |
| Character | 252 | Watchdog timers |
| Character | 253 | Media devices (video) |
| Character | 254 | Real-time clock (rtc) |

Observe the device numbers in the size column with an ls directory listing or find other abstracts of the device listings in the /sys and /proc directories. Table 9-4 shows some example commands for accessing these lists.

*Table 9-4.* *Example Device Inspection Commands*

| Directory | Description |
|-----------|-------------|
| ls -lA /dev | Use this command to see the top level of the /dev directory. |
| ls -lAR /dev | Recursively list all the subdirectories in the /dev hierarchy |
| ls -lA /dev/block | All block devices listed by number |
| ls -lA /dev/char | All character devices listed by number |
| ls -lA /sys/dev/block | A more detailed listing of all block devices |
| ls -lA /sys/dev/char | A more detailed listing of all character devices |
| cat /proc/devices | Lists the minor device numbers for devices your current process knows about |

The device lists in the /sys/dev directory contain useful addressing information that may change from one ARTIK OS release to another and are different between an ARTIK 5 and 10.

The files you see or the ultimate files at the end of a symbolic link chain are bound to the kernel driver that handles the device. The major number originally identified a driver and the minor number was an instance of a device managed by it. This convention has loosened somewhat and no longer applies in modern Linux systems.

Download and inspect the entire source code for the Linux kernel from the official Git repository. Includable files such as major.h tell you more about the device numbers and how to reference them with manifest constants in your C language application source files. Occasionally you will find a comment in a source file that will clear up some major ambiguity in how things work.

```
https://github.com/torvalds/linux/
https://github.com/torvalds/linux/blob/master/include/uapi/linux/major.h
https://github.com/torvalds/linux/blob/master/include/linux/miscdevice.h
```

Read about device numbering in the kernel at the following links:

```
www.makelinux.net/ldd3/chp-3-sect-2
http://stackoverflow.com/questions/9835850/allocating-device-numbers
www.linux-tutorial.info/modules.php?name=MContent&pageid=94
http://unix.stackexchange.com/questions/124225/are-the-major-minor-number-unique
```

---

■ **Note**   Make sure you check the use of your symbolic links after an OS upgrade. The sysfs documentation recommends against using these symbolic links from within your application because they may disappear or change their target in future releases.

---

# Device Types

The first character on each line of the ls -la listing of the /dev directory indicates what kind of device is being described. Table 9-5 summarizes the range of different device types.

***Table 9-5.*** *Device Type Sentinel Letters*

| Type | Description |
|------|-------------|
| C | Character structured devices |
| B | Block structured devices |
| L | Symbolic links to other device end points to alias the names |
| D | Directories containing collections of devices |

There are two principle types of device nodes: character devices and block devices. This is indicated by the first character in the output of the ls -a command and is a letter "c" or "b" accordingly. The symbolic links are merely pointers to other devices and the directories are containers for managing collections of devices. They are not devices at all.

Within the character device category, some devices are presented by the kernel as regular files. These are generally for accessing hardware. A few of the character devices are connected to sockets and these are used for network access. The block devices are mainly used for bulk storage on disk, within RAM, or on eMMC memory chips and SD cards.

# Block Devices

Block devices are organized into chunks and represent storage containers such as disks. Accessing them via the /dev interface makes them appear to be large, fixed-size files. Write some data at a certain offset within the file and then later read data back from the device at that offset and retrieve the same information. The files never change size and you cannot append data to them to make them bigger because after all, they represent a fixed size disk. All of the block devices are collated together using symbolic links in the /dev/block directory. The names in this directory are the device numbers with the major and minor values separated by a colon. Type this command to see a map of block structured ID values to physical disk and memory devices:

```
ls -la /dev/block
```

This provides a convenient way to access the devices using their device number rather than their name. The block devices visible after booting a Commercial Beta ARTIK 5 are listed in Table 9-6.

*Table 9-6.* *Block Devices in a Commercial Beta ARTIK 5*

| Major | Minor | Path | Description |
|-------|-------|------|-------------|
| 1 | 0 to 15 | /dev/ram0 | RAM disks |
| 7 | 0 to 7 | /dev/loop0 | Loopback devices for mounting files containing file systems |
| 179 | 0 | /dev/mmcblk0 | MMC memory hardware device |
| 179 | 1 | /dev/mmcblk0p1 | MMC memory partition 1 mounted as /boot |
| 179 | 2 | /dev/mmcblk0p2 | MMC memory partition 2 mounted as /usr/lib/modules |
| 179 | 3 | /dev/mmcblk0p3 | MMC memory partition 3 mounted as the root of the file system at / |
| 179 | 8 | /dev/mmcblk0boot0 | U-Boot parameters |
| 179 | 16 | /dev/mmcblk0boot1 | U-Boot loader image |
| 179 | 24 | /dev/mmcblk0rpmb | Secure protected partition |

# Character Devices

Character devices represent most non-disk drive hardware that your kernel knows about and a few special items that are managed within the kernel. Writing some data might be transmitted out through a serial connection to another system. Reading data might accept input coming in from that same serial port. This is the basic mechanism for displaying characters on your screen and receiving keystrokes. Other devices might be associated with hardware pins to which you can attach switches and LED indicators. Writing to these pins might turn on the LED and reading from them might sense a switch value or measure a resistance connected between that pin and the ground plane. All of the character devices are collated together using symbolic links in the /dev/char directory. The names in this directory are the device numbers with the major and minor values separated by a colon. Type this command to see a map of character structured ID values to physical I/O hardware and devices:

```
ls -la /dev/char
```

This provides a convenient way to access the devices using their device number rather than their name. Table 9-7 lists the character devices visible in a Commercial Beta ARTIK 5 just after booting.

*Table 9-7.* *Character Devices in a Commercial Beta ARTIK 5*

| Major | Minor | Path | See also |
|-------|-------|------|----------|
| 1 | 1 | /dev/mem | Memory management |
| 1 | 2 | /dev/kmem | Memory management |
| 1 | 3 | /dev/null | Standard I/O devices |
| 1 | 5 | /dev/zero | Data generators |
| 1 | 7 | /dev/full | Data generators |
| 1 | 8 | /dev/random | Data generators |

*(continued)*

*Table 9-7.* (*continued*)

| Major | Minor | Path | See also |
|---|---|---|---|
| 1 | 9 | /dev/urandom | Data generators |
| 1 | 11 | /dev/kmsg | Kernel messaging mechanisms |
| 3 | 2 | n/a | I2C |
| 5 | 0 | /dev/tty | Serial communications |
| 5 | 1 | /dev/console | Standard I/O devices |
| 5 | 2 | /dev/ptmx | Serial communications |
| 5 | 4 | n/a | Serial UART presented on pins J26-8 (RX<-0) and J26-7 (TX->1) |
| 10 | 44 | /dev/rfkill | Networking |
| 10 | 45 | /dev/usb_accessory | USB interface |
| 10 | 46 | /dev/mtp_usb | USB interface |
| 10 | 47 | /dev/android_adb | Debugging (ADBD) |
| 10 | 48 | /dev/cam_throughput | Debugging (ADBD) |
| 10 | 49 | /dev/display_throughput | Debugging (ADBD) |
| 10 | 50 | /dev/kfc_freq_max | Debugging (ADBD) |
| 10 | 51 | /dev/kfc_freq_min | Debugging (ADBD) |
| 10 | 52 | /dev/cpu_freq_max | Debugging (ADBD) |
| 10 | 53 | /dev/cpu_freq_min | Debugging (ADBD) |
| 10 | 54 | /dev/network_throughput | Debugging (ADBD) |
| 10 | 55 | /dev/bus_throughput | Debugging (ADBD) |
| 10 | 56 | /dev/device_throughput | Debugging (ADBD) |
| 10 | 57 | /dev/memory_throughput | Debugging (ADBD) |
| 10 | 58 | /dev/network_latency | Power management |
| 10 | 59 | /dev/cpu_dma_latency | Power management |
| 10 | 60 | /dev/sw_sync | Memory management |
| 10 | 61 | /dev/uhid | Input devices |
| 10 | 62 | /dev/mali | Graphics |
| 10 | 63 | /dev/ion | Memory management |
| 10 | 130 | /dev/watchdog | Timers |
| 10 | 200 | /dev/net/tun | Networking |
| 10 | 223 | /dev/uinput | Input devices |
| 10 | 229 | /dev/fuse | Disk devices |
| 10 | 234 | /dev/btrfs-control | Disk devices |
| 10 | 235 | /dev/autofs | Disk devices |
| 10 | 236 | /dev/mapper/control | Disk devices |

(*continued*)

**Table 9-7.** (*continued*)

| Major | Minor | Path | See also |
|-------|-------|------|----------|
| 10 | 237 | /dev/loop-control | Disk devices |
| 13 | 64 | /dev/input/event0 | Input devices |
| 29 | 0 | /dev/fb0 | Video |
| 81 | 0 | /dev/video23 | Video |
| 81 | 1 | /dev/video24 | Video |
| 81 | 2 | /dev/video26 | Video |
| 81 | 3 | /dev/video27 | Video |
| 81 | 4 | /dev/video6 | Video |
| 81 | 5 | /dev/video7 | Video |
| 81 | 6 | /dev/video8 | Video |
| 81 | 7 | /dev/video9 | Video |
| 89 | 0 | /dev/i2c-0 | Bus I2C-0 |
| 89 | 1 | /dev/i2c-1 | Bus I2C-1 |
| 89 | 3 | /dev/i2c-3 | Bus I2C-3 |
| 89 | 7 | /dev/i2c-7 | Bus I2C-7 |
| 108 | 0 | /dev/ppp | Networking |
| 116 | 0 | /dev/snd/controlC0 | Audio |
| 116 | 16 | /dev/snd/pcmC0D0p | Audio |
| 116 | 24 | /dev/snd/pcmC0D0c | Audio |
| 116 | 33 | /dev/snd/timer | Audio |
| 204 | 64 | /dev/ttySAC0 | Serial communications |
| 204 | 65 | /dev/ttySAC1 | Serial communications |
| 204 | 66 | /dev/ttySAC2 | Serial communications |
| 204 | 67 | /dev/ttySAC3 | Serial communications |
| 249 | 0 | /dev/ttyGS0 | Serial communications |
| 249 | 1 | /dev/ttyGS1 | Serial communications |
| 249 | 2 | /dev/ttyGS2 | Serial communications |
| 249 | 3 | /dev/ttyGS3 | Serial communications |
| 251 | 0 | /dev/iio:device0 | ADC |
| 252 | 0 | /dev/watchdog0 | Timers |
| 253 | 0 | /dev/media0 | Video |
| 254 | 0 | /dev/rtc0 | Timers |

# Special Devices

Several devices on your ARTIK are neither storage nor hardware accessors. They are provided for assistance when debugging or generating special values. The /dev hierarchy not the ideal place for things like this but history forces us to maintain them here because of legacy applications that expect them to be present. Table 9-8 lists these special devices.

***Table 9-8.*** *Special Devices*

| Device | Description |
| --- | --- |
| /dev/null | A data sink where character streams can be redirected and discarded |
| /dev/zero | An infinite supply of null bytes that you can read forever and never run out |
| /dev/urandom | A pseudo random number generator that cycles through the same random data set when it runs out |
| /dev/random | A pseudo random number generator that blocks when it exhausts its entropy pool. It blocks until it has finished refreshing the supply of new random numbers and then allows your process to continue. |
| /dev/full | A special device emulating a disk drive that behaves as if it is always full |

# Summary

Now that you have explored the /dev file system, you can build on that knowledge later when the SPI bus is better supported. Interacting with SPI requires knowledge of drivers and ioctl() function calls. None of these subsystems are impossibly complex to work on and you will understand them better by experimenting.

# CHAPTER 10

■ ■ ■

# The /proc Virtual File System

Understanding processes is a very important part of your programming skill set. If you understand how to communicate with processes, you can factor your design into multiple components that can run simultaneously but still collaborate with one another. Signal handling and process termination is just as important because closing things in an orderly fashion keeps your system running efficiently. Understanding deadlocking and Parent ➤ Child process relationships helps you prevent runaway and zombie processes, which can quickly bring an entire system down.

## About /proc

The kernel manages the physical devices on the system and schedules when and how the processes running in the computer can access the hardware. The current state of the kernel and the running processes is maintained in the /proc and /run virtual file systems. The kernel creates these file systems as the computer is started up and maintains them when things change.

The kernel organizes the CPU capacity so it is sliced up and granted to many separate processes on a scheduled basis. Without this scheduling mechanism, interactions with a user would spend most of their time waiting for user input. Since the computer is very fast, it can get a lot of things done between every keystroke you type.

The more recent versions of the Linux operating system support the /proc virtual file system. The kernel manages the /proc file system for you to access details about running processes. This exposes the inner workings of each running process to your applications that run in the user space subject to the normal UNIX permissions model. Your application can inspect the inner workings of other processes much more easily by opening a file in the /proc file system than if it needed to create a communications channel by any other means.

Because this is a virtual file system, many of the files appear to have a zero length, but when you open them for reading or cat them to the screen from the bash command line, they deliver a wealth of useful information that your applications can use to adjust how they work. There are many useful utilities that can exploit this information and present it in more attractive forms.

Most of the files in the /proc file system are read only from user space where your applications run. Only the kernel can write to them. A few can be used as a command interface to request that the kernel do something on behalf of a user space application. The contents of the /proc/sys directory are related to the contents of the sysfs file system. Refer to these links for more information about the /proc filesystem:

```
https://en.wikipedia.org/wiki/Procfs
http://manpages.courier-mta.org/htmlman5/proc.5.html
www.kernel.org/doc/Documentation/filesystems/proc.txt
http://man7.org/linux/man-pages/man5/proc.5.html
http://linux.die.net/man/5/proc
www.tldp.org/LDP/Linux-Filesystem-Hierarchy/html/proc.html
```

© Cliff Wootton 2016

C. Wootton, *Samsung ARTIK Reference*, DOI 10.1007/978-1-4842-2322-2_10

127

http://linux.about.com/od/commands/l/blcmdl5_proc.htm
http://wiki.tldp.org/static/kernel_user_space_howto.html
https://access.redhat.com/documentation/en-US/Red_Hat_Enterprise_Linux/6/html/Deployment_
Guide/s1-proc-topfiles.html

# Inspecting /proc

There are two areas to focus your interest on in the /proc file system. The contents of the top-level directory have some named items that represent objects within the kernel. Using the same analogy as the sysfs virtual file system, directories reflect kernel objects, files reflect kernel object properties, and symbolic links reflect relational connections between kernel objects. The other important focus for the /proc file system is the numbered directories which correspond on a one-to-one basis with currently running processes. These appear and disappear as the processes are created and destroyed. Inside each of them are objects that reflect the inner workings of those processes.

Because the /proc file system exists in the user space, you can use the command line tools to browse it and examine the content. Listing 10-1 shows the contents of the /proc file system in a Commercial Beta ARTIK 5 just after booting it. Most of the items listed on the left are processes identified by their PID numbers. The named items are global properties about the operating system or hardware.

***Listing 10-1.*** The /proc File System Hierarchy

ls /proc

| 1    | 1579 | 1675 | 307 | 657 | 756    | buddyinfo   | ioports     | self        |
|------|------|------|-----|-----|--------|-------------|-------------|-------------|
| 10   | 1581 | 1677 | 325 | 660 | 768    | bus         | irq         | slabinfo    |
| 11   | 1584 | 1698 | 368 | 662 | 773    | cgroups     | kallsyms    | softirqs    |
| 12   | 1590 | 17   | 396 | 667 | 783    | cmdline     | key-users   | stat        |
| 13   | 1592 | 1705 | 399 | 668 | 786    | consoles    | kmsg        | swaps       |
| 1348 | 16   | 1711 | 4   | 669 | 8      | cpu         | kpagecount  | sys         |
| 1358 | 1610 | 1719 | 400 | 684 | 808    | cpuinfo     | kpageflags  | sysvipc     |
| 1360 | 1614 | 1737 | 401 | 686 | 809    | crypto      | loadavg     | timer_list  |
| 1361 | 1625 | 18   | 408 | 688 | 810    | devices     | locks       | tty         |
| 14   | 1626 | 19   | 413 | 691 | 812    | device-tree | meminfo     | uid_stat    |
| 1450 | 1628 | 2    | 461 | 692 | 813    | diskstats   | misc        | uptime      |
| 15   | 1632 | 20   | 474 | 693 | 854    | driver      | modules     | version     |
| 1534 | 1633 | 288  | 481 | 694 | 857    | execdomains | mounts      | vmallocinfo |
| 1549 | 1636 | 290  | 5   | 7   | 865    | fb          | net         | vmstat      |
| 1564 | 1644 | 292  | 6   | 749 | 871    | filesystems | pagetypeinfo| zoneinfo    |
| 1572 | 1661 | 299  | 627 | 750 | 9      | fs          | partitions  |             |
| 1576 | 1668 | 3    | 628 | 751 | 978    | interrupts  | sched_debug |             |
| 1578 | 1674 | 305  | 634 | 752 | asound | iomem       | scsi        |             |

# Special Locations Within /proc

The top level of the /proc directory contains useful reference information about the operating system as a whole. There are three categories that define these items:

- Kernel subsystem objects reflected as directory containers

- System-wide properties reflected as regular files

- Relational links to other objects maintained for the current process reflected as symbolic links

# Kernel Subsystems as Objects

Table 10-1 describes the kernel objects that are reflected into the /proc directory. They manage various subsystems and have many properties of their own to access with the cat command or as regular files from your C Language application.

*Table 10-1.* *Kernel Objects Representing Subsystems*

| Collection | Description |
| --- | --- |
| asound | Properties and access to control sound card devices. See the audio discussion in Chapter 22. |
| bus | A collection of directories representing various buses on the computer, such as input/PCI/USB. This has been largely superseded by sysfs under /sys/bus, which is far more informative. |
| cpu | Internal properties of the current CPU the process is running in |
| device-tree | A runtime structured directory tree with a copy of the information in the boot loader device tree that was used to start the kernel |
| driver | A collection of statistics on additional platform-specific drivers |
| fs | A tree of directories relating to the currently mounted file systems. Each subdirectory maps to a type and instance of a file system mount. |
| irq | A map of the interrupt request lines that feed IRQs to the CPUs. This also describes the affinity mapping of interrupts per CPU. Interrupts can drive either or both CPUs in an ARTIK 5. |
| scsi | A list of SCSI and other related disk drives |
| self/net | A collection of network configuration and debugging data |
| sys | Dynamically configurable kernel configuration items |
| sysvipc | Memory sharing and interprocess communication support |
| tty | Details of TTY devices such as UART transceivers |
| uid_stat | Statistics collection for network and data usage by applications |

# System-Wide Properties

Table 10-2 summarizes these global objects and their properties. Use the cat command to display the values contained in the regular files at these special locations. Later, use the C language from within your application to open and read these files.

```
cat /proc/{global_property}
```

A few of these files block your terminal output when you use the cat command to read them. Instead, use the od (Octal Dump) tool to display their contents. The od tool is more flexible and can format the output to show you binary values in octal, decimal, hexadecimal, and as text characters. The items that require this approach are noted in the table.

**Table 10-2.** *The /proc File System Global Properties*

| Global property | Description |
|---|---|
| buddyinfo | Information about the buddy algorithm that handles memory fragmentation |
| cgroups | A summary of process counts running in different control groups |
| cmdline | The kernel boot command used by U-Boot to start up your ARTIK. Observe the boot options here. |
| consoles | A summary of currently open console sessions |
| cpu/alignment | Details of the memory alignment used by the current CPU |
| cpu/swp_emulation | Details about emulation of the deprecated SWP instruction inside the ARM CPU |
| cpuinfo | Describes the CPU architecture in this ARTIK module |
| crypto | Describes a list of available cryptographic modules |
| devices | A list of devices supported by the ARTIK sorted into block and character categories with the device number and generic name. Refer to the /dev virtual filesystem description in Chapter 9 for more information. |
| diskstats | A description of all the logical disk devices |
| driver/rtc | Information about the real-time clock settings |
| driver/snd-page-alloc | Information about the memory allocation for audio devices |
| execdomains | Contains a list of the execution domains (ABI personalities) |
| fb | A list of the available frame buffers for video and graphics use |
| filesystems | A list of the supported filesystems with their device disposition |
| interrupts | Displays a count of interrupts for devices, hardware, and processes that are mapped to interrupts on each of the CPUs |
| iomem | Display the mapping of I/O devices to memory address locations |
| ioports | A list of currently active I/O ports |
| kallsyms | An exported list of symbols representing properties inside the loadable kernel modules |
| key-users | Summary of user sessions |
| kmsg | The kernel message log which is displayed with the dmesg command |
| kpagecount | Related to kernel page map support. Using the cat command to view this file stalls but the od command works fine. |
| kpageflags | Related to kernel page map support. Using the cat command to view this file stalls but the od command works fine. |
| loadavg | Performance statistics describing load averages |
| locks | Contains a list of currently active file locks |
| meminfo | Displays some statistical information about how the kernel is utilizing the available memory |

*(continued)*

*Table 10-2.* (*continued*)

| Global property | Description |
| --- | --- |
| misc | A list of the minor device numbers and device names associated with /dev devices whose major number is 10 |
| modules | A list of currently loaded kernel modules. Some information is given about module dependencies but this is not always accurate. |
| pagetypeinfo | A description of the different kinds of memory pages in the page zone tables |
| partitions | A list of partitions that the kernel has identified |
| sched_debug | A debug listing of running processes and potentially runnable processes per CPU |
| slabinfo | Details of the kernel caches for recently used objects |
| softirqs | Usage statistics for software interrupt requests (IRQs) |
| stat | Information about the kernel and various statistics |
| swaps | Details of the swap file usage. Unless you have set up a swap file to provide additional virtual memory, this file does not contain anything useful. |
| sysvipc/msg | Interprocess messaging data |
| sysvipc/sem | Interprocess semaphore flags |
| sysvipc/shm | Shared memory sections |
| timer_list | Displays information about the timers on all CPUs |
| uptime | The amount of time since the kernel was booted and how much of that time was spent in an idle state |
| version | Displays the kernel version information |
| vmallocinfo | Displays information about virtual memory allocation |
| vmstat | Describes various virtual memory statistics |
| zoneinfo | Descriptions of memory zones. This is useful for analyzing virtual memory behavior. |
| scsi/* | Files containing properties for various disk drives |
| sys/* | Directories containing property descriptions for different aspects of the system. Some of them can be modified. |

# Parent and Child Processes

Tree structures are used a lot in computing to organize resources because they are a simple concept to understand and manage, and so it is with processes. Parent processes can spawn child processes to do some work for them. After delegating that task, the parent waits for the child process to complete and hand back the results.

This mode of operation is called blocking or synchronous execution where the parent is prevented from continuing until the child process exits. Blocking may be useful in some cases but usually you want to get on with something else so the child process can just run in the background and either signal its completion to the parent or deposit the output somewhere for later use. This is called asynchronous execution. Set up signal and event handlers to interlock the processes or monitor a shared data storage area in memory or a file. This is a little more work than implementing a blocking execution but it's much more efficient and interactive.

Asynchronous processes are less prone to locking up the system. If a child process encounters a problem and stalls, any parent that is waiting for it stalls too if a synchronous mode is used. If the child calls back to its parent process and the parent process is waiting for the child to complete, this is a two-way blocking of any further progress. The parent cannot service the child and cannot continue either, because the child never completes the task. This is called deadlocking, and once this starts to happen, your system is on the way to a complete failure if more related processes get into this state. These are problems caused by design inadequacies. Avoid these problems by carefully designing your architecture before you implement anything.

# Creating New Processes

When you type a command in the shell environment, it spawns a child process to run that command in synchronous mode. That child process inherits a lot of the environment from its parent process and there is a certain overhead to creating that process context. If you place an ampersand character (&) at the end of the command line before executing it, the child process is thrown into the background and you can carry on working. It still inherits an environment from its parent even though it is running independently.

Processes can be spawned by the launch daemon and configured so they are created automatically when a connection arrives on a network port. This binding is called a service. It is how FTP and Telnet processes are started on receipt of a connection request. The kernel creates a process context under guidance from the launch daemon and the service configuration. Then the network I/O is bound to that new process's standard I/O devices.

Another way to create processes is with the cron scheduler. This can start new processes at scheduled times or intervals. The processes are created by the kernel in accordance with the configuration you set up in the crontab (cron table).

Spawn new processes from inside your application. This is called forking. Make sure that the process is properly detached from your application so it can run independently if you need it to run asynchronously; otherwise you will create a synchronous (blocking) child process. Study the documentation on the fork() and exec() system function calls to see how to manage child processes from within your application.

# Process Identifier Numbers

As each process is started, it is given a unique process ID number (PID). They are created in ascending order, and when the maximum PID number is reached, the cycle starts again. The allocation scheme skips any PID numbers that belong to currently running processes.

# Listing the Running Processes

List the currently running processes with the ps command. Adding options to the command (ps -ef) shows additional information. An example of the ps command and the output is shown in Listing 10-2.

***Listing 10-2.*** Full Process Listing ps –ef Command Output

```
ps -ef

UID        PID  PPID  C STIME TTY        TIME CMD
root         1     0  0 15:55 ?      00:00:02 /sbin/init
root       854     1  0 15:55 ?      00:00:02 /usr/lib/systemd/systemd-journal
root       978     1  0 15:55 ?      00:00:00 /usr/lib/systemd/systemd-udevd
systemd+  1534     1  0 15:55 ?      00:00:02 /usr/lib/systemd/systemd-timesyn
root      1549     1  0 15:55 ?      00:00:00 /usr/sbin/alsactl -s -n 19 -c -E
dbus      1564     1  0 15:55 ?      00:00:00 /usr/bin/dbus-daemon -system -
root      1572     1  0 15:55 ?      00:00:00 /usr/lib/systemd/systemd-logind
root      1576     1  0 15:55 ?      00:00:02 /usr/sbin/NetworkManager -no-da
root      1578     1  0 15:55 ?      00:00:00 ./brcm_patchram_plus -patchram
avahi     1579     1  0 15:55 ?      00:00:00 avahi-daemon: running [linux.loc
pulse     1581     1  0 15:55 ?      00:00:00 /usr/bin/pulseaudio -system -d
avahi     1590  1579  0 15:55 ?      00:00:00 avahi-daemon: chroot helper
root      1592     1  0 15:55 ?      00:00:00 /usr/sbin/gssproxy -D
root      1610     1  0 15:55 ?      00:00:00 /usr/sbin/sshd -D
systemd+  1614     1  0 15:55 ?      00:00:00 /usr/lib/systemd/systemd-resolve
root      1628     1  0 15:55 ?      00:00:00 /usr/sbin/crond -n
root      1636     1  0 15:55 ?      00:00:00 login - root
root      1644     1  0 15:55 ?      00:00:00 /usr/libexec/bluetooth/bluetooth
root      1674     1  0 15:55 ?      00:00:00 /usr/sbin/wpa_supplicant -c /etc
polkitd   1675     1  0 15:55 ?      00:00:00 /usr/lib/polkit-1/polkitd -no-d
root      1705     1  0 15:55 ?      00:00:00 /usr/lib/systemd/systemd -user
root      1719  1636  0 15:55 ttySAC2 00:00:00 -bash
root      1900  1719  0 16:40 ttySAC2 00:00:00 ps -ef
```

Note the PPID column that indicates which process is the parent. Most processes in this listing are owned by the init process. Note the avahi process running with PID 1590. It has a parent PID 1579, which identifies a daemon that spawned a child process, both of which were running under the avahi user account. This shows how the kernel can create processes running under different user accounts, which makes the permissions model much more flexible. The ps –ef command itself has an entry (PID 1900) and its parent is the bash shell running as PID 1719.

Adding the ww option to the ps command displays in a wide wrapped format to see the command that initiated the process. Listing 10-3 shows an abridged copy of the resulting display. This reveals the CPU and memory usage.

***Listing 10-3.*** Extended ps Command Output With Resource Allocations

```
ps -auxww

USER       PID %CPU %MEM    VSZ   RSS TTY     STAT START   TIME COMMAND
root         1  0.1  0.6  24816  3224 ?       Ss   15:55   0:03 /sbin/init
root       854  0.1  0.3   8436  1904 ?       Ss   15:55   0:02 /usr/lib/systemd/systemd-
journald
root       978  0.0  0.3  11220  1540 ?       Ss   15:55   0:00 /usr/lib/systemd/systemd-
udevd
root      1719  0.0  0.3   5320  1884 ttySAC2 Ss   15:55   0:00 -bash
root      1870  0.0  0.3   8524  1596 ttySAC2 R+   16:30   0:00 ps -auxww
```

In this example, the ps -auxww command shows resource usage but because the PPID column is missing this time, the parent process is hidden. Because some of the options are mutually exclusive, you cannot see all of the information in one listing.

# Sending Signals to Processes

If you know the PID number for a process, you can send signals to it from the command line with the kill command. Your application can also send signals to other processes if it can determine their PID number. The receiving process needs to have a signal handler set up during the initialization phase or these signals are ignored. The kill -9 signal is a process termination instruction and does not need you to set up a signal handler first because it calls the exit() function by default. Add a handler for this signal to invoke cleanup tasks before exiting. Just ensure that you eventually call the exit() function.

Signal handling has been part of the UNIX and C language toolkit since the very earliest systems were created, and there is plenty of tutorial and example documentation about it online. The kill command is misnamed. It ought to be called something more obvious, such as send_signal_to_process, but it has been called kill since the early days because that was originally all it could do. For a good example with some experimental code to try out, go to www.thegeekstuff.com/2012/03/catch-signals-sample-c-code/.

The simple signal handler from the Geek Stuff discussion is shown in Listing 10-4. The handler is attached to the signal management framework because your application starts up by calling the signal() function, which installs a reference to the signal handler and registers it for the required signal type identifiers. If that attachment fails, a message is displayed. Otherwise, when the application goes into the while() loop, you can then try sending it signals. Pressing [**Control**] + [**C**] sends the SIGINT signal to the process and the "received SIGINT" message is displayed.

*Listing 10-4.* A Simple Signal Handler

```
#include<stdio.h>
#include<signal.h>
#include<unistd.h>

void sig_handler(int signo)
{
  if (signo == SIGINT)
  {
    printf("received SIGINT\n");
  }
}

int main(void)
{
  if (signal(SIGINT, sig_handler) == SIG_ERR)
  {
    printf("\nCannot catch SIGINT\n");
  }

  // Allow time to issue a signal to this process
  while(1)
  {
    sleep(1);
  }
  return 0;
}
```

If you put in handlers that intercept SIGKILL and SIGSTOP, you can prevent applications from being stopped at all if you never call the exit() function. This is not a good idea because the only way to stop the application then is to reboot the ARTIK. Those handlers ought to complete their task by calling the exit() function so the application can return in an orderly fashion. Replace this printf() with an exit() function call to configure the handler correctly:

```
printf("\nCannot catch SIGKILL\n");
```

# Zombies

If a parent process ceases execution and the kernel tears it down, any child processes that have not been detached from it are also torn down whether they have completed their work or not. This might not be a great idea because if they are halfway through an update it will be left unfinished. Any connections to remote systems and services are also taken down.

If child processes are not detached and are allowed to complete on their own as if they were a stand-alone process, when they eventually complete and post their exit status for the parent to collect, the parent is no longer running and the child process waits forever to be reaped by a parent that no longer exists. These are called zombie processes because they cannot die and they are not going to do any further useful work either. Unfortunately, they use up a process slot. Eventually, when you have enough of them, the computer stalls because it cannot create any new processes.

Because a child process does not give up its PID number until its exit state has been collected by its spawning parent, processes must go into a zombie state before they are reaped. It is the reaping of the exit status that allows the PID to be reused again later on because the process is now genuinely finished.

The kill command cannot get rid of zombie processes. Unless the system has a mechanism to detect and remove them, they can cause a serious resource leak. In an embedded scenario, this brings your product down and your ARTIK must be power cycled or hard booted to restart it. Read more about processes at the following link to find out the fine points about zombies: https://en.wikipedia.org/wiki/Zombie_process.

Coding defensively and implementing a registry of PID numbers as you create child processes allows you to build an exit() handler into your application. When it receives the quit signal, it can instruct its child processes to close down in an orderly manner. Trade off the benefits of making sure those child processes have exited versus the increased time required to shut down your application.

There are many different ways to create child processes and you may be able to delegate ownership of them to the main system scheduler and give up your parentage. This would then allow the scheduler to reap the PID numbers for you when the child process exits. There is no single approach that works for all scenarios. Design your multiprocess applications to carefully to eliminate these failure modes.

# Special Locations Within /proc/{pid}

Each running process has its own containing subdirectory within the /proc directory. This container is identified by the PID number of the process. Working through an example helps to illustrate how to make use of this process container. Taking the bash shell as an example, the PID number can be identified with this example ps command shown in Listing 10-5.

If you want to avoid seeing the process for your grep command listed (because it contains the same search key), pipe the result to a second grep command to remove it. The -v on the second grep command in the pipeline matches the grep keyword and discards lines that contain it, leaving just the single line that matches the bash shell process.

Refine this further with the cut command to isolate just the PID number if you are building this into a shell script to automate the process. There is a variable number of spaces involved and a tr command squeezes them out first, so the cut commend works more predictably.

If the whole command pipeline is enclosed in back ticks, add a head command to acquire just the first item in the list of returned PID numbers because a secondary bash shell is spawned as a child process and that falls through the filters creating a duplicate entry in the list. This is a prime example of where process spawning can catch you unawares. Simulate the back tick behavior by using round brackets to see this happen. You cannot use the back ticks without assigning them to a variable when diagnosing these problems. The result would be interpreted as a new command because of the way the shell substitution mechanism works for back ticks. The round brackets simulate the same effect without the command being substituted and executed by the shell, so it is easier to debug.

***Listing 10-5.*** Capturing PID Numbers

```
# Simple ps command
ps -ef | grep bash

root 1744   1622  0 07:46 ttySAC2  00:00:01 -bash
root 1918   1744  0 07:57 ttySAC2  00:00:00 grep --color=auto bash

# Suppressing the display of the grep command
ps -ef | grep bash | grep -v grep

root 1744   1622  0 07:46 ttySAC2  00:00:01 -bash

# Adding a tr command to squeeze out multiple space characters
ps -ef | grep bash | grep -v grep | tr -s ' '

root 1744 1622 0 07:46 ttySAC2 00:00:01 -bash

# Adding a cut command to isolate the PID
ps -ef | grep bash | grep -v grep | tr -s ' ' | cut -d' ' -f2

1744

#Simulate the back ticking child process by spawning using round brackets
(ps -ef | grep bash)

root 1744   1622  0 07:46 ttySAC2  00:00:02 -bash
root 1943   1744  0 07:59 ttySAC2  00:00:00 -bash
root 1945   1943  0 07:59 ttySAC2  00:00:00 grep --color=auto bash

# Assigning the PID number to a variable using back ticks
MY_PID=`ps -ef | grep bash | grep -v grep | tr -s ' ' | cut -d' ' -f2 | head -1`

echo ${MY_PID}

1744
```

In this example, the most interesting PID is 1744 running under the root account. Change the working directory to the process container path for your own bash shell (which might have a different PID) with a cd command:

```
cd /proc/1744
```

The contents of this directory are a mixture of readable files, subdirectories, and symbolic links. The symbolic links point at other entities within the file system. These entities are relevant to this process but they might also be relevant to many other processes. The directories manage collections of properties in a hierarchical manner so you can find them more easily. Most of the regular files are readable. Inspect them with a cat command or by opening a file descriptor on them from within your application. A few are writable but usually only by the root account. Listing 10-6 shows the result of using the ls command piped through some grep filters to see just the readable files listed. By now, you should start to see the ease with which the UNIX command line can combine individual commands to create combo commands that are very powerful.

*Listing 10-6.* Regular Files Belonging to a Process

```
ls -la | grep -v "^l" | grep -v "^d" | grep -v "total 0" | sort


-r--------  1 root root 0 Feb 16 16:43 environ
-r--------  1 root root 0 Feb 16 17:12 auxv
-r--------  1 root root 0 Feb 16 17:12 mountstats
-r--r--r--  1 root root 0 Feb 16 16:24 cmdline
-r--r--r--  1 root root 0 Feb 16 16:24 stat
-r--r--r--  1 root root 0 Feb 16 16:24 status
-r--r--r--  1 root root 0 Feb 16 16:45 statm
-r--r--r--  1 root root 0 Feb 16 17:12 cgroup
-r--r--r--  1 root root 0 Feb 16 17:12 limits
-r--r--r--  1 root root 0 Feb 16 17:12 maps
-r--r--r--  1 root root 0 Feb 16 17:12 mountinfo
-r--r--r--  1 root root 0 Feb 16 17:12 mounts
-r--r--r--  1 root root 0 Feb 16 17:12 oom_score
-r--r--r--  1 root root 0 Feb 16 17:12 pagemap
-r--r--r--  1 root root 0 Feb 16 17:12 personality
-r--r--r--  1 root root 0 Feb 16 17:12 smaps
-r--r--r--  1 root root 0 Feb 16 17:12 stack
-r--r--r--  1 root root 0 Feb 16 17:12 syscall
-r--r--r--  1 root root 0 Feb 16 17:12 wchan
-rw-------  1 root root 0 Feb 16 17:12 mem
-rw-r--r--  1 root root 0 Feb 16 17:12 comm
-rw-r--r--  1 root root 0 Feb 16 17:12 coredump_filter
-rw-r--r--  1 root root 0 Feb 16 17:12 oom_adj
-rw-r--r--  1 root root 0 Feb 16 17:12 oom_score_adj
-rw-r--r--  1 root root 0 Feb 16 17:12 sched
--w-------  1 root root 0 Feb 16 17:12 clear_refs
```

# Process Property Collections

Table 10-3 summarizes the directories containing collections of properties. List these in the bash command line shell with an ls command. Import and manage them as arrays of values inside a C language application.

***Table 10-3.*** *Property Collections Belonging to a Process*

| Directory | Description |
|-----------|-------------|
| fd | A collection of symbolic links to currently open files, one for each file that the process has open. If you do not have an lsof command installed, looking in here may tell you the same information. This list also includes the standard I/O files. |
| fdinfo | A collection of additional metadata about the open files listed in the fd property collection. You can cat these or open them as regular files to obtain the file read/write position and flags. |
| net | A collection of network-related properties pertaining to this process |
| ns | A collection of namespaces being used by the process |
| task | This contains a subdirectory for each thread in the process. Each one is named with the thread ID that it manages. This could be useful at quit time when you want to tear everything down and clean up as you exit from a process. |

# Process Properties

Table 10-4 describes the regular files containing process properties. Access them to read a value given that you know the PID number for the target process you want to examine. The path to each of these properties should be formed like this:

/proc/{PID_value}/{property_name}

Just like the global properties in the top level of the /proc filesystem, a few of these files block your terminal output when you use the cat command to read them. Instead, use the od (Octal Dump) tool to display their contents.

***Table 10-4.*** *Process Properties Reflected in Regular Files*

| Property | Description |
|----------|-------------|
| auxv | Auxiliary vector with information passed by the ELF interpreter when the process executable was started. This is a binary value so use the od tool to inspect it. |
| cgroup | A list of the control groups to which the process/task belongs |
| clear_refs | The clear_refs property within a process container is write only. Reading this property is of no use because it is intended for your application to send a message to the kernel to request that it clears some flag bits. This is an advanced memory management topic. |
| cmdline | The command line that initiated the process |
| comm | The name off the process (or thread task). This can be altered from inside the process. |
| coredump_filter | A bit mask that determines which memory segments are written to a core dump when the executable crashes |
| environ | The names and values of environment variables. These are inherited from the parent process and might have been modified during execution. They are discarded when the process exits. |

*(continued)*

*Table 10-4.* (*continued*)

| Property | Description |
|---|---|
| limits | This file displays the values and units of measurement for each of the process's resource limits. |
| maps | A text file with information about mapped files and blocks (heap and stack). This lists the shared libraries that are linked to the application at runtime and where in memory the various items are located. |
| mem | A binary image of the process memory for use with the ptrace tools. Because this is a binary value, you use the od tool to inspect it. |
| mountinfo | Lists additional information about the mount points propagated into the process space according to the permissions controlling whether they can be accessed |
| mounts | A list of mount points propagated into the process space according to the permissions controlling whether they can be accessed |
| mountstats | Statistical information about the mounted file systems |
| oom_adj | This file can be used to adjust the score used to select which process should be killed in an out-of-memory (OOM) situation. |
| oom_score | Contains the current score that the kernel gives to this process for the purpose of selecting a process for the OOM killer |
| oom_score_adj | This file can be used to adjust the badness heuristic used to select which process gets killed in OOM conditions. |
| pagemap | Related to kernel page map support |
| personality | Exposes the execution domain for the current process. Alter this if necessary with the personality() function. |
| sched | Tells you statistical information about the performance of your executable process or thread |
| smaps | Contains statistical information about memory consumption for each of the process's mappings |
| stack | Provides a symbolic trace of the function calls in the kernel stack for a process |
| stat | Status information about the process that is presented by the ps command |
| statm | Status information about the process memory space |
| status | Various properties of the running process which may be useful to examine |
| syscall | Debugging output from internal system calls |
| wchan | The symbolic name corresponding to the location in the kernel where the process is sleeping |

# Process-Related Objects

Table 10-5 summarizes the symbolic links that point at relevant locations within the file system.

*Table 10-5.* *Symbolic Links to PID-Related Objects*

| Symlink | Description |
| --- | --- |
| cwd | The current working directory of the process. Updated by the cd command in the bash shell command line or by calling the POSIX chdir() function from your application. |
| exe | The executable binary that is running the process |
| root | The root of the current filesystem. This is normally / but it may be set to another value if the process is running in a chroot jail to limit its access to the file system. This is sometimes called sandboxing. |

The items listed in Table 10-6 are located in the top-level directory of the /proc filesystem and are directly related to the currently running process. These are provided mainly for convenience when accessing the environment on its behalf. They do not have a PID prefix but they are only visible to the process they describe.

*Table 10-6.* *Symbolic Links to "self"-Related Properties*

| Symbolic link | Description |
| --- | --- |
| mounts | A symbolic link to /proc/self/mounts, which contains a list of mounted file systems accessible to the current process |
| net | A symbolic link to /proc/self/net, which contains a lot of useful debugging information about the network configuration of your ARTIK module |
| self | PID identified container inside the /proc directory that corresponds to the current process being executed. You can write generalized access scripts or commands without needing to know the process number first. |
| self/mounts | Displays a list of mounted file systems accessible to this process |
| self/net/* | A collection of network statistics available individually as files or collectively with a netstat command |

# Inspecting the Process Status

Given that you know the PID for the process you are interested in, examine its status by looking in the /proc/{PID}/status file with a cat command or by reading the regular file from the C language. An example status file is shown in Listing 10-7.

***Listing 10-7.*** Process Status Information

```
cat /proc/1719/status

Name:    bash
State:   S (sleeping)
Tgid:    1719
Pid:     1719
PPid:    1636
TracerPid:      0
Uid:     0       0       0       0
Gid:     0       0       0       0
FDSize: 256
Groups:
VmPeak:     5324 kB
VmSize:     5324 kB
VmLck:         0 kB
VmPin:         0 kB
VmHWM:      1900 kB
VmRSS:      1900 kB
VmData:      188 kB
VmStk:       136 kB
VmExe:       900 kB
VmLib:      1696 kB
VmPTE:         8 kB
VmSwap:        0 kB
Threads:       1
SigQ:    0/3206
SigPnd:  0000000000000000
ShdPnd:  0000000000000000
SigBlk:  0000000000010000
SigIgn:  0000000000380004
SigCgt:  000000004b817efb
CapInh:  0000000000000000
CapPrm:  0000001ffffffff
CapEff:  0000001ffffffff
CapBnd:  0000001ffffffff
Cpus_allowed:   3
Cpus_allowed_list:      0-1
voluntary_ctxt_switches:        712
nonvoluntary_ctxt_switches:     642
```

Some properties here are obvious. The PPID number tells you the parent process ID that started this process running. The FDSize value tells you how many files can be open at once. Various memory performance statistics are also available. This might help you diagnose memory leaks or optimize your memory usage by changing your strategy for malloc() function calls, etc. The number of process threads can also tell you about the internal behavior of your process if you have factored your design by multithreading it.

# Resource Usage Monitoring

One of your application processes might be hogging the CPU and denying other processes the opportunity to do their work. The top command can help find which process is the culprit. If you use the top command with options, it displays a constantly updating display of processes ranked in order of their resource usage. Start the monitoring by typing the top command. Add command line options to alter its behavior. Listing 10-8 shows the example output screen generated by the top command that uses terminal cursor controls to redraw the status line each time it updates.

*Listing 10-8.* Resource Allocation Output From the top Command

```
top
```

```
top - 16:50:11 up 55 min,  1 user,  load average: 0.01, 0.06, 0.06
Tasks: 100 total,   1 running,  99 sleeping,   0 stopped,   0 zombie
%Cpu(s):  0.3 us,  0.7 sy,  0.0 ni, 99.0 id,  0.0 wa,  0.0 hi,  0.0 si,  0.0 st
KiB Mem :   502260 total,   386564 free,    26636 used,    89060 buff/cache
KiB Swap:        0 total,        0 free,        0 used.   459526 avail Mem
```

| PID | USER | PR | NI | VIRT | RES | SHR | S | %CPU | %MEM | TIME+ | COMMAND |
|-----|------|----|----|------|-----|-----|---|------|------|-------|---------|
| 1930 | root | 20 | 0 | 8896 | 1808 | 1320 | R | 1.0 | 0.4 | 0:03.06 | top |
| 1842 | root | 20 | 0 | 0 | 0 | 0 | S | 0.7 | 0.0 | 0:04.73 | kworker/u4+ |
| 307 | root | 20 | 0 | 0 | 0 | 0 | S | 0.3 | 0.0 | 0:04.36 | spi0 |
| 1904 | root | 20 | 0 | 0 | 0 | 0 | S | 0.3 | 0.0 | 0:00.99 | kworker/0:0 |
| 1 | root | 20 | 0 | 24816 | 3224 | 2228 | S | 0.0 | 0.6 | 0:04.05 | systemd |
| 2 | root | 20 | 0 | 0 | 0 | 0 | S | 0.0 | 0.0 | 0:00.01 | kthreadd |
| 3 | root | 20 | 0 | 0 | 0 | 0 | S | 0.0 | 0.0 | 0:00.07 | ksoftirqd/0 |
| 5 | root | 0 | -20 | 0 | 0 | 0 | S | 0.0 | 0.0 | 0:00.00 | kworker/0:+ |
| 7 | root | rt | 0 | 0 | 0 | 0 | S | 0.0 | 0.0 | 0:00.00 | migration/0 |
| 8 | root | 20 | 0 | 0 | 0 | 0 | S | 0.0 | 0.0 | 0:00.75 | rcu_preempt |
| 9 | root | 20 | 0 | 0 | 0 | 0 | S | 0.0 | 0.0 | 0:00.00 | rcu_bh |
| 10 | root | 20 | 0 | 0 | 0 | 0 | S | 0.0 | 0.0 | 0:00.00 | rcu_sched |
| 11 | root | rt | 0 | 0 | 0 | 0 | S | 0.0 | 0.0 | 0:00.22 | watchdog/0 |
| 12 | root | rt | 0 | 0 | 0 | 0 | S | 0.0 | 0.0 | 0:00.23 | watchdog/1 |
| 13 | root | rt | 0 | 0 | 0 | 0 | S | 0.0 | 0.0 | 0:00.00 | migration/1 |
| 14 | root | 20 | 0 | 0 | 0 | 0 | S | 0.0 | 0.0 | 0:00.02 | ksoftirqd/1 |
| 16 | root | 0 | -20 | 0 | 0 | 0 | S | 0.0 | 0.0 | 0:00.00 | kworker/1:+ |

The top command itself will consume a lot of CPU capacity when it runs. It is a very busy process that constantly gathers a list of other processes to parse and rank to create its results. Stop the cyclic refresh and return to the command line prompt by pressing the [**Control**] + [**C**] key combination.

# Altering the Process Priority

Sometimes you may want to increase the priority of a process and decrease the CPU consumed by another. The nice command is provided for you to adjust these relative priorities. Do this from inside your own C language applications with the setpriority() function and see the effects it has on process priorities with the getpriority() function. The nice command is used as a wrapper for a command that you want to run at a different priority when you start it up. If you were running a non-urgent file compression task with

```
tar cvzf archive.tgz largefile
```

you can prefix it with a `nice` command that runs the archiving process at a lower priority, as in

```
nice -n 19 tar cvzf archive.tgz largefile
```

This ensures that the task completes with the same result. It consumes less CPU capacity and allows other normal priority processes to run without being affected by the archiving job. As a non-privileged user, you can run your own processes at a lower priority but only the root user can elevate the priority so a process gets more CPU attention.

The niceness factor is inversely proportional to its value. If you think of this as controlling the latency of the process, it makes more sense. Negative values are higher priority and positive values are lower priority. The default niceness of a process is 10. The most favorable priority is -20, which elevates the priority to its maximum. The least favorable priority setting is 19.

Use the `renice` command to adjust the priority of a currently running process; the priority value can be defined as an absolute or relative value. Read the manual pages for more details.

## Processes vs. Threads

A process has a limited number of resources available. These resources are determined when the kernel is configured. One example is the number of simultaneously open files. Each process has its own set of resources and consuming them in one process does not affect any others.

An alternative to processes is a technique called thread programming. This subdivides a process into individual threads of execution but they all run in the context of a single process. Each thread has access to its parent process's pool of resources, and in this scenario, the total number of resources consumed by the threads cannot exceed that configured for a single process. Assume that a process is allowed to open 256 file buffers. If you create multiple threads and open two file buffers in each one, you cannot have more than 128 threads running unless you close files in the threads that have completed their work. Resource allocation and recycling within the process is more complex with thread programming.

The upside of processes is that they have all of their resources available but they take a few moments to start up. Threads have an advantage that they are faster to create because they do not have a complete process context built for them each time they start. The downside is that they must share resources with their sibling threads. Another advantage of thread programming is the ease with which you can communicate between threads or share memory with multiple threads.

When you build multiprocess or multithreaded applications, the major area of complexity is communicating between them and interlocking mutually exclusive execution paths. The thread-programming model supports a lot of tools to help with this. Interprocess signaling has been supported since the very earliest C language applications were written. Modern techniques also use sockets and listeners when the processes are distributed across several separate systems.

## Summary

Now you have an understanding of processes and how they relate to one another inside the ARTIK. This is a large and complex topic and you can spend a good deal more time finding out about thread programming and interprocess messaging. This will be useful knowledge if your design is factored across multiple processes.

# CHAPTER 11

■ ■ ■

# The /run Virtual File System

As the ARTIK runs, the kernel manages its processes via the /proc directory. There are other state-dependent issues and runtime data structures that need to be maintained but which are not processes. These data structures, logs, files, and various other components are gathered together into the /run directory so they avoid cluttering up the rest of the file system. The Linux file system is becoming much better managed and things are being moved to better locations. You will see the /run directory change as things are moved around within the virtual file systems in future operating system releases.

## About /run

The /run virtual filesystem is a recent addition to Linux and is described in version 3.0 of the Filesystem Hierarchy Standard (FHS). It is created by the init process early on in the boot cycle.

The /run directory contains variable data that is gathered by the kernel and reflected into user space for your application to make use of. This directory contains useful reference information about the running system since it was last booted. It maintains a list of currently logged-in users and details of daemon and agent processes running in the background.

The /run directory is implemented as a temporary file storage system (tmpfs). Although there is a limited capacity for storing bulky data here, your applications can store useful temporary data files in the /run directory. Anything stored here is purged during a shutdown/reboot cycle. This is not the place to keep any persistent configuration data; that should be put in the /etc directory. Historically an application might have used the /var/run directory for temporary files. If you are writing new applications, use the new conventions and locate your runtime temporary data in the /run directory tree. Find out more about the /run directory in the Filesystem Hierarchy Standard at the following links:

```
https://en.wikipedia.org/wiki/Filesystem_Hierarchy_Standard
www.linuxfoundation.org/collaborate/workgroups/lsb/fhs
http://refspecs.linuxfoundation.org/fhs.shtml
```

## Why /run Was Created

Historically, there were several virtual file systems where runtime information about processes and daemons were stored for access by other processes. Moving these items under the single virtual file system reduces the complexity of the operating system and makes it easier to find things. Older software needs to have a small modification to bring it up to date. The need for modification is avoided by creating symbolic links at

© Cliff Wootton 2016
C. Wootton, *Samsung ARTIK Reference*, DOI 10.1007/978-1-4842-2322-2_11

the locations where the legacy applications expect to file files and directories. The modifications are then deferred to when the preventive maintenance is carried out. There are several important reasons why the /run virtual file system is a good idea.

- Fewer temporary file systems are mounted

- Less clutter in the /dev directory

- Removal of the unnecessary /lib/init/rw directory

- Elimination of the suboptimal /var/run directory

- Previously hidden files are now visible to user space

When the operating system boots, some processes must store their temporary runtime data in a file. Historically the /dev filesystem was created very early on in the boot process and since it was guaranteed to be there, some developers would write temporary data there even though it is a bad choice of location for that sort of thing. The /run directory cleans this up a great deal. Also, because it is also now available early in the boot process, moving things there has no detrimental effect but it ensures the /dev directory is much less cluttered with non–device-related data.

The /lib/init/rw directory was another place that was a less elegant location for these runtime data files; if your code references it, you should now move those files to the /run directory.

The /var/run directory was introduced as a temporary filesystem to solve these early boot storage problems but this needed to be created before its parent /var directory existed and that caused unnecessary complexity in the boot manager. Moving this to the /run directory and mounting that earlier in the boot process eliminates some unhelpful work-arounds and makes the mount manager more reliable.

By eliminating the dot prefix on some file names, previously hidden items now become visible to a plain ls command rather than needing to remember to add the list all (-la) options. Systems administrators will find this much more convenient.

With these changes, the /var directory now properly contains persistent runtime data and the /run directory has volatile runtime data. The /etc directory now only contains system configuration information and the /dev directory is much less cluttered with non–device-related data. The lifetime guarantees for the content of each of these directories is also more consistent.

Another benefit of implementing the /run directory is to gradually move to a point where the / root directory can eventually be locked and write protected. This is very desirable from a security perspective.

# Kernel Subsystems as Objects

Kernel objects are reflected by the kernel into directory containers within the /run filesystem. Table 11-1 describes briefly what they all do.

*Table 11-1. Kernel Objects Reflected into the /run Directory*

| Object | Description |
|---|---|
| avahi-daemon | Part of the zero configuration auto-discovery protocol. mDNS is the generic term. On Apple systems, this is equivalent to Bonjour/Rendezvous support. |
| console | There is no documentation for this but it may be reserved for later use by the SELinux support. |
| dbus | A messaging system for interprocess communication |
| faillock | Part of the security mechanisms that record unauthorized login attempts |
| lirc | Infrared remote control support. This would expect some infrared detection hardware to be present. |
| lock | Lock files for running processes |
| log | Logging data should be written here when journaling what happens inside your application |
| mount | Part of the auto-mounter support |
| netreport | Messages pertaining to the network startup are logged here. |
| NetworkManager | This is a dynamic network control and configuration system that attempts to keep network devices and connections up and active when they are available. |
| ppp | Point-to-Point Protocol daemon support |
| pulse | Part of the pulse width audio support |
| sepermit | Part of the future SELinux support. Currently undocumented. |
| setrans | Part of the future SELinux support. Currently undocumented. |
| sysconfig | System configuration files. At present, the ARTIK only maintains some NFS configuration values in here. |
| systemd | Runtime data for the systemctl command to operate on |
| tmpfiles.d | Configuration for creation, deletion, and cleaning of volatile and temporary files |
| udev | Runtime data for udev managed device drivers |
| user | Support for logged-in user accounts managed by systemd |
| wpa_supplicant | Wi-Fi networking support |

# Runtime System Properties

These files are rarely needed but they do convey some useful information. They all live in the top level of the /run directory and their purpose is described in Table 11-2.

*Table 11-2. Runtime System Properties*

| Property | Description |
|---|---|
| agetty.reload | Used by the agetty login support when it needs to reload |
| cron.reboot | Used by the cron scheduler to determine whether a genuine reboot has happened to run boot-time scheduled tasks |
| utmp | Records login and logout transactions |

# Socket Connections

Socket connections are used for interprocess communication or for sending messages to the kernel. The /run filesystem contains several of these connections. The items described in Table 11-3 are reflected into the top level /run directory.

***Table 11-3.*** *Socket Connections*

| Socket | Description |
| --- | --- |
| gssproxy.sock | A UNIX socket connection for communicating with the kernel. This is used by the SELinux support when it is released. |
| rpcbind.sock | The rpcbind utility is a server that converts RPC program numbers into universal addresses. This socket is provided to communicate with it from your application. |

# Process Identifier Files

The /run directory is the correct place to store your process identifier (PID) files. These files might have previously been written to the /etc or /tmp directories. The correct format for a PID file is

/run/{application_name}.pid

The internal format of this PID file should be an ASCII coded decimal number representing the process identifier followed by a newline character.

Programs that read PID files should ignore extra whitespace and leading zeroes and should be able to cope with a missing trailing newline. Additional lines in the PID file should be ignored. This forces you to adopt a more flexible application naming strategy if more than one copy of your application can run simultaneously. Extend the {application_name} value to describe the multiple instances. This avoids a namespace collision that would wipe out earlier records of PID numbers when second and subsequent instances of your application start running and consequently record their PID. Watch for possible namespace collisions if you are installing applications from other third parties.

In a shell script, use the $$ internal variable that the bash shell maintains to get the PID number. This command could be incorporated into a shell script to note the PID while it is running:

echo $$ > /run/my_application.pid

There is a built-in variable that was originally intended to serve the same purpose. It is called $BASHPID but there are problems with this if you use it in a sub-shell that is spawned in a child process that does not reinitialize the bash command line as it is started up. The child process would inherit a $BASHPID value from its parent process and use the wrong PID number.

Listing 11-1 shows how to accomplish the same thing from inside your own C language application. Wrap this code in a reusable function if you are building a library of useful tools.

**Listing 11-1.** Storing a PID Number with the C Language

```
// Open a PID file for writing
FILE *myPidFd;

if((myPidFd = fopen("/run/my_application.pid", "w")) == NULL)
{
  printf("Error: unable to write PID file\n");
  return false;
}

// Store the PID value
fprintf(myPidFd, "%d\n", getpid());

// Close the PID file
fclose(myPidFd);
```

Some PID files are created by system processes that are started automatically as the ARTIK is booted. Table 11-4 describes the ones that are already there. This is an important list.

**Table 11-4.** PID Files for Currently Running Processes

| PID file | Description |
| --- | --- |
| alsactl.pid | Part of the ALSA audio support |
| brcm_patchram_plus.pid | Bluetooth support process |
| crond.pid | Cron scheduler daemon process |
| dhclient-p2p0.pid | DHCP client support and peer-to-peer networking |
| gssproxy.pid | Remote procedure call support |
| sm-notify.pid | Reboot notification to collaborating networked devices |
| sshd.pid | Secure shell command line support |

Use unique names for your own applications to avoid a namespace collision. A neat solution to this problem is to build the target PID file name with a prefix made by reversing the items in your own Internet domain name. This makes it very clear who owns the PID file, so a collision is very unlikely because each application developer has a private namespace. You can then add an optional suffix to identify multiple instances of your application. This approach avoids the need to keep a register of child processes because the prefix can be used to create a filtered list of PID files. For example, an Apress application might have a PID file name like this:

```
com.apress.example_application.suffix.pid
```

# Updating Legacy Applications

If you are planning to recycle some old code from a legacy application and deploy it on your ARTIK, check that you do not have any hard-coded references to the legacy paths in the file system. If you hard code references to /var/run, your application will cease to work if that path is eventually deprecated and removed. Refer to /run instead of /var/run. For the time being, a symbolic link protects you. Update your code as a routine maintenance task to avoid these issues. Table 11-5 lists some old versus new canonical paths to be aware of and check for if the OS is upgraded. These are planned changes that the kernel developers are working on. It would not be a huge task to use the refactoring tools in a modern coding IDE to seek out these items and fix them once and for all.

**Table 11-5.** *Old vs. New Canonical Paths*

| Old path | New path |
|---|---|
| /var/run | /run |
| /var/lock | /run/lock |
| /dev/shm | /run/shm |
| /tmp | Later this becomes /run/tmp (but continue to use /tmp via a symlink) |
| Various runtime data locations | /run |
| User temporary data | /run/user/{UID} |
| /lib/init/rw | /run |
| /dev/.* | /run/* |
| /dev/shm/* | /run/* |
| Any writable files in the /etc directory | /run/* |
| /etc/lvm/cache/ | /run/lvm/cache/ |
| /etc/mtab | /run/mtab |
| /etc/network/run/ifstate | /run/network/ifstate |
| /etc/adjtime | /run/adjtime (this is expected to change soon) |
| /etc/lvm/cache/ | /run and /run/lock |
| /etc/mtab | /proc/self/mounts |
| /etc/network/run/ifstate | /run/network/ifstate |

Creating environment variables and defining them in a containing shell script that runs your application is a good way to solve this problem and make your application more portable. Then your application can import the environment variables and use their contents without having any hard-coded paths in them at all. Create an environment variable in the bash shell:

```
export VARIABLE=value
```

There should not be any space characters between the variable and the equals sign (=) and the value. If your value has spaces embedded in it, then the whole value should be enclosed in straight quotes ("). Environment variables are accessed by prepending the dollar sign ($) just like other shell variables. When they are defined in an export command, the dollar sign is omitted.

Now inside your C language application code you can read that environment variable with the getenv() function provided by the stdlib library. Listing 11-2 shows an example to test in your ARTIK.

*Listing 11-2.* Reading an Environment Variable From the C Language

```
#include <stdio.h>
#include <stdlib.h>

int main()
{
  printf("Reading environment variables\n");
  const char* myEnvVar = getenv("VARIABLE");
  printf("VARIABLE :%s\n", myEnvVar);
  printf("end test\n");
}
```

Compile the code example and run it. The first time it runs, the text string '(null)' is presented because the environment variable has not been exported yet. After exporting that environment variable, the value is reflected into the application and displayed by the printf() function. Listing 11-3 shows these steps.

*Listing 11-3.* Reading an Environment Variable With bash

```
gcc -Wall test.c -o test

./test

Reading environment variables
VARIABLE :(null)
end test

$ export VARIABLE=value

./test

Reading environment variables
VARIABLE :value
end test
```

# Summary

Understanding the runtime environment is important for improving the performance of your user space applications. The /run file system provides useful resources you can check from inside your application while it is running. Then you can make informed decisions about how to alter its behavior responsively.

## CHAPTER 12

■ ■ ■

# System Administration

Learn how to do systems administration for your development workstation and your ARTIK module in order to optimize its configuration for your needs. This is a career enhancing skill; it's also necessary for getting the best performance from your ARTIK module. There are plenty of online resources to teach you the systems administration skills you will need, but this chapter offers some initial information.

## How to Be a Sys Admin

One of the major benefits of running Fedora as your development workstation operating system is the opportunity to rehearse these tasks before attempting them on your ARTIK. Read through the systems administrator guide in the Fedora documentation library. There are some items that are particularly relevant to your ARTIK in the Fedora version 22 sys admin guide. See `https://docs.fedoraproject.org/en-US/Fedora/22/html/System_Administrators_Guide/index.html`.

The available admin tasks may be affected by the operating system configuration that Yocto imposes as the Fedora OS is built for the ARTIK. For now, assume that all of the capabilities of the Fedora OS are available until you discover something that you cannot do. These are the sort of things you should learn about:

- Setting up the system locale so the OS can use the right localization settings

- Setting the right keyboard layout if you are interacting via a terminal emulator

- Configuring the date and time

- Managing user accounts, especially if you are communicating with other systems

- Managing user groups

- Managing packages for installation

- Configuring services (agents and Daemons)

- Configuring OpenSSH to maintain the security

- Configuring VNC if you want to do remote desktop access (only relevant if your ARTIK is running a GUI)

- Administering the built-in Apache web server

- Administering the built-in e-mail server (you may have already noticed the messages from SendMail as it starts up during the ARTIK boot process)

- Administering directory servers to run LDAP

© Cliff Wootton 2016
C. Wootton, *Samsung ARTIK Reference*, DOI 10.1007/978-1-4842-2322-2_12

- Administering file servers for sharing with Samba and FTP

- Configuring printers

- Setting up automatic time synchronization with NTP

- Monitoring and analyzing the system performance

- Automating system tasks

- Configuring kernel modules, devices, and drivers

- Installing software with dnf

Here are some systems administration tricks and tips to save you time. Most systems administration work is very simple, often only needing a one-line command unless you are installing major new software items. System administrators often only need to check something occasionally or turn it on and off.

# Identifying an ARTIK Module

There are a variety of different ways to discover what kind of ARTIK your application is running in. The /proc filesystem provides at least two regular files whose contents you can cat to the screen in the bash command line. Access them from a C language application instead by opening and reading the file. Listing 12-1 shows the results of inspecting these files.

***Listing 12-1.*** Determining the ARTIK Model

```
cat /proc/device-tree/compatible
```

```
samsung,artik5samsung,exynos3250
```

```
cat /proc/device-tree/model
```

```
Samsung ARTIK5 board based on EXYNOS3250
```

Check out the following links for more about the kernel support for your Samsung ARTIK hardware. These links document the source code used to build the kernel. There may be new documents introduced in this library as the ARTIK engineers roll out more open source material. Download and study the rest of the ARTIK OS source code now that Samsung has made it available to the developer community.

```
https://github.com/SamsungARTIK
https://github.com/torvalds/linux/blob/master/Documentation/arm/Samsung-S3C24XX/Overview.txt
https://github.com/torvalds/linux/blob/master/Documentation/arm/Samsung-S3C24XX/S3C2412.txt
https://github.com/torvalds/linux/blob/master/Documentation/arm/Samsung-S3C24XX/S3C2413.txt
```

# Detecting the OS Version

Knowing what version of the operating system you are running is useful, especially when you are looking for additional software to install. Some packages have dependencies based on your operating system version. Make sure you download the right one. The uname command tells you what kind of Linux you are running and something about the CPU cores you have available. The output shown in Listing 12-2 illustrates this, but the

results may be different for your system depending on the kind of ARTIK you have and its vintage.
The /proc/version file describes the version of the operating system and some additional properties.
Although the ARTIK runs a Fedora-based OS, the GCC compiler is reported as being Ubuntu compatible. Your
system may display a different GCC compiler version. The contents of the /boot directory are also interesting.

***Listing 12-2.*** Identifying the OS Version

```
uname -a
Linux dhcppc1 3.10.9 #1 SMP PREEMPT Mon Nov 9 13:34:01 KST 2015 armv7l armv7l armv7l GNU/
Linux

cat /proc/version
Linux version 3.10.9 (linuxpark@mozart) (gcc version 4.8.2 (Ubuntu/Linaro 4.8.2-16ubuntu4) )
#1 SMP PREEMPT Mon Nov 9 13:34:01 KST 2015

ls /boot
exynos3250-artik5.dtb  uInitrd  zImage
```

# Determining the Kernel Version

It is useful to know what version of the kernel you are running. This command tells you:

```
uname -r
```

On a Commercial Beta ARTIK 5, this displays the value 3.10.9, which corresponds to the name of a
directory inside the /lib/modules directory. Inside that directory are the modules that are built in to the
currently installed kernel. Installing the latest ARTIK firmware from Samsung would affect this value unless
it is released to deploy a minor patch update without updating the kernel version.

# Dynamically Changing the Host Name

By default the host name in your ARTIK 5 is localhost. You can see this if you type the hostname command.
To alter the host name, write a new value to the /proc/sys/kernel/hostname virtual file location. It makes
sense to constrain your host names to just using the following characters:

- Uppercase letters (A-Z)
- Lowercase letters (a-z)
- Numbers (0-9)
- Dashes (-)
- Underscores (_)
- Periods (.)

You might be able to use other characters but they can be misinterpreted as meta-characters if you use
the host name as a command line parameter. The hostname command displays the current value. Listing 12-3
illustrates how to change the host name from a shell command line. This is just a temporary change. Modify
your network configuration to make it permanent and persistent after a reboot.

*Listing 12-3.* Changing the hostname Property From the Command Line

```
hostname [Return]

localhost

echo "ARTIK-5" > /proc/sys/kernel/hostname [Return]

hostname [Return]

ARTIK-5
```

This approach might be useful if you have a collection of ARTIK modules that collaborate in a grid, mesh, or cluster but are based on the same OS installation image. They could register with a central controlling node and take on a name that is granted by the central system. This would allow your entire herd of ARTIK modules to deploy themselves to distributed tasks in an entirely dynamic fashion. It would be interesting to see a large grid of ARTIK modules clustered together as a massively parallel computer.

Listing 12-4 provides the source of a small application that does the same thing in C language. Open a new source file, call it rename_host.c, save the file, and compile it with GCC. Now use the hostname command to check the current host name. Run your new compiled application and check that the name was changed by using the hostname command again.

*Listing 12-4.* Altering the hostname Property From the C Language

```c
#include <string.h>
#include <unistd.h>

int main()
{
  char myHostname[] = "MY-ARTIK";

  sethostname(myHostname, strlen(myHostname));

  return 0;
}
```

■ **Note** This technique for changing the host name only works for the current session. The host name reverts to the original value when the ARTIK is rebooted unless you permanently reconfigure it in the conventional way.

# Setting the Correct Date

Your ARTIK module may display the wrong date when it is booted. Unless it has a battery backup or you configure your ARTIK to call a timeserver to set the time automatically, you must set the date and time manually every time it boots. Use the date command with the -s option to set the date. Substitute the right date and time values instead of the placeholders shown here when you type it on the ARTIK command line.

```
date -s '2016-M-D HH:MM:SS'
```

# Uploading Files

Once you have your ARTIK configured for IP networking, use the IP address to send files to it from your desktop workstation. The scp command is specifically designed for that task. You use it from the UNIX command line on your desktop system. Use the Cygwin terminal application to use the scp command on a Windows workstation.

The source file to copy can be anywhere on your local workstation but you need a UNIX path to reach it. The account name needs to have sufficient privileges to write to the destination directory where you are copying the files. In most ARTIK-based examples, the root account is used. The IP address is where your ARTIK is configured to exist on your Local Area Network (LAN). The destination directory indicates where to deposit the file inside the ARTIK module. The format of an scp command is

```
scp {source_file_to_copy} {account}@{IP address}:/{destination_directory}
```

Use the scp command to copy the hello.c source file from a development workstation to the /tmp directory in a target ARTIK module:

```
scp /my_files/hello.c root@192.168.1.57:/tmp
```

# Downloading Files

Use the scp tool to bring files back from an ARTIK module to your hosting development workstation. Just switch the parameters around the other way. The remote directory is described as a source rather than a destination:

```
scp {account}@{IP_address}:/{source_file_path} {local_directory}
```

Use scp to copy the hello.c source file back to a development workstation from a target ARTIK module where it was living in the /tmp directory:

```
scp root@192.168.1.57:/tmp/hello.c /my_files
```

# Examining the System Configuration

The getconf command can be used to display all of the system configuration variables that are currently defined. The kernel configuration file is not available from /proc/config.gz on an ARTIK because the kernel was compiled with that option turned **OFF**. The getconf tool may reveal what would have been in that file. Adding the -a option displays all the configuration parameters. Because there are so many lines of output, pipe the results through the more utility to see them one page at a time. Type this command to view the configuration:

```
getconf -a | more
```

The getconf tool is useful in other ways. Read the manual page at www.unix.com/man-page/linux/1/getconf/ for more details.

# Checking the Memory Usage

Your application code may use significant amounts of the available memory. Configuring additional services in the OS core may increase this memory usage. Use the free command when you are logged in to your ARTIK to see how much memory is being used. Listing 12-5 illustrates the memory usage captured immediately after booting an ARTIK 5 module.

*Listing 12-5.* Free Memory Report

```
free -m
```

```
          total used free shared buff/cache available
Mem:       490   33  388      0        68        442
Swap:        0    0    0
```

# Viewing Process Memory Maps

If you know the Process ID (PID) number for a process, the memory allocation map for that process is available in the /proc/{PID} directory in the procfs virtual file system. This example assumes the bash shell is running as PID 1719. This example command displays the memory map for the running process. Listing 12-6 shows how to deduce which shared libraries are linked to an application, where in memory its various components are located, and some information about permissions and flags.

*Listing 12-6.* Memory Map for a Process

```
cat /prod/1719/maps

b6a88000-b6c88000 r--p 00000000 b3:03 5710    /usr/lib/locale/locale-archive
b6c88000-b6c94000 r-xp 00000000 b3:03 996     /usr/lib/libnss_files-2.21.so
b6c94000-b6ca3000 ---p 0000c000 b3:03 996     /usr/lib/libnss_files-2.21.so
b6ca3000-b6ca4000 r--p 0000b000 b3:03 996     /usr/lib/libnss_files-2.21.so
b6ca4000-b6ca5000 rw-p 0000c000 b3:03 996     /usr/lib/libnss_files-2.21.so
b6ca5000-b6de5000 r-xp 00000000 b3:03 5411    /usr/lib/libc-2.21.so
b6de5000-b6de7000 r--p 00140000 b3:03 5411    /usr/lib/libc-2.21.so
b6de7000-b6de8000 rw-p 00142000 b3:03 5411    /usr/lib/libc-2.21.so
b6de8000-b6deb000 rw-p 00000000 00:00 0
b6deb000-b6e08000 r-xp 00000000 b3:03 866     /usr/lib/libgcc_s-5.1.1-20150618.so.1
b6e08000-b6e17000 ---p 0001d000 b3:03 866     /usr/lib/libgcc_s-5.1.1-20150618.so.1
b6e17000-b6e18000 rw-p 0001c000 b3:03 866     /usr/lib/libgcc_s-5.1.1-20150618.so.1
b6e18000-b6e1c000 r-xp 00000000 b3:03 5232    /usr/lib/libdl-2.21.so
b6e1c000-b6e2b000 ---p 00004000 b3:03 5232    /usr/lib/libdl-2.21.so
b6e2b000-b6e2c000 r--p 00003000 b3:03 5232    /usr/lib/libdl-2.21.so
b6e2c000-b6e2d000 rw-p 00004000 b3:03 5232    /usr/lib/libdl-2.21.so
b6e2d000-b6e49000 r-xp 00000000 b3:03 2147    /usr/lib/libtinfo.so.5.9
b6e49000-b6e59000 ---p 0001c000 b3:03 2147    /usr/lib/libtinfo.so.5.9
b6e59000-b6e5b000 r--p 0001c000 b3:03 2147    /usr/lib/libtinfo.so.5.9
b6e5b000-b6e5c000 rw-p 0001e000 b3:03 2147    /usr/lib/libtinfo.so.5.9
b6e5c000-b6e7b000 r-xp 00000000 b3:03 2378    /usr/lib/ld-2.21.so
b6e7d000-b6e81000 rw-p 00000000 00:00 0
b6e81000-b6e88000 r--s 00000000 b3:03 1943    /usr/lib/gconv/gconv-modules.cache
b6e88000-b6e89000 rw-p 00000000 00:00 0
```

```
b6e89000-b6e8a000 r-xp 00000000 00:00 0       [sigpage]
b6e8a000-b6e8b000 r--p 0001e000 b3:03 2378    /usr/lib/ld-2.21.so
b6e8b000-b6e8c000 rw-p 0001f000 b3:03 2378    /usr/lib/ld-2.21.so
b6e8c000-b6f6d000 r-xp 00000000 b3:03 11982   /usr/bin/bash
b6f7c000-b6f7f000 r--p 000e0000 b3:03 11982   /usr/bin/bash
b6f7f000-b6f84000 rw-p 000e3000 b3:03 11982   /usr/bin/bash
b6f84000-b6faa000 rw-p 00000000 00:00 0       [heap]
be912000-be933000 rw-p 00000000 00:00 0       [stack]
ffff0000-ffff1000 r-xp 00000000 00:00 0       [vectors]
```

# Discovering the Process Limits

Use the ulimit tool to display the current limits for resources available to your processes. This tells you about the maximum number of open files and other useful values that help you with capacity planning. Type this command to see the resource limits in your ARTIK module:

```
ulimit -a
```

# Monitoring Service Status

The system runs various services and background processes to keep things managed and under control. These are called units. View the current disposition and status with systemctl utility. List the unit files with this command. The output shows a list of approximately 230 services and pages the results for you as they are displayed.

```
systemctl list-unit-files
```

# Quitting and Aborting Processes

When you initiate UNIX commands, some of them continue running until you explicitly tell them to stop. Sometimes you do so with a [**Control**] + [**C**] key combination or a [**Control**] + [**D**] combination. If the command spawns a sub-shell, try the exit command to leave that shell and bounce back up to the calling parent shell. Some utilities expect you to type quit or bye to exit. Kill a process by checking for the process ID and using the kill -9 command on it. This sends a signal to the process that halts it right away. This is not an ideal way to stop something but it may be necessary. Here is how:

1.  Find the PID:

    ```
    ps -ef | grep {your_application_name}
    ```

2.  This should display a matching process:

    ```
    501 1185 1 0 2:47pm xxxxxx 0:01.16 /xxx/yyyy
    ```

3.  Note the second number (1185 in this example). This is the PID for your application process. The first number is the parent PID. This may describe your command line shell. This is repeated a few times. The application PID you are interested in is only listed once.

4.  Now kill the process by sending a quit signal. Substitute the correct PID value in this command:

```
kill -9 1185
```

5.  Check that it has gone by listing the processes again.

---

■ **Note** **DO NOT ACCIDENTALLY KILL THE PARENT PROCESS.** If you do, your session might be forcibly aborted. This is a bad thing because it can corrupt files. In extreme cases, it can blow away the partition map and destroy the storage device where the main file system is kept. Rebooting your system is now the only solution unless your application was running in a sub-shell. Run a disk repair with the fsck tool immediately in case something was broken. Make sure that you are killing processes in the correct command line shell. Your ARTIK and development workstation may look very similar unless you take steps to ensure that the differences between terminal sessions are obvious.

---

# Determining the Available CPUs

Find out about the current CPU configuration of your ARTIK module from the /proc/cpuinfo file. This is useful when you are setting up processor affinities to run applications on specific CPU cores. It is also useful when debugging because the processor numbers help you understand scan chains if you use the JTAG debugging tools. The example shown in Listing 12-7 was run on a Type 5 Commercial Beta developer reference board with an ARTIK 520 mounted on it. Your output may be different but will contain similar information.

*Listing 12-7.*  Processor Info Virtual File Listing

```
cat /proc/cpuinfo


processor       : 0
model name      : ARMv7 Processor rev 3 (v7l)
BogoMIPS        : 68.57
Features        : swp half thumb fastmult vfp edsp neon vfpv3 tls vfpv4 idiva idivt
CPU implementer : 0x41
CPU architecture: 7
CPU variant     : 0x0
CPU part        : 0xc07
CPU revision    : 3

processor       : 1
model name      : ARMv7 Processor rev 3 (v7l)
BogoMIPS        : 68.57
Features        : swp half thumb fastmult vfp edsp neon vfpv3 tls vfpv4 idiva idivt
CPU implementer : 0x41
CPU architecture: 7
```

```
CPU variant    : 0x0
CPU part       : 0xc07
CPU revision   : 3

Hardware       : Exynos3
Revision       : 0000
Serial         : 0000000000000000
```

# Detecting Current Processor Speed

Use this command to detect the current processor speed for the primary CPU:

```
cat /sys/devices/system/cpu/cpu0/cpufreq/cpuinfo_cur_freq
```

This example refers to cpu0. The secondary CPU on an ARTIK 5 is identified as cpu1; it has a different set of properties. An ARTIK 10 would list even more CPUs. There is much more for you to learn regarding the internals of your ARTIK module, so go explore!

# Managing Processor Affinity

In a multiple CPU scenario, it is technically possible to ensure a process runs in a specific CPU. The advice in some online articles is that you are unlikely to be able to outsmart the scheduler, which decides where your applications and threads execute.

On the other hand, some developers must manage this carefully and the scheduler may not know enough about your intent to do the best job. The Linux operating system provides the taskset command that you can use from the bash shell to control which of the available CPU cores is used. With the taskset command, view the current CPU affinity of a running process or instruct a new process to run on the specified CPU. The example in Listing 12-8 shows how the ps command lists the processes running under the logged-in user. The taskset command then examines the bash shell to see its processor affinity by using the PID value.

*Listing 12-8.* Example taskset Command Inspection

```
ps

PID  TTY      TIME     CMD
1765 ttySAC2  00:00:01 bash
2225 ttySAC2  00:00:00 ps

taskset -p 1765

pid 1765's current affinity mask: 3
```

Processor affinity is defined as a bit mask with each bit representing a single CPU. Setting more bits allows the application process to run on more CPUs at the discretion of the scheduler. Setting a single bit forces processes to only run on the indicated CPU, thereby defeating the scheduler. The mask value 3 (binary 0011) shown in Listing 12-8 has two bits set because on the Commercial Beta ARTIK 520 module, there are two CPUs. The bash shell can run on either processor. Setting the mask value to 1 (binary 0001) or 2 (binary 0010) forces bash to run on only one of the processors. Listing 12-9 shows how to force bash onto one CPU and then reset the affinity back to normal with a bit mask value 3 (binary 0011).

***Listing 12-9.*** Altering the CPU Affinity of a Process

```
taskset -p 02 1765
pid 1765's current affinity mask: 3
pid 1765's new affinity mask: 2

taskset -p 03 1765
pid 1765's current affinity mask: 2
pid 1765's new affinity mask: 3
```

C language application programmers can use the sched_setaffinity() function to control process-based CPU affinities or the pthread_setaffinity_np() and pthread_attr_setaffinity_np() functions to manage thread-based CPU affinities. Set a process up so it is forced to run on a single dedicated CPU. Then it runs at its maximum execution speed. Calling the sched_setaffinity() function and migrating a process to a CPU it is not currently running on asks the scheduler to move it to the specified CPU when it next has the opportunity to intervene. Read these online reference materials for more details:

```
https://en.wikipedia.org/wiki/Processor_affinity
https://technolinchpin.wordpress.com/2015/11/06/linux-smp-cpu-affinity-settings/
http://linux.die.net/man/2/sched_setaffinity
http://linux.die.net/man/3/pthread_setaffinity_np
http://linux.die.net/man/3/pthread_attr_setaffinity_np
```

# Monitoring Internal Temperature

There is no documentation currently available that describes how to monitor the temperature inside the ARTIK module, so it is necessary to inspect the /sys virtual file system to discover a temperature monitoring value. Type this command to find the temperature sensor devices:

```
find /sys -name temp\*
```

A Commercial Beta ARTIK 5 lists only one temperature-sensing device:

```
/sys/devices/virtual/thermal/thermal_zone0/temp
```

Now cat this file to read the temperature:

```
cat /sys/devices/virtual/thermal/thermal_zone0/temp
```

My ARTIK module reported a value of 32000. In a room where the ambient temperature was about 25 degrees C, my ARTIK CPU felt only slightly warm to the touch. As a result, I think this must be a reading of 32 degrees Celsius. This suggests that the temperature is measured in degrees Celsius and scaled by 1000:1 so it is always an integer.

Construct a simple C language application to read the temperature of the CPU and scale the result, as shown in Listing 12-10. A cooling fan can be triggered via a GPIO pin to switch on when the temperature rises above a certain limit.

***Listing 12-10.*** C Language Temperature Measurement

```
#include <stdio.h>
#include <stdbool.h>
#include <stdlib.h>
```

```c
int main()
{
  FILE *myTempFd;
  char myResult[10];

  // Open the thermometer file
  if((myTempFd = fopen("/sys/devices/virtual/thermal/thermal_zone0/temp", "r")) == NULL)
  {
    printf("Error: cannot open thermometer for reading\n");
    return false;
  }

  // Read the temperature value
  fgets(myResult, 6, myTempFd);

  // Close the thermometer
  fclose(myTempFd);

  // Convert the value to an integer before returning it to your application:
  printf("Temperature is: %2.2f\n", atof(myResult)/1000.0);
}
```

# Summary

There are many more systems administration skills you should learn. The few examples here were inspired by exploring the /proc and /run virtual filesystems. The feedback that the kernel writes into these directories is very informative. You need to know what is there and where it lives. Building useful tools once you know these facts becomes very easy.

# CHAPTER 13

■ ■ ■

# AXT Module Connectors

Your ARTIK module has hundreds of input and output pins for connecting to the outside world. The Samsung engineers have chosen a very robust and compact connector format for this: the Panasonic AXT connectors are very high quality and very reliable. You need to know about their physical characteristics and where to buy them if you plan on making your own baseboards for the ARTIK to plug into. This chapter also summarizes all of the pin descriptions for these connectors and it covers the connections to the Commercial Beta ARTIK 5 and 10 modules.

## Physical Connections

The connections are all brought out of the ARTIK modules via several Panasonic AXT multi-pin connectors on the underside. This avoids soldering connections directly onto the ARTIK modules. Build receptacles for these connectors on your interface inside the product you want to empower with the ARTIK. Allow sufficient vertical space in your mechanical design to accommodate these connectors and the ARTIK when it is plugged into them. Look at the developer reference boards to see the connectors underneath your ARTIK module; the configuration of these connectors is different for each version of the ARTIK module. The placement of these connectors is very critical and you must ensure your manufacturing processes are accurate to avoid damaging your ARTIK module when you plug it in.

The latest data sheets for the model 520 and 1020 ARTIK modules provide current information about the physical dimensions of the modules and their connectivity. A summary is provided here for reference. Download the data sheets here after signing on with your Samsung developer account at `https://developer.artik.io/downloads`.

## Panasonic AXT Connectors

The ARTIK modules themselves have a lot of connections delivered via the Panasonic AXT connectors on the underside of the module. When you want to build a product and embed an ARTIK into your hardware, make sure you manufacture your boards with very precise positioning of these sockets and ensure that the correct signals are connected to the pins.

Because the Panasonic AXT connectors are not keyed, they can be inserted the wrong way when they are used on their own. This is unlikely with the ARTIK 5 and 10 module configurations because the connectors only mate properly when you have the ARTIK module oriented correctly. Include an outline of the ARTIK module on your circuit board artwork to indicate the correct orientation.

The Panasonic AXT connectors have been developed for high-density connections with surface mounted components. The developer board schematics and the data sheets have complete details of the pinouts for these connectors.

## Looking More Closely

Gaynor Bromley at Panasonic kindly gave me the 3D image of the AXT connector shown in Figure 13-1 to illustrate the two parts more clearly. The header is surface mounted to the underside of your ARTIK when it is manufactured. The receptacle is the part to incorporate into your product design. Soldering them onto a surface mount printed circuit board by hand is very challenging.

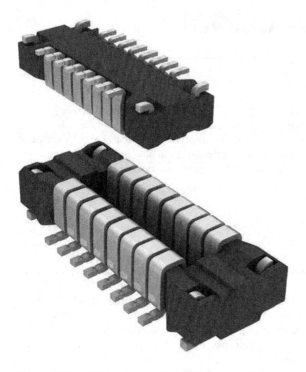

*Figure 13-1.* *AXT header and socket (Courtesy of Panasonic Electric Works)*

## AXT 40-Pin Connector

A pair of 40-pin AXT connectors (AXT340124/AXT440124) is used as a debug interface on the ARTIK 10 modules. They are mounted at right angles to the other two larger connectors. See Figure 13-2. The combination of these four connectors makes it very clear which way the ARTIK 10 should be plugged in. One of the connectors is optional and the data sheets suggest that ARTIK 10 modules may be supplied with only one of these connectors. Doing so will sacrifice the JTAG debugging connections, which you may want on a development system but which should be removed from production devices to prevent people reverse engineering your code.

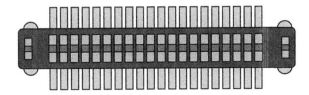

***Figure 13-2.*** *AXT 40-pin connector*

## AXT 60-Pin Connector

Three 60-pin connectors (AXT360124/AXT460124) are used on an ARTIK 5 for the main connections. Their layout makes it impossible to plug the ARTIK 5 into the developer reference board the wrong way. See Figure 13-3.

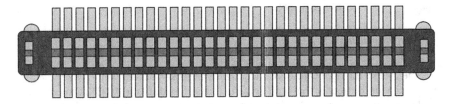

***Figure 13-3.*** *AXT 60-pin connector*

## AXT 80-Pin Connector

There is a pair of 80-pin AXT connectors (AXT380124/AXT480124) on the underside of the ARTIK 10 module. This ARTIK module also has two 40-pin debugging connectors arranged so the module cannot be plugged in the wrong way. See Figure 13-4.

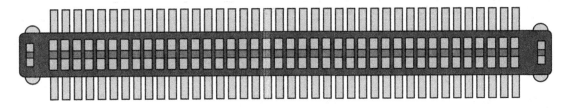

***Figure 13-4.*** *AXT 80-pin connector*

## Ordering AXT Connectors

Order the right kind of receptacles to plug your ARTIK into. Obtain these from Digi-Key, where you bought your ARTIK module. Make sure you purchase the right kind of connector. They each have a part number that is constructed from the connector specification. See Figure 13-5.

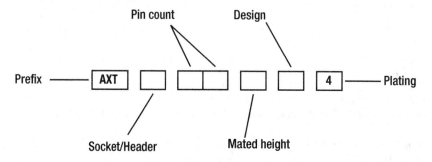

*Figure 13-5.* *AXT part number construction*

To construct a part number, select the right values for each digit. The socket/header value is 3 for the socket for your circuit board and 4 for the header that is soldered to the underside of the ARTIK. Choose 40, 60, or 80 for the pin count, depending on which ARTIK you are working with. The pin spacing is always on a pitch of 0.4mm. The next value indicates the mated height of the header and socket when plugged together. The socket part number can have the value 1 or 2. The value 1 indicates the lowest profile. The header can be 1, 2, or 3 but the values are different for the socket and the header. Make sure you use the correct one. See Table 13-1 for a summary of the mated heights available. The design value describes whether there is a pickup cover. This is always the value 2. The last digit is always 4 and indicates that the pins should be nickel plated for good connectivity.

*Table 13-1.* *Alternative Mated Height AXT Connector Choices*

| Height | Socket selector | Header selector | Notes |
|---|---|---|---|
| 1.5 mm | 1 | 1 | Recommended low profile |
| 2.0 mm | 1 | 2 | Not possible with ARTIK headers as supplied |
| 2.5 mm | 2 | 1 | High profile |
| 3.0 mm | 2 | 3 | Not possible with ARTIK headers as supplied |

The recommended mating height in the ARTIK data sheets is 1.5mm or 2.5mm. This is because a type 1 header is used when the ARTIK modules are manufactured. Choosing the low-profile option allows your design to fit into a thinner container. There may be important constraints on how thin your container can be and still allow sufficient airflow around the ARTIK to keep the operating temperature at an optimum level. This is difficult to predict because it is a function of how hard your application software is working the CPU. The more CPU effort, the hotter your ARTIK runs and the more airflow is needed to keep it cool. Your industrial engineers should run tests to ascertain the optimum height profile for these connectors.

Table 13-2 lists the part number for the sockets and headers for each ARTIK to save having to work out the part numbers. These are very good quality sockets and you may have other uses for them in your projects. The schematic diagrams are labeled with the AXT part numbers for high-profile sockets.

***Table 13-2.*** *Example AXT Part Numbers*

| Module | Pins | Height | Socket | Header |
|--------|------|--------|--------|--------|
| ARTIK 5 | 40 | Low profile | AXT340124 | AXT440124 |
| ARTIK 5 | 60 | Low profile | AXT360124 | AXT460124 |
| ARTIK 10 | 40 | Low profile | AXT340124 | AXT440124 |
| ARTIK 10 | 80 | Low profile | AXT380124 | AXT480124 |
| ARTIK 5 | 40 | High profile | AXT340224 | AXT440124 |
| ARTIK 5 | 60 | High profile | AXT360224 | AXT460124 |
| ARTIK 10 | 40 | High profile | AXT340224 | AXT440124 |
| ARTIK 10 | 80 | High profile | AXT380224 | AXT480124 |

Download the Panasonic P4S data sheet that describes the AXT connectors from www3.panasonic.biz/ac/e_download/control/connector/base-fpc/catalog/con_eng_p4s.pdf.

The link to the Digi-Key catalogue pages for purchasing the Panasonic AXT sockets and headers is www.digikey.com/product-search/en/connectors-interconnects/rectangular-board-to-board-connectors-arrays-edge-type-mezzanine/1442154?k=panasonic+axt.

# AXT Connections, Pins, and I/O

Most of the connections to the ARTIK modules are made via the Panasonic AXT multi-pin surface mounted connectors. These connectors are on the underside of the ARTIK. On top are some miniature co-axial sockets for wireless antenna connections.

The developer reference boards bring the signals from the AXT connections out to a variety of other different kinds of headers and sockets for video, audio, and GPIO (Arduino services). Knowing what sort of connector they are is not always easy if you are unfamiliar with the range of connectors in use. There are some clues on the developer board schematics, and a little forensic research yields the necessary information and connection details. Not all of the AXT connector pins on the ARTIK are available on the hardware I/O header connectors.

Some helpful Illustrator files of some of the connectors, pinouts, and general arrangements of the ARTIK modules are provided in the source kit for this book. They may help you when you are designing your own circuit boards.

On top of the ARTIK modules, the wireless antenna connections use miniature co-axial connections and jumper cables to the antenna mount points that use SMA connectors. Provide a connection from these miniature co-axial connectors if you want to use wireless antennas in your own hardware product designs. They are described in more detail in Chapter 15.

In the AXT pinout tables, some pins have notes that indicate the pin has an alias and is known as something else. This reflects the different GPIO functions that pins can be set into. GPIO supports eight different multiplexed function states and pins can be configured to be in any one of these states, which causes them to operate in a completely different way. Do not arbitrarily alter these states unless you are working with pins that will be used for public access. Altering the function state of a GPIO from I2C to Input could stop the audio codec chip or Ethernet controller chip from working because they have GPIO pins reserved for managing their behavior. Refer to the data sheets for tables that show these different GPIO functions and how they are mapped to the AXT pins.

---

■ **Note**    There is a subtle warning note in the data sheet suggesting that activating wireless communications in your ARTIK without having the antennas installed first may damage your ARTIK.

---

# ARTIK 5 - Connectors

The ARTIK 5 has three 60-pin Panasonic AXT connectors on the underside of the module, which is illustrated in Figure 13-6. Your design needs to have three matching AXT sockets that these connectors can plug into. Take special care to connect the right circuits to each pin. All three connectors have 60 pins but they are oriented so it impossible to plug the ARTIK module into the sockets the wrong way. Make sure you provide sufficient clearance for the module to sit securely inside your product. Add retaining clips for environments that are subject to vibration but be careful that they do not damage the ARTIK or create short circuits on the ARTIK module. Visit the developer downloads page to obtain the data sheets, which contain mechanical drawings that show the layout of these connectors when you incorporate them into your product.

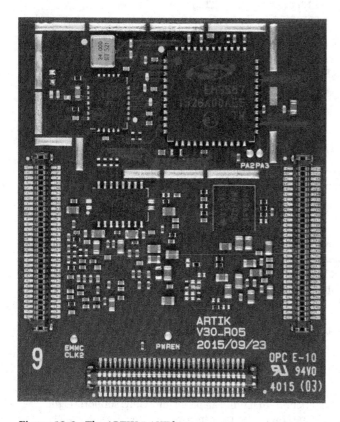

*Figure 13-6.* *The ARTIK 5 AXT base connectors*

# Connector Locations

The sources of information on pinouts for the AXT connectors on an ARTIK 5 are the data sheet, the product briefing, and the schematic diagrams for the Type 5 developer reference board. The illustrations in the data sheet show which end of the connectors is the reference or key location that determines where pin 1 is. Figure 13-7 shows the position of the connectors on an ARTIK 5 with the reference pin indicated by a small triangle as viewed from the top of the ARTIK module. The J numbers that denote each connector are printed on the developer reference board.

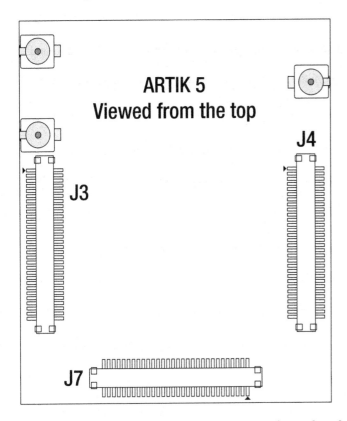

*Figure 13-7. AXT connectors on Type 5 developer reference boards*

The tables in the product data sheet describe the pinouts for these connectors in more detail. Consult the second page of the Type 5 developer board schematic diagram for additional connection details. This page is labeled **Module Interface** and shows the three AXT connector pin assignments. Those pinout diagrams are shown here. Always check your reference information against the latest version of the schematics, data sheets, and the information provided by Samsung.

The ARTIK model 520 data sheet renumbers one of these connector labels and uses a value that is inconsistent with all the other published sources of information. The developer reference board schematics are consistent with the screen-printed labels on the Commercial Beta Type 5 board but the data sheet is not. This book is consistent with the circuit schematics and board artwork as observed on a Commercial Beta Type 5 board shipped from Digi-Key. The ARTIK 520 data sheet uses a different connector numbering scheme from an uncertain source. Table 13-3 shows how these connector labels are mapped from the two conflicting sources.

***Table 13-3.*** *ARTIK 5 AXT Connector Labeling Conflicts*

| Consistent | Data sheet | Description |
|---|---|---|
| J3 | J3 | Main connector A |
| J4 | J4 | Main connector B |
| J7 | J5 | Debug connector |

# Connector J3

Connector J3 is one of the two main connectors for delivering signals in and out of the ARTIK 5 module and onwards to the hosting environment. Most of its signals are related to GPIO controls. The Arduino pins are driven from here. Figure 13-8 shows the signals on the J3 pins and has been replicated from the developer reference board schematic diagrams.

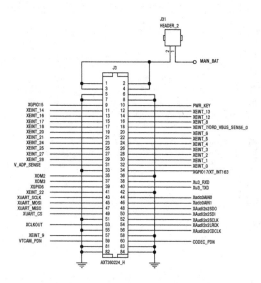

***Figure 13-8.*** *ARTIK 5 - J3 pinout assignments*

The AXT connector J3 pinouts are listed and described in Table 13-4. Although this is a 60-pin connector, there is a stabilizing solder tag on each corner, which is also accessible as a connector pin. To number these consistently when the 80-pin connectors are described, the four extra pins are numbered 81-84 so they do not interfere with the other pin numbers. These pinout values are taken from the board schematic and cross-checked against the data sheets. The Arduino connections are buffered via a voltage translation chip but are otherwise directly connected.

*Table 13-4.* *AXT Connector J3 Pinouts*

| Pin | Name | Notes |
|-----|------|-------|
| J3-1 | MAIN_BAT | Main battery supply; switched via Jumper J31 HEADER_2 |
| J3-2 | MAIN_BAT | Main battery supply; switched via Jumper J31 HEADER_2 |
| J3-3 | MAIN_BAT | Main battery supply; switched via Jumper J31 HEADER_2 |
| J3-4 | MAIN_BAT | Main battery supply; switched via Jumper J31 HEADER_2 |
| J3-5 | GND | Ground |
| J3-6 | GND | Ground |
| J3-7 | GND | Ground |
| J3-8 | GND | Ground |
| J3-9 | XGPIO15 | External GPIO1 operation of the Ethernet controller chip |
| J3-10 | PWR_KEY | PMIC power on key. This pin is connected to the power (boot) button, which triggers a reboot of the ARTIK if it is in the pre-boot state. Assert an active **HIGH** value on this pin to boot the ARTIK. |
| J3-11 | XEINT_14 | GPIO or Arduino pin 13 on connector J27-5 |
| J3-12 | XEINT_13 | GPIO or Arduino pin 12 on connector J27-6 |
| J3-13 | XEINT_16 | Ethernet chip IRQ to CPU |
| J3-14 | XEINT_12 | SigFox low-power wireless transmitter reset |
| J3-15 | XEINT_17 | Charge status interrupt (CHG_IRQ) |
| J3-16 | XEINT_8 | GPIO or Arduino pin 11 on connector J27-7 |
| J3-17 | XEINT_18 | SPI-TO-UART IC for SPI bus emulation RESET |
| J3-18 | XEINT_7 | USB device select (a.k.a. DRD_VBUS_SENSE_0) |
| J3-19 | XEINT_20 | SPI-TO-UART IC for SPI bus emulation IRQ |
| J3-20 | XEINT_6 | GPIO or Arduino pin 10 on connector J27-8. This pin is 3.3v tolerant in input mode. |
| J3-21 | XEINT_21 | LCD backlight enable |
| J3-22 | XEINT_5 | GPIO or Arduino pin 9 on connector J27-9. This pin is 3.3v tolerant in input mode. |
| J3-23 | XEINT_24 | Turns device on |
| J3-24 | XEINT_4 | GPIO or Arduino pin 8 on connector J27-10. This pin is 3.3v tolerant in input mode. |
| J3-25 | XEINT_25 | Fuel gauge interrupt |
| J3-26 | XEINT_3 | GPIO or Arduino pin 7 on connector J26-1. This pin is 3.3v tolerant in input mode. |
| J3-27 | XEINT_27 | Stereo jack insert detection (a.k.a. JACK_DET) |
| J3-28 | XEINT_2 | GPIO or Arduino pin 4 on connector J26-4 and J512-4. This pin is 3.3v tolerant in input mode. |
| J3-29 | XEINT_28 | Ethernet controller chip select (CS) line |

*(continued)*

*Table 13-4.* (*continued*)

| Pin | Name | Notes |
|-----|------|-------|
| J3-30 | XEINT_1 | GPIO or Arduino pin 3 on connector J26-5 and J512-3. This pin is 3.3v tolerant in input mode. |
| J3-31 | V_ADP_SENSE | AC power detect |
| J3-32 | XEINT_0 | GPIO or Arduino pin 2 on connector J26-6 and J512-2. This pin is 3.3v tolerant in input mode. |
| J3-33 | GND | Ground |
| J3-34 | XGPIO17 | Power management external IC interrupt (a.k.a. XT_INT163) |
| J3-35 | XOM2 | Boot from SD when this pin is **HIGH** |
| J3-36 | GND | Ground |
| J3-37 | XOM3 | Boot from eMMC when this pin is **HIGH** |
| J3-38 | Xu3_RXD | GPIO or Arduino pin RX<-0 on connector J26-8 and J511-11. Also known as GPIO port GPA1. UART 3 received data input. |
| J3-39 | XGPIO6 | **SD3503** Z-Wave serial interface chip reset |
| J3-40 | Xu3_TXD | GPIO or Arduino pin TX->1 on connector J26-7 and J511-10. Also known as GPIO port GPA1. UART 3 transmitted data output. |
| J3-41 | XEINT_22 | 27MHz oscillator enable |
| J3-42 | GND | Ground |
| J3-43 | XUART_SCLK | SPI-TO-UART IC for SPI bus emulation of serial clock |
| J3-44 | Xadc0AIN0 | Analog ADC input A0 on connector J24-1 and J510-2 |
| J3-45 | XUART_MOSI | SPI-TO-UART IC for SPI bus emulation of master out, slave in |
| J3-46 | Xadc0AIN1 | Analog ADC input A1 on connector J24-2 and J510-3 |
| J3-47 | XUART_MISO | SPI-TO-UART IC for SPI bus emulation of master in, slave out |
| J3-48 | XAudi2s2SDO | Bus I2S-2 audio serial data output on connector J511-6 |
| J3-49 | XUART_CS | SPI-TO-UART IC for SPI bus emulation of chip select |
| J3-50 | XAudi2S2SDI | Bus I2S-2 audio serial data input on connector J511-3 |
| J3-51 | GND | Ground |
| J3-52 | XAudi2S2SCLK | Bus I2S-2 audio serial clock on connector J511-1 |
| J3-53 | XCLKOUT | I2S audio clock |
| J3-54 | XAudi2S2LRCK | Bus I2S-2 audio left right sample clock on connector J511-2 |
| J3-55 | GND | Ground |
| J3-56 | XAudi2S2CDCLK | Bus I2S-2 audio CD clock on connector J511-7 |
| J3-57 | XEINT_9 | GPIO configuration of Ethernet controller chip |
| J3-58 | GND | Ground |
| J3-59 | VTCAM_PDN | Video camera power down |
| J3-60 | CODEC_PDN | AK4953EQ audio codec IC power down |

(*continued*)

***Table 13-4.*** *(continued)*

| Pin | Name | Notes |
|-----|------|-------|
| J3-81 | GND | Ground |
| J3-82 | GND | Ground |
| J3-83 | GND | Ground |
| J3-84 | GND | Ground |

# Connector J4

Connector J4 is one of the two main connectors for delivering signals in and out of the ARTIK 5 module and onwards to the hosting environment. The camera interface is driven by this connector. Micro SD cards are also controlled from here. Figure 13-9 shows the signals on the J4 pins connected to the base of the ARTIK 5 module.

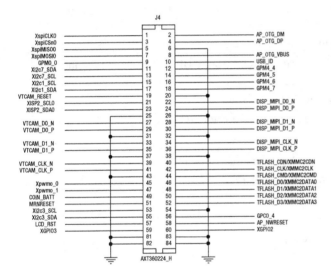

***Figure 13-9.*** *ARTIK 5 - J4 pinout assignments*

The AXT connector J4 pinouts are listed in Table 13-5. These values are also taken from the board schematic and cross-checked against the data sheets. Always check an authoritative and up-to-date source when you are developing hardware board designs.

*Table 13-5. AXT Connector J4 Pinouts*

| Pin | Name | Notes |
|-----|------|-------|
| J4-1 | XspiCLK0 | Bus SPI-0 clock |
| J4-2 | AP_OTG_DM | USB 2.0 interface DM line (a.k.a. AP_USB_DM) |
| J4-3 | XspiCSn0 | Bus SPI-0 chip select |
| J4-4 | AP_OTG_DP | USB 2.0 interface DP line (a.k.a AP_USB_DP) |
| J4-5 | XspiMISO0 | Bus SPI-0 master in, slave out |
| J4-6 | GND | Ground |
| J4-7 | XspiMOSI0 | Bus SPI-0 master out, slave in |
| J4-8 | AP_OTG_VBUS | USB 2.0 interface VBUS line (a.k.a AP_USB_VBUS) |
| J4-9 | GPM0_0 | LCD data clock (a.k.a. PSR_TE) |
| J4-10 | USB_ID | USB 2.0 interface ID line |
| J4-11 | Xi2c7_SDA | Bus I2C-7 Arduino serial data line (SDA). GPD0 connected to connector J27-2. |
| J4-12 | GPM4_4 | SigFox **ATA8520** SPI bus emulation |
| J4-13 | Xi2c7_SCL | Bus I2C-7 Arduino serial clock line (SCL). GPD0 connected to connector J27-1. |
| J4-14 | GPM4_5 | SigFox **ATA8520** SPI bus emulation |
| J4-15 | Xi2c1_SCL | Bus I2C-1 serial clock line on connector J511-5 |
| J4-16 | GPM4_6 | SigFox **ATA8520** SPI bus emulation |
| J4-17 | Xi2c1_SDA | Bus I2C-1 serial data line on connector J511-4 |
| J4-18 | GPM4_7 | SigFox **ATA8520** SPI bus emulation |
| J4-19 | VTCAM_RESET | Video camera reset |
| J4-20 | GND | Ground |
| J4-21 | XISP2_SCL0 | Bus I2C-2 serial clock line |
| J4-22 | DISP_MIPI_D0_N | MIPI display DO_N line |
| J4-23 | XISP2_SDA0 | Bus I2C-2 serial data line |
| J4-24 | DISP_MIPI_D0_P | MIPI display DO_P line |
| J4-25 | GND | Ground |
| J4-26 | GND | Ground |
| J4-27 | VTCAM_D0_N | MIPI video camera DO_N line |
| J4-28 | DISP_MIPI_D1_N | MIPI display D1_P line |
| J4-29 | VTCAM_D0_P | MIPI video camera D0_P line |
| J4-30 | DISP_MIPI_D1_P | MIPI display D1_P line |
| J4-31 | GND | Ground |
| J4-32 | GND | Ground |
| J4-33 | VTCAM_D1_N | MIPI video camera D1_N line |

*(continued)*

*Table 13-5.* (*continued*)

| Pin | Name | Notes |
|-----|------|-------|
| J4-34 | DISP_MIPI_CLK_N | MIPI display clock N line |
| J4-35 | VTCAM_D1_P | MIPI video camera D1_P line |
| J4-36 | DISP_MIPI_CLK_P | MIPI display clock P line |
| J4-37 | GND | Ground |
| J4-38 | GND | Ground |
| J4-39 | VTCAM_CLK_N | MIPI video camera clock N line |
| J4-40 | XMMC2CDN | SD card CDN line (a.k.a TFLASH_CDN) |
| J4-41 | VTCAM_CLK_P | MIPI video camera clock P line |
| J4-42 | XMMC2CLK | SD card data clock (a.k.a TFLASH_CLK) |
| J4-43 | GND | Ground |
| J4-44 | XMMC2CMD | SD card CMD line (a.k.a TFLASH_CMD) |
| J4-45 | Xpwmo_0 | Pulse width modulated output channel 0. Arduino pin ~5 on header pin J26-3 and J513-4. |
| J4-46 | XMMC2DATA0 | SD card data bit 0 (a.k.a TFLASH_D0) |
| J4-47 | Xpwmo_1 | Pulse width modulated output channel 1. Arduino pin ~6 on header pin J26-2 and J513-3. |
| J4-48 | XMMC2DATA1 | SD card data bit 1 (a.k.a. TFLASH_D1) |
| J4-49 | COIN_BATT | Auxiliary backup coin battery 3-volt input |
| J4-50 | XMMC2DATA2 | SD card data bit 2 (a.k.a TFLASH_D2) |
| J4-51 | AP_NRESET | Cold ARTIK 520 module reset by PMIC. RST signal on connector J25-3 and J510-7 (a.k.a. RST/MRNRESET). |
| J4-52 | XMMC2DATA3 | SD card data bit 3 (a.k.a TFLASH_D3) |
| J4-53 | Xi2c3_SCL | Bus I2C-3 serial clock line on connector J510-6 |
| J4-54 | GND | Ground |
| J4-55 | Xi2c3_SDA | Bus I2C-3 serial data line on connector J510-5 |
| J4-56 | GPC0_4 | LCD display identification |
| J4-57 | LCD_RST | LCD display reset |
| J4-58 | AP_NWRESET | Warm reset from PMIC (for development purposes) |
| J4-59 | XGPIO3 | GPIO configuration of Ethernet controller chip |
| J4-60 | XGPIO2 | GPIO reset of Ethernet controller chip |
| J4-81 | GND | Ground |
| J4-82 | GND | Ground |
| J4-83 | GND | Ground |
| J4-84 | GND | Ground |

# Connector J7

Connector J7 is mainly concerned with driving the Ethernet controller chip. The data lines and GPIO control signals come from here for the networking chip. The JTAG debugging interface is also driven from here, although some of the JTAG signals appear to have a prefix suggesting they are part of the ZigBee support. Future documentation releases may clarify whether these are dual mode pins or not. Figure 13-10 shows the signals on the J7 pins on the base of the ARTIK 5 module.

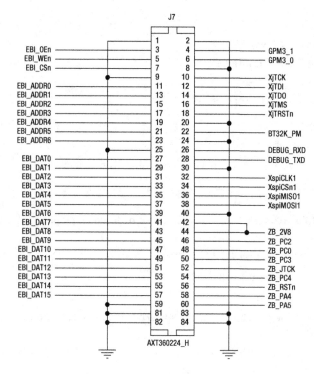

***Figure 13-10.*** *ARTIK 5 - J7 pinout assignments*

The AXT connector J7 pinouts are listed in Table 13-6. These values are taken from the board schematic and cross-checked against the data sheets. Be sure to check an authoritative and up-to-date source for the latest values and check that they correspond to the same revision of the ARTIK module you are deploying.

*Table 13-6.* *AXT Connector J7 Pinouts*

| Pin | Name | Notes |
|-----|------|-------|
| J7-1 | GND | Ground |
| J7-2 | GND | Ground |
| J7-3 | EBI_OEn | Ethernet chip RDN line |
| J7-4 | GPM3_1 | Test point on connector J512-6 |
| J7-5 | EBI_Wen | Ethernet chip WRN line |
| J7-6 | GPM3_0 | Test point on connector J512-5 |
| J7-7 | EBI_CSn | Ethernet chip select line |
| J7-8 | GND | Ground |
| J7-9 | GND | Ground |
| J7-10 | XjTCK | JTAG debug clock |
| J7-11 | EBI_ADDR0 | Ethernet controller address bus bit 0 |
| J7-12 | XjTDI | JTAG debug TDI line |
| J7-13 | EBI_ADDR1 | Ethernet controller address bus bit 1 |
| J7-14 | XjTDO | JTAG debug TDO line |
| J7-15 | EBI_ADDR2 | Ethernet controller address bus bit 2 |
| J7-16 | XjTMS | JTAG debug TMS line |
| J7-17 | EBI_ADDR3 | Ethernet controller address bus bit 3 |
| J7-18 | XjTRSTn | JTAG debug reset line |
| J7-19 | EBI_ADDR4 | Ethernet controller address bus bit 4 |
| J7-20 | GND | Ground |
| J7-21 | EBI_ADDR5 | Ethernet controller address bus bit 5 |
| J7-22 | BT32K_PM | 32 kHz clock for Bluetooth controller on connector J513-1 |
| J7-23 | EBI_ADDR6 | Ethernet controller address bus bit 6 (Not used) |
| J7-24 | GND | Ground |
| J7-25 | GND | Ground |
| J7-26 | DEBUG_RXD | AP debug UART received data (RxD) |
| J7-27 | EBI_DAT0 | Ethernet controller data bus bit 0 |
| J7-28 | DEBUG_TXD | AP debug UART transmitted data (TxD) |
| J7-29 | EBI_DAT1 | Ethernet controller data bus bit 1 |
| J7-30 | GND | Ground |
| J7-31 | EBI_DAT2 | Ethernet controller data bus bit 2 |
| J7-32 | XspiCLK1 | Bus SPI-1 test point for clock line on connector J511-14 |
| J7-33 | EBI_DAT3 | Ethernet controller data bus bit 3 |
| J7-34 | XspiCSn1 | Bus SPI-1 test point for control select line on connector J511-15 |

(*continued*)

*Table 13-6.* (*continued*)

| Pin | Name | Notes |
|-----|------|-------|
| J7-35 | EBI_DAT4 | Ethernet controller data bus bit 4 |
| J7-36 | XspiMISO1 | Bus SPI-1 test point for master in, slave output on connector J511-12 |
| J7-37 | EBI_DAT5 | Ethernet controller data bus bit 5 |
| J7-38 | XspiMOSI1 | Bus SPI-1 test point for master out, slave input on connector J511-13 |
| J7-39 | EBI_DAT6 | Ethernet controller data bus bit 6 |
| J7-40 | GND | Ground |
| J7-41 | EBI_DAT7 | Ethernet controller data bus bit 7 |
| J7-42 | ZB_2V8 | ZigBee 2.8v/300mA ref. Shorted to pin J7-44 (a.k.a VLDO18). |
| J7-43 | EBI_DAT8 | Ethernet controller data bus bit 8 |
| J7-44 | ZB_2V8 | ZigBee 2.8v/300mA ref. Shorted to pin J7-42 (a.k.a VLDO18). |
| J7-45 | EBI_DAT9 | Ethernet controller data bus bit 9 |
| J7-46 | ZB_PC2 | JTAG debug data out |
| J7-47 | EBI_DAT10 | Ethernet controller data bus bit 10 |
| J7-48 | ZB_PC0 | JTAG debug reset |
| J7-49 | EBI_DAT11 | Ethernet controller data bus bit 11 |
| J7-50 | ZB_PC3 | JTAG debug data in |
| J7-51 | EBI_DAT12 | Ethernet controller data bus bit 12 |
| J7-52 | ZB_JTCK | JTAG debug clock line |
| J7-53 | EBI_DAT13 | Ethernet controller data bus bit 13 |
| J7-54 | ZB_PC4 | JTAG debug mode select |
| J7-55 | EBI_DAT14 | Ethernet controller data bus bit 14 |
| J7-56 | ZB_RSTn | JTAG debug reset line |
| J7-57 | EBI_DAT15 | Ethernet controller data bus bit 15 |
| J7-58 | ZB_PA4 | JTAG debug GPIO control |
| J7-59 | GND | Ground |
| J7-60 | ZB_PA5 | JTAG debug GPIO control |
| J7-81 | GND | Ground |
| J7-82 | GND | Ground |
| J7-83 | GND | Ground |
| J7-84 | GND | Ground |

■ **Note**    The ARTIK 520 data sheet incorrectly describes this as connector J5. This is inconsistent with the developer reference board schematic diagrams and the labels printed on the Commercial Beta Type 5 board.

# ARTIK 10 - Connectors

The ARTIK 10 has four Panasonic AXT connectors on the underside of the module that is illustrated in Figure 13-11. Your design needs to have matching AXT sockets that these connectors can plug into. Take special care to connect the right circuits to each pin. Two of the connectors have 80 pins and the smaller ones have 40 pins. They are oriented so it impossible to plug the ARTIK module into the sockets the wrong way. Make sure you provide sufficient clearance for the module to sit securely inside your product. Add retaining clips for environments that are subject to vibration but be careful they do not damage the ARTIK or create short circuits on the ARTIK module. Visit the developer downloads page to obtain the data sheets, which contain mechanical drawings that show the layout of these connectors when you incorporate them into your product.

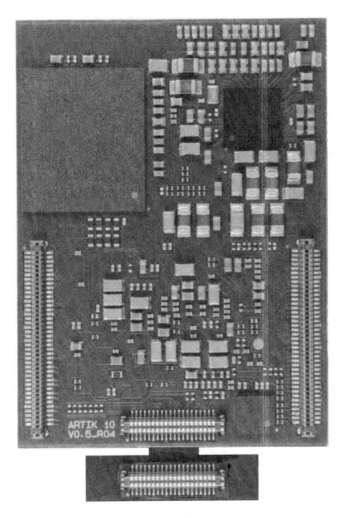

**Figure 13-11.** *The ARTIK 10 AXT base connectors*

## Connector Locations

The ARTIK 10 data sheet is the most authoritative document on connector pinouts. Refer also to the schematic diagrams for the Type 10 developer reference board. Some additional information can also be deduced from the product illustrations that Samsung released as part of the developer documentation. Figure 13-12 shows the position of the connectors on an ARTIK 10 with the reference pin indicated by a small triangle as viewed from the top of the ARTIK module. The J numbers that denote each connector are printed on developer reference board.

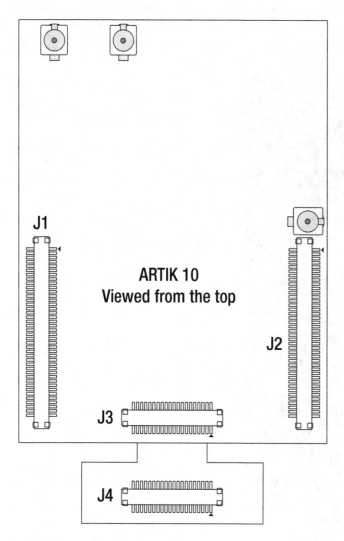

**Figure 13-12.** *AXT connectors on the Type 10 developer reference boards*

The tables in the product data sheet describe the pinouts for these connectors in more detail. Consult the second page of the Type 10 developer board schematic diagram for connection details. This page is labeled **Module Interface** and shows the three AXT connector pin assignments. Those pinout diagrams are shown here. Always check your reference information against the latest version of the schematics, data sheets, and the information provided by Samsung.

The ARTIK model 1020 data sheet renumbers these connector labels and uses values that are inconsistent with all of the other published sources of information. The developer reference board schematics are consistent with the silkscreen-printed labels on the Commercial Beta Type 10 board but the data sheet is not. This book is consistent with the circuit schematics and board artwork as observed on a Commercial Beta Type 10 board shipped from Digi-Key. The ARTIK 1020 data sheet uses a different connector numbering scheme from an uncertain source. Table 13-7 shows how these connector labels are mapped from the two conflicting sources.

*Table 13-7.* *ARTIK 10 AXT Connector Labeling Conflicts*

| Consistent | Data sheet | Description |
| --- | --- | --- |
| J1 | J3 | Main connector A |
| J2 | J4 | Main connector B |
| J3 | J1 | Debug connector |
| J4 | J9 | Optional auxiliary debug connector |

# Connector J1

Connector J1 is one of the two main connectors for delivering signals in and out of the ARTIK 10 module and onwards to the hosting environment. This connector carries a lot of GPIO and other peripheral interface signals. Figure 13-13 shows the signals on the J1 pins on the ARTIK 10 module.

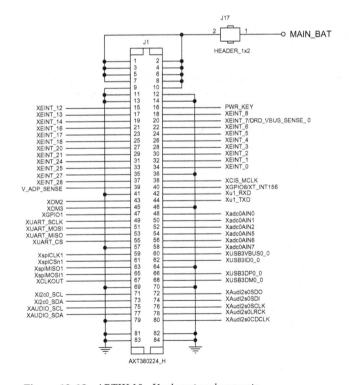

*Figure 13-13.* *ARTIK 10 - J1 pinout assignments*

The AXT connector J1 pinouts are listed in Table 13-8. Although this is an 80-pin connector, on each corner there is a solder tag, which is also accessible as a connector pin. The four extra pins are numbered 81-84 so they do not interfere with the other pin numbers. The sense indicates whether the pin is an input or an output. These values are taken from the board schematic and cross-checked against the data sheets.

***Table 13-8.*** *AXT Connector J1 Pinouts*

| Pin | Name | Notes |
|---|---|---|
| J1-1 | MAIN_BAT | Main battery supply; switched via jumper J17 HEADER_1x2 |
| J1-2 | MAIN_BAT | Main battery supply; switched via jumper J17 HEADER_1x2 |
| J1-3 | MAIN_BAT | Main battery supply; switched via jumper J17 HEADER_1x2 |
| J1-4 | MAIN_BAT | Main battery supply; witched via jumper J17 HEADER_1x2 |
| J1-5 | MAIN_BAT | Main battery supply; switched via jumper J17 HEADER_1x2 |
| J1-6 | MAIN_BAT | Main battery supply; switched via jumper J17 HEADER_1x2 |
| J1-7 | MAIN_BAT | Main battery supply; switched via jumper J17 HEADER_1x2 |
| J1-8 | MAIN_BAT | Main battery supply; witched via jumper J17 HEADER_1x2 |
| J1-9 | GND | Ground |
| J1-10 | MAIN_BAT | Main battery supply; switched via jumper J17 HEADER_1x2 |
| J1-11 | GND | Ground |
| J1-12 | GND | Ground |
| J1-13 | GND | Ground |
| J1-14 | GND | Ground |
| J1-15 | XEINT_12 | MIPI LCD error detect |
| J1-16 | PWR_KEY | PMIC power on key. This pin is connected to the power (boot) button, which triggers a reboot of the ARTIK if it is in the pre-boot state. Assert an active **HIGH** value on this pin to boot the ARTIK. |
| J1-17 | XEINT_13 | GPIO or Arduino pin 12 on connector J27-6 |
| J1-18 | XEINT_8 | GPIO or Arduino pin 11 on connector J27-7 |
| J1-19 | XEINT_14 | GPIO or Arduino pin 13 on connector J27-5 |
| J1-20 | XEINT_7 | USB 3.0 VBUS line (a.k.a. DRD_VBUS_SENSE_0 and EXT_INT40)) |
| J1-21 | XEINT_16 | GPIO interface on connector J512-5 |
| J1-22 | XEINT_6 | GPIO or Arduino pin 10 on connector J27-8 |
| J1-23 | XEINT_17 | Charge status interrupt (CHG_IRQ) |
| J1-24 | XEINT_5 | GPIO or Arduino pin 9 on connector J27-9 |
| J1-25 | XEINT_18 | UART reset (a.k.a. XUART_RST) |
| J1-26 | XEINT_4 | GPIO or Arduino pin 8 on connector J27-10 |
| J1-27 | XEINT_20 | UART IRQ (a.k.a. XUART_IRQ) |
| J1-28 | XEINT_3 | GPIO or Arduino pin 7 on connector J26-1 |
| J1-29 | XEINT_21 | LCD display TP reset (a.k.a. TP_RST) |

(*continued*)

*Table 13-8.* (*continued*)

| Pin | Name | Notes |
| --- | --- | --- |
| J1-30 | XEINT_2 | GPIO or Arduino pin 4 on connector J26-4 and J512-4 |
| J1-31 | XEINT_24 | LCD display TP interrupt (a.k.a. TP_INT) |
| J1-32 | XEINT_1 | GPIO or Arduino pin 3 on connector J26-5 and J512-3 |
| J1-33 | XEINT_25 | Fuel gauge interrupt (a.k.a. EXT_INT43, FG_INT, and UHOST_ID) |
| J1-34 | XEINT_0 | GPIO or Arduino pin 2 on connector J26-6 and J512-2 |
| J1-35 | XEINT_27 | Stereo jack insert detection (a.k.a. JACK_DET) |
| J1-36 | GND | Ground |
| J1-37 | XEINT_28 | Wi-Fi/Bluetooth LVDS reset (a.k.a LVDS_RST) |
| J1-38 | XCIS_MCLK | Rear camera (3L2) MCLK |
| J1-39 | V_ADP_SENSE | AC power detect |
| J1-40 | XGPIO6 | Front camera (6B2) MCLK (a.k.a. XT_INT156) |
| J1-41 | GND | Ground |
| J1-42 | Xu1_RXD | GPIO or Arduino pin RX<-0 on connector J26-8 and J511-11. Also known as GPIO port GPA0. UART 1 received data input. |
| J1-43 | XOM2 | Boot from SD when this pin is **HIGH** |
| J1-44 | Xu1_TXD | GPIO or Arduino pin TX->1 on connector J26-7 and J511-10. Also known as GPIO port GPA0. UART 1 transmitted data output. |
| J1-45 | XOM3 | Boot from eMMC when this pin is **HIGH** |
| J1-46 | GND | Ground |
| J1-47 | XGPIO1 | Front camera (6B2) power down (a.k.a. FRONT CAM_PD) |
| J1-48 | Xadc0AIN0 | Analog input A0 on connector J24-1 and J510-2 |
| J1-49 | XUART_SCLK | General purpose UART, serial clock |
| J1-50 | Xadc0AIN1 | Analog input A1 on connector J24-2 and J510-3 |
| J1-51 | XUART_MOSI | General purpose UART, master out, slave in |
| J1-52 | Xadc0AIN2 | Analog input A2 on connector J24-3 |
| J1-53 | XUART_MISO | General purpose UART, master in, slave out |
| J1-54 | Xadc0AIN5 | Analog input A3 on connector J24-4 |
| J1-55 | XUART_CS | General purpose UART, control select |
| J1-56 | Xadc0AIN6 | Analog input A4 on connector J24-5 |
| J1-57 | GND | Ground |
| J1-58 | Xadc0AIN7 | Analog input A5 on connector J24-6 |
| J1-59 | XspiCLK1 | Bus SPI 1 clock line used for LPWR/Wi-Fi/Bluetooth/SigFox on connector J511-14 |
| J1-60 | XUSB3VBUS0_0 | USB 3.0 DRD channel 0 |
| J1-61 | XspiCSn1 | Bus SPI-1 control select line used for LPWR/Wi-Fi/Bluetooth/SigFox on connector J511-15 |

(*continued*)

*Table 13-8.* (*continued*)

| Pin | Name | Notes |
| --- | --- | --- |
| J1-62 | XUSB3ID0_0 | USB 3.0 Identification for DRD channel 0 |
| J1-63 | XspiMISO1 | Bus SPI-1 master in, slave out used for LPWR/Wi-Fi/Bluetooth/SigFox on connector J511-12 |
| J3-64 | GND | Ground |
| J1-65 | XspiMOSI1 | Bus SPI-1 master out, slave in used for LPWR/Wi-Fi/Bluetooth/SigFox on connector J511-13 |
| J1-66 | XUSB3DP0_0 | USB2.0 backward-compatible P channel in USB3.0 |
| J1-67 | XCLKOUT | 24MHz Audio CDCLK output |
| J1-68 | XUSB3DM0_0 | USB2.0 backward-compatible M channel in USB3.0 |
| J1-69 | GND | Ground |
| J1-70 | GND | Ground |
| J1-71 | Xi2c0_SCL | Bus I2C-0 used by FUEL subsystem (PMIC) |
| J1-72 | Audi2s0SDO | Bus I2S-0 audio serial data output on connector J511-6 |
| J1-73 | Xi2c0_SDA | Bus I2C-0 used by FUEL subsystem (PMIC) |
| J1-74 | Audi2s0SDI | Bus I2S-0 audio serial data input on connector J511-3 |
| J1-75 | Xi2c1_SCL | Bus I2C-1 serial clock line used by audio subsystem (a.k.a. XAUDIO_SCL) on connector J511-5 |
| J1-76 | Audi2s0SCLK | Bus I2S-0 audio serial data clock line on connector J511-1 |
| J1-77 | Xi2C1_SDA | Bus I2C-1 serial data line used by audio subsystem (a.k.a. AUDIO_SDA) on connector J511-4 |
| J1-78 | Audi2s0LRCLK | Bus I2S-0 audio left/right clock line on connector J511-2 |
| J1-79 | GND | Ground |
| J1-80 | Audi2s0CDCLK | Bus I2S-0 audio CD clock line on connector J511-7 |
| J1-81 | GND | Ground |
| J1-82 | GND | Ground |
| J1-83 | GND | Ground |
| J1-84 | GND | Ground |

■ **Note**  The ARTIK 1020 data sheet incorrectly describes this as connector J3, which is inconsistent with the developer reference board schematic diagrams and the labels printed on the Commercial Beta Type 10 board.

## Connector J2

Connector J2 is one of the two main connectors for delivering signals in and out of the ARTIK 10 module and onwards to the hosting environment. This connector carries a lot of A/V signals. Figure 13-14 shows the signals on the J2 pins.

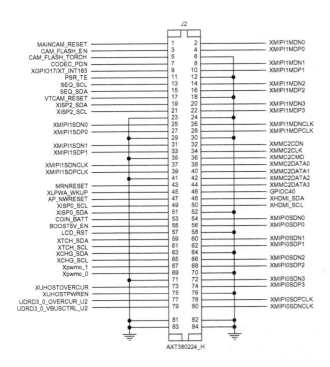

**Figure 13-14.** *ARTIK 10 - J2 pinout assignments*

The AXT connector J2 pinouts are listed in Table 13-9. These values are also taken from the board schematic and cross-checked against the data sheets. Always check an authoritative and up-to-date source when you are developing hardware board designs.

**Table 13-9.** *AXT Connector J2 Pinouts*

| Pin | Name | Notes |
|-----|------|-------|
| J2-1 | MAINCAM_RESET | Camera reset |
| J2-2 | XMIPI1MDN0 | Used for MIPI DSI |
| J2-3 | CAM_FLASH_EN | Camera flash enable |
| J2-4 | XMIPI1MDP0 | Used for MIPI DSI |
| J2-5 | CAM_FLASH_TORCH | Camera flash bulb use as torch |
| J2-6 | GND | Ground |
| J2-7 | CODEC_PDN | Audio codec power down |
| J2-8 | XMIPI1MDN1 | LCD display MIPI DSI1 DN1 channel 1 |
| J2-9 | XGPIO17 | SigFox low-power control on connector J512-6. LPWA INT (a.k.a XT_INT163). |
| J2-10 | XMIPI1MDP1 | LCD display MIPI DSI1 DN1 channel 1 |
| J2-11 | PSR_TE | Display synchronization |

(*continued*)

*Table 13-9.* (*continued*)

| Pin | Name | Notes |
|-----|------|-------|
| J2-12 | GND | Ground |
| J2-13 | SEQ_I2C_SCL | Bus I2C-5 Serial Clock Line |
| J2-14 | XMIPI1MDN2 | LCD display MIPI DSI1 DN2 channel 2 |
| J2-15 | SEQ_I2C_SDA | Bus I2C-5 Serial Data Line |
| J2-16 | XMIPI1MDP2 | LCD display MIPI DSI1 DN2 channel 2 |
| J2-17 | VTCAM_RESET | Video camera reset |
| J2-18 | GND | Ground |
| J2-19 | XISP2_SDA | Bus I2C-2 camera Serial Data Line |
| J2-20 | XMIPI1MDN3 | LCD display MIPI DSI1 DN3 channel 3 |
| J2-21 | XISP2_SCL | Bus I2C-2 camera Serial Clock Line |
| J2-22 | XMIPI1MDP3 | LCD display MIPI DSI1 DN3 channel 3 |
| J2-23 | GND | Ground |
| J2-24 | GND | Ground |
| J2-25 | XMIPI1SDN0 | MIPI camera CSI1 SDN0 channel 0 |
| J2-26 | XMIPI1MDNCLK | LCD display MIPI DSI1 DNCLK |
| J2-27 | XMIPI1SDP0 | MIPI camera CSI1 SDP0 channel 0 |
| J2-28 | XMIPI1MDPCLK | LCD display MIPI DSI1 DPCLK |
| J2-29 | GND | Ground |
| J2-30 | GND | Ground |
| J2-31 | XMIPI1SDN1 | MIPI camera CSI1 SDN1 channel 1 |
| J2-32 | XMMC2CDN | SD card CDN card detect (a.k.a. TFLASH_CDN) |
| J2-33 | XMIPI1SDP1 | MIPI camera CSI1 SDP1 channel 1 |
| J2-34 | XMMC2CLK | SD card clock line (a.k.a. TFLASH_CLK) |
| J2-35 | GND | Ground |
| J2-36 | XMMC2CMD | SD card CMD line (a.k.a. TFLASH_CMD) |
| J2-37 | XMIPI1SDNCLK | MIPI camera CSI1 SDN clock |
| J2-38 | XMMC2DATA0 | SD card data bit 0 (a.k.a. TFLASH_D0) |
| J2-39 | XMIPI1SDPCLK | MIPI camera CSI1 SDP clock |
| J2-40 | XMMC2DATA1 | SD card data bit 1 (a.k.a. TFLASH_D1) |
| J2-41 | GND | Ground |
| J2-42 | XMMC2DATA2 | SD card data bit 2 (a.k.a. TFLASH_D2) |
| J2-43 | AP_NRESET | Cold ARTIK 1020 Module reset by PMIC. RST signal on connector J25-3 and J510-7 (a.k.a. RST/MRNRESET) |
| J2-44 | XMMC2DATA3 | SD card data bit 3 (a.k.a. TFLASH_D3) |

(*continued*)

*Table 13-9.* (*continued*)

| Pin | Name | Notes |
|-----|------|-------|
| J2-45 | XLPWA_WKUP | SigFox LPWA WAKEUP. The data sheet describes this as an LCD_ID or Vsync line, which is contradictory. |
| J2-46 | GPIOC40 | Power management GPIO |
| J2-47 | AP_NWRESET | Warm reset from PMIC (for development purposes) |
| J2-48 | Xi2c7_SDA | Bus I2C-7 Serial Data Line used for HDMI (a.k.a XHDMI_SDA) |
| J2-49 | XISP0_SCL | Bus I2C-0 camera Serial Clock Line |
| J2-50 | Xi2C7_SCL | Bus I2C-7 Serial Clock Line used for HDMI (a.k.a. XHDMI_SCL) |
| J2-51 | XISP0_SDA | Bus I2C-0 camera Serial Data Line |
| J2-52 | GND | Ground |
| J2-53 | COIN_BATT | Auxiliary backup coin battery 3-volt input |
| J2-54 | XMIPI0SDN0 | MIPI CSI0 DN0 channel 0 used for 3L2 CAM |
| J2-55 | BOOST5V_EN | USB 3.0 booster 5v power supply enable |
| J2-56 | XMIPI0SDP0 | MIPI CSI0 DP0 channel 0 used for 3L2 CAM |
| J2-57 | LCD_RST | LCD display reset |
| J2-58 | GND | Ground |
| J2-59 | Xi2c8_SDA | Bus I2C-8 Serial Data Line used for touch interface (a.k.a. XTCH_SDA) |
| J2-60 | XMIPI0SDN1 | MIPI CSI0 DN1 channel 1 used for 3L2 CAM |
| J2-61 | Xi2C8_SCL | Bus I2C-8 Serial Clock Line used for touch interface (a.k.a. XTCH_SCL) |
| J2-62 | XMIPI0SDP1 | MIPI CSI0 DP1 channel 1 used for 3L2 CAM |
| J2-63 | XCHG_SDA | Change I2C SDA lines to 1V8 signaling |
| J3-64 | GND | Ground |
| J2-65 | XCHG_SCL | Change I2C SCL lines to 1V8 signaling |
| J2-66 | XMIPI0SDN2 | MIPI CSI0 DN2 channel 2 used for 3L2 CAM |
| J2-67 | Xpwmo_1 | Pulse width modulated output channel 1. Arduino pin ~6 on header pin J26-2 and J513-3. |
| J2-68 | XMIPI0SDP2 | MIPI CSI0 DP2 channel 2 used for 3L2 CAM |
| J2-69 | Xpwmo_0 | Pulse width modulated output channel 0. Arduino pin ~5 on header pin J26-3 and J513-4. |
| J2-70 | GND | Ground |
| J2-71 | GND | Ground |
| J2-72 | XMIPI0SDN3 | MIPI CSI0 DN3 channel 3 used for 3L2 CAM |
| J2-73 | XUHOSTOVERCUR | USB host over current detection |
| J2-74 | XMIPI0SDP3 | MIPI CSI0 DP3 channel 3 used for 3L2 CAM |
| J2-75 | XUHOSTPWREN | Used for resetting the **AX88760** Ethernet and USB controller |

(*continued*)

**Table 13-9.** (*continued*)

| Pin | Name | Notes |
|-----|------|-------|
| J2-76 | GND | Ground |
| J2-77 | UDRD3_0_OVERCUR_U2 | USB 3.0 over current detection and control |
| J2-78 | XMIPI0SDPCLK | MIPI CSI0 DPCLK used for 3L2 CAM |
| J2-79 | UDRD3_0_VBUSCTRL_U2 | USB 3.0 VBUS control |
| J2-80 | XMIPI0SDNCLK | MIPI CSI0 DNCLK used for 3L2 CAM |
| J2-81 | GND | Ground |
| J2-82 | GND | Ground |
| J2-83 | GND | Ground |
| J2-84 | GND | Ground |

■ **Note**    The ARTIK 1020 data sheet incorrectly describes this as connector J4, which is inconsistent with the developer reference board schematic diagrams and the labels printed on the Commercial Beta Type 10 board.

## Connector J3

Connector J3 is mainly concerned with delivering HDMI video and a few miscellaneous GPIO outputs. Figure 13-15 shows the signals on the J3 pins.

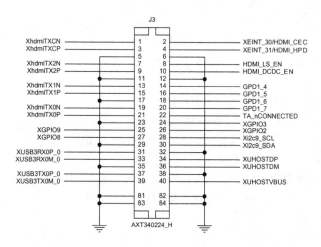

**Figure 13-15.** *ARTIK 10 - J3 pinout assignments*

The AXT connector J3 pinouts are listed in Table 13-10. These values are taken from the board schematic and cross-checked against the data sheets. Be sure to check an authoritative and up-to-date source for the latest values and check that they correspond to the same revision of the ARTIK module you are deploying.

**Table 13-10.** *AXT Connector J3 Pinouts*

| Pin | Name | Notes |
|---|---|---|
| J3-1 | XhdmiTXCN | HDMI transmit clock minus signal |
| J3-2 | XEINT_30 | HDMI Consumer Electronics Control signal for controlling the TV display remotely using AV.link messages (a.k.a HDMI_CEC) |
| J3-3 | XhdmiTXCP | HDMI transmit clock plus signal |
| J3-4 | XEINT_31 | HDMI hot plug detection (a.k.a. HDMI_HPD) |
| J3-5 | GND | Ground |
| J3-6 | GND | Ground |
| J3-7 | XhdmiTX2N | HDMI TMDS channel 2 minus signal |
| J3-8 | HDMI_LS_EN | HDMI load switch enable control via GPIO |
| J3-9 | XhdmiTX2P | HDMI TMDS channel 2 plus signal |
| J3-10 | HDMI_DCDC_EN | HDMI DC to DC step up control via GPIO |
| J3-11 | GND | Ground |
| J3-12 | GND | Ground |
| J3-13 | XhdmiTX1N | HDMI TMDS channel 1 minus signal |
| J3-14 | GPD1_4 | Generic data bit 0 |
| J3-15 | XhdmiTX1P | HDMI TMDS channel 1 plus signal |
| J3-16 | GPD1_5 | Generic data bit 1 |
| J3-17 | GND | Ground |
| J3-18 | GPD1_6 | Generic data bit 2 |
| J3-19 | XhdmiTX0N | HDMI TMDS channel 0 minus signal |
| J3-20 | GPD1_7 | Generic data bit 3 |
| J3-21 | XhdmiTX0P | HDMI TMDS channel 0 plus signal |
| J3-22 | TA_nCONNECTED | PMIC generated power up event signal |
| J3-23 | GND | Ground |
| J3-24 | XGPIO3 | Generic GPIO interface |
| J3-25 | XGPIO9 | SigFox power enable (a.k.a. SPI CS) |
| J3-26 | XGPIO2 | Generic GPIO interface |
| J3-27 | XGPIO8 | Z-Wave reset |
| J3-28 | Xi2c9_SCL | Bus I2C-9 Arduino compatible external bus on connector J27-1 and J510-6 |
| J3-29 | GND | Ground |
| J3-30 | Xi2c9_SDA | Bus I2C-9 Arduino compatible external bus |
| J3-31 | XUSB3RX0P_0 | USB3.0 DRD channel 0 receive plus on connector J27-2 and J510-5 |
| J3-32 | GND | Ground |

*(continued)*

*Table 13-10.* (*continued*)

| Pin | Name | Notes |
|-----|------|-------|
| J3-33 | XUSB3RX0M_0 | USB3.0 DRD channel 0 receive minus |
| J3-34 | XUHOSTDP | USB differential data plus for driving the **AX88760** Ethernet and USB controller |
| J3-35 | GND | Ground |
| J3-36 | XUHOSTDM | USB differential data minus for driving the **AX88760** Ethernet and USB controller |
| J3-37 | XUSB3TX0P_0 | USB3.0 DRD channel 0 transmit plus |
| J3-38 | GND | Ground |
| J3-39 | XUSB3TX0M_0 | USB3.0 DRD channel 0 transmit minus |
| J3-40 | XUHOSTVBUS | USB VBUS |
| J3-81 | GND | Ground |
| J3-82 | GND | Ground |
| J3-83 | GND | Ground |
| J3-84 | GND | Ground |

■ **Note**   The ARTIK 1020 data sheet incorrectly describes this as connector J1, which is inconsistent with the developer reference board schematic diagrams and the labels printed on the Commercial Beta Type 10 board.

# Connector J4

Connector J4 carries all the JTAG debugging signals. This connector can be omitted to save money by removing the need for a second 40-pin AXT connector. It sacrifices JTAG support as a consequence. This will enhance the security of your shipping product because your competitors will find it harder to reverse engineer your code design by attaching a JTAG debugger. The pin labeling prefixes on the schematic diagram seems to indicate that some ZigBee signals are delivered from this connector. The signal names tally with JTAG pinouts as documented by Segger J-Link reference materials and the ZigBee naming conventions may not be relevant. Figure 13-16 shows the signals on the J4 pins.

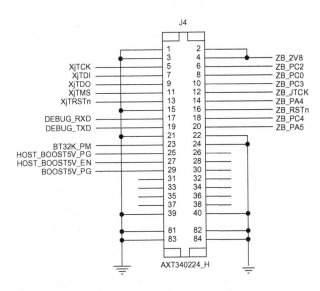

**Figure 13-16.** *ARTIK 10 - J4 pinout assignments*

The auxiliary AXT connector J4 pinouts are listed in Table 13-11. These values are also taken from the board schematic and cross-checked against the data sheets. Check an authoritative and up-to-date source for the latest values.

**Table 13-11.** *AXT Connector J4 Pinouts*

| Pin | Name | Notes |
|-----|------|-------|
| J4-1 | GND | Ground |
| J4-2 | ZB_2V8 | ZigBee 2.8v/300mA ref. Shorted to pin J4-4. (a.k.a. PVDD_LDO28_2V8). |
| J4-3 | GND | Ground |
| J4-4 | ZB_2V8 | ZigBee 2.8v/300mA ref. Shorted to pin J4-2. (a.k.a. PVDD_LDO28_2V8). |
| J4-5 | XjTCK | JTAG debug clock |
| J4-6 | ZB_PC2 | JTAG debug data out |
| J4-7 | XjTDI | JTAG debug TDI line |
| J4-8 | ZB_PC0 | JTAG debug reset |
| J4-9 | XjTDO | JTAG debug TDO line |
| J4-10 | ZB_PC3 | JTAG debug data in |
| J4-11 | XjTMS | JTAG debug TMS line |
| J4-12 | ZB_JTCK | JTAG debug clock line |
| J4-13 | XjTRSTn | JTAG debug reset line |
| J4-14 | ZB_PA4 | JTAG debug GPIO control |
| J4-15 | GND | Ground |

(*continued*)

*Table 13-11.* (*continued*)

| Pin | Name | Notes |
|-----|------|-------|
| J4-16 | ZB_RSTn | JTAG debug reset line |
| J4-17 | DEBUG_RXD | AP debug UART received data (RxD) |
| J4-18 | ZB_PC4 | JTAG debug mode select |
| J4-19 | DEBUG_TXD | AP debug UART transmitted data (TxD) |
| J4-20 | ZB_PA5 | JTAG debug GPIO control |
| J4-21 | GND | Ground |
| J4-22 | GND | Ground |
| J4-23 | BT32K_PM | 32 kHz clock for Bluetooth controller (a.k.a. AP_32.768) on connector J513-1 |
| J4-24 | GND | Ground |
| J4-25 | HOST_BOOST5V_PG | Host boost PG |
| J4-26 | N/C | Not connected |
| J4-27 | HOST_BOOST5V_EN | Host boost enable control |
| J4-28 | N/C | Not connected |
| J4-29 | BOOST5V_PG | Boost PG |
| J4-30 | N/C | Not connected |
| J4-31 | N/C | Not connected |
| J4-32 | N/C | Not connected |
| J4-33 | N/C | Not connected |
| J4-34 | N/C | Not connected |
| J4-35 | N/C | Not connected |
| J4-36 | N/C | Not connected |
| J4-37 | N/C | Not connected |
| J4-38 | N/C | Not connected |
| J4-39 | GND | Ground |
| J4-40 | GND | Ground |
| J4-81 | GND | Ground |
| J4-82 | GND | Ground |
| J4-83 | GND | Ground |
| J4-84 | GND | Ground |

■ **Note** The ARTIK model 1020 data sheet mentions that the J4 debug connector is optional. It not always present in product photographs and is not described in the main introductory paragraphs of the data sheet. It carries JTAG signals to support a serial hardware debug mechanism. The data sheet also incorrectly describes this as connector J9.

# Summary

This information was collated by examining the data sheets and developer reference board schematics. While no reference resource is ever perfect and complete from every reader's point of view, the information here may save you a little time. Always refer back to the Samsung-provided resources since they are the authoritative fount of all knowledge regarding the ARTIK. Your principle reference sources should be the Samsung published ARTIK product data sheets and developer reference board schematics. There are some minor caveats and discrepancies to bear in mind as you read them, which are mentioned in this book where it is relevant.

# CHAPTER 14

▉ ▉ ▉

# Hardware I/O Connections

The ARTIK embodies an Arduino-compatible support architecture for running sketches and driving external hardware. This is presented by implementing Arduino-compatible headers on the developer reference boards. These headers are positioned so you can install Arduino shields on them to extend the hardware capabilities. This chapter describes the pinouts on these hardware I/O headers. There is also some extended coverage about JTAG debugging that builds on what was described in *Beginning Samsung ARTIK*.

## Pins and Programmable I/O

The ARTIK 5 and ARTIK 10 modules and their developer reference boards provide a range of programmable signal pins to access directly from your application. Some of them are reconfigurable for different purposes while others are dedicated pins for interacting with the built-in hardware. The various input/output pin types are listed with cross-references to detailed coverage elsewhere in this book:

- GPIO: These single bit digital input and output pins can be programmed in a variety of different ways, which are discussed in Chapter 17. Some are dedicated to controlling peripheral hardware chips such as the Ethernet controller or audio and video codecs.

- Analog input: Uses IIO conventions for reading variable voltage values. This is covered in Chapter 18.

- PWM output: Variable frequency and duty cycle pulse trains are output by these pins. Pulse width modulated output is discussed in Chapter 19.

- Serial communications with UART and other complex highly integrated chips.

- I2C: Interfaces for managing peripheral devices discussed in Chapter 20.

- I2S: These interfaces for exchanging audio data with a built-in hardware audio codec chip are discussed in Chapter 22.

- SPI: For controlling peripheral devices and displays. This is discussed in Chapter 21.

- MIPI: For managing displays and cameras. This is discussed in Chapter 23.

The layout of these connection headers is designed to be compatible with the Arduino standard design. This should facilitate the attachment of special-purpose Arduino shields.

The pins on these headers are buffered from the ARTIK pinouts on the AXT connectors with voltage level converter chips. Refer to the developer board schematics and design these same level-converting components into your own boards. They protect the ARTIK while converting the voltage from your ARTIK to Arduino-compatible levels.

© Cliff Wootton 2016
C. Wootton, *Samsung ARTIK Reference*, DOI 10.1007/978-1-4842-2322-2_14

# Hardware I/O Pins and Headers

The Type 5 and 10 developer reference boards have a group of headers that are very similar to the ones on an Arduino board. They are a superset of the Arduino headers and many additional I/O connections are brought out from the ARTIK modules via their Panasonic AXT connectors and presented here for you to access them more easily. This is where you can interact with I2C peripherals.

There are eight headers in all. Some are mounted close enough together that they appear to be one component. Indeed, they may even be implemented using one single longer header component, as is the case with connectors J511 and J513.

Figure 14-1 shows the general arrangement of these connectors with their physical pin numbering indicated for a Commercial Beta developer reference board. Although the Type 5 and Type 10 boards have some differences regarding the locations of other connectors, switches, and jumpers, this group of Arduino-compatible headers is located consistently on both types of boards.

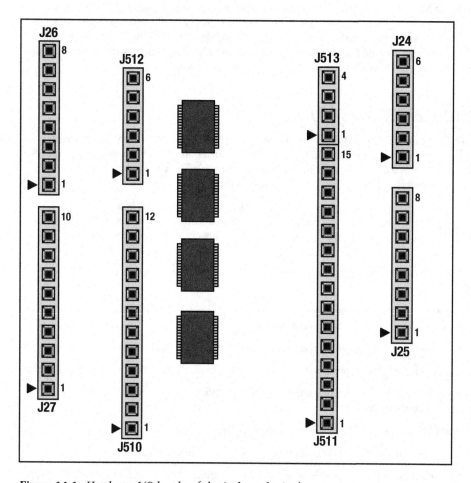

*Figure 14-1.* Hardware I/O headers (physical numbering)

Each header has a small triangle that indicates which end is the reference pin. This is always physical pin number 1. Pin 1 of connector J24 is described as J24-1 and is counted from the reference pin marked with the small triangle at the end of the connector. The developer reference board schematic diagrams label the pins, and the board artwork has similar but not identical names printed beside each connector.

---

■ **Note** The position of these headers was different on the earlier versions of the developer reference boards and they were not physically compatible with Arduino shields.

---

# Arduino Names vs. Pin Numbers

A symbolic name is usually assigned to the pins and printed on the artwork of the developer reference board. Because the Arduino pin names are composed of simple numeric values, describing the pins can be ambiguous. For example, if you refer to Arduino pin 6 on connector J26, the physical pin number is J26-2. In this book, the convention is to indicate the physical pin location and the symbolic name together when there is a chance of confusion. The physical connector label and its pin number is first, followed by the symbolic name/label in brackets:

{connector_label} - {pin_number} ({symbolic_name})

The Arduino serial data receive connection named as Arduino RX<-0 is presented on pin 8 of connector J26. The RST line is connected to pin 3 of connector J25. They are described like this so the physical and symbolic names are described at the same time and you can use either according to your preferences. Table 14-1 provides a useful cross-reference list. The small infinity symbol is similar to the Arduino logo and indicates that an integer number is an Arduino label and not a physical pin number:

- J26-8 (RX<-0)
- J25-3 (RST)
- J26-2 (~6)
- J26-5 (∞3)

*Table 14-1.* *Arduino Pin Names vs. ARTIK Header Pin Numbers*

| Arduino name | Header pin |
| --- | --- |
| RX<-0 | J26-8 |
| TX->1 | J26-7 |
| ∞2 | J26-6 |
| ∞3 | J26-5 |
| ∞4 | J26-4 |
| ~5 | J26-3 |
| ~6 | J26-2 |
| ∞7 | J26-1 |
| ∞8 | J27-10 |
| ∞9 | J27-9 |

(*continued*)

*Table 14-1.* (*continued*)

| Arduino name | Header pin |
|---|---|
| ∞10 | J27-8 |
| ∞11 | J27-7 |
| ∞12 | J27-6 |
| ∞13 | J27-5 |
| GND | J27-4 |
| VREF | J27-3 |
| SDA | J27-2 |
| SCL | J27-1 |
| A0 | J24-1 |
| A1 | J24-2 |
| A2 (ARTIK 10 only) | J24-3 |
| A3 (ARTIK 10 only) | J24-4 |
| A4 (ARTIK 10 only) | J24-5 |
| A5 (ARTIK 10 only) | J24-6 |
| VIN | J25-8 |
| GND | J25-7 |
| GND | J25-6 |
| 5v | J25-5 |
| 3v3 | J25-4 |
| RESET | J25-3 |
| IOREF | J25-2 |
| N/C (No connection) | J25-1 |

■ **Note**    The VREF signal on connector J27-3 is sometimes labeled AREF on Arduino boards and circuit diagrams because it is a reference voltage for the analog inputs.

# Mapping Pins to Connection Headers

The ARTIK 5 and 10 modules are mounted on the Type 5 and Type 10 developer reference boards and their connection headers are organized in a very similar layout. Groups of pins are wired using multi-pin headers that are identical to the type used on an Arduino. Table 14-2 summarizes these header connectors although there are a few minor differences between the two models.

**Table 14-2.** *Hardware I/O Header Connectors*

| Connector | Pin count | Purpose |
|---|---|---|
| J24 | 6 | Analog input pins |
| J25 | 8 | Power supply, ground, and reset lines |
| J26 | 8 | Arduino pins (0 to 7) |
| J27 | 10 | Arduino pins (8 to 13) and some additional GPIO functionality |
| J510 | 12 | ADC interface |
| J511 | 15 | SPI, UART, I2C, and I2S interfaces |
| J512 | 6 | GPM and interrupt lines |
| J513 | 4 | PWM and clock output |

# Pinout Diagrams

The physical pin numbers are shown on the left of the connector and the printed labels are shown on the right. The labels are similar to the names of the signals coming out of the Panasonic AXT connectors on the underside of the ARTIK modules.

The tables following the pinout diagrams list the connections with useful supplementary information. The pins are listed in numerical order, which is the reverse of how they appear on the developer reverence board if you rotate it so the headers are on the left and nearest to you and power cable is at the bottom. This is the natural orientation for reading the labels printed on the board artwork.

Most of these headers are connected directly to pins on the Panasonic AXT connectors underneath the ARTIK modules. The pin numbers are listed for the ARTIK 5 and ARTIK 10 modules accordingly. There may be a voltage level converter chip between these connectors and the ARTIK itself. They also serve to protect the ARTIK against accidental damage. This information is available from the schematic diagrams but it helps to draw it together in a tabular form.

Refer to the schematic diagrams to see how these level converters are deployed to incorporate them into your own hardware designs. The developer reference boards have many useful ideas for additional circuits that augment the ARTIK modules. Since you have the schematics available, adapt them for use in your own hardware.

The tables in this chapter also have a few items of commentary or useful notes as they pertain to each circuit. The Panasonic AXT connector pinouts are listed in Chapter 13 with extracts from the circuit schematics.

# J24 - Analog Input

The J24 hardware I/O header groups all the analog input pins together. The ARTIK 5 has just two channels while the ARTIK 10 supports six. The pinout names on the ARTIK 10 AXT connectors suggest that more channels might be available because the connections are numbered 0 to 7 with two missing items in between. There are only six channels accessible for use. Figure 14-2 illustrates the layout of the J24 header and Table 14-3 lists the pinout details. The label column refers to the screen-printing on the developer reference board. The AXT columns list the Panasonic connectors that these signals are derived from.

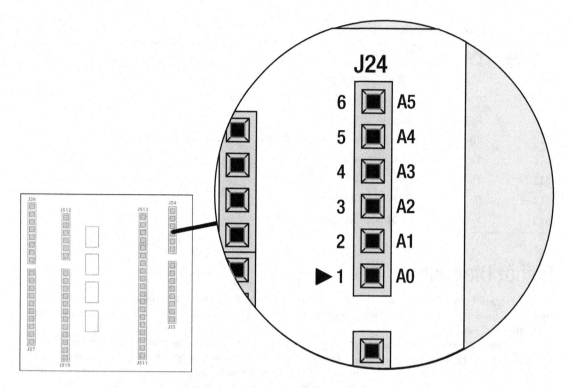

**Figure 14-2.** *Location of J24 header pins*

**Table 14-3.** *Pinouts for Header J24*

| Pin | Label | AXT (A5) | AXT (A10) | Description |
|-----|-------|----------|-----------|-------------|
| J24-1 | A0 | J3-44 | J1-48 | Analog input channel 0. Also connected to J510-2. |
| J24-2 | A1 | J3-46 | J1-50 | Analog input channel 1. Also connected to J510-3. |
| J24-3 | A2 | | J1-52 | Analog input channel 2 (ARTIK 10 only) |
| J24-4 | A3 | | J1-54 | Analog input channel 5 (ARTIK 10 only) |
| J24-5 | A4 | | J1-56 | Analog input channel 6 (ARTIK 10 only) |
| J24-6 | A5 | | J1-58 | Analog input channel 7 (ARTIK 10 only) |

# J25 - Power Supply, Ground, and Reset

Figure 14-3 shows the layout and position of connector J25 on the developer reference board and Table 14-4 describes the connections. Only one of these connections is routed back to the ARTIK module via the AXT connectors to implement a reset line.

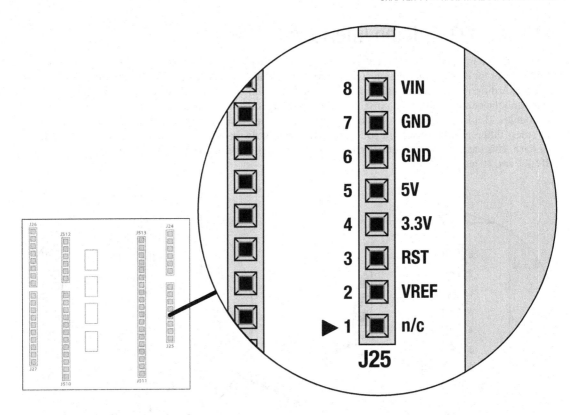

**Figure 14-3.** *Location of J25 header pins*

**Table 14-4.** *Pinouts for Header J25*

| Pin | Label | AXT (A5) | AXT (A10) | Description |
|-----|-------|----------|-----------|-------------|
| J25-1 | n/c | | | No connection |
| J25-2 | VREF | | | Externally supplied reference voltage (not labeled on board and also called IOREF in some documentation) |
| J25-3 | RST | J4-51 | J2-43 | Reset line into the ARTIK AP_NRESET/MRNRESET pin. Also connected to J510-7. |
| J25-4 | 3.3V | | | Main 3.3-volt supply |
| J25-5 | 5V | | | Main 5-volt supply always on |
| J25-6 | GND | | | Ground |
| J25-7 | GND | | | Ground |
| J25-8 | VIN | | | DC 5-volt supply switched by jumper J30. Connect a switch to these two pins to control the 5-volt supply to this connector. |

# J26 and J27 Arduino Interface

The pins shown in Figure 14-4 on the J26 and J27 headers are mainly concerned with Arduino-compatible interfacing or for direct manipulation via the sysfs virtual file system as GPIO pins. When you access them using the Arduino IDE to create a sketch that runs in the Arduino emulation, the mapping of the pins to their symbolic names is done in a portable way that manages the differences between ARTIK 5 and ARTIK 10 modules. This is also resilient to operating system upgrades. If you use the sysfs approach, carefully map these differences because your code is then interacting via the kernel-provided base address of each interface. This base address is prone to change from one OS release to another and is often different in ARTIK 5 and 10 modules.

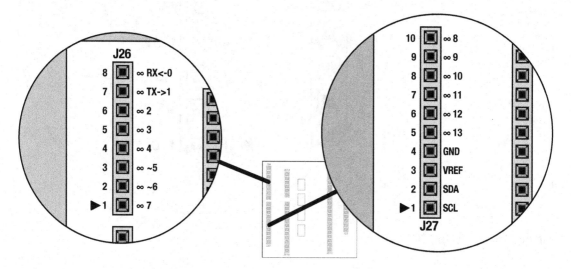

***Figure 14-4.*** *Location of J26 and 27 header pins*

These pins are driven directly from the ARTIK module via a voltage level converter/buffering chip (**TXS0108EPWR**). Refer to Chapter 13 to see how they map to the ARTIK module connections via the Panasonic AXT connectors. The Arduino compatible pins on J26 and J27 in the illustration are prefixed with a small infinity symbol because this is similar to the Arduino logo and helps to remove any ambiguity regarding pin numbers. By convention in this book, the pin numbers are shown on the left of the connector and the labels on the right. Table 14-5 lists the connections on headers J26 and J27 and also cross references to the AXT connector pins.

***Table 14-5.*** *Pinouts for Headers J26 and J27*

| Pin | Label | AXT (A5) | AXT (A10) | Description |
|-----|-------|----------|-----------|-------------|
| J26-1 | ∞7 | J3-26 | J1-28 | Arduino pin 7 (XEINT_3). This pin is 3.3v tolerant in input mode. |
| J26-2 | ~6 | J4-47 | J2-67 | Arduino pin ~ 6 (Xpwmo_1). Also presented on J513-3. |
| J26-3 | ~5 | J4-45 | J2-69 | Arduino pin ~ 5 (Xpwmo_0). Also presented on J513-4. |
| J26-4 | ∞4 | J3-28 | J1-30 | Arduino pin 4 (XEINT_2). This pin is 3.3v tolerant in input mode. Also presented on J512-4 as INT2. |
| J26-5 | ∞3 | J3-30 | J1-32 | Arduino pin 3 (XEINT_1). This pin is 3.3v tolerant in input mode. Also presented on J512-3 as INT1. |
| J26-6 | ∞2 | J3-32 | J1-34 | Arduino pin 2 (XEINT_0). This pin is 3.3v tolerant in input mode. Also presented on J512-2 as INT0. |
| J26-7 | TX->1 | J3-40 | J1-44 | Arduino pin TX->1. Connected to UART3 (Xu3_TXD) on an ARTIK 5 and UART1 (Xu1_TXD) on an ARTIK 10. Controlled via the Serial object in Arduino IDE. Also presented on J511-10. |
| J26-8 | RX<-0 | J3-38 | J1-42 | Arduino pin RX<-0. Connected to UART3 (Xu3_RXD) on an ARTIK 5 and UART1 (Xu1_RXD) on an ARTIK 10. Controlled via the Serial object in Arduino IDE. Also presented on J511-11. |
| J27-1 | SCL | J4-13 | J3-28 | Bus I2C-7/I2C-9 Serial Clock Line (Xi2c7_SCL on ARTIK 5, Xi2c9_SCL on ARTIK 10). This pin is also connected to J510-6 on an ARTIK 10. |
| J27-2 | SDA | J4-11 | J3-30 | Bus I2C-7/I2C-9 Serial Data Line (Xi2c7_SDA on ARTIK 5, Xi2c9_SDA on ARTIK 10). This pin is also connected to J510-5 on an ARTIK 10. |
| J27-3 | VREF | | | External reference voltage input |
| J27-4 | GND | | | Ground |
| J27-5 | ∞13 | J3-11 | J1-19 | Arduino pin 13 (XEINT_14). Can be used as the SCLK line when using the Arduino SPI library. |
| J27-6 | ∞12 | J3-12 | J1-17 | Arduino pin 12 (XEINT_13). Can be used as the MISO line when using the Arduino SPI library. |
| J27-7 | ∞11 | J3-16 | J1-18 | Arduino pin 11 (XEINT_8). Can be used as the MOSI line when using the Arduino SPI library. |
| J27-8 | ∞10 | J3-20 | J1-22 | Arduino pin 10 (XEINT_6). This pin is 3.3v tolerant in input mode. Can be used as the Slave Select (SS) line when using the Arduino SPI library. |
| J27-9 | ∞9 | J3-22 | J1-24 | Arduino pin 9 (XEINT_5). This pin is 3.3v tolerant in input mode. |
| J27-10 | ∞8 | J3-24 | J1-26 | Arduino pin 8 (XEINT_4). This pin is 3.3v tolerant in input mode. |

There are four important caveats regarding the connections on this header:

- If you are writing software to interact with the RX<-0 and TX->1 serial lines, the UART names are different on the ARTIK 5 and 10 modules. UART3 is used on an ARTIK 5 and UART1 is used on an ARTIK 10. These are differently named UARTs within the ARTIK OS. They live at different base addresses for access to the driver and are managed on different peripheral buses.

- Similarly, the SCL and SDA lines use different I2C devices on the two ARTIK modules. On the ARTIK 5, bus I2C-7 is used; on the ARTIK 10, bus I2C-9 is used. Program your application to talk to the correct one if you are sharing the same code across both ARTIK module types.

- The ARTIK 5 presents two different I2C bus signals on connectors J27 and J510. The ARTIK 10 uses the same I2C bus on both connectors. On an ARTIK 10, you might mistakenly assume you can connect a separate set of peripherals on J510 but they are affected by changes you make to J27. The ARTIK 5 lets you control them independently.

- Be aware of the reversed ordering of Arduino pin numbers vs. connector physical pin numbers.

## J510 - Auxiliary Analog ADC input

Figure 14-5 shows the layout and position of connector J510 on the developer reference board. The pinouts for this connector are detailed in Table 14-6. The ADC signals are connected to the same source as the ones on connector J24. You can connect your circuits to either of them.

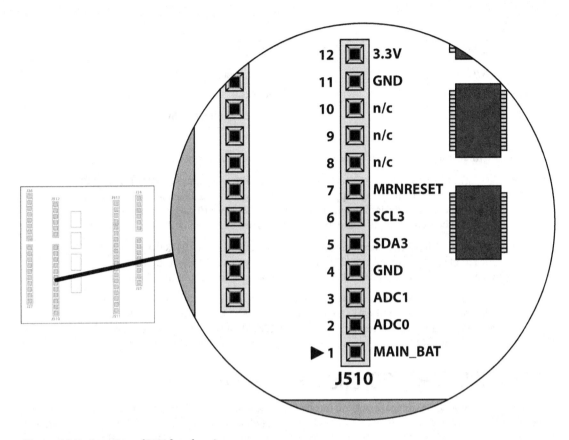

**Figure 14-5.** *Location of J510 header pins*

**Table 14-6.** *Pinouts for Header J510*

| Pin | Label | AXT (A5) | AXT (A10) | Description |
|-----|-------|----------|-----------|-------------|
| J510-1 | MAIN_BAT | | | Main power supply (3.8v) |
| J510-2 | ADC0 | J3-44 | J1-48 | ADC input channel 0. Also connected to J24-1. |
| J510-3 | ADC1 | J3-46 | J1-50 | ADC input channel 1. Also connected to J24-2. |
| J510-4 | GND | | | Ground |
| J510-5 | SDA3 | J4-55 | J3-30 | Bus I2C-3/I2C-9 Serial Data line (Xi2c3_SDA on ARTIK 5, duplicate connection to Xi2c9_SCL on ARTIK 10) |
| J510-6 | SCL3 | J4-53 | J3-28 | Bus I2C-3/I2C-9 Serial Clock Line (Xi2c3_SCL on ARTIK 5, duplicate connection to Xi2c9_SDA on ARTIK 10) |
| J510-7 | AP_NRESET | J4-51 | J2-43 | Reset line into the ARTIK RST/MRNRESET pin. Also connected to J25-3 |
| J510-8 | N/C | | | No connection |
| J510-9 | N/C | | | No connection |

*(continued)*

***Table 14-6.*** (*continued*)

| Pin | Label | AXT (A5) | AXT (A10) | Description |
|---|---|---|---|---|
| J510-10 | N/C | | | No connection |
| J510-11 | GND | | | Ground |
| J510-12 | DC 3.3V | | | Reference voltage (3.3v) |

There are three important caveats regarding the connections on this header:

- The SDA3 and SCL3 connections are mapped to an otherwise unused I2C3 on an ARTIK 5. On the ARTIK 10, they are mapped to I2C9, which is also connected to the J27 header. This connection model is different between the ARTIK 5 and 10 developer boards. The artwork labels on a Type 10 board imply that this is bus I2C-3, which it is not.

- If you are driving the I2C interface on J510-6/J510-7, then on an ARTIK 5 it will not affect the I2C interface on connector J27. On an ARTIK 10, you will affect any peripherals connected to J27 as well as J510 because the pins are electrically one and the same.

- The naming of the reset lines is context dependent. Arduino conventions call it the RST pin. ARTIK calls it the AP_NRESET or MRNRESET depending on whether you are reading a data sheet for the ARTIK 5 or ARTIK 10 or consulting the reference board schematics.

# J511 - SPI, UART, I2C, and I2S Interfaces

There are a few minor typographical errors on the artwork of the Commercial Beta developer reference boards. They are not of any great consequence and have been corrected on these illustrations. They are also due in part to the placement of some surface mounted components that hide the label text. Figure 14-6 shows the layout of the J511 connector on the developer reference board while Table 14-7 lists the pinouts for it.

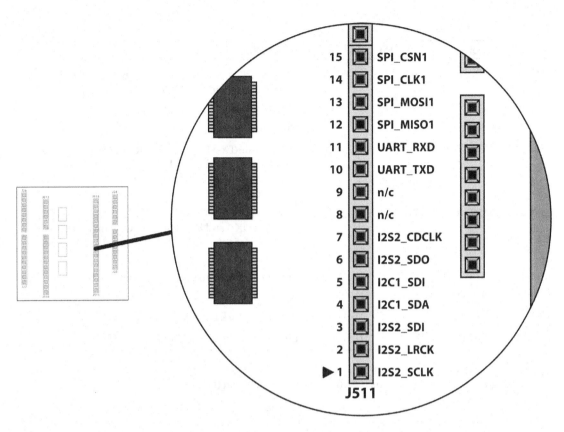

*Figure 14-6.* *Location of J511 header pins*

*Table 14-7.* *Pinouts for Header J511*

| Pin | Label | AXT (A5) | AXT (A10) | Description |
| --- | --- | --- | --- | --- |
| J511-1 | I2S2_SCLK | J3-52 | J1-76 | Bus I2S-2/I2S-0 audio Serial Clock Line (XAudi2s2SCLK on ARTIK 5, XAudi2s0SCLK on ARTIK 10) |
| J511-2 | I2S2_LRCK | J3-54 | J1-78 | Bus I2S-2/I2S-0 audio Left-Right Clock Line (XAudi2s2LRCK on ARTIK 5, XAudi2s0LRCK on ARTIK 10) |
| J511-3 | I2S2_SDI | J3-50 | J1-74 | Bus I2S-2/I2S-0 audio Serial Data Input (XAudi2s2SDI on ARTIK 5, XAudi2s0SDI on ARTIK 10) |
| J511-4 | I2C1_SDA | J4-17 | J1-77 | Bus I2C-1 Serial Data Line (Xi2c1_SDA). Controls the Audio codec hardware codec chip. |
| J511-5 | I2C1_SCL | J4-15 | J1-75 | Bus I2C-1 Serial Clock Line (Xi2c1_SCL). Controls the Audio codec hardware codec chip. |
| J511-6 | I2S2_SDO | J3-48 | J1-72 | Bus I2S-2/I2S-0 Serial Data Out (XAudi2s2SDO on ARTIK 5, XAudi2s0SDO on ARTIK 10) |

(*continued*)

*Table 14-7.* (*continued*)

| Pin | Label | AXT (A5) | AXT (A10) | Description |
|---|---|---|---|---|
| J511-7 | I2S2_CDCLK | J3-56 | J1-80 | Bus I2S-2/I2S-0 audio CD Clock Line (XAudi2s2CDCLK on ARTIK 5, XAudi2s0CDCLK on ARTIK 10) |
| J511-8 | N/C | | | No connection |
| J511-9 | N/C | | | No connection |
| J511-10 | UART_TXD | J3-40 | J1-44 | Arduino pin TX->1. Connected to UART3 (Xu3_TXD) on an ARTIK 5 and UART1 (Xu1_TXD) on an ARTIK 10. Controlled via the Serial object in Arduino IDE. Also presented on J26-7. |
| J511-11 | UART_RXD | J3-38 | J1-42 | Arduino pin RX<-0. Connected to UART3 (Xu3_RXD) on an ARTIK 5 and UART1 (Xu1_RXD) on an ARTIK 10. Controlled via the Serial object in Arduino IDE. Also presented on J26-8. |
| J511-12 | SPI_MISO1 | J7-36 | J1-63 | Bus SPI-1 Master in, slave out (XspiMISO1) |
| J511-13 | SPI_MOSI1 | J7-38 | J1-65 | Bus SPI-1 Master out, slave in (XspiMOSI1) |
| J511-14 | SPI_CLK1 | J7-32 | J1-59 | Bus SPI-1 Clock Line (XspiCLK1) |
| J511-15 | SPI_CSN1 | J7-34 | J1-61 | Bus SPI-1 Clock Select Line(XspiCSn1) |

There are two important caveats regarding the connections on this header:

- The I2S-2 audio connections on an ARTIK 5 are connected to I2S-0 on an ARTIK 10 according to the circuit schematics for the developer reference boards. All of the photographs currently available show the labeling on the Type 10 developer reference board to be identical to that on the Type 5. Therefore the labels shown in Figure 14-6 and Table 14-7 are still relevant although the internal connections are different.

- The naming of bus I2C-1 on J511-4/J511-5 is different between the ARTIK 5 and 10 schematic diagrams. According to the data sheets, they seem to go to the same bus I2C-1 connection via the AXT connectors on both ARTIK modules.

# J512 - GPM and Interrupts

This connector groups the GPM and interrupt connections together. Figure 14-7 shows the layout of connector J512 on the developer reference board while Table 14-8 describes the pinouts.

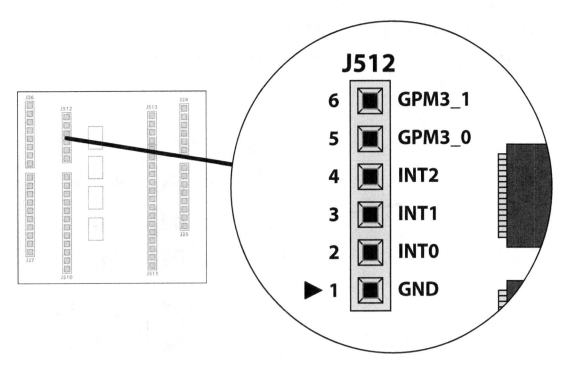

**Figure 14-7.** *Location of J512 header pins*

**Table 14-8.** *Pinouts for Header J512*

| Pin | Label | AXT (A5) | AXT (A10) | Description |
|---|---|---|---|---|
| J512-1 | GND | | | Ground |
| J512-2 | INT0 | J3-32 | J1-34 | Arduino pin 2 (XEINT_0). Also presented on J26-6. |
| J512-3 | INT1 | J3-30 | J1-32 | Arduino pin 3 (XEINT_1). Also presented on J26-5. |
| J512-4 | INT2 | J3-28 | J1-30 | Arduino pin 4 (XEINT_2). Also presented on J26-4. |
| J512-5 | GPM3_0 | J7-6 | J1-21 | Connected to GPM3_0 on ARTIK 5 and XEINT_16 on ARTIK 10. |
| J512-6 | GPM3_1 | J7-4 | J2-9 | Connected to GPM3_1 on ARTIK 5 and XGPIO_17/XT_INT163 on ARTIK 10. |

There is one important caveat regarding this header connector:

- The interrupt signals on pins J512-2, J512-3, and J512-4 are the same as some of the Arduino pins. Be aware of these duplicated connections in case you inadvertently drive the wrong lines. You may be interacting with the Arduino pins but not realizing that equipment connected to these interrupt pins via connector J512 is also being affected.

# J513 - PWM and Clock Output

Connector J513 carries the PWM and clock outputs. The position and layout of the connector is shown in Figure 14-8 and Table 14-9 lists the pinouts.

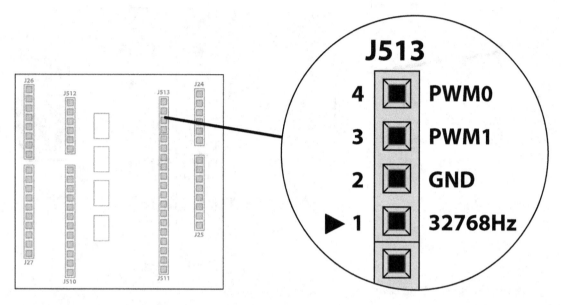

**Figure 14-8.** *Location of J513 header pins*

**Table 14-9.** *Pinouts for Header J513*

| Pin | Label | AXT (A5) | AXT (A10) | Description |
|-----|-------|----------|-----------|-------------|
| J513-4 | PWM0 | J4-45 | J2-69 | Arduino pin ~ 5 (Xpwmo_0). Also presented on J26-3. |
| J513-3 | PWM1 | J4-47 | J2-67 | Arduino pin ~ 6 (Xpwmo_1). Also presented on J26-2. |
| J513-2 | GND | | | Ground |
| J513-1 | 32768Hz | J7-22 | J4-23 | 32 kHz clock output (BT32K_PM) |

There is one important caveat regarding this header connector:

- Older versions of the developer reference boards used for the Alpha and Beta prototypes have their PWM connections reversed compared with the Commercial Beta versions. The Commercial Beta PWM pin connections are considered to be the definitive configuration.

# JTAG Support

*Beginning Samsung ARTIK* briefly describes the Segger J-Link tools for hardware debugging. They can be connected to the JTAG connector on your developer reference board. As that book was being completed, the Commercial Beta of the ARTIK 5 modules had just gone on sale and the ARTIK 10 was still to be launched. Some months later, now that the ARTIK 10 is released, a few developers are beginning to use J-Link debuggers and they find that the ARTIK 10 devices are not listed in the Eclipse IDE. The Eclipse support for the Segger J-Link debugger is documented in great detail at the following links:

```
http://gnuarmeclipse.github.io/debug/jlink/
http://gnuarmeclipse.github.io/debug/jlink/install/
```

This is not the complete story, and if your device is not listed, you cannot select it when you configure a debugging session. Developers have reported that the generic devices do not work either. Because the ARTIK modules have multiple cores, targeting the right CPU requires a little extra configuration to set up a scan chain. Segger has published useful guidance on GDB techniques and other helpful documentation here and there are other useful resources to check out. There is no single source of reference for this debugging approach. Various pieces of information are collated together here to paint a more complete picture of how JTAG works in a multi-core setting:

```
www.segger.com/IDE_Integration_Eclipse.html
www.segger.com/j-link-software.html
www.segger.com/ozone.html
www.segger.com/jlink-gdb-server.html
https://en.wikipedia.org/wiki/JTAG
```

## JTAG Connector

The JTAG support in the ARTIK is compatible with the JTAG interface protocol. Your J-Link may not work correctly if you try to use the SWO interface protocol. Make sure that you deactivate any SWO settings and checkboxes in case they are interfering with the JTAG configuration in your IDE debugger. Figure 14-9 illustrates the J12 connector on both the Type 5 and Type 10 developer reference boards. This is where the JTAG interface connects to a hardware debugger such as the Segger J-Link. The pinouts are summarized in Table 14-10 and are pin-for-pin correct when checked against the pinout documentation in the J-Link user manual.

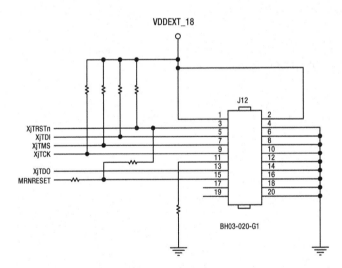

**Figure 14-9.** *Developer board AXT connector J12*

***Table 14-10.*** *AXT Connector J12 Pinouts*

| Pin | Label | Description |
|---|---|---|
| J12-1 | VDDEXT_18 | Target reference voltage used to check whether the device is powered up |
| J12-2 | VDDEXT_18 | Target reference voltage the same as J12-1. The Segger J-Link does not connect anything to this pin. |
| J12-3 | XjTRSTn | Reset signal asserted by the J-Link to reset the target CPU |
| J12-4 | GND | Ground |
| J12-5 | XjTDI | Serial data input to the target CPU |
| J12-6 | GND | Ground |
| J12-7 | XjTMS | Sets the JTAG mode on the target CPU |
| J12-8 | GND | Ground |
| J12-9 | XjTCK | Serial Clock Line providing timing synchronization from the J-Link to the target CPU |
| J12-10 | GND | Ground |
| J12-11 | RTCK | Return clock handshake, which is not implemented on the ARTIK. Grounded via a pull-down resistor to indicate that return clock pulses are not echoed back to the J-Link. |
| J12-12 | GND | Ground |
| J12-13 | XjTDO | Serial data output from the target CPU back to the J-Link |
| J12-14 | GND | Ground |
| J12-15 | AP_NRESET | Cold reset. This RST/MRNRESET signal also appears on connector J25-3 and J510-7. The J-Link can use this to assert a reset on the target CPU. |
| J12-16 | GND | Ground |
| J12-17 | DBGRQ | Not connected in the ARTIK or at the J-Link. Reserved for sending a debug request signal but not currently used. |
| J12-18 | GND | Ground |
| J12-19 | 5V_IN | Some J-Link devices can provide a 5v power supply to the target hardware but this is not connected in an ARTIK, which has its own independent power supply. |
| J12-20 | GND | Ground |

These pinout labels conform to the JTAG interface protocol. They are not compatible with the SWO interface setting in your J-Link command line.

## Adding a New J-Link Device

Segger is aware that new devices may not be supported initially. They provide instructions for manually adding new devices to the database. Once the devices become more popular, their support will be added to a later version of the Eclipse J-Link plug-ins. Check the online resources periodically to see if the J-Link supports your ARTIK modules and deprecate your custom modifications when there is official support for them. The list of currently supported devices is available on the Segger web site at www.segger.com/jlink_supported_devices.html.

Although there are many Samsung devices in the list, the ARTIK models are not included, nor are the Exynos processors on which they are based. Because of the Commercial Beta state of the ARTIK 5 and 10, this is not a surprise. The Samsung support team and the engineers in the Research and Development labs are aware of the need for this support to be added.

If you visit the Segger downloads page, there are some useful manuals describing how J-Link debuggers work. The J-Link Manual (UM08001_JLinkARM.pdf) is particularly helpful because it describes how to add a new item to the devices database XML file that the Eclipse IDE uses to build the device selection menus. Download a copy from www.segger.com/downloads/jlink.

To add a new device to the database currently used by the J-Link tools, you need locate the XML file called JLinkDevices.xml, which is located in the same directory as your J-Link settings file. The location of these items depends on how you installed your IDE and what platform you are using it on as a development workstation. This article may help: http://stackoverflow.com/questions/17431989/where-does-eclipse-store-preferences.

When you find the JLinkDevices.xml file, the internal structure should look similar to Listing 14-1. If <device> tags are there already, create a new one at the same level so it becomes a sibling. This device corresponds to a single chip that might contain several CPU cores.

***Listing 14-1.*** Adding Content to the JLinkDevices.xml File

```
<Database>
  <Device>
  <ChipInfo Vendor="..."
            Name="..."
            WorkRAMAddr="..."
            WorkRAMSize="..."
            Core="..." />
  <FlashBankInfo Name="..."
                 BaseAddr="..."
                 MaxSize="..."
                 Loader="..."
                 LoaderType="..." />
  </Device>
</Database>
```

You must provide Vendor, Name, and Core values. These are mandatory properties for all devices. The <FlashBankInfo> tag is optional but if it is included, you must also provide the WorkRAMAddr and WorkRAMSize properties inside the <ChipInfo> tag and populate your <FlashBankInfo> tag with the Name, BaseAddr, MaxSize, Loader, and LoaderType properties. Table 14-11 lists the important tags in this file and what they are used for.

***Table 14-11.*** *Important J-Link Configuration Tags*

| Tag | Description |
| --- | --- |
| <Database> | The main outer container object for the whole database |
| <Device> | One of these objects per device in the database. All devices are considered equal. There is no nesting to create groups. |
| <ChipInfo> | Describes basic information about the device |
| <FlashBankInfo> | Describes an optional flash memory store for bulk transfer of settings and memory contents |

Table 14-12 lists some potential values for creating your own configuration. This needs to be officially sanctioned as the right solution after the Samsung and Segger engineers have collaborated to prove that it works.

*Table 14-12.* *Example Properties for an ARTIK 10*

| Tag | Property | Value |
|-----|----------|-------|
| <ChipInfo> | Vendor | Samsung |
| <ChipInfo> | Name | Exynos5433 |
| <ChipInfo> | Core | JLINK_CORE_CORTEX_A15 |
| <ChipInfo> | WorkRAMAddr | Base address of where in memory the J-Link should read and write |
| <ChipInfo> | WorkRAMSize | The extent of the working memory starting at WorkRAMAddr that the J-Link can access |

Because the ARTIK 10 has a mix of processors, it may be necessary to create configuration profiles for A7 and A15 as separate items. The Core value is set differently in each case. Then as you create the scan chains for the debugging server processes, call up the right profile for your target CPU.

---

■ **Note**    The **Cortex-A15** is not listed in the Segger user manual as a supported type but that document may not have been updated to include it because it is listed as an available configuration on the supported devices page on the Segger web site.

---

## Testing J-Link Connectivity

There are two interface protocols that J-Link uses to communicate with the target device. The command line interface parameter (-if) can select either JTAG or SWD mode when starting the debugging session. The pin labeling on the J12 connector on the developer reference boards suggest the ARTIK expects to be driven with the -if JTAG parameter value. Make sure you select this in the Eclipse Debugger setup UI panels.

If after creating a new device in your device database you still cannot get your Segger J-Link to work with the ARTIK, contact the Segger support engineers at mailto:support@segger.com.

The Segger discussion forum also carries a lot of useful help regarding the J-Link devices. Access it here to see if your questions have already been covered: http://forum.segger.com/index.php?page=Index.

## Multi-Core Debugging

Debugging a single CPU may work without any problems. The ARTIK 10 has a quad-core **Cortex-A15** and a quad-core **Cortex-A7** while the ARTIK 5 has a dual-core **Cortex-A7**. Debugging multi-core targets would seem to be an impossibly difficult task but the J-Link guidelines suggest that it is not very hard to do.

Before attempting to debug a multi-processor scenario, you may also want to read about processor affinity in Chapter 12, which describes how applications can be assigned to run on specific CPUs.

# Setting Up a Scan Chain

The J-Link ARM user guide available from the Segger web site describes multi-core debugging techniques that are only slightly more complex than debugging a single core. Accomplish them with one single Segger J-Link connected to your target system. The scan chain needs to be configured to include the CPU cores you want to debug. The default configuration expects only one CPU core. Multiple CPU cores are daisy chained using their TDI and TDO connections and are configured as a scan chain by the client debugging system. Figure 14-10 shows how the CPU cores are coupled in a scan chain.

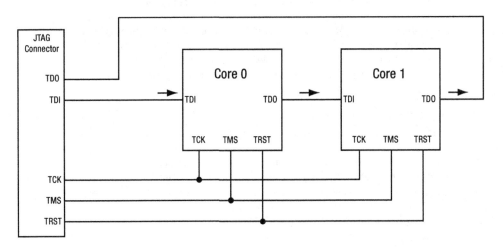

**Figure 14-10.**  *Scan chain coupling*

# How the Scan Chain Works

The scan chain works in a similar way to the SPI shift register technique described in Chapter 21. The bits are pushed into the TDI input and come out of the TDO output with one bit moved each clock cycle. If the internal register is 8 bits wide, it needs eight clock cycles to shift all the bits to the correct destination. Data input and output happen simultaneously.

A scan chain with multiple devices attaches the TDO output of the first CPU core to the TDI input of the second. To shift the bits into the register inside the second core, they must be shifted through the first core to arrive in the correct register in the target core. Therefore, extra clock cycles are needed to move the data down the chain until it reaches the target register. The length of that chain is passed as a parameter so the J-Link can execute the right number of clock cycles. The target device is then alerted that the data has arrived. It is critical that you specify exactly the right number of instruction register bits prior to each target device or this cannot work. The default mode with a single device has zero prior bits and the target device is zero. Unless the scan chain is described in the GDBServer command line, you can only reach the first CPU for debugging. Figure 14-10 shows a simple case with just two devices in the scan chain.

The JTAG clock, mode, and reset lines are shared in parallel. The same value goes to all cores and they must all run in the same mode and be reset at the same time. The data is delivered via the TDI line to the first core as would be case for the single CPU model. The first CPU forwards messages via the TDO line to the TDI of the next processor in the chain. The last CPU delivers an aggregated message flow from the TDO line back to the JTAG connector. This all still appears to be one CPU to the J-Link debugging tools.

To correctly configure the debugging session, the position of the target device in the scan chain and the total number of bits in the Instruction Registers (IR) prior to the target device must be defined. The ARM document linked here says that the IR is 4 bits long. This value is important because the data is shifted serially through the scan chain. The right number of shift cycles must be executed to move information from the JTAG connector to the instruction register in the target CPU core. The scan chain can accommodate different devices. If there is a mixed architecture, some of the IR values may be different. Describe the sum of the IR bits between the JTAG connector TDI pin and the TDI input pin of your target device. Then the J-Link will know how many shift cycles to execute to move the data to the intended target before triggering it to read them.

If you have not ensured that your application is running in the expected target CPU, you may not be debugging the code you expect to. See the discussion on processor affinities in Chapter 12 to see how to attach processes to specific CPU cores using the `taskset` command from the `bash` command line. Alternatively, call the `sched_setaffinity()` function in your application to control the processor affinity from there. Also, see http://infocenter.arm.com/help/index.jsp?topic=/com.arm.doc.ddi0413c/Babeagge.html.

The scan chain is configured using a dialog called up under the project settings or on the command line when the GDB server is started. Use the Segger version of the GDB server, which is installed as part of their kit. If the dialog in the project settings does have the necessary UI elements to configure the scan chain, include this additional command line option for the GDB server start up instructions on the debugger configuration page:

```
jtagconf {IR_Pre} {core_number}
```

where {IR_Pre} is the sum of the IR bits to the left of the target device and the {core_number} is the number of cores to the left of the device, which is coincidentally the same as the core number shown in Figure 14-10. This is covered in the UM08001_JLink.pdf manual on the Segger Downloads page and the GDB Server manual (UM08005_JLinkGDBServer.pdf). Table 14-13 lists the potential values for the two cores shown in Figure 14-10.

***Table 14-13.*** *Scan Chain Configuration Values*

| Target | GDB Server conf |
| --- | --- |
| Core 0 | jtagconf 0 0 |
| Core 1 | jtagconf 4 1 |

Without being able to test this, an informed guess suggests that the ARTIK 5 and 10 CPU cores could be addressed with the scan chain configuration shown in Table 14-14. This assumes that the two quad-core CPUs are chained together internally but it is uncertain whether the ARTIK 10 A15 core is placed before the A7 or vice versa. The scan chain in an ARTIK 5 is easier to deduce because it only has a pair of A7 cores.

***Table 14-14.*** *Assumed ARTIK Scan Chain Values*

| ARTIK | Target | GDB Server conf |
| --- | --- | --- |
| 5 | Core 0 | jtagconf 0 0 |
| 5 | Core 1 | jtagconf 4 1 |
| 10 | CPU 0 - Core 0 | jtagconf 0 0 |
| 10 | CPU 0 - Core 1 | jtagconf 4 1 |
| 10 | CPU 0 - Core 2 | jtagconf 8 2 |
| 10 | CPU 0 - Core 3 | jtagconf 12 3 |
| 10 | CPU 1 - Core 0 | jtagconf 16 4 |
| 10 | CPU 1 - Core 1 | jtagconf 20 5 |
| 10 | CPU 1 - Core 2 | jtagconf 24 6 |
| 10 | CPU 1 - Core 3 | jtagconf 28 7 |

> ▓ **Note**    You can obtain the topology manually by inspecting the whole /sys/devices/system/cpu directory
> tree and displaying the contents of the /proc/cpuinfo file. The contents of these resources are somewhat
> arcane and not well documented online. There may be some clues regarding the organization of the cores if
> you inspect the /sys/devices/system/cpu/cpu0/topology directory (there is also one for cpu1). The Portable
> Hardware Locality tools (hwloc) may also provide some help. The lstop command in that toolkit should list the
> cores and organization of your CPUs but you will need to download the source code and build the tools first.

Also, see these links:

```
http://stackoverflow.com/questions/4284898/how-do-i-find-information-about-the-parallel-
architecture-of-my-cpu
www.open-mpi.org/projects/hwloc/
www.ibm.com/support/knowledgecenter/linuxonibm/liaat/liaattunproctop.htm
```

## Configuring Multiple Debuggers

Each debugging session needs its own GDB server running in the development workstation. They can all connect via the same J-Link device but they must have unique port numbers, which should be configured in the Debug configuration page in the Eclipse IDE. These GDB servers normally run on a local development machine. They can be run remotely provided you can resolve the IP address and port numbers for the remote instance.

As you create each GDB Server, add the jtagconf value to the additional parameters UI input cell to define the scan chain settings.

If you run multiple debug sessions at the same time, they are all gathered together in the Eclipse IDE Debug view. They are all visible at once and you can choose the one you want to view.

Another approach to distributed debugging that might be relevant if you have a multi-ARTIK configuration is to have several J-Link devices, one for each ARTIK, and connect them to the same development workstation. Eclipse is not able to cope with this without running multiple instances of the IDE. You need one for each J-Link. Ensure that the GDB Server port addresses do not collide. Then define which J-Link is associated with each IDE instance by inputting the serial number or IP address to identify it.

## If It Still Does Not Work!

If you have tried everything, here are some possible issues to check:

- Have you installed the J-Link server and documentation pack available from the Segger Downloads page?

- Have you set up your scan chain correctly with the jtagconf parameters added to the GDB server startup commands?

- Have you checked to see if there any spurious SWO interface configuration items are still turned on?

- Have you tried the CDT plug-in with its built-in GDB server support?

- Can CDT be remapped to use the Segger GDB Server to get the benefits of both packages?

- Debugging need not be done inside Eclipse IDE at all. Have you considered using the Segger Ozone J-Link debugger, which runs as a standalone application?

- Using J-Link with Eclipse is currently supported via GDB but a new technology is emerging that make embedded debugging easier to do. The TCF framework is designed from the ground up for embedded systems. There are plug-ins for this already available and development of this technology is moving forward quite rapidly. Experiment with this approach to see if you get better results.

# Summary

Chapter 13 examined the Panasonic AXT connectors on your ARTIK modules. This chapter looks outward via the hardware I/O headers and JTAG debugging features. You need to understand both aspects of the ARTIK connectivity to make the best design decisions.

# CHAPTER 15

# Antennas

If your project needs to operate a wireless communications system, you need to attach antennas to it. There are two important factors to consider. Firstly, the ARTIK boards need the mini-coaxial connectors to be coupled to approved antennas for broadcasting a wireless signal. Secondly, the SMA connectors on the developer board must have the correct kind of antennas installed. This chapter covers the relevant information regarding antennas.

## Antenna Specifications

The antennas that you fit must comply with FCC regulations on antenna design. This is important for the USA market, and other national standards bodies take this seriously too. The correct specifications for the antennas supplied with your ARTIK are summarized in Table 15-1.

***Table 15-1.*** *Antenna Specifications*

| Property | Specification |
| --- | --- |
| Antenna type | Dipole antenna |
| Antenna peak gain | 2.7 dBi |
| Frequency | 2.4GHz, 5GHz (for Wi-Fi, BT, ZigBee) |
| Connector type | SMA-M |

The FCC regulatory compliance statement relevant to the USA is as follows:

> *Replacement antennas must be of the same type, must be of equal or less gain than an antenna previously authorized under the same grant of certification (A3LATKM052000 for ARTIK 5), and must have similar in-band and out-of-band characteristics (consult specification sheet for cutoff frequencies). Any new antenna type, or higher gain antenna, approved under Part 15 requires a Class II permissive change, and the requirements of paragraph 15.203 must be met.*

© Cliff Wootton 2016
C. Wootton, *Samsung ARTIK Reference*, DOI 10.1007/978-1-4842-2322-2_15

The Canadian IC compliance statement has a slightly different text but has the same constraints regarding the prohibition of more powerful antenna usage:

> *This radio transmitter (649E-ATKM052000 for ARTIK 5) has been approved by Industry Canada to operate with the antenna types listed above with the maximum permissible gain indicated. Antenna types not included in this list, having a gain greater than the maximum gain indicated for that type, are strictly prohibited for use with this device. (RSS-GEN clause 8.3)*

The UK position on wireless transmissions is managed by the HM Government department known as Ofcom (Office of Communications). They have published a range of documents regarding IoT broadcasting. Go to their web site at www.ofcom.org.uk and use the search tools to find documents that match the string "Internet of Things."

# About the Antenna Connections

The ARTIK modules have a lot of the wireless networking capabilities built-in but they lack enough real estate to create a large enough antenna to increase the range to a useful distance. This is easily solved by attaching external antennas.

The ARTIK 5 and 10 modules have small miniature coaxial connectors on the top of the module. These are for connecting to external antennas to ensure good signal quality. Implement them in your own product designs if you need Wi-Fi connectivity. The schematics show a resistor in the circuit between the ARTIK and the SMA-F antenna mount.

---

■ **Note**    There is a subtle warning note in the data sheet suggesting that activating wireless communications in your ARTIK without having the antennas installed first may damage your ARTIK.

---

# SMA Connectors

The SMA connectors are a standard antenna connection profile. Make sure that you purchase the correct kind of connector to attach antennas or extension cables. The FCC Part 15 regulations state that it must be impossible to fit a non-compliant antenna if end users replace broken components. You must operate the equipment in compliance with the FCC regulations in those territories that they regulate. Other territories may have their own compliance regulations, which are likely to be very similar.

The coupling is a screw-on type but the mating connection might be an internal (nut) or external (bolt) thread. To make things more complex, the central connection may be a pin (male) or socket (female). This gives rise to four possible variations. The connectors on the board are SMA-F external (bolt) threads with female sockets for the center pin. Buy antennas with an SMA-M internal (nut) thread and a male pin for the center connector. Figure 15-1 shows one of the connectors on the developer reference board.

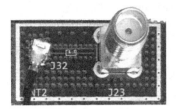

*Figure 15-1.* *SMA connector on a developer reference board*

Study the FCC regulations if you are manufacturing equipment for sale in the USA that has built-in antennas or ones that are attached externally as part of the design. Study part 15 of the regulations. There are severe penalties for manufacturing and shipping non-compliant products. If you are only working on this as a hobbyist, you are permitted to experiment without regulatory approval. Find out more about the FCC regulations that may apply to you at https://en.wikipedia.org/wiki/Title_47_CFR_Part_15.

Other countries also have regulations about radio frequency emissions and they may be slightly different than the FCC regulations regarding frequencies and signal strengths. Always endeavor to keep within these regulations to avoid the expense of having to recall or rework your products after they are shipped to customers.

# Locating the SMA Connectors

Although the Type 5 and 10 developer reference boards are laid out slightly differently and have a few component differences, the SMA antenna connections are in approximately the same place. Figure 15-2 shows the location of each SMA connector.

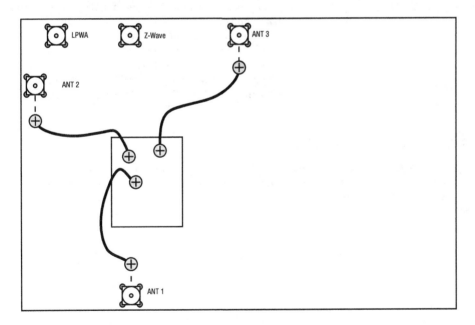

*Figure 15-2.* *Antenna locations on developer reference boards*

Table 15-2 lists the connector J numbers for each board, which are slightly different. There are also some minor caveats to take into consideration; note that there may also be some minor labeling errors on the developer reference board artwork.

**Table 15-2.** *Antenna Connector Numbers*

| Label | Type 5 | Type 10 | Description |
|-------|--------|---------|-------------|
| ANT 1 | J28 | J514 | This is a 5 GHz Wi-Fi antenna connector. The Type 5 circuit schematic describes this as a second CPU ZIGBEE ANT whilst on the Type 10 it is described as CPU WIFI ANT. The printing on the Type 5 developer reference board is confusing because there is a spurious J6 label closest to this connector and the J28 label is nearer to another component. The circuit schematics are taken to be the definitive description. |
| ANT 2 | J23 | J28 | This is a combo 25 GHz Wi-Fi and Bluetooth antenna connection. The circuit schematic describes this as CPU WIFI ANT. |
| ANT 3 | J21 | J21 | This antenna supports the ZigBee transmissions. The circuit schematic describes this as CPU ZIGBEE ANT. |
| Z-WAVE | J16 | J16 | This is for connecting a Z-Wave antenna. The Z-Wave functionality is implemented on the developer reference board. Reproduce this in your product design if you need it. The Type 5 and 10 designs are very similar when you compare the circuit schematics. |
| LPWA | J15 | J15 | This is for connecting an LPWA antenna. Use the small antenna on this SMA connector. It correctly matches the wavelength of the LPWA broadcasts. The LPWA functionality is implemented on the developer reference board. Reproduce this in your product design if you need it. The design is slightly different when you compare the Type 5 and Type 10 circuit schematics. |

# Miniature Coaxial Connectors

The radio frequency (RF) signals for Wi-Fi must be taken off the ARTIK modules separately to the Panasonic AXT multi-pin connectors mounted on the base of the module. This is to avoid interference between the RF and the sensitive high-speed digital signals on the multi-pin connectors. It is impractical to mount the SMA-F antenna sockets directly onto the ARTIK modules so these connections are made via short coaxial cables from miniature connectors on the top surface of the ARTIK modules. The coaxial cable provides RF screening for compliance with the FCC regulations and noise immunity. The connections are made via a **U.FL-R-SMT** Hirose connector. Obtain them from the usual suppliers. Figure 15-3 shows the top and side views of the miniature co-axial connector.

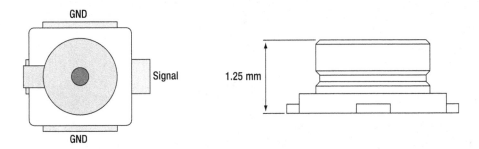

***Figure 15-3.*** *Miniature coaxial connector*

Refer to the following URLs for data sheets to find out more about these connectors to incorporate them into your product design:

```
www.farnell.com/datasheets/307202.pdf
www.wellshow.com/
www.rfcoaxcable.com/
www.digikey.com/product-detail/en/hirose-electric-co-ltd/U.FL-R-SMT(10)/H9161CT-ND/2135256
```

The antenna connectors are named the same on the ARTIK 5 and 10 modules. Table 15-3 lists the names and purpose of each miniature coaxial connector.

***Table 15-3.*** *ARTIK Module Antenna Connectors*

| Antenna | Used for |
| --- | --- |
| ANT1 | 5 GHz Wi-Fi |
| ANT2 | Combo 2.5 GHz Wi-Fi and Bluetooth |
| ANT3 | ZigBee transmissions |

The locations of the miniature coaxial connectors on an ARTIK 5 module are shown in Figure 15-4 and the ARTIK 10 in Figure 15-5. They are arranged differently on each ARTIK module but they serve the same purpose.

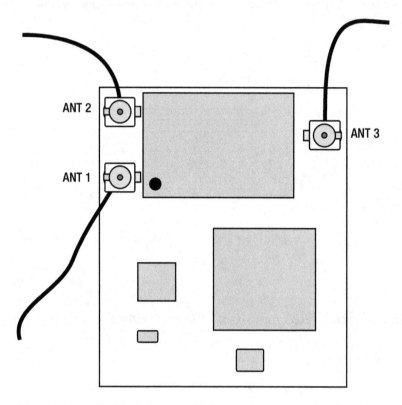

***Figure 15-4.*** *ARTIK 5 miniature coaxial connectors*

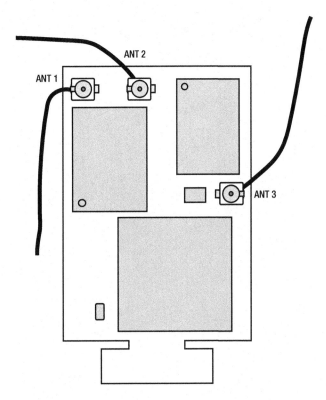

***Figure 15-5.*** *ARTIK 10 miniature coaxial connectors*

# Summary

Although this chapter is small and may appear trivial, the penalties for shipping non-compliant products are quite severe and expensive to remedy. You owe it to yourself to make sure the radio frequency emissions from your ARTIK-based product are compliant with all the government regulations in the territories where you intend to sell your designs.

# CHAPTER 16

■ ■ ■

# The API Kits

There is no single Application Programming Interface (API) in the ARTIK operating system. In fact, there are many. What you want to accomplish with your ARTIK dictates which of the available API tools, SDKs, and libraries you should use to build your application. Most of the API support comes in the form of well-known open source libraries that have been used by developers for years. The major benefit of this is the scope of online resources that are already available. Samsung has accomplished a major achievement by condensing an entire Linux workstation into something the size of a large postage stamp. You can exploit this power by using the API kits that are already built-in to the ARTIK, or you can add more.

## Samsung-Provided API Support

A lot of new software components are being made available to support the release of the Commercial Beta ARTIK 520 and 1020 modules. Although at the time of writing the API support for proprietary Samsung technologies is not yet released, the engineers are hard at work getting it ready; by the time you read this, the API support should start to be delivered via the developer web site. Combining the Samsung API support with the open source components should provide you with everything you need to build powerful and sophisticated solutions.

## Documents to Gather

Before you commence any serious development work, it is a good idea to gather the technical resources from the Samsung developer web site. Find the technical specification data sheets and product briefing documents on the Samsung developer web site. They contain useful information. The developer board schematic diagrams also tell you about the connectivity of your ARTIK and provide prototype designs of auxiliary circuits you can add around an ARTIK and incorporate into your own designs. The operating system source code is now available on the Git repository, which you can map into your development workstation and download.

Other useful information can be found in the most unexpected places. There are third-party web sites with details of alternative operating systems for the ARTIK. They often have useful details about the internals, although they are described in the context of a different OS. When they relate to the hardware, the information is likely to be close to what to expect when running the ARTIK OS. The home web sites for the main operating system components also have useful material that helps you better understand your ARTIK internals. After all, a great deal of the ARTIK design is based on open source projects.

The available documentation varies from one ARTIK model to another. The following links take you to useful starting points within the Samsung developer documentation web site. You must be logged in via a developer account to access them. Registering for one is very easy. Explore these resources thoroughly and get to know what is available. Check from time to time to collect new items as they are added.

© Cliff Wootton 2016
C. Wootton, *Samsung ARTIK Reference*, DOI 10.1007/978-1-4842-2322-2_16

```
https://developer.artik.io/
www.artik.io/gettingstarted
www.artik.io/developer/documentation
https://developer.artik.io/downloads
```

# Where Are the APIs?

With a product as versatile and complex as an ARTIK, the APIs come in a variety of different forms. Often they are not described as an API. Your task as an application programmer is to use any of them to interact with the ARTIK while adding your unique functionality into the mix. They are the handles and levers your application can operate to control the ARTIK module. Some of them let your application listen for messages from the ARTIK to tell you what it is doing. Table 16-1 describes the important interfacing mechanisms.

*Table 16-1.* *Application Programming Interface Mechanisms*

| Interface | Description |
| --- | --- |
| Configuration files | Alter the parameters in these files to control the behavior of the system. |
| Compiled object code libraries | Link the object files, libraries, and frameworks to your application when you compile it. Object files result from compiling a single file. Libraries are collections of those object files in a single container, and a framework is a more structured set of code that manages a subsystem within the ARTIK OS. |
| Arduino sketch source code | Run this code natively inside the ARTIK via the Arduino emulator. |
| Physical files | These are files in the physically manifested parts of the file system to open and read or write to. Typically they live in the /etc or /var directories, but there may be other places to look for them if you have installed additional software. |
| Virtual regular files | The kernel creates these virtual files within the virtual file systems that it builds as the ARTIK is started up. They map to objects inside the kernel so your application can access them from user space. The virtual file systems are mounted as the /sys, /run, /proc, and /dev directories. Additionally, the kernel debug support is mounted as the /sys/kernel/debug directory. |
| Compiled Arduino sketches | Cross-compile these sketches inside the Arduino IDE using the ARTIK board manager and the libArduino plug-in. |
| Temboo (via Arduino IDE) | Build your code on the Temboo web site and then download it to your development workstation. Load it into the Arduino IDE, which you will already have configured with the ARTIK libArduino plug-in. Cross- compile it and install the executable binary on your ARTIK module. |
| Temboo (Native) | Build your code on the Temboo web site and then download it to your ARTIK, compile it natively, and link it against the Temboo libraries when they are supported. |
| Node.js | Interact with regular files inside the /sys directory (sysfs virtual file system) |
| Python | Interact with regular files inside the /sys directory (sysfs virtual file system) |
| GPIO | Interact with regular files inside the /sys directory (sysfs virtual file system). Or map the GPIO kernel memory into your application and operate on it directly. |

(*continued*)

*Table 16-1.* (*continued*)

| Interface | Description |
|---|---|
| Analog input | Use the `sysfs` regular files from `bash` shells or the C language. The same techniques work for Node.js and Python. It is possible to interact directly via the kernel but the complexity usually outweighs the advantage. The new IIO subsystem may also come into play when using ADC to measure sensor inputs. |
| PWM Output | Use the Arduino interface or access the individual PWM channels via `sysfs`. |
| I2C | Use the I2C tools to manipulate the I2C interface or reverse engineer the source code of those tools to interact directly with the kernel from the C language using `ioctl()` function calls on the `/dev` device for the I2C bus you want to interact with. |
| SPI | The user space support for SPI is not yet implemented in the ARTIK modules. Later you can interact with video-related subsystems via the `ioctl()` functions. There may also be some `sysfs` support added later for accessing the ARM MALI GPU. |
| Power management | There are opportunities to access the power management capabilities with the `systemctl` command, Arduino functions, and also via the GPIO and I2C interfaces. |
| I2S audio | The audio facilities are best managed via the ALSA library. Since that is an open source kit and well supported, audio interaction from your application should be straightforward. |
| Video | The video support is managed via the Video4Linux open source project. The built-in support is not yet complete as of the Commercial Beta but more features will be implemented in later releases. |

# Compiled Object Code Libraries

There are supporting object code libraries to bind into a compiled application written in the C language or one of its derivatives. If you are using an interpreted language such as Python or Node, these libraries are accessible via a language binding. The Fortran library expects all parameters passed to function calls to be delivered by reference rather than value. If you want to pass literal constants, they must be converted to an indirect reference to the value. Fortran needs a very thin layer of glue code inserted as a shim to convert the function arguments to the correct format to reuse libraries that were originally written for C language programmers. Your C language applications can be natively coupled to the library more directly. Figure 16-1 shows how the different kinds of language bindings fit together.

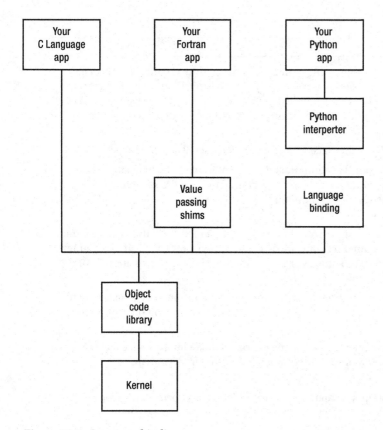

*Figure 16-1. Language bindings*

# I/O Structure

Your application code relies on libraries of pre-written software to provide fundamental capabilities that themselves are built on foundations lower down in the operating system. When you print a single character to console, it translates eventually to a series of bits being sent out on a serial interface or a packet being transmitted via a network connection. If you had to be concerned with the minutiae of that, you would never finish writing your application. The parts of the library toolkit that you care about live in the user space with your application code. The lower levels of those libraries have conduits that talk to the kernel, where more privileged actions occur. To simplify things a lot, the activity in the kernel can be subdivided into three categories:

- Character streams

- Block read/write

- Hardware interactions

Character streams can be incoming keystrokes from your keyboard or outgoing characters to a console screen. There are other variations on this where characters are read from a file or written out to another. The streams may be connected to remote systems via a network and presented to your application as a regular file for access. Character streams are also used when you interact with the regular files in the virtual file systems.

Block read/write is for bulk transfer of data to and from storage devices. This includes virtual disks, network-mounted storage, removable disks, and physically attached devices. By making them all look like regular files, your application code is greatly simplified. It can do many more things without needing specialized code to support them.

Hardware interactions manifest your calls to a library as a voltage level on a pin being raised to a logical **HIGH** value or grounded to zero volts to represent a logical **LOW**. You may be outputting a variable analog voltage but even this is described digitally inside your application. Reading the input-sensed values from the hardware is managed here too. Hardware interaction also includes the control of peripheral devices attached to the CPU such as the audio and video subsystems and the graphics processing unit (GPU). There are a variety of alternatives for this, such as I2C, I2S, IIO, and SPI. Figure 16-2 illustrates a simplified structural organization of these I/O interfaces; the hardware-interfacing mechanisms are covered in their own chapters.

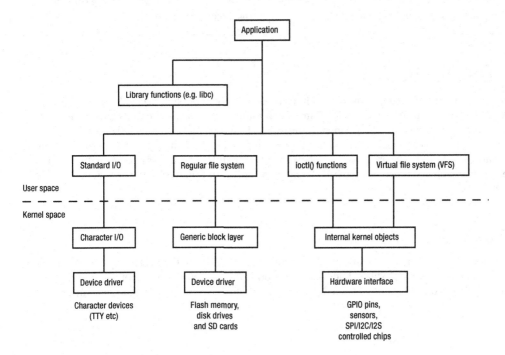

*Figure 16-2. I/O interface organization*

# Finding Out About Devices

Using your forensic and reverse engineering skills, consult the Device Tree Source code and kernel configuration files in the Exynos version of the Linux kernel and compare them against what you find inside the ARTIK. Go to https://github.com/torvalds/linux/blob/master/arch/arm/boot/dts/exynos3250-artik5.dtsi. They describe the device configuration that the kernel uses at boot time to build the /dev file system. Later, the kernel loads additional modules. Make sure you look at the included files that are cited in the main source file for the device tree. Some shared functionality is defined in the files that applies to several similar Exynos architectures.

## Temboo

The Temboo tools are a huge help because they generate working code that you can learn from. This code shows you how to access the Arduino-compatible pins in your ARTIK module directly from the C Language or Node.js and other languages. The early prototype ARTIK support in the Temboo tools was covered in the companion book, *Beginning Samsung ARTIK*. Access more detailed information at the Temboo web site at www.temboo.com/.

---

■ **Note**   The Temboo library is not yet included in the Commercial Beta operating system for the ARTIK modules. Until that support is complete and working by default, you can use Temboo to generate Arduino-compatible code that you can load into the Arduino IDE and cross-compile ARTIK compatible apps using the libArduino plug-in available from the Samsung ARTIK developer resources web page.

---

## Where Else to Look

Because the ARTIK operating system is based on Linux, there are a lot of publicly accessible resources on the World Wide Web with lots of helpful advice. Some open source technologies are well documented and others less so. Search for related topics and inspect the internals of your ARTIK once you know what to look for. After you assimilate that knowledge and understand the technology, you are ready to experiment with an idea. It is not always easy but it is very satisfying when you get something to work as a result of the learning experience. If you are the first one to explore that technology, post your findings for the benefit of the rest of the ARTIK community.

## Summary

This chapter looked at the overall API support that is built into the ARTIK. In the next few chapters, the peripheral interface buses will be explored one at a time. You may not need to know about all of them at first, but it is very likely you will eventually need to interact with them as your design goals become more ambitious.

■ ■ ■

# CHAPTER 17

# General Purpose Input/Output (GPIO)

The General Purpose Input/Output (GPIO) interfaces supported by the ARTIK modules have evolved out of a simple need to sense an input pin value or set an output pin value from within your application. This is expanded to include a variety of peripheral bus systems for controlling external devices and much more sophisticated ways to manage input and output. The term GPIO has itself evolved to mean much more than it used to. Hardware engineers use the term to describe a simple 1-bit input/output pin. The kernel developers see GPIO as being much broader than that. The latest innovations in pin multiplexing inside the kernel allow GPIO pins to be highly configurable and properties such as drive voltage, bias, and debouncing control are becoming accessible to the application developer. Pin multiplexing is dealt with at the end of this chapter because it is such an advanced topic.

## About GPIO in the ARTIK

This chapter also examines the inner workings of the `pinctrl` driver to help you understand the foundations. This explains why base address values are important. It also explains how to interact with the GPIO pins from your own application.

The GPIO interface provides digital I/O channels to use for reading data from external hardware or writing values out to it. The data you write could be simple digital information setting the state of an output **HIGH** or **LOW**. When you read a value, the digital inputs tell you the binary state of a connection.

The GPIO interface is used for controlling strictly digital outputs or reading digital inputs. The kernel controls this interface via the `pinctrl` device described in the `sysfs` virtual file system. Because the ARTIK is based in part on the Arduino specification, the GPIO may appear to have some analog capabilities but GPIO interfaces are simple binary switching pins whose value can only be **HIGH** or **LOW**. Pseudo analog output is accomplished using a pulse width modulated (PWM) output whose duty cycle is modified to change the perceived brightness of an LED. The PWM output is described in detail in Chapter 19.

The Samsung ARTIK data sheets describe type A and B GPIO pins. The Type A GPIO pins in an ARTIK expect the input voltage to be no greater than 1.8v to indicate a **HIGH** value. The Type B pins can cope with a 3.3v input to indicate a **HIGH** value. This is a purely Samsung convention described only in the data sheets for each ARTIK module. Find out more about GPIO at the electronics stack exchange at `http://electronics.stackexchange.com/questions/104456/`

## Pin Modes

After you have exported the GPIO hardware pins to the user space, they can be set into input or output mode. You use input mode to read a switch or sensor and output mode to control a light or motor. Table 17-1 summarizes the sort of things you might control or manage with GPIO.

***Table 17-1.*** *Example Use of GPIO by Signal Type and Direction*

| Description | Mode | Value |
|---|---|---|
| Is a window or door open? | Input | A switch pulls the GPIO pin up to Vcc when the window is closed. |
| Is it day or night? | Input | Measure the voltage drop across a light-dependent resistor. |
| Turning a light on or off | Output | Drive a lighting controller via a transistor or thyristor circuit. |
| Set the brightness of an LED | Output | PWM pseudo analog strobed output with higher duty cycle indicating a brighter LED. |

Choosing whether to switch things **HIGH** or **LOW** when you are sensing may affect the current drain on your design. What percentage of the time is a high voltage asserted and what are the implications for battery capacity?

GPIO controls can be used to switch the operation of peripheral hardware chips whose values are driven by other interface types such as I2C or I2S. Complex chips such as the Ethernet controller or the audio codec on the developer reference board use these hybrid combinations of interface controls.

## Digital Input

Define the GPIO pin you want to control as an input and then read the value. There are two possible values when you are sensing a digital input:

- **LOW**: Pulled down to Ground (0v)

- **HIGH**: Pulled up to Vcc level

---

■ **Note** On some earlier prototype boards, these values were reversed and **HIGH** was 0v and **LOW** was Vcc. The Commercial Beta developer reference boards work correctly.

---

See this Samsung developer tutorial for a working example of how to read a digital input connected to a button: https://developer.artik.io/documentation/tutorials/read-a-button.html.

If a pin has its operating mode set to input, writing a value to it has no effect. Internally, the kernel discards the bits that map to an input pin. If you have a mixture of input and output pins in a GPIO port register, you may be able to condense your code and possibly even avoid a Read ➤ Modify ➤ Write operation in favor of a simple write. To do this, you must know the correct values for all the output pins so some caching logic inside your application may be necessary. Caching presents problems because the pin state or value may change, which would invalidate your cache. Caching data in this context is always risky. Consider each individual case on its own merits.

You might observe that your digital read only ever reports a 1 value. Reading a digital input pin should return a binary 1 or 0 depending on the state of the sensor or switch that is connected to it. Internally, the pins are pulled up to a 3.3v level with a 10KΩ resistance. Your hardware needs to defeat this and ground the pin to ensure that it returns a zero value. Then the GPIO value and the Arduino `digitalRead()` function should return the correct result. This behavior may also occur when you read the digital inputs in other contexts.

## Digital Output

Define the GPIO pin you want to control as an output and then write the value. The same **LOW** and **HIGH** values apply to digital input and output. When you assert a **LOW** value on a GPIO output pin, it is pulled down to 0v as if it had been shorted to ground. Asserting a **HIGH** value pulls it up to Vcc. Your code design affects how fast you can cycle the changes. Refer to these Samsung developer articles relating to digital outputs:

https://developer.artik.io/documentation/tutorials/blink-an-led.html
www.artik.io/2015/09/artik-gpio-using-digital-outputs/

# Exploring GPIO

The GPIO functionality is implemented via two instances of the pinctrl kernel driver module. These are loaded during the ARTIK boot process. Although Samsung gives them names, only the base address of these drivers is visible from the user space. That base address is sufficient to identify each driver and the interfaces it is responsible for managing. Each driver is a container for a set of GPIO ports. Those ports have names, which can be used as keys to navigate the GPIO hierarchy in the sysfs file system and kernel.

Each port contains several registers, each containing a bitmap that corresponds to GPIO pins to which you can connect hardware. Port GPX0 bit 1 is connected to header J26 pin 3 and delivers the XEINT_1 interface from your ARTIK module through a voltage level convertor/buffer to the connector. Bit 1 in all of the associated registers within GPX0 manages different aspects of that GPIO. Usually you only access a MODE and DATA register but in some hardware implementations, GPIO offers several other registers within the named port. Figure 17-1 shows how this is all integrated together inside the ARTIK.

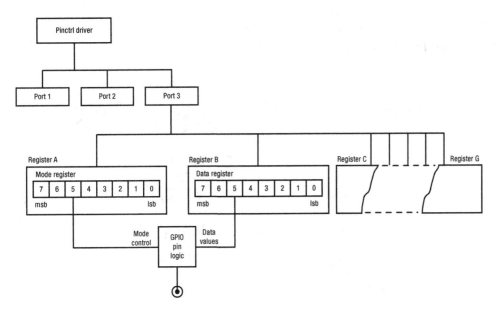

***Figure 17-1.*** *GPIO organization*

# Developer Board GPIO Pinouts

Program the GPIO interfaces from a language that accesses sysfs as if it were regular files. Use the appropriate pin export numbers, signal names, and kernel level I/O port addresses for the individual pins.

Although the pins are arranged in the same physical layout on the Type 5 and Type 10 developer reference boards, the pin addresses are exported to different locations in the virtual file system when viewed as sysfs-accessible GPIO pins. Modify your application source code to cope with this. Figure 17-2 illustrates the pin layout of the Arduino compatible pins on J26 and J27 while Figure 17-3 shows the analog input pins on J24. The analog input pins are described in Chapter 18. The labels on the board are the Arduino-compatible names for the pins. Your application accesses the pins using I/O port addresses through the sysfs interface or directly via the kernel.

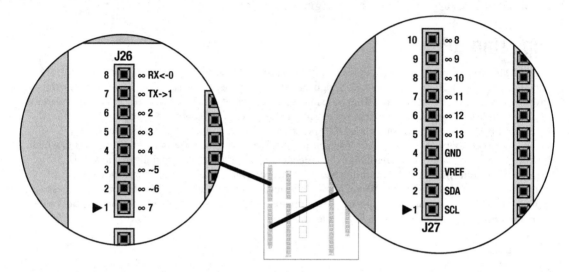

*Figure 17-2.* *Type 5 and 10 Arduino pins (J26 and J27)*

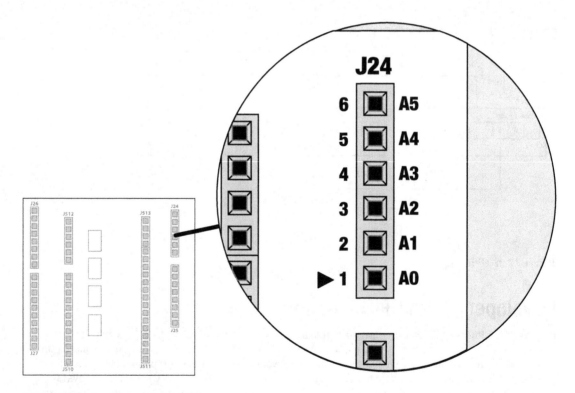

*Figure 17-3.* *Analog input pins (J24)*

Table 17-2 lists the available Arduino-compatible GPIO and I2S/I2C pin connections on a Type 5 or 10 developer reference board.

*Table 17-2.* *Arduino-Compatible Header Pins on a Developer Reference Board*

| Header | Label | Description |
| --- | --- | --- |
| J26-8 | RX<-0 | Arduino serial RX input via the Serial object |
| J26-7 | TX->1 | Arduino serial TX output via the Serial object |
| J26-6 | ∞2 | Arduino-compatible pin 2 |
| J26-5 | ∞3 | Arduino-compatible pin 3. Some Arduino devices implement an additional PWM here but the ARTIK does not. |
| J26-4 | ∞4 | Arduino-compatible pin 4 |
| J26-3 | ~5 | Use for PWM output with the analogWrite() function. |
| J26-2 | ~6 | Use for PWM output with the analogWrite() function. |
| J26-1 | ∞7 | Arduino-compatible pin 7 |
| J27-10 | ∞8 | Arduino-compatible pin 8 |
| J27-9 | ∞9 | Arduino-compatible pin 9. Some Arduino devices implement an additional PWM here but the ARTIK does not. |
| J27-8 | ∞10 | Arduino-compatible pin 10. Some Arduino devices implement an additional PWM here but the ARTIK does not. |
| J27-7 | ∞11 | Arduino-compatible pin 11. Some Arduino devices implement an additional PWM here but the ARTIK does not. |
| J27-6 | ∞12 | Arduino-compatible pin 12 |
| J27-5 | ∞13 | Arduino-compatible pin 13 |
| J27-4 | GND | Ground |
| J27-3 | VREF | Reference voltage for ADC converters |
| J27-2 | SDA | Bus I2C-7 SDA |
| J27-1 | SCL | Bus I2C-7 SCL |
| J24-1 | A0 | Analog input channel 0 |
| J24-2 | A1 | Analog input channel 1 |
| J24-3 | A2 | Analog input channel 2 (ARTIK 10 only) |
| J24-4 | A3 | Analog input channel 3 (ARTIK 10 only) |
| J24-5 | A4 | Analog input channel 4 (ARTIK 10 only) |
| J24-6 | A5 | Analog input channel 5 (ARTIK 10 only) |
| J25-8 | Vin | Reference voltage for analog inputs |
| J25-7 | GND | Ground |
| J25-6 | GND | Ground |
| J25-5 | 5V | 5v supply |
| J25-4 | 3.3V | 3.3v supply |
| J25-3 | RESET | External reset pin |
| J25-2 | IOREF | Reference voltage for I/O signals (a.k.a VREF) |
| J25-1 | N/C | No connection |

In addition to the Arduino-compatible header pins, the developer reference boards also have some auxiliary GPIO and peripheral interfacing pins, which are listed in Table 17-3. The circuit schematics describe these as test points and debugging connectors.

**Table 17-3.** *Auxiliary Test and Debugging Header Pins*

| Header | Label | Description |
|--------|-------|-------------|
| J510-1 | MAIN_BAT | Main battery voltage output |
| J510-2 | ADC0 | Analog to digital converter 0 |
| J510-3 | ADC1 | Analog to digital converter 1 |
| J510-4 | GND | Ground |
| J510-5 | SDA3 | Bus I2C-3 SDA |
| J510-6 | SCL3 | Bus I2C-3 SCL |
| J510-7 | AP_NRESET | Master reset pin (a.k.a. RST/MRNRESET) |
| J510-8 | N/C | No connection |
| J510-9 | N/C | No connection |
| J510-10 | N/C | No connection |
| J510-11 | GND | Ground |
| J510-12 | 3.3V | 3.3v supply |
| J511-1 | I2S2_SCLK | Bus I2S-2 SCLK Serial Clock line |
| J511-2 | I2S2_LRCK | Bus I2S-2 LRCK Left-Right Clock line |
| J511-3 | I2S2_SDI | Bus I2S-2 SDI Serial data in line |
| J511-4 | I2C1_SDA | Bus I2C-1 SDA |
| J511-5 | I2C1_SCL | Bus I2C-1 SCL |
| J511-6 | I2S2_SDO | Bus I2S-2 SDO Serial data out line |
| J511-7 | I2S2_CDCLK | Bus I2S-2 CDCLK CD clock line |
| J511-8 | N/C | No connection |
| J511-9 | N/C | No connection |
| J511-10 | UART_TXD | Serial interface out |
| J511-11 | UART_RXD | Serial interface in |
| J511-12 | SPIMISO1 | Bus SPI-1 MISO |
| J511-13 | SPIMOSI1 | Bus SPI-1 MOSI |
| J511-14 | SPICLK1 | Bus SPI-1 CLK |
| J511-15 | SPICSN1 | Bus SPI-1 CSN |
| J512-1 | GND | Ground |
| J512-2 | INT0 | Interrupt 0 |
| J512-3 | INT1 | Interrupt 1 |
| J512-4 | INT2 | Interrupt 2 |

*(continued)*

*Table 17-3.* (*continued*)

| Header | Label | Description |
|--------|-------|-------------|
| J512-5 | GPM3_0 | GPIO I/O pin 0 |
| J512-6 | GPM3_1 | GPIO I/O pin 1 |
| J513-1 | 32763 Hz | 32 kHz clock output (BT32K_PM) |
| J513-2 | GND | Ground |
| J513-3 | PWM1 | Pulse Width Modulated output 1 |
| J513-4 | PWM0 | Pulse Width Modulated output 0 |

# Reserved Pins

Although there are many programmable pins on the ARTIK modules, some pins are reserved for dedicated functionality. These may be connected to other hardware inside the module or devices on the developer reference board that extend the capabilities of the ARTIK. A few are not connected to anything although they may be used later. The Audio codec chip is controlled by reserved GPIO pin numbers. They configure the codec to receive audio samples delivered via a separate I2S interface. This hybrid mode of operation is not unusual in embedded systems. A combination of control mechanisms is often used to manage complex peripheral hardware.

Download a copy of the schematic diagrams and the data sheets for your developer reference board and study them carefully to identify the various connectors. Get to know these diagrams and data sheets well because they have a lot of useful knowledge embedded within them. They are the most reliable source of pinout descriptions for each of the connectors. There are currently only schematic diagrams for the Type 5 and Type 10 boards: `https://developer.artik.io/downloads`.

Samsung make a special point about some of these pins not being tampered with. If they are predefined as input or output pins, modifying their behavior is dangerous and according to Samsung, you may damage your ARTIK module or deactivate critical components such as the Ethernet controller or the audio and video codec hardware. This is particularly of concern if you are writing kernel level code. Samsung also mentions shared control registers as an area where you can cause problems when you write your own kernel level code. Shared registers are where a specific bit is reserved for special functionality. The implications of this are that not only are there reserved pins but there are reserved values that can be asserted onto some pins. Writing the wrong value may contain a binary digit (bit) value, which is incorrect for that port. You could repurpose them if for example your product does not need the audio codec. That frees up some useful GPIO and I2C lines.

Always use a Read ➤ Modify ➤ Write approach when setting values on these registers. This way you preserve the current values on the registers and only alter the ones you intend. Do not cache your values because they may be changed by other processes and your cached value would then be incorrect and would undo the change made by the other party. These kinds of bugs are notoriously difficult to trace and fix.

# Active Levels

The general-purpose physical I/O pins on an ARTIK module can be programmed dynamically to become either an input or a driven output by setting their MODE before you try to read or set their value.

When pins are used for output, the ARTIK drives them **HIGH** or **LOW**. A **LOW** value is considered to be equivalent to grounding the pin and setting it to 0v. A **HIGH** value is equivalent to Vcc, hence it is not a fixed value but relative to a supplied voltage. This designation is fixed by the Samsung engineering design and cannot be altered or reprogrammed. A **HIGH** value is anything greater than 66% of the Vcc reference voltage. If you need it to work the opposite way, invert the value using external hardware 74 series logic circuits.

Most of the pins work with a Vcc value of 1.8v (GPIO Type A). They do not like being driven with a higher voltage. You must be careful that any sensors you attach do not try to exceed that value without adding protective buffer circuits before connecting to the pins.

A small group of pins (GPIO Type B) can cope with a 3.3v input without requiring protective buffer circuits. These are managed via kernel port GPX0 and are attached to ARTIK pins XEINT0 to XEINT6. When programmed as an output, they still only assert 1.8v on the pin when it is driven active **HIGH**. You still need protective buffers if you want to exceed 3.3v as an input level.

Internally, a pull-up or pull-down resistor is wired to the pin so it assumes the default value when it is not being driven **HIGH** or **LOW**. A pull-down resistor needs to be driven **HIGH** to change the state of a pin and a pull-up resistor needs to be driven **LOW** to change the state of the pin. This is described as being active **HIGH** or active **LOW**.

The active **HIGH** or **LOW** designation does not affect the values of data that are read from the pins when they are set to input mode; the correct signal state is always returned (never an inverted one).

All of the GPIO pins on ARTIK are active-**HIGH** unless otherwise stated. Other programmable pins may operate differently and are noted in the ARTIK data sheets for each module type.

You may consider adding your own pull-up or pull-down resistors to stop the inputs from floating when you design your hardware and to assist the internal ones. These define a default value for the input which your sensor or switch needs to override. The stabilizing resistors must be a value of around 50KΩ to avoid too high a current drain and to allow driving circuits to override them without imposing an excessive load on the ARTIK. Depending on your sensors, you may need to use a different value.

---

■ **Note**    Earlier Alpha prototype developer reference boards had an active **LOW** output on their Arduino pins. Setting the pin value to **HIGH** forced the output voltage to zero instead and setting it to **LOW** raised the pin voltage to 3.3v.

---

# Slewing Rates

It is natural to assume the switching signals have an instantaneous change in value. In the real world, this transition takes a finite amount of time. The value of the resistors chosen may affect the signal rise or fall time of the GPIO pins when the value is changed. Signals may rise more quickly than when they fall if the pins are driven **HIGH** from a default pulled-down **LOW** state. Figure 17-4 shows how these transitions may not be as steep in both cases. The slope of these rise and fall times is called the slewing rate of the circuit. This determines how fast you can drive the signals because the slewing rate takes a finite time. You may want to observe these waveforms with an oscilloscope if timing becomes critical to your design.

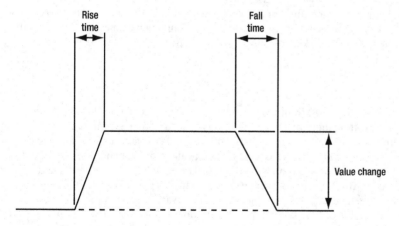

***Figure 17-4.**  Slewing rates*

# Resonant Circuits

Take into account resonant frequencies when you design switching circuits. The physics of waveforms is well understood and covered under the general topic of the Fourier series. Jean-Baptiste Joseph Fourier was a French mathematician who deduced that a complex waveform can be deconstructed into the component sine wave harmonics. When a signal changes from **LOW** to **HIGH** or vice versa, a square wave edge is created by combining an infinite number of harmonics of a fundamental Sine wave. If the design of your hardware has any resonant qualities, some of those frequencies may coincide leading to problems. If you try to improve the slewing rate of the circuit by switching faster, it introduces more frequency coefficients into the switching signal. If the circuit becomes resonant, a ringing effect can occur, which causes overshoots and instabilities in the edge detection. In extreme cases, this can lead to multiple triggers of the edge detecting logic. It is akin to debouncing keyboard inputs although that is a mechanical artifact. Figure 17-5 shows a transition with a high degree of resonant coupling.

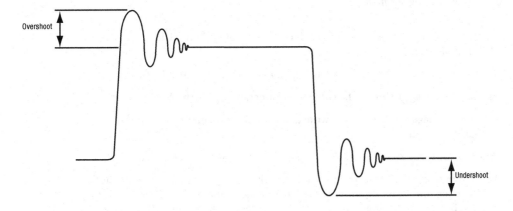

*Figure 17-5.* *Ringing artifact with resonant circuits*

If you want to understand the mathematics behind the Fourier analysis, these articles tell you how the algorithms work in detail:

```
https://en.wikipedia.org/wiki/Fourier_series
https://en.wikipedia.org/wiki/Fourier_transform
https://en.wikipedia.org/wiki/Fourier_analysis
```

# Interacting With the Hardware

There are several ways to interact with the GPIO interface. When you run an Arduino sketch inside the ARTIK, it interacts with the kernel via the Arduino interpreter. Compiled applications and bash shell command scripts can use the regular files in the sysfs virtual file system. Use a memory-mapped approach to interact more closely with the kernel. The speed advantages are minimal but the code may be more compact. Figure 17-6 shows how these different mechanisms relate to one another.

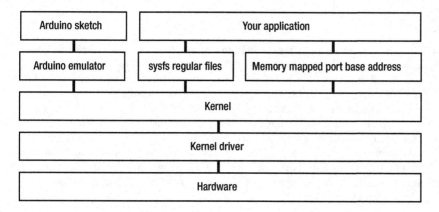

*Figure 17-6.* *GPIO interfacing hierarchy*

- Implement your application as an Arduino sketch using Arduino IDE and run it in the Arduino emulator.

- Cross-compile your Arduino sketch using libArduino and the Arduino IDE.

- Use the C language to link to the GPIO utility functions inside the ARTIK library.

- Use any language that can read or write to regular files and interface via the sysfs virtual file system.

- Talk directly to the kernel-level I/O using device driver and port addresses.

- Use Temboo to generate your source code and then compile it natively inside the ARTIK when the library support is added to the OS. Alternatively, build an Arduino-compatible sketch with Temboo and cross-compile it in the Arduino IDE. Temboo uses the above methods so it is not really an alternative way of programming but it is a much easier way to write prototype code.

Start your project design by using the Arduino IDE with its built-in GPIO functions. Then migrate your design to use sysfs calls. When you have the project debugged and working with sysfs, introduce kernel-level efficiency improvements. Attempting to do this too early can sometimes cause unforeseen difficulties during development because you cannot tell whether any problems arise from flaws in your design or mistakes you have made in the kernel-level programming. By keeping things simple at first and then moving steadily forward, the complexity introduced at each step is incremental and much easier to manage.

This chapter focuses on accessing the GPIO pins via the sysfs interface first and then illustrates how to use kernel-level I/O ports.

# Hardware Header Pin Numbers

Programming via the sysfs interface uses the GPIO export numbers. See Tables 17-4 and 17-5 for a summary of the export numbers mapped to pins. This is based on the contents of the /sys/kernel/debug/gpio file. Inspect it in your own ARTIK to check whether the pin numbers are the same or not. Use the values you find in that debugging file if they are different to the ones listed here; these are for a Commercial Beta ARTIK 5.

**Table 17-4.** *ARTIK 5 GPIO Export Numbers*

| Pin number | Label (Arduino pin names) | ARTIK 5 GPIO Export number |
|---|---|---|
| J26-1 | ∞7 | 124 |
| J26-2 | ~6 | 33 |
| J26-3 | ~5 | 32 |
| J26-4 | ∞4 | 123 |
| J26-5 | ∞3 | 122 |
| J26-6 | ∞2 | 121 |
| J26-7 | TX->1 | 13 |
| J26-8 | RX<-0 | 12 |
| J27-1 | SCL | 35 |
| J27-2 | SDA | 34 |
| J27-3 | VREF | Not a GPIO pin |
| J27-4 | GND | Not a GPIO pin |
| J27-5 | ∞13 | 135 |
| J27-6 | ∞12 | 134 |
| J27-7 | ∞11 | 129 |
| J27-8 | ∞10 | 127 |
| J27-9 | ∞9 | 126 |
| J27-10 | ∞8 | 125 |

**Table 17-5.** *ARTIK 10 GPIO Export Numbers*

| Pin number | Label (Arduino pin names) | ARTIK 10 GPIO Export number |
|---|---|---|
| J26-1 | ∞7 | 11 |
| J26-2 | ~6 | 204 |
| J26-3 | ~5 | 203 |
| J26-4 | ∞4 | 10 |
| J26-5 | ∞3 | 9 |
| J26-6 | ∞2 | 8 |
| J26-7 | TX->1 | 176 |
| J26-8 | RX<-0 | 175 |
| J27-1 | SCL | 188 |
| J27-2 | SDA | 187 |
| J27-3 | VREF | Not a GPIO pin |
| J27-4 | GND | Not a GPIO pin |

*(continued)*

***Table 17-5.*** (*continued*)

| Pin number | Label (Arduino pin names) | ARTIK 10 GPIO Export number |
|---|---|---|
| J27-5 | ∞13 | 22 |
| J27-6 | ∞12 | 21 |
| J27-7 | ∞11 | 16 |
| J27-8 | ∞10 | 14 |
| J27-9 | ∞9 | 13 |
| J27-10 | ∞8 | 12 |

# Using Arduino Emulation

Possibly the most simple approach to accessing the pins on your developer reference board is to use the Arduino emulation. Avoid the complexities of device address mapping and use the same source code across both the ARTIK 5 and 10 modules. The GPIO pins can be configured as digital inputs or outputs. They are equivalent to Arduino named pins 2 to 4 and 7 to 13. These are not pin numbers but symbolic Arduino-compatible names. Be careful not to confuse these pin names with the pin numbers on the header connectors because they are in reverse order with respect to each other. To interact with a GPIO pin, define whether it is an input or output and then read or write to it accordingly. This technique is well documented in the Arduino resources available online. Later, convert your designs from this approach to use the sysfs interfaces when your project becomes more advanced.

Tables 17-6 and 17-7 summarize the GPIO- and Arduino-related connections available on the AXT connectors underneath your ARTIK module. The connections for the ARTIK 5 and 10 are each shown in their own tables. Refer to the data sheets for more information about voltage levels and other detailed specifications regarding these pins.

***Table 17-6.*** *ARTIK 5 GPIO and Arduino AXT Pinouts*

| AXT pin | Name | Function |
|---|---|---|
| J3-11 | XEINT_14 | General-purpose interrupt or IO/Arduino pin 13 |
| J3-12 | XEINT_13 | General-purpose interrupt or IO/Arduino pin 12 |
| J3-16 | XEINT_8 | General-purpose interrupt or IO/Arduino pin 11 |
| J3-20 | XEINT_6 | General-purpose interrupt or IO/Arduino pin 10 |
| J3-22 | XEINT_5 | General-purpose interrupt or IO/Arduino pin 9 |
| J3-24 | XEINT_4 | General-purpose interrupt or IO/Arduino pin 8 |
| J3-26 | XEINT_3 | General-purpose interrupt or IO/Arduino pin 7 |
| J3-28 | XEINT_2 | General-purpose interrupt or IO/Arduino pin 4 |
| J3-30 | XEINT_1 | General-purpose interrupt or IO/Arduino pin 3 |
| J3-32 | XEINT_0 | General-purpose interrupt or IO/Arduino pin 2 |
| J3-38 | Xu3_RXD | Arduino pin 0 (RX<-0) |
| J3-40 | Xu3_TXD | Arduino pin 1 (TX->1) |

(*continued*)

***Table 17-6.*** (*continued*)

| AXT pin | Name | Function |
|---|---|---|
| J3-44 | Xadc0AIN0 | Analog ADC Input 0 |
| J3-46 | Xadc0AIN1 | Analog ADC Input 1 |
| J4-11 | Xi2c7_SDA | Bus I2C-7 SDA |
| J4-13 | Xi2c7_SCL | Bus I2C-7 SCL |
| J4-45 | Xpwmo_1 | General purpose interrupt or IO or PWM output/Arduino pin 6 |
| J4-47 | Xpwmo_0 | General purpose interrupt or IO or PWM output/Arduino pin 5 |

***Table 17-7.*** *ARTIK 10 GPIO and Arduino AXT Pinouts*

| AXT pin | Name | Function |
|---|---|---|
| J1-17 | XEINT_13 | General-purpose interrupt or IO/Arduino pin 12 |
| J1-19 | XEINT_14 | General-purpose interrupt or IO/Arduino pin 13 |
| J1-18 | XEINT_8 | General-purpose interrupt or IO/Arduino pin 11 |
| J1-22 | XEINT_6 | General-purpose interrupt or IO/Arduino pin 10 |
| J1-24 | XEINT_5 | General-purpose interrupt or IO/Arduino pin 9 |
| J1-26 | XEINT_4 | General-purpose interrupt or IO/Arduino pin 8 |
| J1-28 | XEINT_3 | General-purpose interrupt or IO/Arduino pin 7 |
| J1-30 | XEINT_2 | General-purpose interrupt or IO/Arduino pin 4 |
| J1-32 | XEINT_1 | General-purpose interrupt or IO/Arduino pin 3 |
| J1-34 | XEINT_0 | General-purpose interrupt or IO/Arduino pin 2 |
| J1-42 | Xu1_RXD | Arduino pin 0 (RX<-0) |
| J1-44 | Xu1_TXD | Arduino pin 1 (TX->1) |
| J1-48 | Xadc0AIN0 | Analog ADC input |
| J1-50 | Xadc0AIN1 | Analog ADC input |
| J1-52 | Xadc0AIN2 | Analog ADC input |
| J1-54 | Xadc0AIN5 | Analog ADC input |
| J1-56 | Xadc0AIN6 | Analog ADC input |
| J1-58 | Xadc0AIN7 | Analog ADC input |
| J2-67 | Xpwmo_1 | General purpose interrupt or IO or PWM output/Arduino pin 6 |
| J2-69 | Xpwmo_0 | General purpose interrupt or IO or PWM output/Arduino pin 5 |

# GPIO Via sysfs

A more sophisticated alternative to the Arduino solution is to drive the GPIO via the sysfs virtual file system that the kernel builds when the ARTIK OS is started up. This makes the GPIO interface objects inside the kernel available to your own applications as a collection of regular files that are accessible from the user space. Your code must take into account platform differences. The GPIO pin mapping base addresses may also change if the OS is upgraded and the kernel maps the devices differently.

The generic Linux `sysfs` functionality is very easy to use for many application scenarios. Translating to `sysfs`-style access from an Arduino-style approach is not very complicated if you built an earlier prototype using the Arduino IDE. Later, refactor your design to use the kernel-based memory mapped GPIO technique. There are two key benefits to using the `sysfs` virtual file system interface:

- Access to each GPIO pin is via a simple regular file read or write. Determine the correct path for the GPIO you want to access.

- There are many useful symbolic links and reference files you can inspect to connect the various components together. Building a map of pins to device drivers is not complex, although it may take a few steps. This helps you build a dynamic mechanism to figure out where things are.

---

■ **Note**    The Linux kernel uses the term `pinctrl` in place of GPIO. When you are searching for useful entities in `sysfs`, look out for files whose name contains the strings `pinctrl` and `gpio`.

---

The kernel reflects the GPIO from a secure, protected, kernel-controlled environment and presents them to you as a virtual file system containing regular files. Those files have properties that control whether you can read or write to them. The existence of a virtual file tells you whether a feature is present on the board. Virtual file systems respond in ways that normal files do not. Writing a value to a virtual file is intercepted by the file system manager. It sends a message to the kernel rather than storing the value in a physical file within the file system. Read this document first to understand some basic concepts and then try experimenting: www.kernel.org/doc/Documentation/gpio/sysfs.txt.

Read it again after experimenting to reinforce the learning experience. Each time you go through a read-and-experiment cycle, you build a more complete mental model of the technology you are learning about. Practice and repetition works for engineering just as effectively as for learning a musical instrument. The GPIO related entities are shown in Figure 17-7.

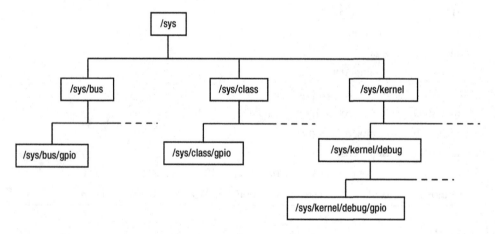

*Figure 17-7.*  *GPIO entity map*

# Using the sysfs Interface

Configure various properties of the GPIO pins via the sysfs virtual file system. The GPIO ports must be registered (exported) to user space, which reserves them for your application. Then define the input/output mode to read or write data. Once you have a working solution using sysfs, make performance improvements by aggregating the calls more efficiently.

If your application loads the CPU down so it is spending all its time servicing your needs, the system as a whole suffers from lower performance. You may choose to build kernel-level extension modules to apply changes to groups of pins. Attach a logic matrix to several pins and use various combinations of pin values (binary 1 and 0) to map an address space so the matrix can control a larger number of devices. Operating on those shared addressing lines should be done collectively. A kernel extension would certainly improve CPU performance over the alternative of controlling each wire singly. You would also solve some awkward race hazard timing issues at the same time. The performance improvements over accessing sysfs directly from a compiled C language application are less noticeable when you interact with dedicated pins.

Get it to work first using simple techniques. Make it faster later. Kernel programming is challenging and you must know what you are doing first or you may render your ARTIK unbootable. Recovery may be possible by reinstalling the OS but this puts everything back to the factory defaults. Table 17-8 lists some useful GPIO related locations within the sysfs virtual file system.

***Table 17-8.*** *Useful GPIO Locations in the sysfs File System*

| Location | Description |
|---|---|
| /sys/class/gpio | Control interface for programming GPIO via sysfs. Contains a list of chips, which is a superset of the chips across all drivers. |
| /sys/devices/*pinctrl | The kernel device driver objects for each of the GPIO drivers |
| /sys/devices/11400000. pinctrl/gpio | A list of chip objects for this driver. Each driver has a different collection and the drivers are named differently on ARTIK 5 and 10 because their base address are different. The driver base address might move if the OS is upgraded. |
| /sys/kernel/debug/gpio | A regular file containing a map of exportable GPIO numbers vs. port names |
| /sys/kernel/debug/pinctrl | Readable files with lists of pins showing how they map to the GPIO ports and their function |

# GPIO Drivers

In the ARTIK 5 and 10, the kernel installs two instances of the pinctrl driver, each of which manages a different group of ports. The GPIO drivers are named differently between the ARTIK 5 and 10 modules types. They are listed in the /sys/devices directory with the pinctrl suffix. Use this command to list the GPIO drivers in your ARTIK. This command works regardless of your model or OS vintage:

```
ls -1 /sys/devices/ | grep pinctrl
```

Table 17-9 summarizes the base addresses and GPIO driver names. These driver names do not show up in the file system so the find command cannot locate them.

***Table 17-9.*** *GPIO Driver Base Addresses*

| GPIO driver | ARTIK 5 base address | ARTIK 10 base address |
| --- | --- | --- |
| gpio0 | 0x11400000 | 0x13400000 |
| gpio1 | 0x11000000 | Not used |
| gpio2 | Not used | Not used |
| gpio3 | Not used | 0x14010000 |

The mapping in this table is probably best managed by creating manifest constants and including them within your application. The downside of this approach is that it is static and gives rise to a maintenance overhead that you must document and check with every upgrade. Several code examples are given in this book that show you how to generate base addresses dynamically for an algorithmic approach.

# Device Base Addresses

When the kernel loads device drivers, it allocates an area of memory for them to work in. The order and number of kernel drivers is a variable quantity and there are no guarantees about drivers being installed at a specific address when the OS is upgraded. Therefore, the kernel publishes a list of base addresses in the sysfs file system for your application to reference. Listing 17-1 shows the contents of the /sys/devices directory from a Commercial Beta ARTIK 5. Other models and revisions list something similar, but the base addresses are different.

***Listing 17-1.*** Driver Base Addresses in the /sys/devices Directory

```
ls /sys/devices
```

```
10000000.chipid              11e20000.sysmmu            13860000.i2c
10010000.sysreg_localout     120a0000.fimc_is_sensor    13870000.i2c
10023c00.pd-cam              12180000.fimc_is           13890000.i2c
10023c40.pd-mfc              12260000.sysmmu            138d0000.i2c
10023c60.pd-g3d              12270000.sysmmu            13920000.spi
10023c80.pd-lcd0             12280000.sysmmu            13970000.i2s
10023ca0.pd-isp              122a0000.sysmmu            139d0000.pwm
10030000.clock-controller    122b0000.sysmmu            205f000.firmware
10050000.mct                 122c0000.sysmmu            amba.0
10060000.watchdog            122d0000.sysmmu            artik_zb_power.7
10070000.rtc                 12480000.usb              bluetooth.4
100c0000.tmu                 12510000.dwmmc0           breakpoint
10481000.interrupt-controller 12520000.dwmmc1          gpio_keys.5
11000000.pinctrl             12530000.dwmmc2           ion.1
11400000.pinctrl             125b0000.usb2phy          mdev_output.2
11830000.jpeg                126c0000.adc              platform
11850000.gsc                 13000000.mali             software
11860000.gsc                 13400000.mfc              sound.6
11a20000.sysmmu              13620000.sysmmu           system
11a30000.sysmmu              13800000.serial           tracepoint
11a60000.sysmmu              13810000.serial           virtual
11c00000.fimd_fb             13820000.serial           wlan.3
11c90000.smies               13830000.serial
```

The GPIO devices have a symbolic name of pinctrl. There are two of them visible in the device listings. These are certainly different for ARTIK 5 and 10 modules. They could potentially change if the operating system is upgraded, which is very likely because Fedora is always evolving.

If your application is going to be deployed on ARTIK 5 and 10 modules, the effort of creating a dynamic mechanism to generate the physical paths to the GPIO channels may be worthwhile. Work out a way to auto discover their paths without building any static dependencies into the code by exploiting the device naming conventions. There are no devices with the GPIO port identifiers in their names. The base address can be generated from a search for the pinctrl drivers. This command lists the /sys/devices directory and filters out the two interesting items in a Commercial Beta ARTIK 5:

```
ls /sys/devices | grep pinctrl
```

```
11000000.pinctrl
11400000.pinctrl
```

These represent the two GPIO drivers gpio0 (11400000) and gpio1 (11000000). The numbering of the devices is reversed with respect to the ordering of the base address values. This illustrates an important caveat that you should never assume that things are presented in the same order or in a consistent manner within an operating system. Their positions are usually dictated by the order in which the kernel creates things at boot time, and if there is any predictability in that ordering, it would come from the kernel configuration files and device tree. It is always better to check things before making assumptions. Working things out dynamically at runtime is not particularly hard, provided you know where to look for the information. Another place to look for informative help is in the drivers directory. The following command lists the contents of the Samsung pinctrl driver container. The same two items are listed as symbolic links with several kernel driver interface controls.

```
ls /sys/bus/platform/drivers/samsung-pinctrl
```

# GPIO Chip Numbers

Tracing the GPIO pin numbers that the kernel can control involves a few steps to inspect and reverse engineer what the kernel has mapped into the sysfs virtual file system. In the /sys/class/gpio directory, there is an item representing each of the GPIO control chips. These are mapped to the port names. The GPIO pin numbers, base addresses, and offsets are then deduced from this basis. Each item in /sys/class/gpio is structured in the same way as shown for gpiochio0 in Figure 17-8.

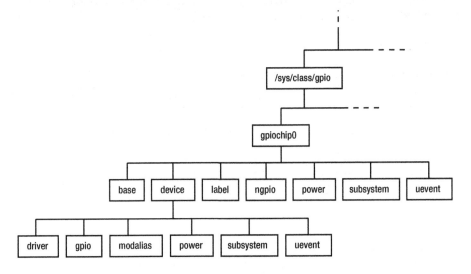

*Figure 17-8.* *GPIO chip object internal structure*

Get a list of chip numbers with this command:

```
ls -1 /sys/class/gpio/
```

Finding out how the chips map to the rest of the GPIO architecture helps you to develop a dynamic approach to GPIO interfacing, which should be robust enough to be portable across ARTIK modules and OS upgrades. Define a chip number in a shell variable:

```
MY_CHIP=0
```

Or define a wildcard match to generate output listings for all chips by setting the variable to this value:

```
MY_CHIP=*
```

Given a chip number or wild card, this shell command line instruction finds the port name each chip controls. The kernel documentation suggests this is just for diagnostic use and may not always be unique, but on inspection, it seems to behave consistently in a Commercial Beta ARTIK 5.

```
cat /sys/class/gpio/gpiochip${MY_CHIP}/label
```

This variant of the same command tells you the base GPIO export number for each chip:

```
cat /sys/class/gpio/gpiochip${MY_CHIP}/base
```

The range of GPIO export numbers for a chip is described by the ngpio value. This is how many GPIO pins the controller manages. For chip 0, whose base GPIO number is 0, there are eight GPIO signals associated with that chip. By adding ngpio to the base value, the base value for the next chip in the GPIO hierarchy is calculated in a relative fashion. This command shows you the ngpio values:

```
cat /sys/class/gpio/gpiochip${MY_CHIP}/ngpio
```

If you need the GPIO driver, the modalias value in the device directory displays the driver base address to use as a key to locate a driver description or just use the base address in your application. This command shows you the pinctrl device name containing the driver base address:

```
cat /sys/class/gpio/gpiochip${MY_CHIP}/device/modalias
```

Add a little post processing to deliver only the base address:

```
cat /sys/class/gpio/gpiochip${MY_CHIP}/device/modalias | cut -c10-17
```

Table 17-10 summarizes the results of using these commands to show how the chip numbers map to other properties.

***Table 17-10.*** *Mapping GPIO Chip Numbers to Labels and Base Addresses*

| GPIO chip | Label | Base | N-GPIO | Modalias |
|---|---|---|---|---|
| gpiochip0 | gpa0 | 0 | 8 | platform:11400000.pinctrl |
| gpiochip85 | gpa1 | 8 | 6 | platform:11400000.pinctrl |
| gpiochip145 | gpb | 14 | 8 | platform:11400000.pinctrl |
| gpiochip22 | gpc0 | 22 | 5 | platform:11400000.pinctrl |
| gpiochip27 | gpc1 | 27 | 5 | platform:11400000.pinctrl |
| gpiochip32 | gpd0 | 32 | 4 | platform:11400000.pinctrl |
| gpiochip36 | gpd1 | 36 | 4 | platform:11400000.pinctrl |
| gpiochip40 | gpe0 | 40 | 8 | platform:11000000.pinctrl |
| gpiochip48 | gpe1 | 48 | 8 | platform:11000000.pinctrl |
| gpiochip56 | gpe2 | 56 | 3 | platform:11000000.pinctrl |
| gpiochip59 | gpk0 | 59 | 8 | platform:11000000.pinctrl |
| gpiochip67 | gpk1 | 67 | 7 | platform:11000000.pinctrl |
| gpiochip74 | gpk2 | 74 | 7 | platform:11000000.pinctrl |
| gpiochip8 | gpl0 | 81 | 4 | platform:11000000.pinctrl |
| gpiochip81 | gpm0 | 85 | 8 | platform:11000000.pinctrl |
| gpiochip93 | gpm1 | 93 | 7 | platform:11000000.pinctrl |
| gpiochip100 | gpm2 | 100 | 5 | platform:11000000.pinctrl |
| gpiochip105 | gpm3 | 105 | 8 | platform:11000000.pinctrl |
| gpiochip113 | gpm4 | 113 | 8 | platform:11000000.pinctrl |
| gpiochip121 | gpx0 | 121 | 8 | platform:11000000.pinctrl |
| gpiochip129 | gpx1 | 129 | 8 | platform:11000000.pinctrl |
| gpiochip137 | gpx2 | 137 | 8 | platform:11000000.pinctrl |
| gpiochip14 | gpx3 | 145 | 8 | platform:11000000.pinctrl |

Build a table of these values inside your application to do a reverse lookup from the label containing a port name to yield a GPIO base number or driver base address.

# Interacting With sysfs

The code to interact with the GPIO interfaces is not very complicated. All of the interactions involve reading and writing to regular files. Table 17-11 summarizes the directory structure for sysfs managed GPIO pins.

***Table 17-11.*** *Managed GPIO Pins*

| Path | Description |
|------|-------------|
| /sys/class/gpio | This is where the export and unexport hooks live. There are also objects here that represent the GPIO chips that control the hardware. Any exported GPIO pins are also placed here. |
| /sys/class/gpio/export | Write a pin number to this file to export that GPIO pin to user space. |
| /sys/class/gpio/unexport | Write a pin number to this file to relinquish that GPIO pin from user space and hand it back to the kernel for another process to use. |
| /sys/class/gpio/gpio* | Exported pin numbers appear at this location where the asterisk represents the pin number. |
| /sys/class/gpio/gpio*/direction | Write the value of in or out to this location to determine the kind of access you want to use the GPIO pin for. |
| /sys/class/gpio/gpio*/value | Read or write the value for a GPIO pin. |
| /sys/class/gpio/gpio*/edge | Define the kind of edge triggering to use or view the current value. |
| /sys/class/gpio/gpio*/active_low | Manage whether the GPIO is active_low or active_high. |
| /sys/class/gpio/gpiochip* | One directory per hardware chip that implements the GPIO interface |
| /sys/class/gpio/gpiochip*/label | A diagnostic value that describes what port the chip is allocated to. |
| /sys/class/gpio/gpiochip*/base | The starting GPIO index number managed by this chip. |
| /sys/class/gpio/gpiochip*/ngpio | The number of GPIO pins managed by this chip. |

# Using bash With sysfs

In the command line shell, use the echo command to generate the value you want to send and then use I/O redirection to send the output to the target regular file. This example tells the kernel to export pin 19 to the user space:

```
echo 19 > /sys/class/gpio/export
```

In fact, any command line tool, sequence of commands, or shell functions that can generate the required output can be used. The sysfs interface is easy enough to use that many developers never contemplate memory mapped I/O via the kernel.

If you want to acquire the value of a pin, read the regular file using a C language application or perhaps use the command line cat command to take the file contents and display them on the screen:

```
cat /sys/class/gpio/gpio19/value
```

Any command line tool that can read from a regular file can be used, depending on what you are trying to accomplish.

# /sys/kernel/debug/gpio

The kernel debugging tables can be a great help when you are working out the mapping of devices in your ARTIK. Although this book is based around a Commercial Beta ARTIK 5 for its examples, the same techniques should work for an ARTIK 10. Becoming familiar with these resources helps you find the differences when you write code for each ARTIK or if things change after an OS upgrade.

The /sys/kernel/debug/gpio file is a read-only file containing a debugging table of how the GPIO interfaces are all allocated inside the ARTIK kernel. The output of this is slightly different for the ARTIK 5 and 10 modules. This tells you a lot of hidden information about the GPIO internals. Deduce the pin export numbers vs. the GPIO port names. Listing 17-2 shows the content of the file.

***Listing 17-2.*** Kernel Debug GPIO Listing

```
cat /sys/kernel/debug/gpio

GPIOs 0-7, platform/11400000.pinctrl, gpa0:
GPIOs 8-13, platform/11400000.pinctrl, gpa1:
GPIOs 14-21, platform/11400000.pinctrl, gpb:
GPIOs 22-26, platform/11400000.pinctrl, gpc0:
 gpio-25  (PDNA                ) out hi

GPIOs 27-31, platform/11400000.pinctrl, gpc1:
GPIOs 32-35, platform/11400000.pinctrl, gpd0:
GPIOs 36-39, platform/11400000.pinctrl, gpd1:
GPIOs 40-47, platform/11000000.pinctrl, gpe0:
GPIOs 48-55, platform/11000000.pinctrl, gpe1:
GPIOs 56-58, platform/11000000.pinctrl, gpe2:

GPIOs 59-66, platform/11000000.pinctrl, gpk0:
 gpio-61  (dev-pwr             ) out hi

GPIOs 67-73, platform/11000000.pinctrl, gpk1:
GPIOs 74-80, platform/11000000.pinctrl, gpk2:
GPIOs 81-84, platform/11000000.pinctrl, gpl0:
GPIOs 85-92, platform/11000000.pinctrl, gpm0:
GPIOs 93-99, platform/11000000.pinctrl, gpm1:
GPIOs 100-104, platform/11000000.pinctrl, gpm2:
GPIOs 105-112, platform/11000000.pinctrl, gpm3:
GPIOs 113-120, platform/11000000.pinctrl, gpm4:
GPIOs 121-128, platform/11000000.pinctrl, gpx0:

GPIOs 129-136, platform/11000000.pinctrl, gpx1:
 gpio-136 (bten_gpio           ) out hi

GPIOs 137-144, platform/11000000.pinctrl, gpx2:
 gpio-140 (WLAN_REG_ON         ) out hi
 gpio-144 (power key           ) in  hi

GPIOs 145-152, platform/11000000.pinctrl, gpx3:
 gpio-147 (WLAN_HOST_WAKE      ) in  lo
 gpio-149 (spi0.0              ) out hi
 gpio-151 (bthostwake_gpio     ) in  hi
 gpio-152 (btwake_gpio         ) out lo
```

# Accessing GPIO with the C Language

All of the interactions involve reading and writing to regular files. In the C language, you do this by opening a file and retaining a handle to the file buffer. The file can be opened in read, write, or read/write combined mode. These are character files rather than the binary format alternative.

To save space, only the fundamental working parts of some of these example listings are shown here. Take the functional aspects of the code and embed it inline into your own applications or place a function wrapper around it to make something reusable and call it whenever you need it.

## Using Boolean Data Types in C

Some of the examples in Samsung developer documentation show functions returning a Boolean value of true or false and a function prototype with a return value specified as a bool data type. For this to work properly, add this line at the top of your source files where you define the rest of the system includes:

```
#include <stdbool.h>
```

Without this include file you cannot use lines such as

```
bool myBinaryVariable;
myBinaryVariable = true;
bool myTestFunction() { ...function body... }
```

This Boolean support may also be particularly helpful if you decide to use the kernel memory-mapped approach to driving your GPIO pins.

## Finding a GPIO Base Address

According to the Linux kernel development team plans, the /sys/class/gpio directory is expected to disappear eventually. For now, it is a useful place to look for GPIO device mapping. This directory contains symbolic links to the devices to examine from a shell script. The script in Listing 17-3 yields a base address given a GPIO chip number.

***Listing 17-3.*** Finding a Base Address From a Chip Number in bash

```
CHIPNUM=145

ls -la /sys/class/gpio    |
  grep ${CHIPNUM}         |
  sed 's/\.pinctrl.*$//' |
  sed 's/^.*devices.//'
```

The ls command and its piped counterparts are split over several lines so they are easier to read. They should be typed on a single line when you execute the command. The CHIPNUM variable is used to define it in a variety of ways.

Use the same mechanism from the C language that worked in bash but wrap the call in a function to reuse it in a variety of different ways. If you embed the bash solution inside a C language function, hard-code the complete command or pass the port number in from outside and generate the bash command dynamically.

This small command line tool needs to be typed into a file in your ARTIK module and compiled there with the built-in GCC compiler. Go to the temporary directory and work there unless you have a more permanent place you want to test this example:

```
cd /tmp
```

Now create a source file called gpiobaseaddress.c with your vi editor and type in the code shown in Listing 17-4.

***Listing 17-4.*** GPIO Base Address Extraction Tool

```c
#include <stdio.h>
#include <stdlib.h>
#include <string>

int main( int argc, char *argv[] )
{

  FILE *fp;
  char myResult[16];
  char myFormat[96];
  char myCommand[96];

// Build the format string
// You can do this with a single literal but this method
// avoids confusing line wraps in the book listing
strcpy(myFormat, "ls -la /sys/class/gpio");
strcat(myFormat, " | grep %s");
strcat(myFormat, " | sed 's/..pinctrl.*$//'");
strcat(myFormat, " | sed 's/^.*devices.//'");

  // Manufacture a command line from the first argument
  sprintf(myCommand, myFormat, argv[1]);

  // Open the command for reading
  fp = popen(myCommand, "r");

  if (fp == NULL)
  {
    printf("Failed to run command\n" );
    exit(1);
  }

  // Read and output the result
  while (fgets(myResult, sizeof(myResult)-1, fp) != NULL)
  {
    printf("%s", myResult);
  }

  // Close and quit
  pclose(fp);

  return 0;
}
```

Now compile the source and run the tool to see the base address of the ADC interface and then test to see that it works for other chip addresses (see Listing 17-5).

***Listing 17-5.*** Running the Base Address Tool

```
gcc -Wall gpiobaseaddress.c -o gpiobaseaddress

./gpiobaseaddress 145
1100000

./gpiobaseaddress 27
1140000
```

In both cases, the base address is written out. These test values have been chosen to display both of the base addresses in a Commercial Beta ARTIK 5. Check your listing for other values.

Install this tool somewhere more permanent and invoke it from within a shell script. Perhaps even enclose the call to action in back ticks to substitute the result and assign it to a variable. By doing so, you have just decoupled your shell script from any changes that Samsung make to the base address of your devices because now you are accessing them symbolically.

## Pin Export to the User Domain

Before you can use an interface, you need to tell the kernel to export it into your user space. While you have it exported, nobody else can grab it and take control. This is neat because it provides a kind of locking mechanism that avoids contention between two opposing processes. Once the GPIO is exported, a new directory is created with that GPIO number. When you unexport the GPIO after you have finished with it, the directory is removed and the GPIO is then available for other processes to acquire. Make sure you relinquish it when you are done.

The file system permissions conditionally allow you to do these operations on the GPIO pins it manages. Open the /sys/class/gpio/export file and write a GPIO pin number to it. Listing 17-6 is an example bash script fragment that writes to a GPIO pin.

***Listing 17-6.*** Exporting a GPIO Pin Using bash

```
MY_PIN_NUMBER=19
echo ${MY_PIN_NUMBER} > /sys/class/gpio/export
```

To accomplish the same thing in the C language, open a file and write the export instruction to it. Listing 17-7 shows you how.

***Listing 17-7.*** Writing to a GPIO Pin With C Language

```
#include <stdio.h>
#include <stdbool.h>

// Declare the variables
FILE *myGPIoExportFd;

// Define the target pin number
myGPIOPinNumber = 19;

// Open a messaging channel to the kernel
```

```
if((myGPIoExportFd = fopen("/sys/class/gpio/export", "w")) == NULL)
{
  printf("Error: unable to export GPIO pin\n");
  return false;
}

// Tell the kernel which pin to use
fprintf(myGPIoExportFd, "%d\n", myGPIOPinNumber);

// Close the kernel messaging channel
fclose(myGPIoExportFd);
```

## Previously Exported GPIO Pins

There are couple of GPIO interfaces that are already exported by the time your application is able to make use of them. These reserved GPIO interfaces are part of the Wi-Fi support, which is accessed through other mechanisms if it needs to be reconfigured. Because they have already been exported, your application cannot interfere with them. They are listed in Table 17-12.

*Table 17-12.* *Previously Exported GPIO Pins*

| GPIO | Reserved by |
|------|-------------|
| /sys/class/gpio/gpio140 | WLAN_REG_ON |
| /sys/class/gpio/gpio147 | WLAN_HOST_WAKE |

## Creating a Dynamic Path to an Exported Pin

Exporting a GPIO into the user-accessible domain creates a new node within the sysfs virtual file system that represents that pin. Write to that node to send messages to the kernel to configure the pin direction or send a value to it on your behalf. The path to the new node is

```
/sys/class/gpio/gpio{pin_number}
```

Use the built-in bash string concatenation tools to manufacture a path and store it in a variable:

```
MY_PIN_NUMBER=19
MY_PIN_PATH="/sys/class/gpio/gpio${MY_PIN_NUMBER}"
```

Use this fragment of C language code to dynamically create a path to an exported pin container. The sprintf() function can manufacture a path name from the pin number:

```
myGPIOPinNumber = 19;
sprintf(myGPIOPinPath, "/sys/class/gpio/gpio%d", myGPIOPinNumber);
```

## Pin Active LOW Setting

Give that GPIO pin some instructions by writing to subdirectories within it. The pin mode or direction (for this node) is controlled by this virtual file system location. Write the values shown in Table 17-13 to the active_low property:

```
/sys/class/gpio/gpio{pin_number}/active_low
```

*Table 17-13.* *Active LOW Parameter Settings*

| Value | Behavior |
|-------|----------|
| 0 | Configures the GPIO to be active **LOW**, pulled down to ground unless a **HIGH** value is asserted to drive it. |
| 1 | Configures the GPIO to be active **HIGH**, pulled up to Vcc unless a **LOW** value is asserted to drive it. Any non-zero value selects this behavior. |

## Pin Direction Setting

Give that GPIO pin some instructions by writing to subdirectories within it. The pin mode or direction (for this node) is controlled by this virtual file system location:

```
/sys/class/gpio/gpio{pin_number}/direction
```

When you write the out value to the direction setting, it asserts a default value on the pin as if you had written to the value property at the same time. This default value sets the pin **LOW**; it might not be the default that you want. Optionally, write the values low or high to set the pin into output mode and at the same time set the default value. The values listed in Table 17-14 can be written to this regular file to indicate the pin direction.

*Table 17-14.* *GPIO Direction Parameter Values*

| Direction value | Action |
|-----------------|--------|
| in | Defines the GPIO pin as an input to read values from it |
| out | Defines the GPIO as an output to write values to it. By default, the pin is set **LOW** (0). |
| low | Defines the GPIO as an output and at the same time force set the value **LOW** (0) |
| high | Defines the GPIO as an output and at the same time force set the value **HIGH** (1) |

■ **Note** This property does not exist if the kernel cannot support changing the direction of a GPIO. The property is also not available if the GPIO was exported by kernel code that does not explicitly allow user space applications to reconfigure the direction of this GPIO interface.

Write the message 'out' or 'in' depending on whether the code controls something or reads a sensor value. Write the required mode value to the direction virtual file, as shown in Listing 17-8. Save this as a shell script if you need it often.

*Listing 17-8.* Setting the GPIO Mode From bash

```
MY_PIN_NUMBER=19
MY_PIN_MODE_PATH="/sys/class/gpio/gpio${MY_PIN_NUMBER}/direction"

MY_PIN_DIRECTION="out"
echo ${MY_PIN_DIRECTION} > ${MY_PIN_MODE_PATH}
```

The same thing can be implemented in the C language by accessing a regular file. Write the message out or in as shown in Listing 17-9.

***Listing 17-9.*** Setting a GPIO Pin Mode from the C Language

```
#include <stdio.h>
#include <stdbool.h>

// Declare variables
FILE *myGPIOPinModeFd;

// Manufacture a path
myGPIOPinNumber = 19;
sprintf(myGPIOPinModePath, "/sys/class/gpio/gpio%d/direction", myGPIOPinNumber);

// Select one of these values to choose a mode
// Uncomment the one you want to use
myGPIOPinMode = "out";
//myGPIOPinMode = "in";
//myGPIOPinMode = "high";
//myGPIOPinMode = "low";

// Open the direction configuration for the GPIO node
if((myGPIOPinModeFd = fopen(myGPIOPinModePath, "w")) == NULL)
{
  printf("Error: cannot open pin direction\n");
  return false;
}

// Set the pin mode with the passed in direction
fprintf(myGPIOPinModeFd, "%s\n", myGPIOPinMode);

// Close the direction configurator
fclose(myGPIOPinModeFd);
```

# Digital Value Reading

If you want to acquire the value of a pin, read the regular file using a C language application or perhaps use the command line cat command to take the file contents and display them on the screen.

To read the value of the GPIO pin, just set the pin mode for input, open the path to the value configurator, and read in the value from the virtual file. The following values are available from an input GPIO pin:

- 0: **LOW**

- 1: **HIGH**

When you set the pin mode for a GPIO to be an input, the value can be acquired by reading from a special path within the GPIO node in the virtual file system:

/sys/class/gpio/gpio{pin_number}/value

Use a cat command to acquire the value and enclose it in back ticks (`) to assign the result to a bash shell variable. Listing 17-10 shows you the sequence of bash commands.

***Listing 17-10.*** Reading a Digital Value From bash

```
MY_PIN_NUMBER=19
MY_PIN_VALUE_PATH="/sys/class/gpio/gpio${MY_PIN_NUMBER}/value"

MY_RESULT=`cat ${MY_PIN_VALUE_PATH}`

echo ${MY_RESULT}
```

In the C language, the same thing is accomplished by opening and reading the virtual file directly. Acquire the value from the GPIO pin with an fgets() function that is configured to read just two characters at a time. Listing 17-11 provides an example code fragment to read a GPIO pin.

***Listing 17-11.*** Reading a GPIO pin Value With the C Language

```
#include <stdio.h>
#include <stdbool.h>

// Declare the variables
FILE *myGPIOPinValueFd;
char myResult[6];

// Manufacture a path to the pin value
sprintf(myGPIOPinValuePath, "/sys/class/gpio/gpio%d/value", myGPIOPinNumber);

// Open the value configuration for the GPIO node
if((myGPIOPinValueFd = fopen(myGPIOPinValuePath, "r")) == NULL)
{
  printf("Error: cannot open pin value for reading\n");
  return false;
}

// Read the pin value
fgets(myResult, 2, myGPIOPinValueFd);

// Close the value configurator
fclose(myGPIOPinValueFd);

// Convert the value to an integer before returning it to your application:
myIntegerResult = atoi(myResult);
```

# Digital Value Setting

When you set the pin mode for a GPIO to be an output, the value can be set by writing to a special path within the GPIO node in the virtual file system. The same path is used for reading inputs and writing outputs. Set the output to one of the values listed in Table 17-15.

```
/sys/class/gpio/gpio{pin_number}/value
```

***Table 17-15.*** *Output Pin Values*

| Value | Meaning |
|---|---|
| 0 | **LOW** |
| 1 | **HIGH** |
| Any other non zero value | **HIGH** |

Use the echo command in bash (as shown in Listing 17-12) to set the pin to the required value.

***Listing 17-12.*** Setting an Output Pin Value From bash

```
MY_PIN_NUMBER=19
MY_PIN_VALUE_PATH="/sys/class/gpio/gpio${MY_PIN_NUMBER}/value"

MY_NEW_PIN_VALUE="1"
echo ${MY_NEW_PIN_VALUE} > ${MY_PIN_VALUE_PATH}
```

Listing 17-13 shows how to set the value on that GPIO with the C language having already synthesized the path to reach it.

***Listing 17-13.*** Setting a GPIO Pin Value in the C Language

```
#include <stdio.h>
#include <stdbool.h>

// Declare variables
FILE *myGPIOPinValueFd;

// Manufacture a path to the pin value
sprintf(myGPIOPinValuePath, "/sys/class/gpio/gpio%d/value", myGPIOPinNumber);

// Select one of these values to set on the pin
// Uncomment the one you want to use
myNewGPIOPinValue = 1;  // Represents HIGH
//myNewGPIOPinValue = 0; // Represents LOW

// Open the value configuration for the GPIO node
if((myGPIOPinValueFd = fopen(myGPIOPinValuePath, "w")) == NULL)
{
  printf("Error: cannot open pin value for writing\n");
  return false;
}

// Set the pin value with the passed in setting
fprintf(myGPIOPinValueFd, "%d\n", myNewGPIOPinValue);

// Close the value configurator
fclose(myGPIOPinValueFd);
```

# Edge Detecting

Taking the value-reading example further, the virtual file edge can be used instead of the value file to detect rising or falling edges. Detecting button press or button release actions becomes much easier because state management and button changes become atomic functions. Atomic functionality encapsulates things so only a single line of code is necessary where an entire function was required before. Atomic functions are less likely to be interrupted by other things happening in the system.

This mechanism could be used to detect and trigger different behavior when a button is pressed or released. This is analogous to a mouseDown and mouseUp event in a web browser event handler.

This virtual file path only exists if the driver for the GPIO supports this functionality. Inspect the file system embedded in your ARTIK to see if this feature is available. The read path for detecting an edge on the same example {pin_number} is /sys/class/gpio/gpio{pin_number}/edge.

The values listed in Table 17-16 can be set to define the behavior of the edge detection when the pol() function is called. Read back the values to see what was previously set.

***Table 17-16.*** *Edge-Detecting Behavior Settings*

| Edge detect type | Description |
| --- | --- |
| none | Edge detection is inactive. |
| rising | The poll() function returns when the value changes from a 0 to a 1. |
| falling | The poll() function returns when the value changes from a 1 to a 0. |
| both | The poll() function returns when the value changes in either direction. Be careful not to get a double trigger since you are now looking for both edges. |

If the pin can be configured to generate an interrupt and has been set up that way by default. Use the poll() function on the value file. The poll() function blocks until the value changes and then returns whenever the interrupt was triggered. If you use the poll() function, set the events POLLPRI and POLLERR. If you use the select() function to create a non-blocking interrupt listener, set the file descriptor in the exceptfds property. After the poll() function returns, either use lseek() to reset the file pointer to the beginning of the sysfs file and read the new value or close the file and reopen it to read the value. If you omit the call to lseek(), your file reading end position will prevent your read call from seeing the new value.

# Releasing Exported Pins

When you are done with using a GPIO, release it for use by other applications by writing the pin number to the unexport file location. Listing 17-14 shows you how to do this from a bash command line.

***Listing 17-14.*** Releasing a GPIO Pin Using bash

```
MY_PIN_NUMBER=19
echo ${MY_PIN_NUMBER} > /sys/class/gpio/unexport
```

In the C language, this is very similar to the earlier example where the GPIO was exported. Listing 17-15 shows the modified version of the code.

***Listing 17-15.*** Releasing GPIO Pin Using the C Language

```
#include <stdio.h>
#include <stdbool.h>
```

```
// Declare the variables
FILE *myGPIoUnexportFd;

// Define the target pin number
myGPIOPinNumber = 19;

// Open a messaging channel to the kernel
if((myGPIoUnexportFd = fopen("/sys/class/gpio/unexport", "w")) == NULL)
{
  printf("Error: unable to unexport GPIO pin\n");
  return false;
}

// Tell the kernel which pin to relinquish
fprintf(myGPIoUnexportFd, "%d\n", myGPIOPinNumber);

// Close the kernel messaging channel
fclose(myGPIoUnexportFd);
```

## Continuous Reads and Writes

If your application loops to set or get the value of a in a continuous fashion, reset the file pointer after each operation. This would normally be set to the beginning of the file when you open the file. If your reading and writing cycle opens and closes the file each time, this is not a problem. This is somewhat inefficient and keeping the file open makes more sense in a loop.

If you open the value file for get the current GPIO status (1 or 0), after the first read operation, the file pointer moves to the next position in the file. The subsequent read carries on where it left off because the file pointer has not been moved. After all, you want a file to spool out some new data each time you read some of it into your applications. When reading a GPIO interface, it must always read or write from the start of the file. Reset the file pointer to the beginning of the file before each read by using the lseek() function:

```
lseek(fp, 0, SEEK_SET);
```

If you open and close GPIO value file every time read it, this additional lseek() function call is unnecessary. Opening and closing the file introduces an unwanted delay if you do so on a continuous basis.

## Trailing Carriage Returns

When you read data from the GPIO interface, the returned string is terminated by the newline character (\n). Make sure you trim off that trailing newline character if it is there because the code you pass the result to may not expect it.

# Access Directly Via the Kernel

Your application interacts with the GPIO internal registers to control the mode of operation and read or write values. The kernel captures your calls and returns status information on the hardware managed by each module. The kernel can also pass your values to the hardware on your behalf. The GPIO internal registers are accessed through addressable ports. When the GPIO interface is accessed via the kernel, the registers are grouped into collections called ports. Each port group is discussed separately in this section. These ports are only of consequence when accessing GPIO via the kernel. The other modes of access (sysfs and Arduino) organize the collection of GPIO pins differently. There are several ports of interest for the programmable pins. The tables below provide programming information arranged by internal port groupings.

Implement low-level coding to reduce GPIO handling times, which helps to reduce the amount of CPU time spent on those tasks. This should lead to significant improvements in system efficiency. Fixed-purpose pins whose functionality is reserved can also be programmed at the kernel level. This may not yield any performance benefits and using the simpler sysfs method might be fast enough for your needs.

The amount of CPU time your application code uses for handling GPIO pins affects the performance of the platform as a whole. You may find it is worth the additional effort of writing kernel-based drivers to optimize performance for a particular kind of GPIO usage. Custom driver code may be able to set a group of related pins in a single write operation, instead of acting on each pin change individually. This will make the pin access more atomic. When the driver function is called, all pins are operated on together and the delay between configuring each one would be minimized.

Figure 17-9 illustrates the basic components of the GPIO drivers and ports and how they relate to one another inside the kernel.

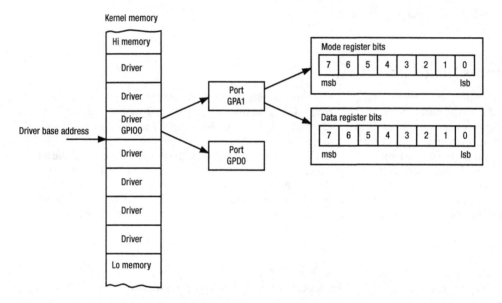

*Figure 17-9.* *GPIO drivers and ports*

The driver and port naming can be confusing because there are GPIO drivers with very similar names to the GPIO ports. Become familiar with the structure of these drivers, ports, and the registers associated with them.

## GPIO Ports

The Samsung developer documentation lists only a few ports, but by inspecting the debugfs virtual file system that the kernel creates, it is possible to discover others. Knowing that they exist answers some of the questions already posed on the ARTIK developer forums about where things are.

This may be useful later for exploiting the graphics and video support. Talking to the ARM MALI GPU graphics chip or the video camera and display/HDMI ports is not yet fully supported from the user space in the Commercial Beta and there is no ARTIK-specific documentation available at the moment.

Use the following commands to display a list of port names mapped to each driver (gpio0 and gpio1 in an ARTIK 5) with a list of pin numbers associated with them. Substitute the appropriate driver base address values for an ARTIK 10.

```
cat /sys/kernel/debug/pinctrl/11400000.pinctrl/gpio-ranges
cat /sys/kernel/debug/pinctrl/11000000.pinctrl/gpio-ranges
```

The kernel and operating system are prepared to manage many more GPIO pins than the ARTIK 5 implements. To interact with the GPIO interfaces owned by a port, first calculate the port address. The results for a Commercial Beta ARTIK 5 are aggregated and summarized in Table 17-17. Only the documented port addresses are listed. Given that ports GPA1 and GPD0 are documented, the rest of the offsets can be deduced for the remaining ports supported by driver GPIO0. The undocumented address offsets are less certain for driver GPIO1.

***Table 17-17.*** *GPIO Port Names and Ranges (ARTIK 5)*

| Driver | Port | GPIOs | Pins | Offset |
|--------|------|-------|------|--------|
| gpio0 | gpa0 | 0 - 7 | 0 - 7 | |
| gpio0 | gpa1 | 8 - 13 | 8 - 13 | 0x0008 |
| gpio0 | gpb | 14 - 21 | 14 - 21 | |
| gpio0 | gpc0 | 22 - 26 | 22 - 26 | |
| gpio0 | gpc1 | 27 - 31 | 27 - 31 | |
| gpio0 | gpd0 | 32 - 35 | 32 - 35 | 0x0028 |
| gpio0 | gpd1 | 36 - 39 | 36 - 39 | |
| gpio1 | gpe0 | 40 - 47 | 0 - 7 | |
| gpio1 | gpe1 | 48 - 55 | 8 - 15 | |
| gpio1 | gpe2 | 56 - 58 | 16 - 18 | |
| gpio1 | gpk0 | 59 - 66 | 19 - 26 | |
| gpio1 | gpk1 | 67 - 73 | 27 - 33 | |
| gpio1 | gpk2 | 74 - 80 | 34 - 40 | |
| gpio1 | gpl0 | 81 - 84 | 41 - 44 | |
| gpio1 | gpm0 | 85 - 92 | 45 - 52 | |
| gpio1 | gpm1 | 93 - 99 | 53 - 59 | |
| gpio1 | gpm2 | 100 - 104 | 60 - 64 | |
| gpio1 | gpm3 | 105 - 112 | 65 - 72 | |
| gpio1 | gpm4 | 113 - 120 | 73 - 80 | |
| gpio1 | gpx0 | 121 - 128 | 81 - 88 | 0x0300 |
| gpio1 | gpx1 | 129 - 136 | 89 - 96 | 0x0308 |
| gpio1 | gpx2 | 137 - 144 | 97 - 104 | |
| gpio1 | gpx3 | 145 - 152 | 105 - 112 | |

To develop a dynamic solution, work out the driver base address and use the correct offset value based on the port name to work out the port address using a simple formula:

```
{port_address} = {driver_base_address} + {port_offset}
```

Table 17-18 summarizes the port offsets that have been described by Samsung in the developer documentation. They are different for the ARTIK 5 and 10. Combining the offset and base address yields the port address to access the correct register.

***Table 17-18.*** *Computing the Port Address*

| ARTIK | Port name | Driver | Base addr | Offset | Port addr |
|-------|-----------|--------|-----------|--------|-----------|
| 5 | GPX0 | gpio1 | 0x11000000 | 0x0300 | 0x11000300 |
| 5 | GPX2 | gpio1 | 0x11000000 | 0x0308 | 0x11000308 |
| 5 | GPA1 | gpio0 | 0x11400000 | 0x0008 | 0x11400008 |
| 5 | GPD0 | gpio0 | 0x11400000 | 0x0028 | 0x11400028 |
| 10 | GPX0 | gpio0 | 0x13400000 | 0x0300 | 0x13400300 |
| 10 | GPX1 | gpio0 | 0x13400000 | 0x0308 | 0x13400308 |
| 10 | GPA0 | gpio3 | 0x14010000 | 0x0000 | 0x14010000 |
| 10 | GPA2 | gpio3 | 0x14010000 | 0x0010 | 0x14010010 |
| 10 | GPB2 | gpio3 | 0x14010000 | 0x0028 | 0x14010028 |

Figure 17-10 shows how these port addresses are mapped into the driver's memory space inside the kernel.

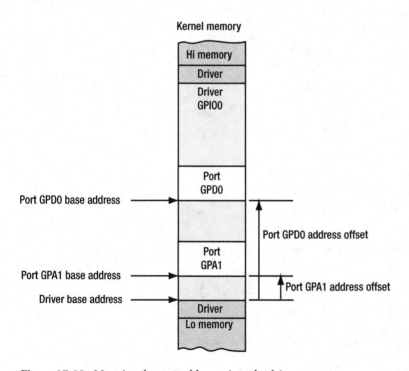

***Figure 17-10.*** *Mapping the port addresses into the driver memory*

# Shared Registers

Within each port base address block are a collection of different registers. Only the MODE and DATA register addresses have been published in the Samsung developer documentation. Reading about GPIO programming in the online resources suggests there is much more to GPIO programming than this. Knowing about MODE and DATA is sufficient to work out the base address and the values for reading and writing to it. The gpio.h include file documents the registers in more detail. This header file is part of the kernel source code for the ARTIK OS.

Because the GPIO pins convey a simple binary value to indicate whether they are on or off, each pin can be represented internally by a single bit in a control or data register. Figure 17-11 shows how a GPIO pin is mapped to a bit within a shared register at a port address.

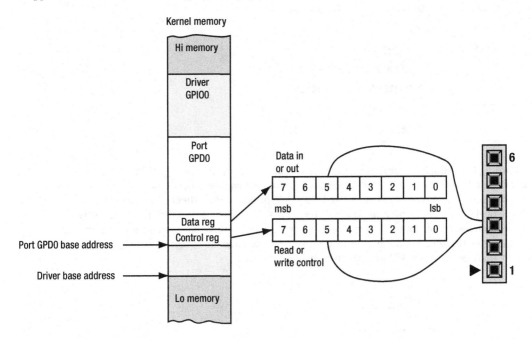

**Figure 17-11.** *Mapping GPIO pins to port address registers*

Because the pins are mapped onto specific bits within the value written to each port address, you cannot write a value for the pin you are setting. Instead, use Read ➤ Modify ➤ Write coding to acquire the current value, set the bit you want to, and then write it back.

In a few rare cases, the pins are mapped so you can safely write to the pins without needing to read the others first to preserve their state. Reading inputs is benign and does not change any pin values. Consequently, reading cycles can repeat faster than write cycles. This might be important if you are trying to sample a rapidly changing pin value and then play it back out again. In that case, adjust your read cycles so they are slow enough to be played back within a Read ➤ Modify ➤ Write timing throughput capacity.

# GPIO Registers

The GPIO control registers are maintained separately to the ones you read or write values to. The port addresses are similar. At the most fundamental level, kernel drivers access the hardware pin MODE and DATA ports directly to control the GPIO behavior. You would set the MODE first and then access the DATA. In some cases, the MODE value can be assumed to be a default and the corresponding data value can be written directly.

Table 17-19 shows the port names for ARTIK 5 and 10 modules with the corresponding MODE and DATA registers. The MODE register address is the port base address with a zero offset so they are the same value. The DATA register is offset by 0x0001. The corresponding bits in each register are mapped to the same pins on the GPIO interface.

**Table 17-19.** *MODE and DATA Register Addresses*

| ARTIK | Port name | MODE addr | DATA addr |
|-------|-----------|-----------|-----------|
| 5 | GPXO | 0x11000300 | 0x11000301 |
| 5 | GPX1 | 0x11000308 | 0x11000309 |
| 5 | GPA1 | 0x11400008 | 0x11400009 |
| 5 | GPDO | 0x11400028 | 0x11400029 |
| 10 | GPXO | 0x13400300 | 0x13400301 |
| 10 | GPX1 | 0x13400308 | 0x13400309 |
| 10 | GPAO | 0x14010000 | 0x14010001 |
| 10 | GPA2 | 0x14010010 | 0x14010011 |
| 10 | GPB2 | 0x14010028 | 0x14010029 |

According to the documentation on generic GPIO access, there may be other port addresses for different functionality. The offset of eight memory locations between each port base address suggests that there can be eight different registers associated with each port. The data sheets describe GPIO ports as having one of eight possible functional states. These registers may be used to facilitate that behavior but there is no documentation about it at present. Inspect the kernel source code to deduce what the other registers are from the kernel configuration. Figure 17-12 shows how the registers are mapped into the block of memory managed as a port within the driver inside the kernel.

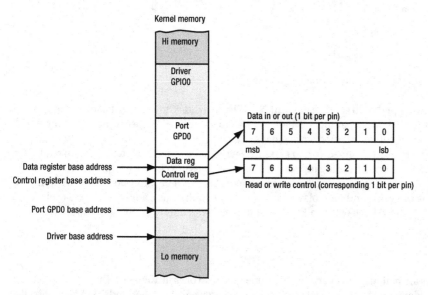

*Figure 17-12.* *Mapping registers to ports*

# Mapping the Bits

The port registers expect an 8-bit value to be used to set a mode or read/write values. It helps to have some manifest constants defined for the pins. It might also be useful to include this line at the top of your source files to use the Boolean data types in the C language:

```
#include <stdbool.h>
```

Knowing how to perform simple decimal-to-hexadecimal and binary arithmetic is a skill worth knowing. There are times when you can exploit simple mathematical tricks to perform binary operations. Table 17-20 lists the 16 hexadecimal digits and their equivalent binary values.

***Table 17-20.*** *Hexadecimal Digits vs. Binary Values*

| | |
|---|---|
| 0 - 0000 | 8 - 1000 |
| 1 - 0001 | 9 - 1001 |
| 2 - 0010 | A - 1010 |
| 3 - 0011 | B - 1011 |
| 4 - 0100 | C - 1100 |
| 5 - 0101 | D - 1101 |
| 6 - 0110 | E - 1110 |
| 7 - 0111 | F - 1111 |

Compare the binary equivalent values for 1, 2, 4, and 8. By multiplying the decimal equivalent by 2, the binary value performs a leftwards shift towards the most significant bit. Dividing by 2 performs a rightwards shift towards the least significant bit. Adding values together performs a Boolean OR operation. Knowing these tricks lets you write very concise code, which performs well. The C language also has mechanisms for operating on bit-fields to directly manipulate each bit in the value. Figure 17-13 shows two registers being combined through a bitwise Boolean operator with the result being placed in a third register.

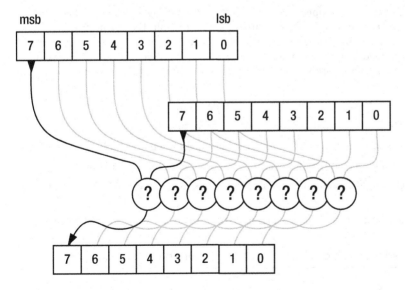

***Figure 17-13.*** *Bit-wise operators*

Table 17-21 lists the C language bitwise operators. Getting to know these binary operators can significantly help your application code design. There are some neat tricks you can do by adding or subtracting one integer value from another to invert bits or multiplying and dividing by 2 to accomplish simple bit-shifting tasks.

**Table 17-21.** *Bitwise Operators*

| Operator | Example | Description |
|---|---|---|
| & | c = a & b | This operator yields the Boolean result of evaluating a AND b. The bit patterns in both variables are compared bit by bit. Where there is a 1 bit in both, the result has a 1-bit value. Where either or both bits are zero, the corresponding bit in the result is zero too. In this example, the result is assigned to variable c and variables a and b are unchanged. |
| \| | c = a \| b | This operator yields the Boolean result of evaluating a OR b. The same bit-by-bit test is applied but in this case, a 1 bit results if there is a 1 in either a or b. The result only has a zero in the corresponding bit if neither a or b has a 1 in the bit value. The result is stored in variable c, leaving a and b unchanged. |
| ^ | c = a ^ b | This operator yields the Boolean result of evaluating a XOR b. This is similar to the a OR b case except that only one of them can be set to 1. If both are zero or if both are 1, the result in the corresponding bit in variable c is zero. |
| << | c = a << b | The bit pattern in variable a is shifted leftwards towards the most significant bit by a count specified in variable b. The result is stored in variable c. If you shift by too many steps, the values fall out of the left hand end and your register contains zero. Shifting left by 1 step is equivalent to multiplying the value by 2 in the decimal domain. |
| >> | c = a >> b | The bit pattern in variable a is shifted rightwards towards the least significant bit by a count specified in variable b. The result is stored in variable c. If you shift by too many steps, the values fall out of the right hand end and your register contains zero. Shifting right by 1 step is equivalent to dividing the value by 2 in the decimal domain. |
| &= | a &= b | The compound operators apply an expression using both values but replace the contents of the leftmost variable with the result. This is a destructive form of evaluation because the original values for the left most item are not retained. This operator performs the a AND b expression and stores the result in variable a. Variable b is left unchanged. The value on the left must be a variable. |
| \|= | a \|= b | The result of evaluating a OR b is stored in variable a. |
| ^= | a ^= b | The result of evaluating a XOR b is stored in variable a. |
| <<= | a <<= b | Variable a is shifted leftwards by the number of steps in variable b. |
| >>= | a >>= b | Variable a is shifted rightwards by the number of steps in variable b. |
| invert all bits | a ^= 0xFF | Use the XOR operator with an all 1's bit mask to invert every bit in variable a. |
| clear all bits | a = 0 | Assign a zero value to set all bits to 0 in variable a. |
| set all bits | a = 0xFF | Assign the value 0xFF (decimal 255) to set all bits to 1 in variable a. |

Incorporate the fragment of code in Listing 17-16 to define masks for pins which you can use with an AND operator to extract the pin value for a single header pin. Any non-zero result after masking with these values means the pin has a **HIGH** value. A zero result means it is **LOW**.

***Listing 17-16.*** Bit-Mask Manifest Constants

```
// Define 1-bit masks for filtering each individual bit
#define MASK_BIT_0 0x01
#define MASK_BIT_1 0x02
#define MASK_BIT_2 0x04
#define MASK_BIT_3 0x08
#define MASK_BIT_4 0x10
#define MASK_BIT_5 0x20
#define MASK_BIT_6 0x40
#define MASK_BIT_7 0x80


// Define masks to exclude each individual bit
#define EXCLUDE_BIT_0 0xFE
#define EXCLUDE_BIT_1 0xFD
#define EXCLUDE_BIT_2 0xFB
#define EXCLUDE_BIT_3 0xF7
#define EXCLUDE_BIT_4 0xEF
#define EXCLUDE_BIT_5 0xDF
#define EXCLUDE_BIT_6 0xBF
#define EXCLUDE_BIT_7 0x7F


// Combo masks
#define MASK_NO_BITS  0x00
#define MASK_ALL_BITS 0xFF


// Binary values
#define ARTIK_PIN_TRUE  1
#define ARTIK_PIN_FALSE 0
```

Use the code in Listing 17-17 to return a true (**HIGH**) value or false (**LOW**) value for a specific pin. In the C language, a false result is represented by an integer having a zero value. A true result is any non-zero integer. This is convenient because the bits can be masked using a simple Boolean AND operator to get a true or false result. This does work but it leads to multiple values for true and avoiding any potential errors later is best done at source. Wrap the test inside a function that returns a fixed, consistent, and known value for true. Creating a manifest constant helps to make the code somewhat self-documenting.

***Listing 17-17.*** Example Bit Testing Function

```
#include <stdbool.h>

#define ARTIK_PIN_TRUE true
#define ARTIK_PIN_FALSE false

int pinState(port_value, pin_mask)
{
  if(port_value & pin_mask)
  {
```

```
    return ARTIK_PIN_TRUE;
  }
  return ARTIK_PIN_FALSE;
}
```

Extend this function wrapping to pass in port names or symbolic identifiers based on the header names and then map them inside the function with switch()/case mechanisms to further abstract your code and decouple it from the hardware.

## Port GPX0

The GPX0 port has a single reserved signal allocated to bit 7. This bit is reserved for internal use as a USB status sense function by the ARTIK 10 module. It is not used at all in an ARTIK 5 module. Do not change the functionality of bit 7. Because the default state of the remaining bits is set to be output, they are ready to have values written to them. Writing a value to a bit that is configured for input ignores any value that attempts to change the setting. Therefore, as long as a GPIO device driver leaves MODE bit 7 set as INPUT, it could set any remaining GPIO output pin values with a single DATA write. This has a helpful performance benefit because a Read ➤ Modify ➤ Write cycle is replaced with a single write.

Table 17-22 lists the mapping of the bits to the header pins and also lists the signal names from the Panasonic AXT connectors on the underside of the ARTIK modules. Refer to Chapter 13 for details of the AXT connector pinouts. Some of those pins drive the Arduino digital pins on the J26 and J27 headers. The small infinity symbol (∞) denotes an Arduino pin name because they have a numeric label that could be confused with the physical pin number.

*Table 17-22.* *GPX0 Pins and Signals Mapped to Bits*

| BIT | MODE | Signal name | Header pin | Mask |
|-----|------|-------------|------------|------|
| 7 | Input | DRD_VBUS_SENSE_0 (ARTIK 10) | - | 0x80 |
| 6 | In/Out | XEINT_6 | J27-8 (∞10) | 0x40 |
| 5 | In/Out | XEINT_5 | J27-9 (∞9) | 0x20 |
| 4 | In/Out | XEINT_4 | J27-10 (∞8) | 0x10 |
| 3 | In/Out | XEINT_3 | J26-1 (∞7) | 0x08 |
| 2 | In/Out | XEINT_2 | J26-4 (∞4) | 0x04 |
| 1 | In/Out | XEINT_1 | J26-5 (∞3) | 0x02 |
| 0 | In/Out | XEINT_0 | J26-6 (∞2) | 0x01 |

If you use the bitwise AND expression with the 0x7F value to mask your read and write values, it will exclude any spurious values from bit 7. Use the manifest constants you defined earlier for the pin masks to set or clear the bits in the value you want to read or write. Although it is somewhat risky, if you have internally cached the values you are writing out to the pins, write to the DATA register to set new values. Make sure you know if the cached value has been invalidated or you may introduce a hard-to-find bug. If you want to preserve existing values and you have not cached them, a Read ➤ Modify ➤ Write is called for. The relevant addresses for GPX0 are different in the ARTIK 5 and 10 modules and are listed in Table 17-23.

*Table 17-23.* *Base Addresses for Port GPX0*

| Module | Address | Description |
|--------|---------|-------------|
| ARTIK 5 | 0x11000300 | Port base address |
| ARTIK 5 | 0x11000300 | MODE control register |
| ARTIK 5 | 0x11000301 | DATA value register |
| ARTIK 10 | 0x13400300 | Port base address |
| ARTIK 10 | 0x13400300 | MODE control register |
| ARTIK 10 | 0x13400301 | DATA value register |

# Port GPX1

The GPX1 port has multiple reserved signals, mixed with some other pins that you may want to configure for input and output use. Be careful to mask out some of the pins when you are defining the modes or setting output values on the GPIO pins. Always use Read ➤ Modify ➤ Write actions when changing the MODE or DATA port settings on this register to preserve the existing values. The modify part of this process involves some bit masking to protect the current values of the pins so they do not get changed inadvertently.

Table 17-24 lists the mapping of the bits to the header pins and also lists the signal names from the Panasonic AXT connectors on the underside of the ARTIK modules. Refer to Chapter 13 for details of the AXT connector pinouts. Some of those pins drive the Arduino digital pins on the J26 and J27 headers. The small infinity symbol (∞) denotes an Arduino pin name because they have a numeric label that could be confused with the physical pin number.

*Table 17-24.* *GPX1 Pins and Signals Mapped to Bits*

| Bit | MODE | Signal name | Header pin | Mask |
|-----|------|-------------|------------|------|
| 7 | Output | BT_REG_ON | - | 0x80 |
| 6 | In/Out | XEINT_14 | J27-5 (∞13) | 0x40 |
| 5 | In/Out | XEINT_13 | J27-6 (∞12) | 0x20 |
| 4 | N/C | XEINT_12 | - | 0x10 |
| 3 | Output | XGPIO17/XT_INT163 | - | 0x08 |
| 2 | Input | V_ADP_SENSE | - | 0x04 |
| 1 | N/C | XEINT_9 | - | 0x02 |
| 0 | In/Out | XEINT_8 | J27-7 (∞11) | 0x01 |

If you use the bitwise AND expression with the 0x73 value to mask your read and write values, it will exclude any spurious values that affect bits 7, 3 and 2. Use the manifest constants you defined earlier for the pin masks to set or clear the bits in the value you want to read or write. The relevant addresses for GPX1 are different in the ARTIK 5 and 10 modules and are listed in Table 17-25.

*Table 17-25.* *Base Addresses for Port GPX1*

| Module | Address | Description |
|--------|---------|-------------|
| ARTIK 5 | 0x11000308 | Port base address |
| ARTIK 5 | 0x11000308 | MODE control register |
| ARTIK 5 | 0x11000309 | DATA value register |
| ARTIK 10 | 0x13400308 | Port base address |
| ARTIK 10 | 0x13400308 | MODE control register |
| ARTIK 10 | 0x13400309 | DATA value register |

## Port GPA0

The GPA0 port is only used on an ARTIK 10 and provides access to control a Universal Asynchronous Receiver Transmitter (UART). This is mapped to the Arduino RX and TX serial pins. Table 17-26 summarizes the four connections on this UART.

*Table 17-26.* *UART Signal Names*

| Signal | Description |
|--------|-------------|
| RTS | Request to send |
| CTS | Clear to send |
| TXD | Outgoing transmitted data stream |
| RXD | Incoming received data stream |

The RTS and CTS lines are for hardware handshaking between the two participating serial devices. In the case of UART1 in an ARTIK 10, the RTS and CTS connections are not brought out to a header pin so you cannot implement hardware handshaking. Serial interfaces perform very well with software handshaking. The receiving system can send an XOFF message to the other end, which suspends transmission until it is told to resume with an XON message. The XOFF and XON messages are only sent when the receiving data buffers are full and the processing is unable to keep up with the data being received. Design your serial protocols to be efficient and economical so software flow control is less likely to be needed.

If a hardware handshake on the serial interface is necessary, use spare GPIO pins on the header that are not used for anything else. Then read their data values and use them to set the RTS and CTS lines. However, this is not a particularly neat solution.

Four pins are reserved for UART Xu1 and the other four are reserved to control the internal onboard Bluetooth UART.

Avoid interfering with the Bluetooth UART as it is managed very well via the Bluetooth drivers and networking software configuration.

Table 17-27 lists the mapping of the bits to the header pins and also lists the signal names from the Panasonic AXT connectors on the underside of the ARTIK modules. Refer to Chapter 13 for details of the AXT connector pinouts. Some of these pins drive the Arduino digital pins on the J26 and J27 headers.

***Table 17-27.*** *GPA0 Pins and Signals Mapped to Bits*

| BIT | MODE | Signal name | Header pin | Mask |
|-----|------|-------------|------------|------|
| 7 | Output | Xu1_RTS | - | 0x80 |
| 6 | Input | Xu1_CTS | - | 0x40 |
| 5 | Output | Xu1_TXD | J26-7 (TX->1) | 0x20 |
| 4 | Input | Xu1_RXD | J26-8 (RX<-0) | 0x10 |
| 3 | Output | BT_UART_RTSn | - | 0x08 |
| 2 | Input | BT_UART_CTSn | - | 0x04 |
| 1 | Output | BT_UART_TXD | - | 0x02 |
| 0 | Input | BT_UART_RXD | - | 0x01 |

If you use the bitwise AND expression with the 0x0F or 0xF0 values to mask your read and write values, it will separate your operations so they only apply to one of the UARTS. Use the manifest constants you defined earlier for the pin masks to set or clear the bits in the value you want to read or write. If you have internally cached the values you are writing out to the pins, write to the DATA register to set new values. If you want to preserve existing values and you have not cached them, a Read ➤ Modify ➤ Write is called for. The relevant addresses for GPA0 in the ARTIK 10 modules are listed in Table 17-28.

***Table 17-28.*** *Base Addresses for ARTIK 10 Port GPA0*

| Address | Description |
|---------|-------------|
| 0x14010000 | Port base address |
| 0x14010000 | MODE control register |
| 0x14010001 | DATA value register |

# Port GPA1

The GPA1 port is only used on the ARTIK 5 and not on the ARTIK 10 module. The ARTIK 5 module has a simpler UART interface than the ARTIK 10 and the pins that are not needed for UART control are used for other purposes. This is mapped to the Arduino RX and TX serial pins.

Two of the pins are reserved for controlling bus I2C-3 and two others are reserved for serial input/output for debugging. Because the debugging serial interface is not documented, other than being listed for this GPIO port, it is not clear where this debugging serial interface is physically connected and accessible.

Table 17-29 lists the mapping of the bits to the header pins and also lists the signal names from the Panasonic AXT connectors on the underside of the ARTIK modules. Refer to Chapter 13 for details on the AXT connector pinouts. Some of these pins drive the Arduino digital pins on the J26 and J27 headers.

*Table 17-29.* *GPA1 Pins and Signals Mapped to Bits*

| BIT | MODE | Signal name | Header pin | Mask |
|-----|------|-------------|------------|------|
| 7 | - | Not used | - | 0x80 |
| 6 | - | Not used | - | 0x40 |
| 5 | Output | Xu3_TXD | J26-7 (TX->1) | 0x20 |
| 4 | Input | Xu3_RXD | J26-8 (RX<-0) | 0x10 |
| 3 | Output | Xi2c3_SCL | - | 0x08 |
| 2 | In/Out | Xi2c3_SDA | - | 0x04 |
| 1 | Output | DEBUG_TXD | - | 0x02 |
| 0 | Input | DEBUG_RXD | - | 0x01 |

A bitwise AND expression with the 0x30 value to mask your read and write values will only access the J26 UART pins. Use the manifest constants you defined earlier for the pin masks to set or clear the bits in the value you want to read or write. If you have internally cached the values you are writing out to the pins, write to the DATA register to set new values. If you want to preserve existing values and you have not cached them, a Read ➤ Modify ➤ Write is called for. The relevant addresses for GPA1 in the ARTIK 5 modules are listed in Table 17-30.

*Table 17-30.* *Base Addresses for ARTIK 5 Port GPA1*

| Address | Description |
|---------|-------------|
| 0x11400008 | Port base address |
| 0x11400008 | MODE control register |
| 0x11400009 | DATA value register |

## Port GPA2

The GPA2 port is used to manage bus I2C-9 on an ARTIK 10. This is an external I2C bus that is brought out to a pair of Arduino-compatible pins on header J27. There you have access to the SCL and SDA lines for this interface. This port also has an addition mode of use as an SPI interface. This port is not used on an ARTIK 5 module.

Table 17-31 lists the mapping of the bits to the header pins and also lists the signal names from the Panasonic AXT connectors on the underside of the ARTIK modules. Refer to Chapter 13 for details on the AXT connector pinouts. Some of these pins drive the Arduino digital pins on the J26 and J27 headers.

*Table 17-31.* *GPA2 Pins and Signals Mapped to Bits*

| BIT | MODE | Signal name | Header pin | Mask |
|-----|------|-------------|------------|------|
| 7 | Output | XspiMOSI1 | - | 0x80 |
| 6 | Input | XspiMISO1 | - | 0x40 |
| 5 | Output | XspiCSn1 | - | 0x20 |
| 4 | Output | XspiCLK1 | - | 0x10 |
| 3 | Output | XspiMOSI0/XEXT_SCL | J27-1 (SCL) | 0x08 |
| 2 | Input | XspiMISO0/XEXT_SDA | J27-2 (SDA) | 0x04 |
| 1 | Output | XspiCSn0 | - | 0x02 |
| 0 | Output | XspiCLK0 | - | 0x01 |

A bitwise AND expression with the 0x0C value to mask your read and write values will only operate on pins J27-1 and J27-2. These pins have several possible modes of operation and can be configured as an SPI or I2C interface depending on the GPIO pin multiplex mode. Use the manifest constants you defined earlier for the pin masks to set or clear the bits in the value you want to read or write. If you have internally cached the values you are writing out to the pins, write to the DATA register to set new values. If you want to preserve existing values and you have not cached them, a Read ➤ Modify ➤ Write is called for. The relevant addresses for GPA2 in the ARTIK 10 modules are listed in Table 17-32.

***Table 17-32.*** *Base Addresses for ARTIK 10 Port GPA2*

| Address | Description |
| --- | --- |
| 0x14010010 | Port base address |
| 0x14010010 | MODE control register |
| 0x14010011 | DATA value register |

# Port GPD0

The GPD0 port provides access to the I2C-7 bus interface and the PWM pins on an ARTIK 5. This is known as the external I2C bus and is brought out to a pair of Arduino-compatible pins on the J27 header. The ARTIK 10 maps the corresponding external interface to bus I2C-9 and supports that via GPA2. The other pins on this port are for managing the PWM outputs. The ARTIK 10 maps them to a different port so this discussion is only relevant to an ARTIK 5 module. Inspecting the device tree source code indicates that bus I2C-7 is related to the HDMI video output on an ARTIK 10.

Table 17-33 lists the mapping of the bits to the header pins and also lists the signal names from the Panasonic AXT connectors on the underside of the ARTIK modules. Refer to Chapter 13 for details on the AXT connector pinouts. Some of those pins drive the Arduino digital pins on the J26 and J27 headers. The small tilde symbol (~) denotes a PWM Arduino pin name because they have a numeric label that could be confused with the physical pin number.

***Table 17-33.*** *GPD0 Pins and Signals Mapped to Bits*

| BIT | MODE | Signal name | Header pin | Mask |
| --- | --- | --- | --- | --- |
| 7 | - | N/C | - | 0x80 |
| 6 | - | N/C | - | 0x40 |
| 5 | - | N/C | - | 0x20 |
| 4 | - | N/C | - | 0x10 |
| 3 | Output | Xi2c7_SCL | J27-1 (SCL) | 0x08 |
| 2 | In/Out | Xi2c7_SDA | J27-2 (SDA) | 0x04 |
| 1 | Output | Xpwmo_1 | J26-2 (~6) | 0x02 |
| 0 | Output | Xpwmo_0 | J26-3 (~5) | 0x01 |

If you use the bitwise AND expression with the 0x0C value to mask your read and write values, it will only operate on pins J27-1 and J27-2. A mask of 0x03 only operates on the PWM pins. Use the manifest constants you defined earlier for the pin masks to set or clear the bits in the value you want to read or write. If you have internally cached the values you are writing out to the pins, write to the DATA register to set new values. If you want to preserve existing values and you have not cached them, a Read ➤ Modify ➤ Write is called for. The relevant addresses for GPD0 in the ARTIK 5 modules are listed in Table 17-34.

***Table 17-34.*** *Base Addresses for ARTIK 5 Port GPD0*

| Address | Description |
|---------|-------------|
| 0x11400028 | Port base address |
| 0x11400028 | MODE control register |
| 0x11400029 | DATA value register |

## Port GPB2

The GPB2 port is allocated to an Arduino-compatible PWM control on an ARTIK 10 module. This functionality is mapped to GPD0 on an ARTIK 5 and so GPB2 is not used on that module.

Table 17-35 lists the mapping of the bits to the header pins and also lists the signal names from the Panasonic AXT connectors on the underside of the ARTIK modules. Refer to Chapter 13 for details of the AXT connector pinouts. Some of these pins drive the Arduino digital pins on the J26 and J27 headers. The small tilde symbol (~) denotes a PWM Arduino pin name because they have a numeric label that could be confused with the physical pin number.

***Table 17-35.*** *GPB2 Pins and Signals Mapped to Bits*

| BIT | MODE | Signal name | Header pin | Mask |
|-----|------|-------------|------------|------|
| 7 | - | N/C | - | 0x80 |
| 6 | - | N/C | - | 0x40 |
| 5 | - | N/C | - | 0x20 |
| 4 | - | N/C | - | 0x10 |
| 3 | - | N/C | - | 0x08 |
| 2 | - | N/C | - | 0x04 |
| 1 | output | Xpwmo_1 | J26-2 (~6) | 0x02 |
| 0 | output | Xpwmo_0 | J26-3 (~5) | 0x01 |

If you use the bitwise AND expression with the 0x03 value to mask your read and write values, you will only operate on the PWM pins. Use the manifest constants you defined earlier for the pin masks to set or clear the bits in the value you want to read or write. If you have internally cached the values you are writing out to the pins, write to the DATA register to set new values. If you want to preserve existing values and you have not cached them, a Read ➤ Modify ➤ Write is called for. The relevant addresses for GPB2 in the ARTIK 10 modules are listed in Table 17-36.

***Table 17-36.*** *Base Addresses for ARTIK 10 Port GPB2*

| Address | Description |
|---------|-------------|
| 0x14010028 | Port base address |
| 0x14010028 | MODE control register |
| 0x14010029 | DATA value register |

# Programming Via the Kernel Interface

An alternative to accessing the GPIO pins via sysfs is to communicate directly with the kernel and use I/O port addresses. Compared with the user space access via the sysfs regular files, this is a complex scenario to set up and get working. For a start, it involves direct access to memory, allocation, and reading/writing binary data. It is sufficiently challenging that there are almost no clear examples of how to do this in the online resources for GPIO programming. Most of them open a file descriptor on a sysfs regular file. This is right out there on the so-called "bleeding edge" of technology. There are almost no resources that cover this kind of programming and so a solution must be synthesized by a process of deduction. A good understanding of the internal memory architecture of the Linux operating system is helpful. It is fortunate that the ARTIK OS is based on Linux so the conversion from examples on other platforms is simple. The inspiration for this example was presented on the eLinux web site and developed by Dom and Gert (Gert van Loo): http://elinux.org/RPi_Low-level_peripherals.

The performance gains might be minimal by going down this path. Experienced systems programmers insist that this is the right approach because there are fewer layers between your application and the bare metal. There may be a few edge cases where runtime performance is so critical that this technique is better than using sysfs files. Before assembling the complete example, the individual steps are discussed to explain how this works.

These include files are needed to resolve the calls made to the Linux libraries:

```
#include <stdio.h>
#include <stdlib.h>
#include <fcntl.h>
#include <sys/mman.h>
```

These manifest constants must be defined so the memory allocation can map the memory correctly:

```
#define PAGE_SIZE (4*1024)
#define BLOCK_SIZE (4*1024)
```

Confirm the memory page size value with this command:

```
getconf PAGE_SIZE
```

According to the online resources, the disk block size is 4096. Confirm this by carefully inspecting the kernel source code or just use the default and assume that it is the right value.

Decide on a value to use for the GPIO_BASE manifest constant. This should point at a reference location relative to the virtual memory storage position of the GPIO registers. Use the base address defined for each of the drivers, which is different for each group of GPIO registers (according to their driver parentage). The address is also different between the ARTIK 5 and 10 modules. This value is appropriate for an ARTIK 5 to access ports belonging to the gpio driver:

```
#define GPIO_BASE 0x11400000
```

These examples require a few global variables to be defined to hold handles to resources as they are created. Storing them in global variables makes the code easier to manage. Define these global variables near the top of your source file:

```
FILE *mem_fd;
char *gpio_mem;
unsigned char *gpio_map;
volatile unsigned *gpio;
```

281

The memory in your ARTIK is presented to user space applications via the /dev/mem virtual file. This is a character access file. Open it to get a file descriptor. Then read and write to it provided your process has the necessary permissions from the kernel.

```
if ((mem_fd = open("/dev/mem", O_RDWR|O_SYNC) ) < 0)
{
  printf("cannot open /dev/mem \n");
  exit (-1);
}
```

This uses the open() function, which is a system call rather than the traditional fopen() that user space applications might normally use on a regular file. After the target file path, the flags are a combination bit-mask that defines the file that should be opened for reading and writing and that synchronous I/O should be used to block any further action until the written data has been flushed to the destination.

The file needs to be mapped into your application memory space. This might seem odd but it is necessary to fix the location to remove any offsets due to virtual memory management or kernel virtual file system creation. The location in memory is unpredictable otherwise. It must be in a predictable place so the hardware registers are mapped correctly. These fragments of code allocate sufficient space, map the memory and retain a handle to it:

```
if ((gpio_mem = malloc(BLOCK_SIZE + (PAGE_SIZE-1))) == NULL)
{
  printf("allocation error \n");
  exit (-1);
}
```

The next step in the example code is to confirm that the pointer is located on a 4K boundary. This uses the PAGE_SIZE constant to check it and applies a modulo operator to force it to change if necessary:

```
if ((unsigned long)gpio_mem % PAGE_SIZE)
{
  gpio_mem += PAGE_SIZE - ((unsigned long)gpio_mem % PAGE_SIZE);
}
```

Now that the pointer has been relocated, the memory contents can be mapped to a physical location:

```
gpio_map = (unsigned char *)mmap((caddr_t)gpio_mem,
                        BLOCK_SIZE,
                        PROT_READ|PROT_WRITE,
                        MAP_SHARED|MAP_FIXED,
                        mem_fd,
                        GPIO_BASE);
```

The mapping process is then checked and an early exit called if it did not work properly:

```
if ((long)gpio_map < 0)
{
  printf("mmap error %d\n", (int)gpio_map);
  exit (-1);
}
```

Now that everything works, the pointer is stored as a volatile value in the gpio global variable:

```
gpio = (volatile unsigned *)gpio_map;
```

Perform a memory dump of the gpio allocated space. This should be a benign process because it only reads the memory locations and nothing is written at this stage:

```
int i;
printf("Memory dump\n");
for(i=0; i<10;i++)
{
  printf("GPIO memory address=0x%08x: 0x%08x\n",
                          (unsigned int)gpio+i,
                          *(gpio+i));
}
```

There are no published examples for the next step. The port address comes into play at this point. This must be relative to the address that has been stored in the gpio global variable. If this assumption is wrong, an offset needs to be added or subtracted to align that base address with the memory image that was just mapped.

If port address is wrong, any reads and writes go to the incorrect location. Since this approach directly alters the memory contents in the ARTIK, the results are unpredictable.

The memory dump displays the address where the GPIO memory has been mapped into your application. The start of that address range corresponds to the value you defined in the GPIO_BASE manifest constant because one is mapped onto the other. This could have been defined in a variable that you dynamically generated based on detecting the ARTIK model or inside a function body with it defined as a passed-in parameter. In this code, expect to see the memory mapped to 0x00022000 which does yield a value that looks like a MODE control register value. The next address location at 0x00022001 looks like it might be values read back from a DATA port. Exactly where it is expected, another MODE register appears at address 0x00022008. As an exercise, calculate an offset and modify the formatter in the printf() function so it displays the same base address as GPIO_BASE.

When the example is run, the values returned by the MODE address appear to be 64 bits long. This might be a simple formatting issue with the output.

Based on the same pointer to the driver base address, use the port and register offsets to compute a location to read the GPIO value from. Using the volatile pointer as a reference, this C language expression returns the value of a GPIO register:

```
result = *(gpio + {port_base_address_offset} + {port_register_offset});
```

To store a value into a GPIO register, use the pointer and compute the offset in the same way, then assign the new value to that location:

```
*(gpio + {port_base_address_offset} + {port_register_offset}) = {new value};
```

A Read ➤ Modify ➤ Write would work like this:

```
result = *(gpio + {port_base_address_offset} + {port_register_offset});
result = {some bit manipulated variant of the current value};
*(gpio + {port_base_address_offset} + {port_register_offset}) = result;
```

## Prototype Example Code

The example code that was just explained can be typed in as a single application and compiled for testing. Build this example in your working directory where you try out code examples. Build test examples in the /tmp directory where they are cleaned up automatically. You may want to keep them somewhere else so they can survive after rebooting your ARTIK. Open a new source code file called kernel_gpio.c with your editor. Then type in the code in Listing 17-18 and save the file.

***Listing 17-18.*** Kernel Access to Mapped GPIO Registers

```
// Based on an example found at http://elinux.org/

// Define access to the operating system library functions
#include <stdio.h>
#include <stdlib.h>
#include <fcntl.h>
#include <sys/mman.h>

// Define some manifest constants to describe the memory layout
#define PAGE_SIZE (4*1024)
#define BLOCK_SIZE (4*1024)

// Define the base address for the GPIO registers in virtual memory
#define GPIO_BASE 0x11400000

// Define the global variables
int  mem_fd;
char *gpio_mem
unsigned char *gpio_map;
volatile unsigned *gpio;

// Main application body
int main(int argc, char* argv[])
{

  // Open the kernel provided memory image
  if ((mem_fd = open("/dev/mem", O_RDWR|O_SYNC) ) < 0)
  {
    printf("cannot open /dev/mem \n");
    exit (-1);
  }

  // Allocate some space to map the memory into
  if ((gpio_mem = malloc(BLOCK_SIZE + (PAGE_SIZE-1))) == NULL)
  {
    printf("allocation error \n");
    exit (-1);
  }

  // Adjust the pointer to locate it on a 4K boundary
  if ((unsigned long)gpio_mem % PAGE_SIZE)
  {
   gpio_mem += PAGE_SIZE - ((unsigned long)gpio_mem % PAGE_SIZE);
  }

  // Map the kernel memory image into application memory space
  gpio_map = (unsigned char *)mmap((caddr_t)gpio_mem,
                                    BLOCK_SIZE,
                                    PROT_READ|PROT_WRITE,
                                    MAP_SHARED|MAP_FIXED,
```

```
                                          mem_fd,
                                          GPIO_BASE);

  // Now check that the mapping worked
  if ((long)gpio_map < 0)
  {
    printf("mmap error %d\n", (int)gpio_map);
    exit (-1);
  }


  // Preserve the mapped GPIO pointer
  gpio = (volatile unsigned *)gpio_map;

  // Dump out the contents of the mapped GPIO memory
  int i;
  printf("Memory dump\n");
  for(i=0; i<10;i++)
  {
    printf("GPIO memory address=0x%08x: 0x%08x\n",
                               (unsigned int)gpio+i,
                               *(gpio+i));
  }

// Return a result code
return 0;
}
```

Compile and run your test application with these commands. You should see some output from your application that looks like Listing 17-19. Expect it to be different between an ARTIK 5 and 10 because their GPIO structure is not the same.

***Listing 17-19.*** Example Output From the Kernel GPIO Test Application

```
gcc -Wall kernel_gpio.c -o kernel_gpio
./kernel_gpio

Memory dump
GPIO memory address=0x00022000: 0x22222222
GPIO memory address=0x00022001: 0x000000b3
GPIO memory address=0x00022002: 0x00000000
GPIO memory address=0x00022003: 0x00000000
GPIO memory address=0x00022004: 0x00000000
GPIO memory address=0x00022005: 0x00000000
GPIO memory address=0x00022006: 0x00000000
GPIO memory address=0x00022007: 0x00000000
GPIO memory address=0x00022008: 0x00223322
GPIO memory address=0x00022009: 0x0000003d
```

# GPIO Pin Multiplexing

GPIO pin multiplexing allows the GPIO interfaces to be reconfigured for a variety of different purposes. This helps the system designers when they create the chips because now they can make generic GPIO hardware that can be reconfigured at startup. The support for this is relatively new, incomplete, and somewhat primitive but extremely powerful. Even at this early stage, useful functionality is already available via the kernel debugging virtual file system. Read the kernel documentation for details of how this all works inside the ARTIK.

GPIO pins can be set into one of eight possible multiplexed function states. This is managed by a pin-multiplexing chip that is deeply integrated into the SoC core of your ARTIK module. Reading the contents of the /proc/device-tree/compatible file on a Commercial Beta ARTIK 5 module reveals that it is a samsung,artik5samsung,exynos3250 device. Searching the online kernel sources reveals the exynos3250-pinctrl.dtsi file, which the kernel uses to build the pin-multiplexing configuration at boot time from the device tree.

Each multiplexed function causes the GPIO pin behavior to be reconfigured as it is selected. A lot of the possible combinations are unused at present. The pin behaviors are grouped logically under each function. The ARTIK 5 and 10 data sheets describe eight alternative multiplexed function states with the default being normal GPIO operation. Table 17-37 lists the different functions that the GPIO pins can be configured to.

*Table 17-37.* *Multiplexed GPIO Pin Functions*

| Function | Pin behavior |
| --- | --- |
| F0 | Input mode for detecting switches and sensors |
| F1 | Output mode for setting control pins in peripherals, turning on lights, starting motors |
| F2 | Wakeup interrupts and I2C bus signals |
| F3 | Mostly reserved for future use but some pins used for PCM audio output |
| F4 | Mostly reserved for future use but some pins used for debug tracing |
| F5 | Mainly used for debugging |
| F6 | Mainly used to control the Multi-Function-Codec |
| F7 | External interrupts |

## /sys/kernel/debug/pinctrl

There are three useful directories in the debugfs file system relevant to GPIO pin multiplexing. They are mounted at /sys/kernel/debug/pinctrl on each of the ARTIK modules. They are global property files and containers for the two devices instantiated by the pinctrl driver to manage GPIO pins. User space applications can access all of them via the sysfs virtual file system. They are not named exactly the same for an ARTIK 5 and 10 because they are located at different memory base addresses in each module. Table 17-38 lists the directories for both modules.

*Table 17-38.* *Kernel Debug Support for pinctrl Devices*

| ARTIK module | Path |
| --- | --- |
| 5/10 | /sys/kernel/debug/pinctrl/ |
| 5 | /sys/kernel/debug/pinctrl/11400000.pinctrl |
| 5 | /sys/kernel/debug/pinctrl/11000000.pinctrl |
| 10 | /sys/kernel/debug/pinctrl/13400000.pinctrl |
| 10 | /sys/kernel/debug/pinctrl/14010000.pinctrl |

Each of these directories contains a collection of readable files with useful configuration data about the GPIO structure. Use the cat command to view their contents. You may be able to exploit them to dynamically configure the behavior of your application as it uses the GPIO ports.

If you inspect the contents of the /sys/kernel/debug/pinctrl directory, there are some files that describe the current mapping of the GPIO pins and a pair of directories that reflect the two pinctrl devices. If you cat the files to your screen, the current state of the GPIO pins and what they are used for becomes much clearer. The pinctrl-devices, pinctrl-handles, and pinctrl-maps property files tell you a great deal.

The pinctrl devices in /sys/kernel/debug/pinctrl reflect the internal properties for each pinctrl kernel object. They contain the files listed in Table 17-39.

***Table 17-39.*** *GPIO Configuration Interface*

| Property | Purpose |
|---|---|
| gpio-ranges | Describes which GPIO pin numbers are managed by each GPIO port owned by that driver. Aggregate the contents this file in both device objects to see the entire range. These port numbers become important of you want to find the registers that control each pin when you program GPIO pins via the kernel. |
| pinconf-config | Displays the most recent change to GPIO pin states. Write to this property to set the state of a pin. Identify the device, pin, and state that you want to set. |
| pinconf-groups | Lists the grouping of GPIO pin configurations, which related to the port names used in kernel programming |
| pinconf-pins | List the pins by index number and shows various group membership and other properties |
| pingroups | Lists the groups with the pins that are members of each one |
| pinmux-functions | Debug list of pin multiplex functions as currently configured |
| pinmux-pins | Lists the pins in numbered index order and describes what they are currently allocated to |
| pins | Lists the pins with their state and value properties |

## Modifying the GPIO Pin Multiplexed State

The only one of the regular files in the pinctrl device container that is writable is the pinconf-config file. This is part of the GPIO configuration support, which lets you change the configuration of a GPIO interface. The user space interface to this via sysfs is at a very early stage of development, so for now access it via the debugfs virtual file system mounted at /sys/kernel/debug. This is likely to change in subsequent kernel releases and at some point the control files will be placed in a more suitable location. The current behavior is outlined here for you to start learning about it but arbitrarily altering GPIO pin configurations is likely to cause severe problems. You might make some important internal devices inoperable if you alter the GPIO that controls them. To alter the contents of this file, echo a very specific command format to it. Refer to this kernel source file for details in the comments for the pinconf_dbg_config_write() function: https://github.com/torvalds/linux/blob/master/drivers/pinctrl/pinconf.c.

Only the modify command is supported at this time. Later, the kernel developers plan to implement the add and delete tools. The format of your configuration requests would be based on an echo command:

```
echo "modify {target} {device-name} {state} {name}" > /sys/kernel/debug/pinctrl/{device}/
pinconf-config
```

where {target} is config_pin or config_group. The {device-name} {state} {name} values should be consistent with the pinctrl maps you can obtain by inspecting other files in this part of the tree. Later config_mux and other options will be supported. The file path where this is written needs to identify the device (A or B).

## Learn More About pinctrl Multiplexing

Read the following kernel documentation files for more insight into this advanced GPIO pin multiplexing configuration technique. The bindings document is particularly interesting as it lists the generic properties that expose very sophisticated GPIO configuration opportunities. The DTSI source file for the Exynos3250 device tree describes the pinctrl values for the GPIO pins that the kernel establishes at boot time.

```
https://developer.artik.io/documentation/developer-guide/gpio-mapping.html
https://developer.artik.io/documentation/developer-guide/kernel-gpio.html
www.artik.io/developer/documentation/tutorials/using-gpio-on-artik-10.html
www.kernel.org/doc/Documentation/devicetree/bindings/gpio/gpio.txt
www.kernel.org/doc/Documentation/devicetree/bindings/pinctrl/pinctrl-bindings.txt
www.kernel.org/doc/Documentation/gpio/gpio.txt
www.kernel.org/doc/Documentation/gpio/sysfs.txt
www.kernel.org/doc/Documentation/pinctrl.txt
www.kernel.org/doc/man-pages/online/pages/man2/mmap.2.html
https://github.com/torvalds/linux/blob/master/arch/arm/boot/dts/exynos3250-pinctrl.dtsi
https://github.com/torvalds/linux/tree/master/Documentation/arm/Samsung-S3C24XX
http://falsinsoft.blogspot.co.uk/2012/11/access-gpio-from-linux-user-space.html
http://free-electrons.com/kerneldoc/latest/devicetree/bindings/pinctrl/samsung-pinctrl.txt
```

Explore the contents of the /sys/kernel/debug/pinctrl directory with the cat command. It tells you how the pinctrl driver maps to the GPIO hardware chips.

Read the ARTIK documentation about using GPIO and the programmable I/O pins. Also check out the links to the kernel documentation and the memory-mapping functions. Read the Samsung ARTIK data sheets, developer board schematics, and product briefs for other insights into the GPIO behavior. The ARTIK OS source code may also provide some helpful insight, although the most useful material is in the kernel source code. Because the audio codec chip is controlled by GPIO, there may also be some interesting clues in the publicly available ALSA library and SDK toolkit source code.

# Summary

Understanding GPIO and pin control interfaces immediately gives your application the means to interact with the real world. Even though GPIO is a simple on/off control of a pin, you can accomplish some amazing things with it.

# CHAPTER 18

# Analog Input and IIO

Analog input is used to read a varying signal level from a sensor, which is processed through an analog-to-digital converter (ADC) to generate a raw numeric value. This raw value needs to be scaled to the correct units of measure. Analog input is taken through the ADC pins on the J24 header. ARTIK 5 modules support only two channels of ADC input while the ARTIK 10 supports six.

## Reading Analog Inputs

The analog inputs are managed under the general class of IIO devices. There is an emerging and important subsystem gradually being developed around the management of analog values. The IIO subsystem started out as a prototype developed by Jonathan Cameron but it has now been adopted into the main Linux kernel project.

When you interact with sensors, everything comes down to measuring a value or detecting a binary state. For simple binary on/off states, use the GPIO pins because they are intended for single bit switching tasks. However, GPIO cannot read varying analog voltages so the IIO subsystem has been developed to help make things easier to implement.

Your application can read the incoming values on the analog inputs with simple IIO function calls. These inputs are completely separate to the digital pins. The input is connected to a 12-bit analog-to-digital converter (ADC) which yields a numeric value between 0 and 4096. This is the granularity or resolution of the analog input. The value is measured relative to a reference voltage, which is 1.8v in an ARTIK module. Apply a scaling factor to convert the incoming sample value to the correct units of measure that you need.

The analog value is determined by a valuator control or sensor. Physical sensors are often based around changes in electrical resistance, which translates to your application being able to measure a voltage on an analog input pin. The modern sensor components have a lot of input intelligence and present meaningful values mapped into a range the Arduino and ARTIK modules can easily understand.

---

**Note** Arduino devices typically use a 10-bit ADC resolution (1024 steps) and the ARTIK uses a 12-bit ADC resolution (4096 steps). If you are porting code from an earlier Arduino project, check that the scaling factor is correct before you build the application. Determining the correct algorithm for working out scaling factors is covered later in this chapter.

---

## Analog ADC Pin Connections

The ARTIK 5 supports two 12-bit ADC input pins. This is enough to use the ARTIK to make a stereo recording, but more channels are needed to build a surround sound-compatible solution. The ARTIK 10 is better suited to that scenario. Figure 18-1 shows the J24 connector for a Type 5 and 10 developer reference boards. Although the pins are reserved for six ADC inputs on a Type 5 board, you can see that the signal conditioning components are only present for the two channels that the ARTIK 5 supports.

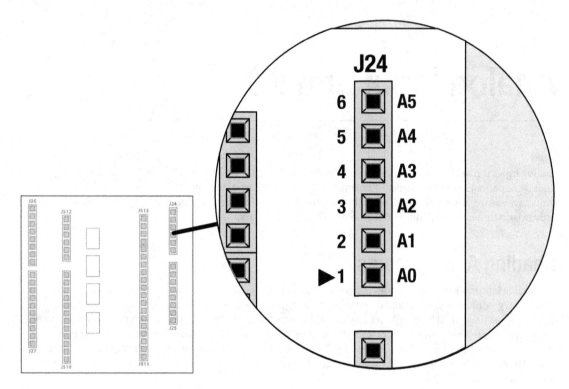

***Figure 18-1.*** *Analog input pins (J24)*

The ARTIK 10 supports six 12-bit analog input channels. This is fine for a 5•1 surround system design to record the audio. Interestingly, the pin names in the Samsung documentation suggest that there may be other inputs that are not yet brought out to an accessible connector. Table 18-1 summarizes the pins on the Type 5 and Type 10 developer reference boards. The label column is the symbolic name of the connectors. The physical pin numbers on each connector are described in the other columns.

***Table 18-1.*** *ADC Pins on Developer Reference Board Jumpers*

| ARTIK Name | Label | Type 5 | Type 10 | Aux |
|---|---|---|---|---|
| ADC0 | A0 | J24-1 | J24-1 | J510-2 |
| ADC1 | A1 | J24-2 | J24-2 | J510-3 |
| ADC2 | A2 | N/A | J24-3 | |
| ADC3 (non-existent) | N/A | N/A | N/A | |
| ADC4 (non-existent) | N/A | N/A | N/A | |
| ADC5 | A3 | N/A | J24-4 | |
| ADC6 | A4 | N/A | J24-5 | |
| ADC7 | A5 | N/A | J24-6 | |

According to the developer board schematic diagrams, physical pins J24-1 and J24-2 are connected to auxiliary test points on connector J510. Connect to either of these locations for ADC0 and ADC1.

---

■ **Note** The labeling of A0 to A5 on the developer reference boards should not be confused with the ADC numbers used internally by the ARTIK. This is not a one-to-one mapping. Refer to Table 18-1 to see how the two environments are reflected.

---

# Analog ADC Input with Arduino IDE

On the Type 5 and Type 10 developer reference boards, header pins J24-1 and J24-2 are available. On the Type 10, J24-3, J24-4, J24-5, and J24-6 can also be used as analog inputs with the Arduino IDE. The analogRead() function, explained in the "ADC Interface" section of the *Samsung GPIO Programming Guide*, makes it very easy to use.

Use the code shown in Listing 18-1 to collect temperature sensor data every second using the analogRead() function. Install a **TMP36** temperature sensor and wire it to your ADC input (analog data comes from the middle pin.)

*Listing 18-1.* Example ADC Input With Arduino IDE

```
#include <stdio.h>

// Declare and initialisevariables
int inputPin = 1;
int currentRun = 0;
const int MAX_RUNS = 10;

int main(void)
{

  while(currentRun < MAX_RUNS){

    int sensorVal = analogRead(inputPin);

    printf("current sensor is %f\n", sensorVal);

    /* Convert sensor data to temperature */

    currentRun++;

    sleep(1);

  }
}
```

# Using sysfs

Notwithstanding the fact that Samsung intend to release a developer library to make the API connection easier, you can still use the sysfs virtual file system to access the ADC pins directly. The kernel presents these pins as regular files to access either from the command line shell or with a high-level language. Open and read or write to the files. Kernel-level monitoring of the ADC pins is also possible, but may not provide a significant advantage over using the standard Linux virtual files provided by sysfs.

# Working Out the Base Address

The sysfs virtual file system base address for analog pins is different for the ARTIK 5 and 10 modules. This is important if you plan to use the same code on ARTIK 5 and 10 modules because your application crashes if you attempt to use the wrong one. Modify your shell scripts and C language application source code when you move between platforms. Alternatively, use a more dynamic automatic detection method. Samsung recommends using a manifest constant in C language applications in their developer resources on this web page:

https://developer.artik.io/documentation/developer-guide/kernel-gpio.html.

A manifest constant does work well enough for many scenarios. However, because it is a static approach, it must be modified when the base address changes. This may happen when the OS is upgraded, at which point your application will cease to work. For an ARTIK 5, define your manifest constant with this line of pre-processor code and use this as a basis to build the path to the raw voltage input file path name:

```
#define SYSFS_ADC_PATH "/sys/devices/126c0000.adc/iio:device0/"
```

The equivalent line for an ARTIK 10 would be this:

```
#define SYSFS_ADC_PATH "/sys/devices/12d10000.adc/iio:device0/"
```

Note the different hexadecimal-coded hardware address. Because this value is accessible as a virtual file, it can be exploited very easily with any language that can open regular files for reading and writing. Modify the file path to accommodate the different base path for an ARTIK 10 and use write values to the virtual file to set pin values. Table 18-2 shows the alternative file system locations.

*Table 18-2.* *Analog Pin Base Addresses*

| Module | Virtual file system address |
| --- | --- |
| ARTIK 5 | /sys/devices/126c0000.adc/iio:device0/in_voltageX_raw |
| ARTIK 10 | /sys/devices/12d10000.adc/iio:device0/in_voltageX_raw |

# Reading a Pin Voltage

To read a pin voltage, locate the address of the ADC for the pin you want to read. Include the pin number within the virtual file system path you compose. This illustration is based on an ARTIK 5 module; alter the address to use this example on an ARTIK 10:

```
/sys/devices/126c0000.adc/iio:device0/in_voltage{pin_number}_raw
```

The complete path to the input for pin 1 is this:

```
/sys/devices/126c0000.adc/iio:device0/in_voltage1_raw
```

Listing 18-2 shows how to acquire the raw voltage value from the bash command line.

*Listing 18-2.* Reading an ADC Pin Voltage with bash

```
MY_ADC_PATH="/sys/devices/126c0000.adc/iio:device0/in_voltage1_raw"

MY_ADC_VALUE=`cat ${MY_ADC_PATH}`
```

```
echo "ADC channel 1 has value: ${MY_ADC_VALUE}"

ADC channel 1 has value: 0
```

Taking this very simple example and translating it to the C language is shown in Listing 18-3. Type it in, compile it, and run the application to prove it works. This version uses the base address for an ARTIK 5 module. If you have an ARTIK 10, change the base address to the correct value or your application will throw a segmentation fault. Put some avoidance code around the fopen() call to exit with an error status to make it more robust.

**Listing 18-3.** Reading an ADC Pin Voltage with the C Language

```c
#include <stdio.h>

int main( int argc, char *argv[] )
{
  char myResult[6];
  FILE *myFp;

  myFp = fopen("/sys/devices/126c0000.adc/iio:device0/in_voltage1_raw", "r");

  if(fgets(myResult, 6, myFp) == NULL)
  {
    return(2);
  }

  fclose(myFp);

  printf("ADC channel 0 has value: %s\n", myResult);

  return(0);
}
```

# Automatic Base Addresses in bash

If you know the symbolic name of the device you want to find the base address for, automatically detect the value and decouple your application from the changes that happen when you move code from an ARTIK 5 to an ARTIK 10 or perhaps when the operating system is upgraded. This fragment of bash command line code tells you the base address for the ADC device driver on your ARTIK. A single hexadecimal number is displayed (this example is from an ARTIK 5).

```
ls /sys/devices | grep adc$ | cut -d'.' -f1
126c0000
```

Call this command during the initialization of bash-scripted applications to detect the base address of the chosen device. One useful feature of the bash shells lets you call a sequence of commands and substitute the resulting value in a variable assignment. This variable is an indirect reference to the base address throughout the rest of the script. The technique is called back ticking. It encloses the command in back tick quotes (`) and evaluates the command at runtime. Then it substitutes the result in place of the back-ticked code.

```
MY_ADC_BASE_ADDRESS=`ls /sys/devices | grep adc$ | cut -d'.' -f1`
```

Use the echo command to display the variable on the screen to check that it was assigned, like so:

```
echo $MY_ADC_BASE_ADDRESS
```

Now substitute this variable whenever the base address where the iio:device0 lives is required. This command lists the contents of the base addressed ADC object container, revealing the accessible properties. The variable is expanded by the shell as it parses the command you typed. The contents of the variable are substituted in its place before evaluating the command for execution.

```
ls -l /sys/devices/$MY_ADC_BASE_ADDRESS*
```

```
lrwxrwxrwx 1 root root    0 May 25 05:45 driver -> ../../bus/platform/drivers/exynos-adc
drwxr-xr-x 3 root root    0 May 25 05:42 iio:device0
-r--r--r-- 1 root root 4096 May 25 05:45 modalias
drwxr-xr-x 2 root root    0 May 25 05:45 power
lrwxrwxrwx 1 root root    0 May 25 05:42 subsystem -> ../../bus/platform
-rw-r--r-- 1 root root 4096 May 25 05:42 uevent
```

---

■ **Note**   If you use variable substitution, it is sometimes useful to enclose the variable name in curly braces ( { } ) to give the bash parser a bit more help in understanding the syntax of your command. Be careful if you nest expressions containing quote characters. If the different kinds of quotes are nested properly, everything works, but be aware of the different way that bash sometimes treats single and double quoted strings. It may affect the order in which things are evaluated. You may need multiple layers of escape characters to deliver a command intact to its destination.

---

Construct the path to the voltage pins and store it in a variable. The pin numbers can also be managed as variables. Assign the result to another variable for use elsewhere in the script by using the back tick technique. Listing 18-4 shows an example script to demonstrate the principle.

***Listing 18-4.***  Reading a Voltage With a Shell Script

```
MY_ADC_BASE_ADDRESS=`ls /sys/devices | grep adc$ | cut -d'.' -f1`
ADC_CHANNEL=0
RAW_VOLTAGE="/sys/devices/${MY_ADC_BASE_ADDRESS}.adc/iio:device0/in_voltage${ADC_CHANNEL}_raw"

MY_RESULT=`cat ${RAW_VOLTAGE}`

echo $MY_RESULT
```

For an ARTIK 5, the ADC_CHANNEL value can be set to 0 or 1. For an ARTIK 10, the value can be 0, 1, 2, 5, 6, or 7. There are no ADC3 and ADC4 channels. This numbering is different from the conventions used when programming in the Arduino IDE.

# Automatic Base Addresses in the C Language

Creating a small function for dynamically generating base addresses is helpful in a variety of ways inside your application. Create a framework or library from these small component functions. Then include it in all your ARTIK projects to save having to write the same code every time.

Listing 18-5 provides the source code for the testing application and the function body. It returns the base address in a string buffer that is passed by reference. A successful result is indicated by a return value of zero (0). A return value of 1 indicates that the process file failed to open. If this happens, it might indicate a problem with your account privileges because this should work without any problems. A return value of 2 indicates that the process generated no resulting data. At the top of the source file containing your function you must include the header files for the standard library calls you intend to use. Define the function prototype first in a header file when building a library. The compiler can then correctly determine the function prototype. The buffer length is defined with a manifest constant so it can be used in several places but only modified in one when it needs to change. Open a new source file called testbaseaddress.c with your vi editor and type in the code.

***Listing 18-5.*** Function Example - getBaseAddress()

```c
// Include standard library header files
#include <stdio.h>
#include <stdlib.h>
#include <string.h>

// Declare the function prototype
int getBaseAddress(char* aSymbolicName, char *aResultString );

// Declare the manifest constants
#define BUFFER_LENGTH 16

// Main body of the test application that calls the helper function
int main( int argc, char *argv[] )
{

  char myBaseAddress[BUFFER_LENGTH];
  int myResult;
  int ii;

  myResult = getBaseAddress("adc", myBaseAddress);

  printf("Base address for ADC is: %s with result %d:\n\n",
         myBaseAddress,
         myResult);

  // Display a character by character dump of the result
  printf("------\n");
  for(ii=0; ii<strlen(myBaseAddress); ii++)
  {
    printf("%d - %d\n", ii, myBaseAddress[ii]);
  }
  printf("------\n");

  return 0;
}

// Helper function to get a base address
int getBaseAddress(char* aSymbolicName, char *aResultString )
{
```

```
  FILE *fp;
  char myCommand[64];

  // Manufacture a command line from the first argument
  sprintf(myCommand,
          "ls /sys/devices | grep %s$ | cut -d'.' -f1",
          aSymbolicName);

  // Open the command for reading
  fp = popen(myCommand, "r");

  if (fp == NULL)
  {
    return(1);
  }

  // Read and output the result
  if(fgets(aResultString, BUFFER_LENGTH, fp) == NULL)
  {
    return(2);
  }

  // Close and quit
  pclose(fp);

  // Clean off the trailing line feed character
  // by shortening the string by one character
  aResultString[strlen(aResultString)-1] = 0;

  return(0);
}
```

A for() loop is included to dump the characters out to see whether there are any spurious meta-characters included. With this debugging output, it was apparent that the child process was adding a line feed to the result being returned. Adding a line at the end of the function to strip this off solved the problem. Always check the values you are getting back from your functions and clean them up before returning them to the caller. Now compile and run the example with these commands to see the base address of the ADC interface:

```
gcc -Wall testbaseaddress.c -o testbaseaddress

./testbaseaddress
```

---

■ **Note**    When you use the printf() function to output a line of text in the ARTIK, be sure to use \n to create your newline breaks because \r does not work in the UNIX command line environment and the output from the printf() function will be suppressed.

---

Now that you have a useful function to get the base address, you may choose to store it in a local variable if you plan to exploit it more than once. This saves the time penalty of frequently accessing the command line to retrieve the same information repetitively.

Another strategy is to store the value in a global variable. There are advantages and disadvantages to using global variables. Provided they are managed carefully, they can be very useful. Storing the values in named properties in a struct, which is referenced from a single global variable, creates the smallest footprint in the global namespace.

# Reading an ADC Value

Use that base address value to construct a path to the target ADC channel. Taking the example code from the Samsung developer web page and adding an auto-detecting mechanism leads to the code in Listing 18-6.

*Listing 18-6.* Reading the ADC Raw Voltage Value

```
#include <stdio.h>

int analogRawRead(int aPinNumber)
{
  FILE *fd;
  char fName[64];
  char val[8];
  int myResult;
  char myBaseAddress[BUFFER_LENGTH];

  myResult = getBaseAddress("adc", myBaseAddress);

  // Open value file
  sprintf(fName,
          "/sys/devices/%s.adc/iio:device0/in_voltage%d_raw",
          myBaseAddress,
          aPinNumber);

  if((fd = fopen(fName, "r")) == NULL)
  {
    printf("Error: cannot open analog voltage value\n");
    return 0;
  }

  fgets(val, 8, fd);
  fclose(fd);

  return atoi(val);
}
```

■ **Note**    The data sheets suggest that the ARTIK modules continuously sample these inputs and cache the readings. When you request the readings, you are picking up the most recent sample and not triggering a fresh sampling action. This is a neat way to decouple the performance of your application code from the sampling process.

## Scaling the Raw Value

This raw value that is read from the pin must be scaled to yield a useful voltage value. There are several factors that can affect how you scale that value. The reference voltage and the resolution of the measurements calibrate the conversion factor. The basic formula is based on the relationship between the measured voltage and the reference. The number of discrete values is determined by the resolution, which depends on the number of bits in your sample values.

```
SampleValue = (Vin/VRef) * Resolution
```

The data sheets for the ARTIK 520 and 1020 describe the pinouts as a 1.8v circuit, which we can substitute into the formula as **VRef**. The accuracy of the samples is measured to 12 bits, so the resolution is 2 raised to the power 12 (4096). Divide the reference voltage by the resolution to determine the value of each increment. This value can then be used to multiply the sampled value to arrive back at the measured voltage. To arrive at a usable value for **Vin**, the formula needs to be transposed to yield the correct result. Substituting the right values yields this. Multiply the scale factor by 1000 to calculate a value in milliVolts instead of Volts.

```
Vin = SampleValue * (VRef / Resolution)
Vin = SampleValue * (1.8 / 4096)
Vin = SampleValue * 0.000439453125
mVin = SampleValue * 0.439453125
```

Encapsulate that conversion in another function to call the earlier one to obtain either value elsewhere in your application. Listing 18-7 returns a pre-scaled result in milliVolts.

***Listing 18-7.*** Reading the Scaled ADC Input Voltage

```
float analogRead(int aPinNumber)
{
  int myRawVoltage;

  myRawVoltage = analogRawRead(int aPinNumber);

  return (myRawVoltage * 0.439453125);
}
```

Read the following useful PDF files and web pages for a full explanation of how the ADC sample value scaling factors work and refer to the descriptions of the ADC circuits in the ARTIK data sheets for the electrical properties and sampling rates, which are different in the ARTIK 520 and 1020 modules:

```
http://tayloredge.com/reference/Electronics/ADCDAC/adcscaler.pdf
www.infoplc.net/files/descargas/rockwell/infoplc_net_plc_analog.pdf
www.ni.com/white-paper/4806/en/
https://en.wikipedia.org/wiki/Analog-to-digital_converter
```

# Using the /sys/bus Devices

An alternative and as yet undocumented approach to reading these ADC inputs is possible by accessing them through a different path. Studying the internals of the kernel and how it maps devices into user space can sometimes reveal useful hidden knowledge. Occasionally, you may get some inspiration for a new approach to coding your application. The sysfs virtual file system built by the kernel places copies of the ADC devices at this location in the bus hierarchy:

```
/sys/bus/iio/devices/iio:device0
```

Because this is a symbolic link to the path described in the Samsung developer documentation, it is the same device. So you can access the same device via the bus hierarchy without needing to decode the base address. All of the maintenance overheads required to cope with managing base addresses can be avoided if this works in a consistent manner in all ARTIK modules and is stable from one release of Fedora to another. The shell script for reading voltages becomes much more compact. Monitor the evolution of the sysfs virtual file system as the OS is upgraded because the kernel maintainers are still planning some important changes to it. See the alternative coding in Listing 18-8.

***Listing 18-8.*** Reading a Voltage From a Shell Script

```
ADC_CHANNEL=0
RAW_VOLTAGE="/sys/bus/iio/devices/iio:device0/in_voltage${ADC_CHANNEL}_raw"

MY_RESULT=`cat ${RAW_VOLTAGE}`

echo "ADC channel 0 has value: ${MY_RESULT}"
```

The C Language solution becomes correspondingly simpler. This is shown in Listing 18-9 and should work on the ARTIK 5 and 10 modules unchanged.

***Listing 18-9.*** Reading an ADC Raw Voltage Value Via the Bus Address

```c
#include <stdio.h>

int analogRawRead(int aPinNumber)
{
  FILE *fd;
  char fName[64];
  char val[8];

  // Open value file
  sprintf(fName,
          "/sys/bus/iio/devices/iio:device0/in_voltage%d_raw",
          aPinNumber);

  if((fd = fopen(fName, "r")) == NULL)
  {
    printf("Error: cannot open analog voltage value\n");
    return 0;
  }

  fgets(val, 8, fd);
  fclose(fd);

  return atoi(val);
}
```

Accessing ADC without needing to know the base address leads to the name property within the iio:device0 object. The base address is there in case it is needed. This command displays the base address for the current ADC interface. According to the official IIO documentation, this property should describe the chip being used. Check that it has not moved after upgrading the OS:

```
cat /sys/bus/iio/devices/iio:device0/name
126c0000.adc
```

# About the New IIO Subsystem

The ADC support is being evolved as part of a subsystem in Linux. The IIO subsystem is being developed by Jonathan Cameron. This work started in 2009 and is adding new and more advanced features with each release. It became part of the Linux kernel core in 2012.

IIO is designed from the ground up to be a powerful ADC support tool. Devices such as accelerometers, light sensors, and gyroscopes all present their measurements as analog values. The measurement must be acquired and scaled from the raw values to the correct units of measurement.

IIO is intended to abstract the differences between sensors manufactured by various manufacturers and currently supports nearly 200 devices. The intention is to create a consistent interface for developers to access hardware sensors like the following:

- Accelerometers

- Magnetometers

- Gyroscopes

- Pressure

- Humidity

- Temperature

- Light

- Proximity

- Activity

- Chemicals

- Heart rate monitors

- Potentiometers and rheostats

Each IIO device knows how many channels are supported, what modes it can operate in, and what hooks are available for the driver. Your application can access all this information through the C language `structs`.

The currently defined modes are managed through manifest constants, which define whether the device supports triggers and whether they are hardware or software implemented. The configuration can also include a buffer for streamed data. The driver hooks include these features:

- Raw one-shot reads

- Raw continuous reads of streamed values

- Scaled value reads

- State change triggered functions

- Time scheduled functions

There are currently two kinds of buffering strategies. One is a First In, First Out (FIFO) buffer, which may become full and unable to process more incoming data. This can either lead to blocking or data loss. The other kind of buffer is a ring buffer. This has infinite capacity and cannot block, but old data may be overwritten by newer incoming values.

Switching on these advanced buffering capabilities introduces new entities into the device container. Those are regular files just like all the other sysfs properties and you interact with them with a read or write operation.

This is still a work in progress within the Linux kernel and the ARTIK engineers are still working on driver implementations in their own labs. The IIO project documentation describes an ideal world where everything is already working. See the following links for more information:

```
http://events.linuxfoundation.org/sites/events/files/slides/lceu15_baluta.pdf
https://archive.fosdem.org/2012/schedule/event/693/127_iio-a-new-subsystem.pdf
www.ohwr.org/projects/zio/wiki/Iio
www.kernel.org/doc/Documentation/ABI/testing/sysfs-bus-iio
https://lwn.net/Articles/463338/
www.kernel.org/doc/Documentation/iio/
```

At the time of writing, only the one-shot mode of voltage reading is supported. The continuous buffering mode is not yet implemented. Additional IIO parameters are planned for later support as the IIO kernel support is upgraded.

---

■ **Note**    Because the IIO subsystem manages analog inputs and needs to respond quickly, some of the kernel-related safety net protection is not implemented because it would slow things down. You may get an error when you try to open the same device twice from your application. Your code should not be trying to do this in any case, but some applications are designed with multiple threads and processes and may be unable to interlock against one another. This suggests the application design needs to be reconsidered, so it is not possible to attempt to open your IIO devices a second time until the previous client has closed its session and relinquished the device.

---

# Summary

Now you have extended your knowledge about interfaces to include analog value inputs. Your project could output analog values by using multiple GPIO pins to drive a digital-to-analog convertor (DAC). Reading analog inputs is easier because the ADC interface is already present courtesy of the IIO support built into the kernel. Move on to the next chapter where you will learn about PWM output.

# CHAPTER 19

■ ■ ■

# Pulse Width Modulated Output

The PWM support in the ARTIK is a direct benefit from implementing the Arduino architecture inside a powerful Linux architecture. The ARTIK PWM works very similarly to the Arduino feature but there are some additional capabilities that a Linux kernel offers in addition to the standard Arduino support. This chapter explores the PWM interface in detail and examines what you can do from your own application by interacting with the sysfs virtual file system to configure the PWM output.

## What Is Pulse Width Modulation?

Pulse width modulation (PWM) is not an analog output at all. It can be described as pulse width strobing when it is used to drive an LED to control the apparent brightness. The human eye has persistence of vision, which this PWM approach exploits. If the retina worked instantaneously and humans had no persistence of vision at all, the individual flashes would be visible. Persistence of vision aggregates the LED illumination and averages it out over time to perceive an apparent dimming effect at lower duty cycles. The pulse width varies according to the value, as shown in Figure 19-1.

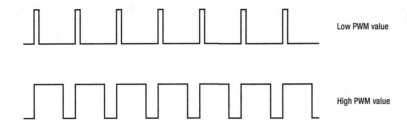

*Figure 19-1.* *Pulse width modulation*

Once you set the value, the pin outputs a continuous stream of pulses whose width is proportional to the value. If you want a genuinely analog varying voltage output, use the digital pins to control the inputs to a digital-to-analog converter (DAC). Adjust the DC voltage output precisely or generate other waveform shapes by converting a stream of digital sample values to voltages. Alternatively, use the audio outputs to generate a control voltage rather than a sound. Read the following online resources to learn more about PWM:

```
https://developer.artik.io/documentation/tutorials/using-gpio-on-artik-10.html
https://developer.artik.io/documentation/developer-guide/kernel-gpio.html#pwm-interface
www.kernel.org/doc/Documentation/pwm.txt
```

# PWM Support in the ARTIK Modules

The ARTIK-5 and ARTIK-10 modules both support two active-high PWM signals to generate periodic waveforms. Internally, the ARTIK supports four PWM outputs but only two are accessible via hardware pin connections. Table 19-1 summarizes the available information on the PWM ports.

*Table 19-1.* *PWM Channels*

| PWM | Signal name | Notes |
|-----|-------------|-------|
| 0 | Xpwmo_0 | Brought out of the ARTIK module via the AXT connector and made available on pin J26-3 (~5) and J513-4 (PWM0) |
| 1 | Xpwmo_1 | Brought out of the ARTIK module via the AXT connector and made available on pin J26-2 (~6) and J513-3 (PWM1) |
| 2 | Xpwmo_2 | No connection from inside the ARTIK module to the outside world |
| 3 | Xpwmo_3 | No connection from inside the ARTIK module to the outside world |

Older versions of the developer reference boards used for the Alpha and Beta prototypes have their PWM connections reversed compared with the Commercial Beta versions. The Commercial Beta PWM pin connections should be considered to be the definitive configuration. See this web page for more details: http://developer.artik.io/documentation/developer-guide/gpio/kernel-gpio.html#pwm-interface.

# PWM Output Connectors

Connector pins J26-3 (~5) and J26-2 (~6) provide programmable PWM outputs compatible with standard Arduino practice. These pins are also duplicated on J513-4 (PWM0) and J513-3 (PWM1). Figure 19-2 shows the connections on a Commercial Beta developer reference board. They are in the same place on the Type 5 and Type 10 developer reference boards. Table 19-2 summarizes the relevant pins on these headers.

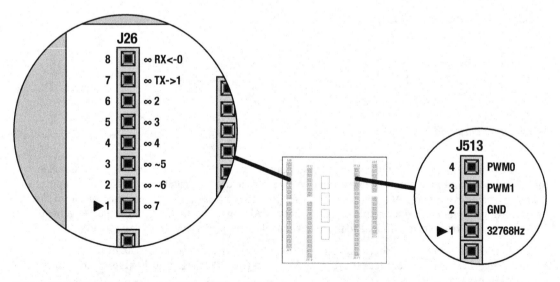

*Figure 19-2.* *PWM pinout connections (J26 and J513)*

*Table 19-2.* *PWM Header Pins*

| Header pin | Label | Notes |
|---|---|---|
| J26-2 | ~6 | Arduino compatible pin 5. Connected to the Xpwmo_1 output on the ARTIK module. Equivalent to pin J513-3. Mapped to Xpwmo_0 on older boards. |
| J26-3 | ~5 | Arduino compatible pin 6. Connected to the Xpwmo_0 output on the ARTIK module. Equivalent to pin J513-4. Mapped to Xpwmo_1 on older boards. |
| J513-3 | PWM1 | Connected to the Xpwmo_1 output on the ARTIK module. Equivalent to pin J26-2. Mapped to Xpwmo_0 on older boards. |
| J513-4 | PWM0 | Connected to the Xpwmo_0 output on the ARTIK module. Equivalent to pin J26-3. Mapped to Xpwmo_1 on older boards. |

# Using PWM with Arduino Calls

In the Arduino IDE, after you have set the digital pin mode to OUTPUT, set the value of that pin to an analog value. Similarly to an Arduino, the ARTIK is not setting a continuously variable analog value but defining the duty cycle of a PWM square wave. This is still strictly speaking a digital output.

Set the pin value with the analogWrite() function. The pulse train runs at a constant rate but the width of the pulses is adjusted to a value proportional to the input value. This pulse train operates at different frequencies according to the kind of device it runs on. The implementation of the ARTIK module hardware is different to the Arduino. Clocks and timers in an ARTIK module run at a different frequency. Check the timings if it is important to your implementation. The same current-limiting concepts that apply in the Arduino environment also apply here. The analogWrite() function syntax is

```
analogWrite({pin_number}, {pin_value});
```

The {pin_number} value is in the range of 0 to 13 and the {pin_value} is between 0 (always off) and 255 (always on):

```
analogWrite(13, 150);
```

The pulse width varies according to the value, as shown in Figure 19-1. When you use the Arduino IDE to code a sketch that you run in the ARTIK, the pin outputs a continuous stream of pulses until you tell it otherwise. Subsequently calling the analogWrite(), digitalRead(), or digitalWrite() functions on that pin halt the output of the PWM pulse train.

# Accessing PWM via sysfs

If you are writing your code outside of the Arduino IDE context, accessing the PWM outputs via sysfs is a useful mechanism when your application is written in the C language or you are working things out with a shell script to experiment with it. This approach works in any language that can access regular files in the sysfs virtual file system. The same techniques for accessing the pins that were used in Chapter 17 for controlling GPIO pinouts also work for PWM programming. The pins are mapped to a different directory in the sysfs virtual file system to keep them separate from the strictly binary GPIO digital pins. Because there is only one PWM chip in the ARTIK, define the base address as a manifest constant in the C language source code or use a dynamic base address discovery technique.

## PWM Entities in sysfs

The PWM interfaces are all grouped together by the kernel and their sysfs files are managed under the PWM class in the /sys/class/pwm directory. Find the PWM device by searching the /sys/devices directory. Longer term, this may be a more reliable solution as /sys/class is gradually being absorbed into the sysfs subsystem support. Use this bash command to extract the base address from the PWM driver:

```
ls /sys/devices/ | grep pwm | cut -d\. -f1
```

The organization of the PWM devices in the sysfs file system is shown in Figure 19-3. There are several paths to PWM-related entities, some of which are symbolic links to the same thing.

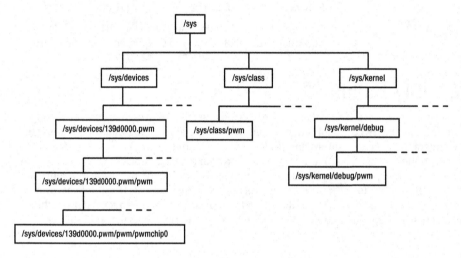

***Figure 19-3.*** *PWM sysfs directory structure*

## /sys/class/pwm/pwmchip0

The PWM chip is reflected into the sysfs file system so your application can operate on it to configure the PWM behavior. This directory contains some important properties. Table 19-3 lists the most interesting items in the top level of the /sys/class/pwm/pwmchip0 directory. Some of these properties are only visible after the channels have been exported to the user space. There are several paths to the same place because of the symbolic linking within sysfs.

**Table 19-3.** *PWM Chip Object Properties*

| Property | Notes |
|----------|-------|
| device | This is a symbolic link to the device object in /sys/devices although the link does not display the target path correctly. |
| export | A writable location where you can request PWM interfaces to be exported to user space |
| npwm | A property that describes how many PWM channels this chip can support |
| power | Power management hooks |
| pwm0 | Connected to the pin labeled Xpwmo_0 on the ARTIK AXT multi-pin interface |
| pwm1 | Connected to the pin labeled Xpwmo_1 on the ARTIK AXT multi-pin interface |
| pwm2 | Programmable but not connected to the outside world |
| pwm3 | Programmable but not connected to the outside world |
| subsystem | A symbolic link to the pwm object in the /sys/class directory |
| uevent | A messaging interface to UDEV to tell it about new devices |
| unexport | A writable location where you can request PWM interfaces to be relinquished from user space |

Type the following command to see a count of how many PWM channels are supported by the ARTIK. Although it presents the value 4, only two of them are available on output pins that you can use. The other two exist inside the ARTIK module but are not connected to an output pin.

```
cat /sys/devices/139d0000.pwm/pwm/pwmchip0/npwm
```

The kernel debug directory contains a file containing the current disposition of the PWM circuits. Type the command in Listing 19-1 to see the contents. The output shows (null) status values while all PWMs are quiescent.

**Listing 19-1.** PWM Channel Status Values

```
cat /sys/kernel/debug/pwm

platform/139d0000.pwm, 4 PWM devices
 pwm-0   ((null)              ):
 pwm-1   ((null)              ):
 pwm-2   ((null)              ):
 pwm-3   ((null)              ):
```

# PWM Channel Properties

Once you have exported a PWM device, it shows up in the /sys/class/pwm/pwmchip0 directory in a directory named pwm0 to pwm3. These directories represent each individual PWM channel object. Each channel has a set of properties for controlling the PWM wave train. The properties are described in Table 19-4.

**Table 19-4.** *PWM Channel Object Properties*

| Property | Notes |
|---|---|
| duty_cycle | The duration of the on time versus the off time. This value must not be greater than the period duration. |
| enable | Setting this value to 1 turns on the PWM waveform output. Setting it to 0 turns it off again. |
| period | The frequency of a PWM waveform is controlled by setting the period value. |
| polarity | Write the value "normal" or "inversed" to switch the polarity of the PWM waveform. This can only be altered while the PWM is disabled. Write a zero (0) value to the enable the property to halt the output before setting this property if the PWM is already running. |
| power | Power management control hooks |
| uevent | A messaging interface to the UDEV driver support when new devices are added |

## PWM Timing Control

The timing values describe the period of the waveform and the duty cycle. Because it is a simple alternating high/low value, the waveform is a square wave. If you just feed this to an amplifier, the square wave sounds somewhat harsh. To do something musical with this output, feed it through wave shaping circuits or just use it as a timing clock for a synthesizer. If you program the PWM channels via sysfs calls, control the frequency by adjusting the period. Figure 19-4 shows the three values that define the pulse train.

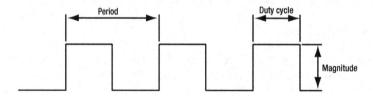

**Figure 19-4.** *Defining the PWM period*

To set a frequency measured in Hz, divide that frequency into 1 billion (1,000,000,000) to get a period duration in nanoseconds (nS).

The duty cycle value must always be less than the period value. If they are the same, it represents a 100% duty cycle and the PWM output is a permanently **HIGH** value. A duty cycle of 0 nS would output a permanently **LOW** value. Because the period is variable, the duty cycle needs to be calculated as a percentage of that period duration. Multiply the period value by the duty cycle percentage to arrive at the right value. Increasing the period value without changing the duty cycle duration alters the percentage and the perceived effect is to dim an LED that is connected and strobed with the PWM waveform.

---

■ **Note**   In an Arduino, the frequency of the PWM outputs shares its timers with the millis() and delay() functions in the Arduino IDE. There may be some effects on the timing of PWM pulses if those functions are used. The ARTIK hardware is somewhat different to that of an Arduino and the effects may not be as pronounced.

---

# Inverting the PWM Waveform

If you program the PWM channels via sysfs calls, invert the waveform via the polarity property. Set it to "inversed" to turn the waveform upside down and "normal" to put things back the way they were by default. Figure 19-5 shows a normal and inverted pulse train.

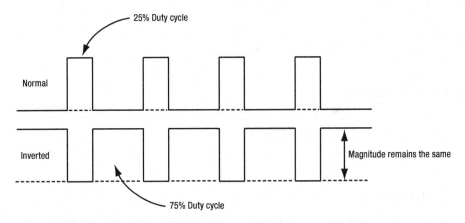

***Figure 19-5.*** *Inverting the PWM waveform*

This inverting functionality suggests some interesting ideas for running two PWM output signals cross phased and fed through a summing circuit to generate interesting musical effects. At present, there is no feasible way to ensure they are synchronized but if they are configured correctly and started at the same time, they should be stable enough to coincide.

# Configuring the PWM Interface with bash

The easiest way to experiment with PWM programming is to use the bash command line shell. Everything can be accomplished with the echo command. If necessary, read property values to check things with the cat command.

## Requesting a Channel Count

Use the cat command to see how many PWM channels are available. The value 4 indicates that the PWM chip can manage four channels but only two of them are brought out from inside the ARTIK module.

```
cat /sys/class/pwm/pwmchip0/npwm
```

## Exporting a Channel to the User Space

The first thing to do is to export a channel from the PWM interface into the user space. Use the commands in Listing 19-2 to see the effect of exporting a channel. Note the appearance of /sys/class/pwm/pwmchip0/pwm0 after executing the commands. The kernel debug display shows it has changed its status. After this, the PWM channel can be configured by altering its properties to set up the wave train.

**Listing 19-2.** Exporting a PWM Channel

```
ls /sys/class/pwm/pwmchip0/
device  export  npwm  power  subsystem  uevent  unexport

MY_PWM_CHANNEL=0
echo ${MY_PWM_CHANNEL} > /sys/class/pwm/pwmchip0/export

ls /sys/class/pwm/pwmchip0/
device  export  npwm  power  pwm0  subsystem  uevent  unexport

cat /sys/kernel/debug/pwm
platform/139d0000.pwm, 4 PWM devices
 pwm-0   (sysfs               ): requested
 pwm-1   ((null)              ):
 pwm-2   ((null)              ):
 pwm-3   ((null)              ):
```

## Setting the Timing Properties for a Channel

The timing control is measured in nS multiples. You must make sure the duration of the duty cycle is always less than the period of the waveform. If you reduce the period value, be careful not to make it less than the duty cycle. Use a function that calculates the duty cycle as a percentage of the duration and set both properties at the same time.

The instructions in Listing 19-3 set the period to a 100th of a second (100 Hz) and a duty cycle of 25%. Use the built-in bc calculator in the bash command line to calculate the value. Enclose that calculation in back ticks to assign the result to a variable. Because the built-in bc command line tool only handles integer values, multiplying by a value of 0.25 will not work. Instead, multiply by 25 and divide by 100 to do an equivalent calculation. The result will be an integer that is rounded down automatically.

**Listing 19-3.** Setting the PWM Timing Controls

```
MY_PWM_CHANNEL=0
MY_DURATION=10000000
MY_DUTY_CYCLE=`echo $(((${MY_DURATION} * 25 / 100))`

echo ${MY_DURATION}    > /sys/class/pwm/pwmchip0/pwm${MY_PWM_CHANNEL}/period
echo ${MY_DUTY_CYCLE} > /sys/class/pwm/pwmchip0/pwm${MY_PWM_CHANNEL}/duty_cycle
```

## Turning On the Output Waveform

Switch the PWM output on by enabling it. The instructions in Listing 19-4 turn it on and the waveform should now be visible on the corresponding output pin. Use the kernel debug output to see the result.

**Listing 19-4.** Turning On the PWM Waveform

```
MY_PWM_CHANNEL=0

echo 1 > /sys/class/pwm/pwmchip0/pwm${MY_PWM_CHANNEL}/enable

cat /sys/kernel/debug/pwm
```

```
platform/139d0000.pwm, 4 PWM devices
 pwm-0   (sysfs                ): requested enabled
 pwm-1   ((null)               ):
 pwm-2   ((null)               ):
 pwm-3   ((null)               ):
```

## Detecting Whether the PWM Is Running

Find out if the PWM is running to invoke the correct logic when you want to invert the waveform. This command line instruction reports a 0 or 1 to indicate whether the PWM is enabled or not:

```
cat /sys/class/pwm/pwmchip0/pwm${MY_PWM_CHANNEL}/enable
```

## Inverting the Waveform

Invert the waveform so the duty cycle describes the **OFF** time rather than the **ON** time. The inverting control can only applied while the PWM is halted. The example in Listing 19-5 can be used before the waveform is enabled.

***Listing 19-5.*** Inverting a PWM Waveform

```
MY_PWM_CHANNEL=0

echo "inversed" > /sys/class/pwm/pwmchip0/pwm${MY_PWM_CHANNEL}/polarity
```

Use this variation to return things to the normal non-inverted condition:

```
echo "normal" > /sys/class/pwm/pwmchip0/pwm${MY_PWM_CHANNEL}/polarity
```

Once you have started the PWM running, Listing 19-6 illustrates how to wrap some disable/enable controls around it so the invert setting can be applied while it is in the correct state.

***Listing 19-6.*** Wrapping PWM Invert Commands Within Enable Calls

```
MY_PWM_CHANNEL=0

echo 0         > /sys/class/pwm/pwmchip0/pwm${MY_PWM_CHANNEL}/enable
echo "inverse" > /sys/class/pwm/pwmchip0/pwm${MY_PWM_CHANNEL}/polarity
echo 1         > /sys/class/pwm/pwmchip0/pwm${MY_PWM_CHANNEL}/enable
```

Add more code to automatically test whether the PWM is running or not and then invoke the appropriate logic.

## Turning Off the Output Waveform

Switch the PWM output off again by disabling it. These instructions turn it off and the waveform should be silenced:

```
MY_PWM_CHANNEL=0

echo 0 > /sys/class/pwm/pwmchip0/pwm${MY_PWM_CHANNEL}/enable
```

## Relinquishing a Channel

When you are finished with the PWM channel, release it back to the pool for other processes to use with this command:

```
MY_PWM_CHANNEL=0

echo ${MY_PWM_CHANNEL} > /sys/class/pwm/pwmchip0/unexport
```

# Programming PWM with the C Language

Accessing the sysfs file system from the C language to control the PWM output is very straightforward. The same techniques you use for the bash command line will work. Wrapping them in C language functions is very straightforward. C language applications retain the input values more easily and percentage calculations use floating point values. Conditional handling and code reuse with function wrappers is also more sophisticated.

## Requesting a Channel Count

Use the example function in Listing 19-7 to see how many PWM channels are available.

*Listing 19-7.* Requesting a PWM Channel Count

```
int pwmChannelCount()
{
  char myResult[6];
  int myIntegerResult;
  FILE *myPWMCountFd;

  // Open the PWM channel count property
  if((myPWMCountFd = fopen("/sys/class/pwm/pwmchip0/npwm", "r")) == NULL)
  {
    printf("Error: cannot open PWM channel count (npwm) for reading\n");
    return false;
  }

  // Read the pin value
  fgets(myResult, 2, myPWMCountFd);

  // Close the PWM channel count property
  fclose(myPWMCountFd);

  // Convert the value to an integer before returning it to your application:
  myIntegerResult = atoi(myResult);

  return myIntegerResult;
}
```

The value 4 is returned to your application when it calls this function. This indicates that the PWM chip can manage four channels but only two of them are brought out from inside the ARTIK module.

# Exporting a Channel to the User Space

The first thing to do is to export the PWM interface into user space. Use the example function in Listing 19-8 to create a new item in the sysfs directory tree that contains the control properties for the channel.

*Listing 19-8.* Exporting a PWM Channel to the User Space

```
bool initialisePWMChannel(int anId)
{
  FILE *myPWMExportFd;

  // Open the PWM export property
  if((myPWMExportFd = fopen("/sys/class/pwm/pwmchip0/export", "w")) == NULL)
  {
    printf("Error: cannot open PWM exporter for writing\n");
    return false;
  }

  // Activate the required PWM channel
  fprintf(myPWMExportFd, "%d\n", anId);

  // Close the PWM export property
  fclose(myPWMExportFd);

  return true;
}
```

After calling this function, operate on that PWM channel by altering its properties to set up the wave train.

# Synthesizing a Path to the PWM Channel Container

Generate a path to the PWM channel container to operate on the properties contained within it. Embed the path generator inside each function that works on the PWM channel or create a utility function to return the path each time you need it. Listing 19-9 shows how to create a path dynamically with the sprintf() function.

*Listing 19-9.* Creating a Dynamic Path to a PWM Channel

```
char myPath[256];
int myChannel;

myChannel = 0;

sprintf(myPath, "/sys/class/pwm/pwmchip0/pwm%d/", myChannel);
```

Use the strcat() function to append the property name or modify the format string each time you use it inside a PWM utility function.

# Setting the Duration Value for a Channel

The period duration control is measured in nS multiples. The example function in Listing 19-10 sets the duration value for a channel.

***Listing 19-10.*** Setting the Duration Value for a PWM Channel

```
bool setPWMDuration(int anId, long int aDuration)
{
  FILE *myPWMDurationFd;
  char myPath[256];

  // Manufacture a path to the PWM period property
  sprintf(myPath, "/sys/class/pwm/pwmchip0/pwm%d/period", anId);

  // Open the PWM period property
  if((myPWMDurationFd = fopen(myPath, "w")) == NULL)
  {
    printf("Error: cannot open PWM period duration for writing\n");
    return false;
  }

  // Activate the required PWM channel
  fprintf(myPWMDurationFd, "%d\n", aDuration);

  // Close the PWM period property
  fclose(myPWMDurationFd);

  return true;
}
```

## Setting the Duty Cycle for a Channel

The duty cycle control is measured in nS multiples. The example function in Listing 19-11 sets the duty cycle for a channel.

***Listing 19-11.*** Setting the Duty Cycle of a PWM Channel

```
bool setPWMDutyCycle(int anId, long int aDutyCycle)
{
  FILE *myPWMDutyCycleFd;
  char myPath[256];

  // Manufacture a path to the PWM duty cycle property
  sprintf(myPath, "/sys/class/pwm/pwmchip0/pwm%d/duty_cycle", anId);

  // Open the PWM duty cycle property
  if((myPWMDutyCycleFd = fopen(myPath, "w")) == NULL)
  {
    printf("Error: cannot open PWM duty cycle for writing\n");
    return false;
  }

  // Activate the required PWM channel
  fprintf(myPWMDutyCycleFd, "%d\n", aDutyCycle);
```

```
// Close the PWM duty cycle property
fclose(myPWMDutyCycleFd);

return true;
}
```

## Setting the Timing Properties for a Channel

You must make sure that the duration of the duty cycle is always less than the period of the waveform. If you reduce the period value, be careful not to make it less than the duty cycle or contrive to set both using a function that calculates the percentage. The example function in Listing 19-12 sets the period to the passed-in value in nanoseconds and calculates an appropriate duty cycle value to use based on the passed-in percentage as a proportion of the duration. This ensures that the duty cycle is always less than the duration and it keeps the values coherent with one another.

*Listing 19-12.* Setting the PWM Channel Timing Values

```
bool setCoherentTimingProperties(int anId, long int aDuration, int aPercentage)
{
  long int myDutyCycle;

  if(!setPWMDuration(anId, aDuration))
  {
    printf("Duration setting failed");
    return false;
  }

  // Calculate the duty cycle as a proportion of the duration period
  myDutyCycle = (aDuration * aPercentage)/100;

  if(setPWMDutyCycle(anId, myDutyCycle))
  {
    printf("Duty cycle setting failed");
    return false;
  }

  return true;
}
```

## Turning On the Output Waveform

Switch the PWM output on by enabling it. The example function in Listing 19-13 turns it on and the waveform should now be visible on the corresponding output pin.

*Listing 19-13.* Turning On the PWM Channel

```
bool enablePWM(int anId)
{
  FILE *myPWMControlFd;
  char myPath[256];

  // Manufacture a path to the PWM enable property
  sprintf(myPath, "/sys/class/pwm/pwmchip0/pwm%d/enable", anId);
```

```
// Open the PWM enable property
if((myPWMControlFd = fopen(myPath, "w")) == NULL)
{
  printf("Error: cannot open PWM enable for writing\n");
  return false;
}

// Enable the required PWM channel
fprintf(myPWMControlFd, "1\n");

// Close the PWM enable property
fclose(myPWMControlFd);

return true;
}
```

## Detecting Whether the PWM Is Running

This is a useful convenience feature, which is exploited with the inverting function example. This function intelligently calls a Disable ➤ Enable cycle in a wrapper around the polarity invert setting. The example function in Listing 19-14 checks the running state of the PWM channel when inverting.

***Listing 19-14.*** Detecting the PWM Channel Enable State

```
bool isPWMRunning(int anId)
{
  char myResult[6];
  int myIntegerResult;
  FILE *myPWMStatusFd;
  char myPath[256];

  // Manufacture a path to the property
  sprintf(myPath, "/sys/class/pwm/pwmchip0/pwm%d/enable", anId);

  // Open the PWM enable property
  if((myPWMStatusFd = fopen(myPath, "r")) == NULL)
  {
    printf("Error: cannot open PWM enable for reading\n");
    return false;
  }

  // Read the pin value
  fgets(myResult, 2, myPWMStatusFd);

  // Close the property file
  fclose(myPWMStatusFd);

  // Convert the value to an integer before returning it to your application:
  myIntegerResult = atoi(myResult);

  return myIntegerResult;
}
```

# Inverting the Waveform

Invert the waveform so the duty cycle describes the **OFF** time rather than the **ON** time. The inverting control can only be applied while the PWM is halted. Testing the current status of the PWM to see if it is running makes this function smart enough to avoid knowing beforehand if the PWM output is stopped. The example function in Listing 19-15 interlocks the polarity invert calls against the enabled state.

***Listing 19-15.*** Inverting the PWM Waveform

```
bool invertPWM(int anId, bool anInvertFlag)
{
  FILE *myPWMPolarityFd;
  char myPath[256];
  bool myPWMStatusFlag;

  myPWMStatusFlag = bool isPWMRunning(int anId);

  // Conditionally switch off the PWM channel
  if(myPWMStatusFlag)
  {
    disablePWM(int anId);
  }

  // Manufacture a path to the PWM polarity property
  sprintf(myPath, "/sys/class/pwm/pwmchip0/pwm%d/polarity", anId);

  // Open the PWM polarity property
  if((myPWMPolarityFd = fopen(myPath, "w")) == NULL)
  {
    printf("Error: cannot open PWM polarity for writing\n");
    return false;
  }

  // Set the required PWM invert value
  if(anInvertFlag)
  {
    fprintf(myPWMPolarityFd, "inversed\n");
  }
  else
  {
    fprintf(myPWMPolarityFd, "normal\n");
  }

  // Close the PWM polarity property
  fclose(myPWMPolarityFd);

  // Conditionally turn the PWM back on
  if(myPWMStatusFlag)
  {
    enablePWM(int anId);
  }

  return true;
}
```

## Turning Off the Output Waveform

Switch the PWM output off again by disabling it. The example function in Listing 19-16 turns it off to silence the waveform.

***Listing 19-16.*** Turning Off the PWM Waveform

```
bool disablePWM(int anId)
{
  FILE *myPWMControlFd;
  char myPath[256];

  // Manufacture a path to the PWM enable property
  sprintf(myPath, "/sys/class/pwm/pwmchip0/pwm%d/enable", anId);

  // Open the PWM enble property
  if((myPWMControlFd = fopen(myPath, "w")) == NULL)
  {
    printf("Error: cannot open PWM enable for writing\n");
    return false;
  }

  // Disable the required PWM channel
  fprintf(myPWMControlFd, "0\n");

  // Close the PWM enable property
  fclose(myPWMControlFd);

  return true;
}
```

## Relinquish a Channel

When you are finished with the PWM channel, release it back to the pool for other processes to use with the example function in Listing 19-17.

***Listing 19-17.*** Giving up the PWM Channel

```
bool destroyPWMChannel(int anId)
{
  FILE *myPWMUnexportFd;

  // Open the PWM unexport property
  if((myPWMUnexportFd = fopen("/sys/class/pwm/pwmchip0/unexport", "w")) == NULL)
  {
    printf("Error: cannot open PWM unexporter for writing\n");
    return false;
  }

  // Deactivate the required PWM channel
  fprintf(myPWMUnexportFd, "%d\n", anId);
```

```
// Close the PWM enexport property
fclose(myPWMUnexportFd);

return true;
}
```

## Utility Helper Function

The example function in Listing 19-18 takes a frequency value measured in Hz and uses it to work out a duration value in nS. This may be more convenient. It also calls the coherent property setting function to ensure the duty cycle is set as a proportion of the computed duration.

***Listing 19-18.*** Frequency Convertor Function

```
bool setPWMFrequency(int anId, int aHzValue, int aPercentage)
{
  long int myDuration;

  // Convert the frequency into a duration
  myDuration = 1000000000/aHzValue;

  // Call the property setting function to set things up
  setCoherentTimingProperties(anId, myDuration, aPercentage);

}
```

# PWM-Related AXT Connections

Tables 19-5 and 19-6 summarize the PWM-related connections available on the AXT connectors underneath your ARTIK module. The connections for the ARTIK 5 and 10 are each shown in their own tables. Refer to the data sheets for more information about voltage levels and other detailed specifications regarding these pins.

***Table 19-5.*** *ARTIK 5 PWM AXT Pinouts*

| AXT pin | Name | Function |
|---------|------|----------|
| J4-45 | Xpwmo_0 | PWM output channel 0. Arduino pin ~5 on header pin J26-3 |
| J4-47 | Xpwmo_1 | PWM output channel 1. Arduino pin ~6 on header pin J26-2 |

***Table 19-6.*** *ARTIK 10 PWM AXT Pinouts*

| AXT pin | Name | Function |
|---------|------|----------|
| J2-67 | Xpwmo_1 | PWM output channel 1. Arduino pin ~6 on header pin J26-2 |
| J2-69 | Xpwmo_0 | PWM output channel 0. Arduino pin ~5 on header pin J26-3 |

# Summary

Adding PWM to your catalog of skills opens more opportunities for driving external hardware. Although it is not truly analog, the PWM output can be used to manage lighting systems and dimming controls. You will need to attach suitable power transistors or thyristors to control high current apparatus using the PWM signals to gate control the current. Added to the GPIO controls, which can turn entire circuits on and off, plus the analog input sending capabilities, your potential for cool, capable, and smart designs is growing all the time.

**CHAPTER 20**

# Inter-Integrated Circuit (I2C)

There are some interesting serial communications technologies for adding peripheral devices. The I2C bus interface is one of the most capable, and there are many sensors and other devices that you can control and monitor with it. This chapter explores the Inter-Integrated Circuit (I2C) support in the ARTIK and extends the published coverage of it to show you the inner workings.

## What Is I2C?

The Inter-Integrated Circuit (I2C) standard was designed to simplify communications between individual chips in highly integrated hardware designs. The original concept and design was by Philips Semiconductor, now known as NXP.

The documentation describes the nodes on an I2C bus as devices but sometimes calls them chips. It makes sense to describe them as devices from a software point of view, but when discussing the hardware, they can be described as chips.

The I2C bus is used inside the ARTIK module for the ARM CPU to talk with the peripheral chips that support the hardware I/O. Some of those chips are implemented on the developer reference board. The taxonomy of the I2C architecture (as found in a Commercial Beta ARTIK 5) is shown in Figure 20-1. This illustrates how the various parts of an I2C implementation relate to one another.

© Cliff Wootton 2016

C. Wootton, *Samsung ARTIK Reference*, DOI 10.1007/978-1-4842-2322-2_20

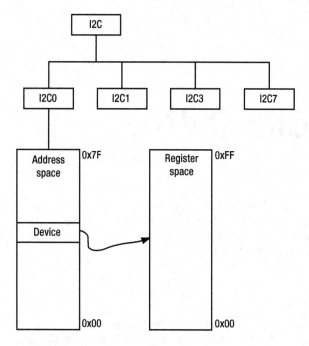

**Figure 20-1.** *Taxonomy of an I2C interface*

The top level I2C device driver owns the whole hierarchy. Within it are a number of separate I2C buses. Each of them has an SCL and SDA pinout from the ARTIK module. Within each bus is a sparsely populated 7-bit address space with devices mapped to the addresses. Usually only a few devices are allocated per bus because the hardware chips themselves only have a limited number of address pins. A chip with only three pins can only exist at one of eight possible addresses. Within each device, the data registers are accessible within an 8-bit range. The lowest numbered register is 0x00 and the highest is 0xFF.

Use the i2cdetect command to see the chips mapped onto a bus as I2C devices. The i2cget command yields the value of a register and the i2cset command sets it to a new value.

Read these online resources for more in depth information about the I2C bus and how it works:

```
https://en.wikipedia.org/wiki/NXP_Semiconductors
https://en.wikipedia.org/wiki/I2C
www.kernel.org/doc/Documentation/i2c/instantiating-devices
```

The data sheets for the model 520 and 1020 ARTIK modules have a lot of detailed specifications of the I2C timings and levels that is useful to know when you drive them from your own applications.

# How Does I2C Work?

The I2C communications are designed to support multiple master nodes connected to a single bus. They automatically sense each other's activity and avoid collisions when they all contend for access at the same time. Multiple slave destinations are supported so a single master can dispatch a message to multiple destinations in one transaction. The bus carries a serial data stream, which reduces the number of wires needed to implement the functionality. Figure 20-2 shows a simplified view of how the bus is implemented.

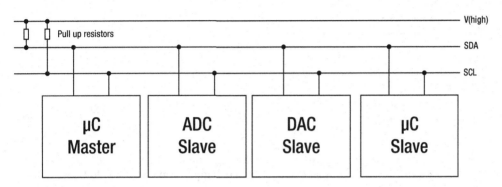

***Figure 20-2.*** *I2C bus layout*

There are two wires in the I2C bus, both pulled up to the power supply voltage rail which makes them **HIGH** by default, so to assert a **LOW** value, the I2C master device needs to drive them to an active-low state.

The Serial Data Line (SDA) carries the information and the Serial Clock Line (SCL) tells the slave devices when it is safe to read it. The I2C master pulls the SCL bus line down while it asserts a value on the SDA bus line. Then the SCL is raised, telling the slaves to collect the data bit that has just been transmitted. The data is mapped to a 7-bit or 10-bit address space of the design. The ARTIK modules use a 7-bit addressing scheme, which allows for 128 distinct chip addresses in the range 0x00 to 0x7F. Typical bus data transfers can take place at 100 Kbits per second in standard mode. Alternatively, a slower 10 Kbits per second data rate can be used to economize the power consumption. The bus can operate at arbitrarily slow speeds, and recent innovations have raised the upper speed limit and allowed for larger address space when I2C is used in an embedded design such as the ARTIK. These performance improvements are possible because the tightly integrated design of embedded systems keeps the signal paths short.

The master node generates the clock signals on the SCL line and initiates the communication. The slave nodes listen for clock signals and respond when addressed by the master. Multiple master nodes can be present and the nodes can change their role from master to slave and back again as determined by the engineering design of the system. Each kind of node can be in transmit or receive mode. See Table 20-1.

***Table 20-1.*** *I2C Node Types and Modes of Operation*

| Node type | Mode | Description |
|-----------|----------|-------------|
| Master | Transmit | The master node is sending data to a slave node. |
| Master | Receive | The master node is receiving data from a slave node. |
| Slave | Transmit | The slave node is sending data to the master node. |
| Slave | Receive | The slave node is receiving data from the master node. |

Messages are transmitted on the bus by sending the most significant bits first. These are framed by start and stop bits. A start bit is indicated by holding the SCL line **HIGH** and transitioning SDA from **HIGH** to **LOW**. See Figure 20-3.

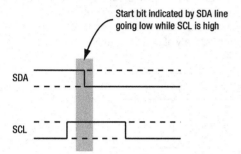

*Figure 20-3.* *I2C start bit indication*

At the end of a message, a stop bit is signified in a similar way but with an SDA transition from **LOW** to **HIGH**. All other transitions of SDA that carry serial data happen while SCL is held **LOW**. See Figure 20-4.

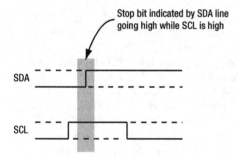

*Figure 20-4.* *I2C stop bit indication*

Initially, a master node is in transmit mode and initiates transactions with the slaves when it chooses to. After sending a start bit, the master transmits the target address value of the slave it wants to communicate with. A final bit to indicate whether it wants to write (0) to the slave or read (1) data from it is followed by a stop bit. The write is signified by a 0 value bit and a read by a 1 value bit. See Figure 20-5 for an illustration of the relative timings between SDA and SCL.

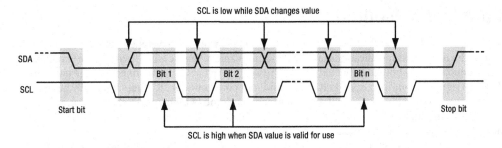

*Figure 20-5. I2C bus timings*

- Data transfer is initiated with a **Start bit** signaled by SDA being pulled **LOW** while SCL stays **HIGH**.

- SDA sets the first data bit level while keeping SCL **LOW**.

- The data is sampled when SCL rises to a **HIGH** value for **Bit 1**.

- This process repeats: SDA transitioning while SCL is **LOW**, and the data being read while SCL is **HIGH** (Bit 2 to Bit n).

- A **Stop bit** is signaled when SDA is pulled **HIGH** while SCL is **HIGH**.

Because these are electrical signals, they may take a finite time to transition from low to high or vice versa. The voltage change vs. the time it takes is called the slewing rate. The longer the bus line, the lower the slewing rate and consequently the slower the bus must operate. To avoid inadvertent value detection, SDA is changed on the SCL falling edge and is sampled and captured on the rising edge of SCL.

Because the protocol is single-ended, it is possible to send out messages that do not correspond to any slaves on the bus. If there is a matching slave, it responds to the message with an ACK signal. The master knows that a slave is present and, depending on whether a read or write is indicated in the initial message, the two nodes communicate. If the master indicates it wants to read data, the slave transmits information while the master listens. Alternatively, if the master wants to write to the slave, it transmits the message while the slave receives the incoming data.

The handshaking happens as each byte is completed. The receiving node transmits an ACK signal to indicate that it received the data. If necessary, the master can assert its authority and send another start bit to seize control of the bus when it wants to interrupt the proceedings. Slave devices can hold the SCL line down to indicate they are busy and cannot yet receive more data. This is called clock stretching.

If there are multiple masters, they will not interrupt one another's transactions while they are engaged in communicating with a slave. It is possible for two masters to initiate a new transaction at the same time. Such collisions are arbitrated automatically by the master nodes detecting that the SDA line has changed state from what it expects as a consequence of another master asserting a value on it. The first master to detect that the SDA does not have the value it expects to see relinquishes control and waits until it sees a Stop bit before attempting to transmit again.

Read the I2C Wikipedia article to find out more about the finer points of this communication protocol: https://en.wikipedia.org/wiki/I2C. There is a pseudo code example of how to program I2C communications.

# I2C on the ARTIK Modules

The data sheets for the model 520 and 1020 ARTIK modules and the Type 5/10 developer reference board schematics have a lot of detailed specifications on the I2C timings and voltage levels. There is some variance in the naming conventions. Study both together very carefully to deduce what I2C bus connections are available.

The ARTIK 10 supports four high-speed I2C buses and four conventional I2C buses internally but not all of these are brought to the outside world via the AXT connectors. Some of them are used for internal control of chips on the ARTIK modules. The ARTIK 5 supports six conventional I2C buses and one additional I2C bus dedicated for use as a camera control interface.

Tables 20-2 and 20-3 list the I2C interfaces for each of the ARTIK 5 and 10 modules based on what is documented in the data sheets and schematic diagrams. The i2cdetect command line tool tells a slightly different story and lists an I2C-0 bus on an ARTIK 5, which is not described in the data sheets or schematics.

**Table 20-2.** *ARTIK I2C Bus Connections*

| Bus | Notes |
| --- | --- |
| I2C-0 | Used internally for the dummy device and power management. No external connection, nor is it described in the data sheet, but it does show up when the i2cdetect tool is used. |
| I2C-1 | Audio Codec chip control and some power management functionality |
| I2C-2 | Used to control the 6B2 camera |
| I2C-3 | External developer accessible bus |
| I2C-4 | Multi-purpose pins also used for SPI, Ethernet, and LPWA |
| I2C-5 | Multi-purpose pins also used for SPI, Ethernet, and LPWA |
| I2C-6 | Multi-purpose pins also used for Audio I2S |
| I2C-7 | Arduino-compatible I2C external bus |

**Table 20-3.** *ARTIK 10 I2C Bus Connections*

| Bus | Notes |
| --- | --- |
| I2C-0 | Used for fuel gauge chip control. Also controls the dummy device and other PMIC functions. |
| I2C-1 | Audio Codec chip control and some power management functionality |
| I2C-2 | Used to control the 5EA camera. Labeled as ISP2. |
| I2C-5 | Appears to not be connected to anything in the developer board according to the schematic. The data sheet describes multiple GPIO functionality for this pin. |
| I2C-7 | Controls the HDMI display |
| I2C-8 | Controls the LCD display |
| I2C-9 | Arduino-compatible I2C external bus |
| ISP0 | Used to control the 3L2 camera. Documented in the data sheet as a second I2C-0 bus but this numbering may not be correct. |

# I2C Tools

There is a small suite of I2C utilities provided with the ARTIK OS by default. They make it very easy to interact with the I2C bus from the bash command line.

i2cdetect: Probes an I2C bus and lists the devices (chips)
i2cget: Gets a register value from an I2C device
i2cset: Sets a register value in an I2C device
i2cdump: Dumps all registers from a I2C device
Read the manual pages about these tools from your bash command line with the man command.

## The Device Detector Tool (i2cdetect)

Use the i2cdetect tool to detect devices on your I2C buses. The simplest variant of this command lists the active I2C buses on your system. Listing 20-1 illustrates how i2cdetect works.

*Listing 20-1.* Using the i2cdetect Tool on an ARTIK 5

```
i2cdetect -l

i2c-0  i2c s3c2410-i2c I2C adapter
i2c-1  i2c s3c2410-i2c I2C adapter
i2c-3  i2c s3c2410-i2c I2C adapter
i2c-7  i2c s3c2410-i2c I2C adapter
```

A variation of the i2cdetect command lists the functionalities supported on each bus. The example in Listing 20-2 examines bus I2C-0 and displays the current disposition.

*Listing 20-2.* Using the i2cdetect Tool to Display a Bus

```
i2cdetect -F 0

Functionalities implemented by /dev/i2c-0:
I2C                              yes
SMBus Quick Command              yes
SMBus Send Byte                  yes
SMBus Receive Byte               yes
SMBus Write Byte                 yes
SMBus Read Byte                  yes
SMBus Write Word                 yes
SMBus Read Word                  yes
SMBus Process Call               yes
SMBus Block Write                yes
SMBus Block Read                 no
SMBus Block Process Call         no
SMBus PEC                        yes
I2C Block Write                  yes
I2C Block Read                   yes
```

The third variant of the i2cdetect command scans the named bus for devices and if they are correctly addressed and powered up, they are displayed in a 16 x 16 address grid. The example command in Listing 20-3 scans bus I2C-0 for recognizable devices. The two devices are indicated by the UU symbols at addresses 0x06 and 0x66.

327

***Listing 20-3.*** Listing the Devices on an I2C Bus

```
i2cdetect -y 0

     0  1  2  3  4  5  6  7  8  9  a  b  c  d  e  f
00:          -- -- -- UU -- -- -- -- -- -- -- -- --
10: -- -- -- -- -- -- -- -- -- -- -- -- -- -- -- --
20: -- -- -- -- -- -- -- -- -- -- -- -- -- -- -- --
30: -- -- -- -- -- -- -- -- -- -- -- -- -- -- -- --
40: -- -- -- -- -- -- -- -- -- -- -- -- -- -- -- --
50: -- -- -- -- -- -- -- -- -- -- -- -- -- -- -- --
60: -- -- -- -- -- -- UU -- -- -- -- -- -- -- -- --
70: -- -- -- -- -- -- -- --
```

# The Value Reading Tool (i2cget)

The `i2cget` tool reads the values of registers in devices that are visible on the I2C bus. Specify a valid bus number, chip address, and register index with the command. An optional mode parameter can be added to alter the way that `i2cget` operates on the data it accesses. The basic `i2cget` command format is

```
i2cget {bus_number} {chip_address} {data_register}
```

Download and read the data sheet for any sensors you are adding to your ARTIK. Somewhere in that data sheet is a list of registers and their values. Look for manufacturer ID codes and test that you get the correct value back for them. This assures you that the sensor chip is working.

The following command reads the byte value from the embedded PMIC (**S2MPS14**) ID register of the ARTIK 5 at register number 0x00 of chip address 0x66 on bus I2C-0:

```
i2cget -f -y 0 0x66 0x0
```

# The Value Setting Tool (i2cset)

The `i2cset` tool writes values to the registers that are visible on the I2C bus. Specify one of the valid bus numbers, chip addresses, and registers with this command. The command format is

```
i2cset {bus_number} {chip_address} {data_register} {value} ...
```

A single value can be written or multiple values in a sequence. An optional mode parameter can be added to alter the way that `i2cset` operates on the data it accesses. Additionally, the `-m` option flag indicates a protective mask, which can be applied to the write so the tool internally performs a Read ➤ Modify ➤ Write operation.

Download and read the data sheet for any sensors you are adding to your ARTIK. Somewhere in that data sheet is a list of registers and their values. Look for manufacturer ID codes and test that you get the correct value back for them. This reassures you that the sensor chip is working. Then you can write values to it.

The following command writes a zero value to an imaginary location at register number 0x10 of chip address 0x50 on bus I2C-0:

```
i2cset -f -y 0 0x50 0x10 0x00
```

## The Register Dump Tool (i2cdump)

The i2cdump tool displays all of the registers belonging to a chip address on an IC bus. The example command in Listing 20-4 forces the i2cdump command to display all 256 registers on chip address 0x06 of bus I2C-0. This is mapped to the dummy device.

***Listing 20-4.*** Example i2cdump Tool Usage

```
i2cdump -y -f 0 0x06


No size specified (using byte-data access)
     0  1  2  3  4  5  6  7  8  9  a  b  c  d  e  f    0123456789abcdef
00: 02 c3 00 f8 2e 2c 4c 20 0a 06 10 00 00 0c 01 01    ??.?.,L ???..???
10: 01 00 00 00 0c 01 01 01 00 00 00 00 00 00 00 00    ?...????........
20: 02 c3 00 f8 2e 2c 4c 20 0a 06 10 00 00 0c 01 01    ??.?.,L ???..???
30: 01 00 00 00 0c 01 01 01 00 00 00 00 00 00 00 00    ?...????........
40: 02 c3 00 f8 2e 2c 4c 20 0a 06 10 00 00 0c 01 01    ??.?.,L ???..???
50: 01 00 00 00 0c 01 01 01 00 00 00 00 00 00 00 00    ?...????........
60: 02 c3 00 f8 2e 2c 4c 20 0a 06 10 00 00 0c 01 01    ??.?.,L ???..???
70: 01 00 00 00 0c 01 01 01 00 00 00 00 00 00 00 00    ?...????........
80: 02 c3 00 f8 2e 2c 4c 20 0a 06 10 00 00 0c 01 01    ??.?.,L ???..???
90: 01 00 00 00 0c 01 01 01 00 00 00 00 00 00 00 00    ?...????........
a0: 02 c3 00 f8 2e 2c 4c 20 0a 06 10 00 00 0c 01 01    ??.?.,L ???..???
b0: 01 00 00 00 0c 01 01 01 00 00 00 00 00 00 00 00    ?...????........
c0: 02 c3 00 f8 2e 2c 4c 20 0a 06 10 00 00 0c 01 01    ??.?.,L ???..???
d0: 01 00 00 00 0c 01 01 01 00 00 00 00 00 00 00 00    ?...????........
e0: 02 c3 00 f8 2e 2c 4c 20 0a 06 10 00 00 0c 01 01    ??.?.,L ???..???
f0: 01 00 00 00 0c 01 01 01 00 00 00 00 00 00 00 00    ?...????........
```

# Accessing I2C via sysfs

The Samsung documentation states that the I2C bus cannot be accessed via the sysfs virtual file system in the same way that user space applications could use it to control GPIO pins. Nevertheless, many of the properties of the I2C bus structures can be inspected by exploring the sysfs directories. Use the Samsung recommended tools to set or get I2C values. You will learn a lot more about I2C by inspecting the values that the kernel reflects into sysfs.

There are a lot of useful locations within the /sys virtual file system. Others are located in the /proc virtual file system. Knowing where they are suggests how to build dynamic self-configuring applications that are resilient to OS upgrades, which is when base addresses are likely to move.

According to the kernel documentation, it is possible to add or delete devices from an I2C bus using sysfs file locations. This is covered shortly under the heading of "Instantiating and Removing Devices."

## I2C Device Nodes

Listing the /sys/bus/i2c/devices directory in the Commercial Beta ARTIK 5 module reveals the currently active I2C devices within each bus system. The built-in chips are accessed within a 7-bit address space. The addresses can range from 0x00 to 0x7F. They are summarized in Table 20-4. Other devices may be visible when you add your own peripherals and sensors or check out this directory on an ARTIK 10 module.

***Table 20-4.*** *I2c Device Nodes*

| Node | Bus | Address | |
|------|-----|---------|---|
| 0-0006 | I2C-0 | 0x06 | Dummy device |
| 0-0066 | I2C-0 | 0x66 | Power management IC |
| 1-0013 | I2C-1 | 0x13 | Stereo audio codec |
| 1-0062 | I2C-1 | 0x62 | Battery level fuel gauge |
| 1-006B | I2C-1 | 0x6B | Battery charger |

# I2C Containers and Properties

Each I2C bus is represented in the `sysfs` virtual file system by a container or object. The properties of that object provide some limited capabilities for interacting with the bus. Look inside the directory to view the properties for one of the bus containers. All the other usual kernel-provided properties are present, such as `name`, `power`, and `uevent`. Table 20-5 enumerates the properties displayed by this command:

```
ls -la /sys/bus/i2c/devices/i2c-3/
```

***Table 20-5.*** *I2C Object Properties*

| Property | Description |
|----------|-------------|
| new_device | Writes a space-separated symbolic name and chip address to create a new device within the I2C bus |
| delete_device | Writes a chip address here to remove a device from the I2C bus |
| Device | This is a symbolic link to the device directory. It can be used to discern the base address for an I2C bus if you need it to memory map the kernel space into your application. |

# Built-in Drivers

The `/sys/bus/i2c/drivers` directory reveals drivers for very specific built-in hardware chips. Use these device part numbers in a web search engine to find data sheets and other resources for them. On an ARTIK, this reveals that the **AK4953** device driver is for a hardware-implemented stereo audio codec. Searching for that chip online reveals a data sheet with much useful information about how it works. Refer to Chapter 22 where that codec chip and other audio-related topics are discussed.

Inside the device driver directories are properties that reveal which I2C bus is used and the chip address. Although this is undocumented material, the address can be deduced by a process of inspection. The Commercial Beta ARTIK 5 reveals the devices listed in Table 20-6.

***Table 20-6.*** *Built-in I2C Devices*

| Device | Bus | Address | Description |
|---|---|---|---|
| ak4953 | I2C1 | 0x13 | Stereo audio codec |
| bq2429x_charger | - | - | Battery charger |
| cw201x | I2C1 | 0x62 | Battery level fuel gauge |
| Dummy | I2C0 | 0x06 | Used to map devices that respond to multiple addresses |
| sec_pmic | I2C0 | 0x66 | Power management IC |

The battery charger is listed as a device but is not allocated an address because it is not plugged in. An address is reserved for it to use when it comes online.

## Instantiating and Removing Devices

If you add new external I2C-compatible chips to your ARTIK, tell the ARTIK about them so it can communicate with them. This kernel reference document shows how to instantiate new devices in several different ways: www.kernel.org/doc/Documentation/i2c/instantiating-devices.

Instantiate a new device from user space with this command line instruction:

```
echo test_device 0x50 > /sys/bus/i2c/devices/i2c-3/new_device
```

The example creates a new device on bus I2C-3 at address 0x50 with a symbolic name of test_device and it manufactures a new container for the device. Verify that it exists with this command, which shows you that a new directory named 3-0050 has been created:

```
ls -la /sys/bus/i2c/devices/i2c-3/
```

For this to be useful there must be some hardware connected to the specified bus. This hardware must also have its address configured to match the address you just used to create the device. If that hardware is not present, then this address will not show up as being activated with the i2cdetect command. If there is a directory present for the device but i2cdetect does not show it as active, perhaps you connected your hardware to the wrong address, or accidentally switched the SDA and SCL connections round or perhaps the device is broken or unpowered. Learning about diagnostic techniques is a useful skill to have at your disposal. Remove the device again later with this command:

```
echo 0x50 > /sys/bus/i2c/devices/i2c-3/delete_device
```

An error message is presented if the device does not exist. This may indicate you typed the device address incorrectly or chose the wrong bus.

# Access I2C from the C Language

The i2ctools are a useful command line solution to access the I2C bus from the bash shell and they simplify things a lot. You can learn how to access the I2C bus from the C language by inspecting the source code for the i2ctools. Make a copy of the open source files, and dismantle the i2cget and i2cset tools to find out how to read and write directly to the I2C bus architecture inside the kernel via the ioctl() function.

This approach works by opening files in the /dev/i2c file system tree. The i2ctools package all this accessibility into a couple of useful files with useful functions. Download the i2ctools package from https://fossies.org/dox/i2c-tools-3.1.2/index.html.

Here is another set of source code archives that contains older versions for comparison: http://i2c-tools.sourcearchive.com.

# Breakout Connections

Tables 20-7 and 20-8 list the I2C interfaces that are presented via breakout connectors on the developer reference boards for the ARTIK 5 and 10 modules based on what is documented in the data sheets and schematic diagrams.

*Table 20-7.* *ARTIK 5 - I2C Bus Breakout Connections*

| Bus | Header (SCL) | Header (SDA) | Notes |
| --- | --- | --- | --- |
| I2C-1 | J511-5 | J511-4 | Audio Codec chip control and some power management functionality |
| I2C-2 | J10-17 | J10-18 | Used to control the 6B2 camera |
| I2C-3 | J510-6 | J510-5 | External developer accessible bus |
| I2C-7 | J27-1 | J27-2 | Arduino-compatible I2C external bus |

*Table 20-8.* *ARTIK 10 - I2C Bus Breakout Connections*

| Bus | Header (SCL) | Header (SDA) | Notes |
| --- | --- | --- | --- |
| I2C-1 | J511-5 | J511-4 | Audio Codec chip control and some power management functionality |
| I2C-2 | J10-18 | J10-17 | Used to control the 5EA camera. Labeled as ISP2. |
| I2C-9 | J27-1 | J27-2 | Arduino-compatible I2C external bus |
| I2C-9 | J510-6 | J510-5 | Duplicate connection for Arduino-compatible I2C external bus. This is different on an ARTIK 10 because the ARTIK 5 presents a separate bus on this connector. |
| ISP0 | J35-18 | J35-20 | Used to control the 3L2 camera. Documented in the data sheet as a second I2C-0 bus but this naming may not be correct. |

The so-called boot mode switch on the developer reference board (SW2-2) appears to be dedicated to enabling a voltage level convertor that couples the internal bus I2C-3 SDA/SCL lines coming out of the ARTIK 5 to the SDA/SCL lines on the J510 external connector where a higher voltage is needed. When SW2-2 is on, the I2C signals are enabled on J510; otherwise they are not driven.

# I2C-Related AXT Connectors

Tables 20-9 and 20-10 summarize the I2C-related connections available on the AXT connectors underneath your ARTIK module. The connections for the ARTIK 5 and 10 are each shown in their own tables. Refer to the data sheets for more information about voltage levels and other detailed specifications regarding these pins.

***Table 20-9.*** *ARTIK 5 - I2C AXT Pinouts*

| Bus | AXT (SCL) | AXT (SDA) | Notes |
| --- | --- | --- | --- |
| I2C-1 | J4-15 | J4-17 | Audio Codec chip control and some power management functionality for fuel gauge |
| I2C-2 | J4-21 | J4-23 | Used to control the 6B2 camera |
| I2C-3 | J4-53 | J4-55 | External developer accessible bus |
| I2C-4 | J4-3 | J4-1 | Multi-purpose pins also used for SPI, Ethernet, and LPWA |
| I2C-5 | J4-7 | J4-5 | Multi-purpose pins also used for SPI, Ethernet, and LPWA |
| I2C-6 | J3-48 | J3-50 | Multi-purpose pins also used for Audio I2S |
| I2C-7 | J4-13 | J4-11 | Arduino-compatible I2C external bus |

***Table 20-10.*** *ARTIK 10 - I2C AXT Pinouts*

| Bus | AXT (SCL) | AXT (SDA) | Notes |
| --- | --- | --- | --- |
| I2C-0 | J1-71 | J1-73 | Used for fuel gauge chip control. Also controls the dummy device and other PMIC functions. |
| I2C-1 | J1-75 | J1-77 | Audio Codec chip control |
| I2C-2 | J2-21 | J2-19 | Used to control the 5EA camera. Labeled as ISP2. |
| I2C-5 | J2-13 | J2-15 | Appears to not be connected to anything in the developer board according to the schematic. The data sheet describes multiple GPIO functionality for this pin. |
| I2C-7 | J2-50 | J2-48 | Controls the HDMI display |
| I2C-8 | J2-61 | J2-59 | Controls the LCD display and touch interface |
| I2C-9 | J3-28 | J3-30 | Arduino-compatible I2C external bus |
| ISP0 | J2-49 | J2-51 | Used to control the 3L2 camera. Documented in the data sheet as a second I2C-0 bus but this naming may not be correct because there is another I2C-0 bus on a different pin. |

In addition to the SDA and SCL lines for each I2C bus, there are two pins that can control the voltage level for the SDA and SCL lines. Refer to the data for more details about this. The pins are summarized in Table 20-11.

*Table 20-11.* *ARTIK 10 - I2C Management and Control*

| AXT Pin | Name | Notes |
| --- | --- | --- |
| J2-63 | XCHG_SDA | Change I2C SD lines to 1v8 signaling |
| J2-65 | XCHG_SCL | Change I2C SCL lines to 1v8 signaling |

# Summary

The I2C bus control of peripheral sensor devices rounds out your interfacing skills very usefully. Now you can interact with some very powerful chips. You may only want to read a temperature value, but you now have all the controls at your disposal to manage complex chips. You only need to add the SPI and I2S buses to have all peripheral interconnect and control options covered.

# CHAPTER 21

# Serial Peripheral Interface (SPI)

The Serial Peripheral Interface Bus (SPI) is a means of communicating between the CPU and the peripheral devices. It is very simple to operate and is used for a variety of devices that connect to the physical world. SD cards, touch screens, liquid crystal displays (LCDs), and analog-to-digital convertors (ADCs) are commonly connected to an SPI bus for extending embedded systems.

A private SPI bus is used for managing the **AX88796C** Ethernet controller chip on the ARTIK 520, and SPI is also used to drive the video display outputs. The programming interface support is not yet available to develop your own user space applications. It is still important to learn about how SPI works so you are equipped to use it later. The data sheets for the model 520 and 1020 ARTIK modules describe the SPI timings.

## How Does SPI Work?

The SPI specification describes a synchronous communication over four wires. The configuration can either be a direct connection between a single master and a single slave or one master and multiple slaves. Figure 21-1 shows the one-to-one configuration.

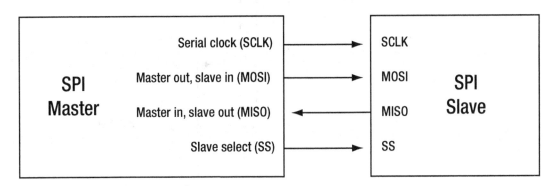

*Figure 21-1.* *SPI single master, single slave configuration*

© Cliff Wootton 2016
C. Wootton, *Samsung ARTIK Reference*, DOI 10.1007/978-1-4842-2322-2_21

A more complex arrangement can be built with one single master and multiple slaves. Figure 21-2 shows this arrangement. Three of the four wires are connected in a bus-like manner to all of the slaves and the slave select line is then extended so each slave can be selected individually.

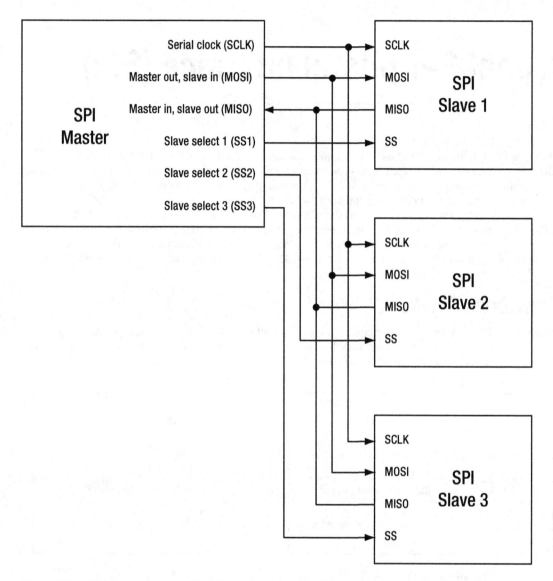

**Figure 21-2.** *SPI single master, multiple slaves configuration*

The SPI bus works best over very short distances. It is ideally suited for use in embedded systems where the components are packed very closely together or even integrated onto a single chip.

# Interfacing Signal Lines

There are four wires connecting the master device to the slave devices. Table 21-1 summarizes the signals they carry.

***Table 21-1.*** *SPI Four Wire Signaling*

| Signal | Description |
| --- | --- |
| SCLK | Serial clock |
| MOSI | Master output, slave input |
| MISO | Master input, slave output |
| SS | Slave select |

- The **serial clock** line is driven by the master. This maintains the synchronous nature of the communications protocol.

- The **master output, slave input** line transfers instructions and data from the master node to the slave.

- The **master input, slave output** line transfers responses from the slave node back to the master.

- The **slave select** line activates the required slave devices so they will see and respond to the messages from the master node. In a simple configuration where there is just one master and one slave, the SS line is hard wired with no selection logic involved because there is only one slave available. This pin can be permanently connected to ground so the single slave is always active. This line is driven active **LOW** by the master. When it is not driven, it is floating **HIGH** via a pull-up resistor. This hardware slave selection technique replaces the chip-addressing techniques used on other kinds of buses.

# Alternative Naming Conventions

The SPI peripheral devices are slaves and may be repurposed from other buses such as I2C. In such an adaption, not all of the connections may have been renamed. There are many manufacturers all over the world and many of them use their own conventions when naming the pins on their SPI-compatible devices. Table 21-2 lists a dictionary of the alternative names you might encounter and maps them to the conventions used by the ARTIK engineering team when they labeled the schematics for the developer reference boards.

**Table 21-2.** *Alternative SPI Signal Naming Conventions*

| Alternative name | ARTIK name |
|---|---|
| CD | SS |
| CLK | SCLK |
| CSB | SS |
| CSN | SS |
| DI | MOSI |
| DIN | MOSI |
| DO | MISO |
| DOUT | MISO |
| EN | SS |
| Master input, Slave output | MISO |
| Master output, slave input | MOSI |
| MRSR | MISO |
| MTST | MOSI |
| nCS | SS |
| nSS | SS |
| SCK | SCLK |
| SDI (on slave devices) | MOSI |
| SDO (on slave devices) | MISO |
| Serial clock | SCLK |
| SI | MOSI |
| SIMO | MOSI |
| Slave Select | SS |
| SO | MISO |
| SOMI | MISO |
| SSn | SS |
| SSQ | SS |
| STE | SS |
| SYNC | SS |

If you use these alternative naming conventions, the SDI on the master should be connected to SDO on the slaves and vice versa. Most devices are selected when the slave select line or the equivalent named pin is pulled **LOW**. In a very few rare cases, you may encounter an active **HIGH** device. A hardware level inverter chip must be introduced between the master and the slave. You may be able to reprogram the driving code, but driving a pin constantly is a waste of energy and is a less-than-ideal choice for battery-driven designs. For very fast signaling, the propagation delays through that inverter become important. Factor them into the design.

# Transmitting Data

The process of communicating between the master and slave is very simple. The master selects a clock frequency that is compatible with the slave devices. This ensures that all devices are operating in synchronization with the master. Initially, though, the clock signal is paused.

The master then uses the slave select (SS) line corresponding to the desired slave device and drives it **LOW** to select that slave. Some devices require a short time to settle. The master may wait until it thinks the slave is ready for a conversation. Then the master can commence transmitting clock pulses on the SCLK line.

During each clock cycle, the master transmits a single bit on the MOSI line to the slave. At the same time, the slave transmits a single bit on the MISO line to the master. The master and slave are simultaneously sending and receiving data in a full duplex fashion. This happens even when data is transmitted only in one direction.

This is usually implemented around a pair of 8-bit shift registers that are coupled end to end to make a 16-bit cyclic buffer with 8 bits in each device. Figure 21-3 shows how this is constructed.

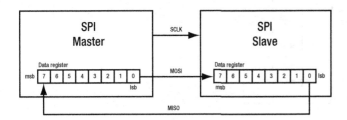

***Figure 21-3.*** *SPI ring buffer arrangement*

After eight clock cycles, the data has been fully exchanged between the master and the slave. Internally, the master writes eight bits of data into its shift register and performs eight clocked shifts, after which the slave can read its shift register to recover the data. At the same time, the data that the slave wrote into its buffer can now be read by the master. This is a compact and simple data transmission technique. Although this example uses 8-bit data registers, touchscreen controllers may use 16-bit values to address a large enough canvas, and ADC inputs might use 12-bit values to resolve the analog waveform to sufficient accuracy. When slaves are not active, they must ignore the clock pulses and must never place data on the MISO line unless they have been asked to by the master. Read this Wikipedia article to find out more about SPI: https://en.wikipedia.org/wiki/Serial_Peripheral_Interface_Bus.

This kernel documentation outlines how the internals work from a technical standpoint: www.kernel.org/doc/Documentation/spi/spidev.

# SPI Internal Architecture

Table 21-3 lists the three registers inside the SPI devices that the CPU can interact with to drive the SPI transmissions.

***Table 21-3.*** *Internal SPI Registers*

| Register | Name |
| --- | --- |
| Data register | SPDR |
| Control register | SPCR |
| Status register | SPSR |

The CPU can read and write data to the SPDR data register. This data is clocked out to the slave devices during a data transmission cycle. The communications process is governed by what the CPU writes to the SPCR control register. One bit of the SPSR status register is also writable when setting the clock frequency. Any feedback from the SPI interface is accessible to the CPU by reading the SPSR status register. Study the ARM documentation for more information about ARM processor internals: http://infocenter.arm.com/.

# Control Register (SPCR)

The control register maintains eight bits of information that the CPU can alter to control the way that the SPI interface operates. All bits can be written, and they can also be read back so a Read ➤ Modify ➤ Write approach can be used. All the bits in this register are set to zero to begin with. Figure 21-4 illustrates how the bits are mapped to the control register. The purpose of each bit in the control register is described in Table 21-4.

| Bit number | 7 | 6 | 5 | 4 | 3 | 2 | 1 | 0 |
|---|---|---|---|---|---|---|---|---|
| Bit mask | 0x80 | 0x40 | 0x20 | 0x10 | 0x08 | 0x04 | 0x02 | 0x01 |
| Label | SPIE | SPE | DORD | MSTR | CPOL | CPHA | SPR1 | SPR0 |
| Access | R/W | R/W | R/W | R/W | R/W | R/W | R/W | R/W |
| Default value | 0 | 0 | 0 | 0 | 0 | 0 | 0 | 0 |

*Figure 21-4.* *Control register SPCR bits*

*Table 21-4.* *SPCR Register Bit Functionality*

| Label | Name | Bit mask |
|---|---|---|
| SPIE | Interrupt enable | 0x80 |
| SPE | SPI enable | 0x40 |
| DORD | Data order | 0x20 |
| MSTR | Master/slave select | 0x10 |
| CPOL | Clock polarity | 0x08 |
| CPHA | Clock phase | 0x04 |
| SPR1 | Clock rate (bit 1) | 0x02 |
| SPR0 | Clock rate (bit 0) | 0x01 |

- When the individual interrupt enable bit for this SPI interface (**SPIE**) is set to 1, an interrupt occurs when the SPI interrupt flag is set in the SPI status register. This can be inhibited if the Global Interrupt Enable flag is not set. This flag is managed by the SREG control register in an AVR micro-controller as found in an Arduino. The ARM CPU in an ARTIK has a similar mechanism that performs the same function.

- The **SPE** bit controls whether the SPI interface is enabled for use. If this bit is not set to 1, you cannot use the SPI interface.

- The **DORD** bit controls which direction the shift register is clocked out. If this bit is set to 1, the least significant bit (LSB) is transmitted first. Otherwise, the most significant bit (MSB) is delivered first. Clearly, your master and slave must both be expecting the bits to arrive in the same order unless you intend to use this as a bit order reversal process.

- The **MSTR** bit determines whether this SPI interface is going to operate as a master or slave device. Although this functionality is dynamic, one would expect the SPI component in the ARTIK CPU to be the master.

- The **CPOL** bit indicates whether the clock line is held **HIGH** or **LOW** during idle time. When there is no activity, the clock line must be maintained in a safe and inactive state. This indicates whether **SCLK** is held **LOW** (0) or **HIGH** (1).

- The **CPHA** bit controls how the clock phase is interpreted. A 0 value indicates that the leading edge when the clock line goes from inactive to active should cause the slave to sample the data. The trailing edge is then be used to set up for the next data arrival. Setting this bit to 1 reverses the meaning of the leading and trailing edges of the clock pulses. In this case, the leading edge triggers the setup and the trailing edge triggers a sample.

- The **SPR1** and **SPR0** bits are used with an additional bit on the status register to define the clock rate for the SPI bus.

## Status Register (SPSR)

The status register contains two bits of information that the CPU can read to find out the current status of the SPI interface. One bit is used to extend the range of available clock rate divider values and the remaining bits are unused and reserved for future use. Although there is only one writable bit, because all the others are set to read only, it may be safe to just write a 0x00 or 0x01 value to clear or set the **SP1X2** bit instead of using a Read ➤ Modify ➤ Write technique. The default state of all the bits in this register is zero to begin with. Figure 21-5 illustrates how the bits are mapped to the status register. The purpose of each bit in the control register is described in Table 21-5.

| Bit number | 7 | 6 | 5 | 4 | 3 | 2 | 1 | 0 |
|---|---|---|---|---|---|---|---|---|
| Bit mask | 0x80 | 0x40 | 0x20 | 0x10 | 0x08 | 0x04 | 0x02 | 0x01 |
| Label | SPIF | WCOL | - | - | - | - | - | SPI2X |
| Access | R | R | R | R | R | R | R | R/W |
| Default value | 0 | 0 | 0 | 0 | 0 | 0 | 0 | 0 |

***Figure 21-5.*** *Status register SPSR bits*

*Table 21-5.* *SPSR Register Bit Functionality*

| Label | Name | Bit mask |
|-------|------|----------|
| SPIF | Interrupt flag | 0x80 |
| WCOL | Write collision occurred | 0x40 |
| Unused | N/A | 0x20 |
| Unused | N/A | 0x10 |
| Unused | N/A | 0x08 |
| Unused | N/A | 0x04 |
| Unused | N/A | 0x02 |
| SPIX2 | Clock rate extension (bit 2) | 0x01 |

- The **SPIF** bit carries an Interrupt flag that is set to a 1 value when the serial transfer is completed.

- The **WCOL** bit contains a write collision flag that is set **HIGH** if the SPI interface detects that the SPDR data register was written to while the previous data value was still being transferred. A premature overwrite of the SPDR could cause corruption of the transmitted data and have unintended consequences when it arrives in the slave. If you detect that this bit is set, then the data should be transmitted again. Whether you are able to tell the slave to abort or disregard the corrupted data depends on the features of the slave device.

- The **SPIX2** bit can be set to 1 to halve the clock divider ratio and hence double the currently defined clock rate that is set by the **SPR0** and **SPR1** bits in the control register.

- All the remaining bits in the status register are unused.

## Clock Rate Setting

The clock rate is set by combining the **SPR0**, **SPR1**, and **SPI2X** bits and using the value as an index into a table of clock rate values. The **SPI2X** bit is contained in the status register and is the only writable bit in that register. The clock rate frequency depends on the attached crystal oscillator. This set of bits controls a clock divider value. See Figure 21-6. The clock rate is determined by this formula:

```
{oscillator_frequency} / {clock_rate_value}
```

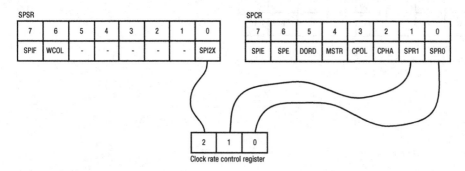

*Figure 21-6.* *SPI clock rate control*

If the status register is never written to, the **SPI2X** value will always be zero. A useful range of values can still be achieved with **SPR0** and **SPR1** on their own. Adding a 1 bit in **SPI2X** halves the division value, thereby doubling the clock rate defined by **SPR0** and **SPR1**. The clock rate settings for all the possible bit value combinations are summarized in Table 21-6.

***Table 21-6.*** *SPI Clock Rate Settings*

| SPI2X | SPR1 | SPR0 | Divide clock rate by |
| --- | --- | --- | --- |
| 0 | 0 | 0 | 4 |
| 0 | 0 | 1 | 16 |
| 0 | 1 | 0 | 64 |
| 0 | 1 | 1 | 128 |
| 1 | 0 | 0 | 2 |
| 1 | 0 | 1 | 8 |
| 1 | 1 | 0 | 32 |
| 1 | 1 | 1 | 64 |

## Data Register (SPDR)

The data register is where CPU puts the data it wants to send to a slave or where it can read the data that a slave device has sent back. The initial default state of the bits in this register is uncertain. They probably contain the most recently transmitted value but there is no guarantee of that. Assume that the results are garbage and are not to be relied on until after a successful transfer has happened. Figure 21-7 illustrates the data register showing where the significant bits are located.

| Bit number | 7 | 6 | 5 | 4 | 3 | 2 | 1 | 0 |
| --- | --- | --- | --- | --- | --- | --- | --- | --- |
| Bit mask | 0x80 | 0x40 | 0x20 | 0x10 | 0x08 | 0x04 | 0x02 | 0x01 |
| Label | MSB | - | - | - | - | - | - | LSB |
| Access | R/W | R/W | R/W | R/W | R/W | R/W | R/W | R/W |
| Default value undefined | X | X | X | X | X | X | X | X |

***Figure 21-7.*** *Data register bits*

Access to the data values happens in the master. The meaning of the values in this register should be interpreted in the context of the slave device after the data has been transferred to it. Slave devices may treat the data differently. Read the data sheets carefully for the peripheral devices that you are connecting to the SPI bus.

Reading values back from the register is only meaningful after a transfer cycle has moved all of the bits from the slave device back to the master. Sense the interrupt pin on the status register to see when it is appropriate to read that data.

## Interacting with an SPI Device

Although the software support is not yet complete, here is an outline of the programming steps that will be required when it is available.

## External Includes

Include these header files to start with. They provide access to all of the library calls needed to interact with SPI.

```
#include <fcntl.h>
#include <unistd.h>
#include <sys/ioctl.h>
#include <linux/types.h>
#include <linux/spi/spidev.h>
```

Inspecting the contents of the /user/include/linux/spi/spidev.h header file tells you about the struct data passed to the kernel to communicate with the SPI driver.

## Global Variables

The next step is to create some global variables for use by the open, close, read, and write function calls:

```
int           spi_cs_fd;
unsigned char spi_mode;
unsigned char spi_bitsPerWord;
unsigned int  spi_speed;
```

Initialize these here or set them via functions in your SPI toolkit once you have constructed it.

## Opening an SPI Device

Open a device and create a file handle on it. Recall that the open() function was used earlier as opposed to the fopen() function when the GPIO device was opened via the kernel. SPI device control works in a similar way. Create a function that initializes your SPIO port and open an ioctrl device at the same time.

```
FILE *spi_cs_fd;
spi_cs_fd = open("/dev/spidev0.1", O_RDWR)
```

Make sure you have a corresponding close() function call for this file descriptor at the end of your SPI interaction.

## Initializing the SPI Port

Once the SPI device is opened, check to see if you have write access to the SPI with this call. A non-zero result indicates that you do not have access.

```
ioctl(*spi_cs_fd, SPI_IOC_WR_MODE, &spi_mode)
```

Check to see if you have read access. Zero indicates success.

```
ioctl(*spi_cs_fd, SPI_IOC_RD_MODE, &spi_mode)
```

Set the word size for write requests with this call:

```
ioctl(*spi_cs_fd, SPI_IOC_WR_BITS_PER_WORD, &spi_bitsPerWord)
```

Set the word size for read requests with this call:

```
ioctl(*spi_cs_fd, SPI_IOC_RD_BITS_PER_WORD, &spi_bitsPerWord)
```

Set the transfer speed (clock rate) for write requests with this call:

```
ioctl(*spi_cs_fd, SPI_IOC_WR_MAX_SPEED_HZ, &spi_speed)
```

Set the transfer speed for read requests with this call:

```
ioctl(*spi_cs_fd, SPI_IOC_RD_MAX_SPEED_HZ, &spi_speed)
```

# Reading and Writing Data

The SPI interface expects to use one transfer operation for each byte that is exchanged between the master and slave. For handling multi-byte messages, use a for() loop to call one write for each byte. An array of SPI struct entities is created so there is one available for each byte in the data. The data buffer is overwritten with the data that is received back from the slave. Listing 21-1 shows the prototype for a function that writes a multi-byte transfer out via SPI.

***Listing 21-1.*** Multi-Byte Transfer to SPI

```
int SpiWriteAndRead (unsigned char *data, int length)
{
  struct spi_ioc_transfer spi[length];
  int i;
  int retVal;

  //One SPI transfer for each byte
  for (i = 0 ; i < length ; i++)
  {
    memset(&spi[i], 0, sizeof (spi[i]));
    spi[i].tx_buf        = (unsigned long)(data + i); // transmit from "data"
    spi[i].rx_buf        = (unsigned long)(data + i) ; // receive into "data"
    spi[i].len           = sizeof(*(data + i)) ;
    spi[i].delay_usecs   = 0 ;
    spi[i].speed_hz      = spi_speed ;
    spi[i].bits_per_word = spi_bitsPerWord ;
    spi[i].cs_change = 0;
  }

  retVal = -1;
  retVal = ioctl(*spi_cs_fd, SPI_IOC_MESSAGE(length), &spi) ;

  if(retVal < 0)
  {
    perror("Error - Problem transmitting spi data..ioctl");
    exit(1);
  }

  return retVal;
}
```

On returning from this function, the data array that you passed the transmit data in with contains the received data. The data buffer length will not change because for every byte that was written, another one is received. The input and output data are always exactly the same length.

This example function is based on an original C++ program written by Hussam Al-Hertani for the Raspberry PI. It was subsequently modified by Adam at IBEX UK Ltd. See www.raspberry-projects.com/pi/programming-in-c/spi/using-the-spi-interface.

## AX88796 Ethernet Controller (ARTIK 520)

The U-Boot messages on an ARTIK 5 reveal that SPI is being used for controlling the Ethernet interface via an **AX88796C** chip. Searching for information about this device reveals that it is an Ethernet controller. These Ethernet services are made available to the ARTIK 520 by the developer board because they are not built into the module. Inspecting the developer reference board schematics reveals that this is controlled via a private SPI interface on the ARTIK module. It feeds back its interrupts and status values via dedicated GPIO pins. The SPI and GPIO support for this is all managed via the EBI data pins on the Panasonic AXT connector J7 on the underside of the ARTIK 5 module. This Ethernet controller chip is located on the developer reference board. If you want to replicate this interface, study the schematic diagrams to help you implement your own Ethernet support in your product design. If you follow the Samsung design very closely, you may be able to avoid the need for writing kernel-level driver code.

## AX88760 USB and Ethernet Controller (ARTIK 1020)

The strategy for driving the Ethernet interface in an ARTIK 1020 is different. The Ethernet support is external but a different controller is used. The **AX88760** controller chip is more sophisticated and also implements the USB interfaces for the ARTIK 1020. Whereas the ARTIK 520 uses a lot of EBI data pins to drive the Ethernet controller chip using address and data lines, the ARTIK 1020 controls the Ethernet controller chip via a USB connection instead of using SPI. The networking support is similar to the way you can add an Ethernet port by plugging in a USB/Ethernet adaptor on a laptop. Refer to the Type 10 developer board schematics to trace the connections back to the relevant AXT connectors for that module. The data sheets also provide some relevant information about the pins on the AXT connectors.

## Arduino and SPI

The ARTIK emulates an Arduino SPI connection on pins J27-8 ($\infty$10), J27-7 ($\infty$11), J27-6 ($\infty$12), and J27-5 ($\infty$13), as shown in Table 21-7. This implementation is compatible with the connections on an Arduino UNO board. Refer to the Arduino documentation regarding the SPI library. Including this into your Arduino sketches is by far the simplest way to experiment with SPI. You can at least exercise your hardware and know that it is working. Then you have something reliable to test your own software against. Developing C language software tests when you are uncertain about the hardware makes the debugging process very ambiguous because the problem could be in either the hardware or the software. Debug your hardware first using this technique to eliminate a major unknown when debugging your C language application. Refer to the Arduino web site for reference information on the SPI control function provided by the SPI library: www.arduino.cc/en/Reference/SPI.

***Table 21-7.*** *Arduino SPI Emulation in an ARTIK*

| Header pin | SPI signal | Description |
|------------|-----------|-------------|
| J27-7 (∞11) | MOSI | Serial data delivered by the master out pin on the ARTIK to the slave input pin of a peripheral |
| J27-6 (∞12) | MISO | Serial data delivered by the slave out pin on a peripheral to the master input pin on an ARTIK |
| J27-5 (∞13) | SCLK | SPI serial clock line |
| J27-8 (∞10) | SS | Slave select |

# Programming via the Arduino SPI Library

Add this line to your Arduino sketches in order to call any of the functions summarized in Table 21-8.

```
#include <SPI.h>
```

Define a pin for slave selection at the start of your sketch:

```
const int slaveSelectPin = 10;
```

Then populate the Arduino setup() function with the necessary initializer code. This sets the slave select pin as an output and initialize the SPI library by calling the begin() function:

```
void setup()
{
  pinMode(slaveSelectPin, OUTPUT);
  SPI.begin();
}
```

Now select the target device connected to the slave select pin by asserting a **LOW** value on the digital output pin:

```
digitalWrite(slaveSelectPin, LOW);
```

While the slave is selected, you can make two transactions with the SPI device. The first defines an address inside the target device where some data is going to be written, and the second sends the data value to be stored there:

```
SPI.transfer(address);
SPI.transfer(value);
```

At the end of the process, deselect the device by asserting a **HIGH** value on the slave select line:

```
digitalWrite(slaveSelectPin, HIGH);
```

# The Arduino SPI library

The SPI interface is programmed by instantiating an SPI object and sending messages to it to control the interface. Table 21-8 summarizes the functions available in the SPI library. Refer to the Arduino web site for complete descriptions of these functions and their parameters.

***Table 21-8.*** *Arduino SPI Functions*

| Function | Purpose |
| --- | --- |
| SPISettings | A helpful auxiliary object to manage settings when calling SPI transaction() functions |
| begin() | Initializes the SPI bus by setting SCLK, MOSI, and SS to outputs, pulling SCLK and MOSI **LOW**, and SS **HIGH**. |
| end() | Disables the SPI bus (leaving the pin modes unchanged) |
| beginTransaction() | Initializes the SPI bus using the passed in SPISettings object |
| endTransaction() | Stops using the SPI bus. Normally this is called after deasserting the chip select in order to allow other libraries to use the SPI bus. |
| setBitOrder() | A deprecated function that sets the order of the bits shifted out of and into the SPI bus |
| setClockDivider() | A deprecated function that sets the SPI clock divider relative to the system clock |
| setDataMode() | A deprecated function that sets the SPI data mode |
| transfer() | SPI transfer is based on a simultaneous send and receive. This delivers new data and returns the data that has been sent back. |
| transfer16() | A 16-bit variant of the 8-bit transfer() function |
| usingInterrupt() | Register interrupts to be called when SPI devices are ready for access |
| shiftOut() | Shifts out a byte of data one bit at a time via the indicated pin. This is a built-in function that is not part of the SPI library. |
| shiftIn() | Shifts in a byte of data one bit at a time via the indicated pin. This is a built-in function that is not part of the SPI library. |

■ **Note**    Some older functions are deprecated and should not be used for new projects. They still work fine but the SPISettings object is a much-improved way to control these configuration details. Because they are deprecated, they may be removed in a later version of the SPI library.

# Multiplexing Digital Pins for SS Addressing

The Arduino documentation suggests that slave select (SS) is available on pin 10 although you can use any available digital pin. Alternatively, the slave device select lines can be emulated using multiple digital pins to select the target peripheral device when you have more than one. Use one GPIO pin per device (which is inefficient) or use them as an address multiplex to extend the number of reachable devices. Add an address decoder chip for that implementation. A 4-to-16 line decoder/demultiplexer (**74154**) will select one of 16 devices in return for only using 4 pins. There are other variants of this decoder with two or three input lines. You can choose exactly the part you need. Understanding the 74 series digital chips will help you solve many problems with an inexpensive chip instead of writing many lines of code. See `https://en.wikipedia.org/ wiki/List_of_7400_series_integrated_circuits` for more information.

# Summary

The ARTIK uses the SPI bus internally to control and manage the Ethernet interfaces that it uses for networking. Theoretically, these SPI buses can be made available to user space applications. The SPI interfaces have been listed in the product specifications and it is just a matter of time before they are released for developers to use in a later operating system upgrade. For now, the coverage in this chapter is based on publicly available knowledge of how generic SPI interfaces work.

■ ■ ■

# CHAPTER 22

# Audio and Inter-IC Sound (I2S)

The ARTIK modules are designed for a variety of purposes. From the outset, the Samsung engineers knew that many developers would want to integrate them into some kind of Audio product or infrastructure. The ARTIK is equipped with Inter-IC Sound (I2S) serial buses for delivering audio samples to a stereo audio codec chip on the developer reference board. You can implement this same chip in your own hardware designs. Layered on top of the kernel support for I2S are the ALSA SDK, library, and toolkit for managing sound recording and playback.

## Audio Capabilities

The ARTIK modules are equipped to manage audio recording and playback. A monaural solid-state microphone is built in to the developer reference board as a default sound source. Connect headphones or a small loudspeaker to the 3.5mm jack socket to hear the audio output. Figure 22-1 shows the location of these components, which are in the same place on the Type 5 and 10 developer reference boards.

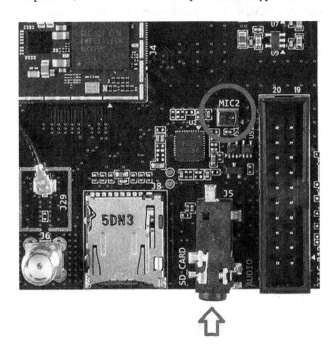

*Figure 22-1.* *Solid-state microphone and jack socket*

© Cliff Wootton 2016
C. Wootton, *Samsung ARTIK Reference*, DOI 10.1007/978-1-4842-2322-2_22

The ARTIK modules are well suited for designs that involve simple sound applications and playing music, perhaps in portable devices. The audio support in the ARTIK 10 has more channels available than the ARTIK 5. The ALSA toolkit is already installed by default and can be upgraded when a new version is available.

The audio in the ARTIK modules is built on an I2S bus architecture. Layering the ALSA toolkit on top of the operating system avoids you having to get involved with the internals of the I2S bus at all. The mPlayer tools are also available. The ffmpeg utility is also installed as a built-in toolkit. Even though ffmpeg is oriented more towards video processing, it is useful for extracting and converting audio files. Consult Wikipedia and download the I2S specification from SparkFun from the following links:

```
https://en.wikipedia.org/wiki/I2S
www.sparkfun.com/datasheets/BreakoutBoards/I2SBUS.pdf
```

# Audio Output

Both the ARTIK 5 and 10 modules drive their stereo audio output via a 3.5mm stereo jack socket mounted on the developer reference board. In both cases, this socket is labeled J5. The ARTIK does not output stereo audio directly. Rather, it controls an audio codec chip (AK4953), which is located just behind the stereo jack socket and labeled U2. The I2S bus standard is used to communicate audio sample data between the ARTIK CPU and this codec chip. There is also some I2C bus control involved to allow the ARTIK CPU to manage and configure the chip. All of this is evident on the circuit schematics, which are very similar for the Type 5 and 10 developer reference boards. The pages are titled differently in the schematics PDF file. In the ARTIK 5 schematics, the page is called **AUDIO-AK4593** while the ARTIK 10 schematic describes it as the **CODEC** page.

The **AK4593** drives the 3.5mm headphone jack but can also drive a small loudspeaker. The connections for the loudspeaker are brought out to a pair of unlabeled test points on the developer reference board. These test points are a pair of small, circular, metallic pads near the corner of the codec chip. Attaching a loudspeaker to them might be difficult without a surface mounted connector that connects to the test points somehow.

The audio is driven through the **AK4593** chip by delivering raw digital data to it at the correct sample rate. Any compression and decompression from MP3 or AAC formats must be done in software inside the ARTIK CPU. There is hardware assistance for audio digital-to-analog conversion, filtering, and mixing to create the output signal and analog recording input that is converted to digital samples.

# Audio Input

To record incoming multi-channel analog audio, use the analog inputs. The developer reference board has a built-in miniature solid-state analog MEMS microphone connected to one of the inputs of the **AK4953** codec chip. This delivers a mono signal to the codec. The other inputs of the codec are shorted to ground to inhibit noise induced by floating pins. If you implement this codec chip in your own product designs, exploit more of its input channels with additional microphones and line input connections. The part number for this microphone is **MOE-C110T42-K1** and an online search reveals the data sheet at http://richwellgroup.com/Private/Files/6355797373201562502005514315.pdf.

# ALSA Audio Support

The foundation of the audio support is built on the Advanced Linux Sound Architecture (ALSA) project. This is a standard set of tools for audio processing in Linux. ALSA provides support for MIDI in addition to the sampled audio support. The MIDI support is not turned on by default in the ARTIK. Adding the necessary connectors and software drivers is necessary first. Access the ALSA project and explore the source code and guidance on using the SDK and tools at the following links:

```
https://wiki.archlinux.org/index.php/Advanced_Linux_Sound_Architecture
www.alsa-project.org/main/index.php/Main_Page
http://alsa.opensrc.org/
www.kernel.org/doc/Documentation/sound/alsa/
http://equalarea.com/paul/alsa-audio.html
www.linuxjournal.com/article/6735
www.alsa-project.org/main/index.php/Asoundrc
http://alsa.opensrc.org/Asoundrc
```

The ALSA API supports several interfaces, which are managed separately:

- Control interface: Manages multiple sound cards

- PCM interface: Controls digital audio capture and playback

- Raw MIDI interface: A standard for electronic musical instruments, which supports Musical Instrument Digital Interface (MIDI). The raw interface works directly with the MIDI events, and the programmer is responsible for managing the protocol and timing. This is not yet configured on the ARTIK.

- Timer interface: Manages timing hardware on sound cards for synchronizing sound events

- Sequencer interface: A high-level interface for MIDI support built on top of the raw MIDI interface, it manages MIDI protocols and timing.

- Mixer interface: Used to route signals and control volume levels.

# Exploring ALSA

The /proc/asound directory contains some useful files that your application can read to find things out about the ALSA library you have installed. Listing 22-1 displays the hardware sound card devices in the ARTIK.

***Listing 22-1.*** Listing Your Sound Cards

```
$ cat /proc/asound/cards

 0 [artikak4953    ]: artik-ak4953 - artik-ak4953
                      artik-ak4953
```

Discover the version of the ALSA library you have installed with the command in Listing 22-2.

***Listing 22-2.*** ALSA Version

```
cat /proc/asound/version

Advanced Linux Sound Architecture Driver Version k3.10.9-00008-g48685d2.
```

The available ALSA devices are shown in Listing 22-3. There are four in an ARTIK 5 by default.

***Listing 22-3.*** ALSA Devices

```
$ cat /proc/asound/devices

  0: [ 0]   : control
```

```
16: [ 0- 0]: digital audio playback
24: [ 0- 0]: digital audio capture
33:         : timer
```

The /proc/asound/pcm and /proc/asound/timers files tell you about the current configuration of your ALSA devices.

## Configuring ALSA

The pre-installed ALSA kit has already been configured and is ready to use. If you download a new ALSA installation, there are references to default sound cards that are not present on an ARTIK. They are for supporting multi-channel surround sound. When ALSA attempts to initialize them, it displays warning messages. If you see the messages in Listing 22-4, modify the ALSA configuration file to comment out the unwanted sound cards.

***Listing 22-4.*** Installing the ALSA Software Library

```
ALSA lib pcm.c:2267:(snd_pcm_open_noupdate) …
... Unknown PCM cards.pcm.front
... Unknown PCM cards.pcm.rear
... Unknown PCM cards.pcm.center_lfe
...
```

Use your vi editor to open the ALSA configuration file /usr/share/alsa/alsa.conf and then comment out the references to the unsupported sound cards by adding a hash character (#) at the start of the line. Listing 22-5 shows what this looks like after editing the file.

***Listing 22-5.*** Commented Out Sound Cards

```
#pcm.front cards.pcm.front
#pcm.rear cards.pcm.rear
#pcm.center_lfe cards.pcm.center_lfe
...
```

You may see other warning messages about unreachable sound servers. These can be ignored because there is no configuration setting to suppress them.

There is also a global ALSA library configuration file called /etc/asound.conf which by default is empty. This configures things for all user accounts on the system. Individual user accounts can customize their own settings via the .asoundrc file in their home directory. Neither needs to be altered to use ALSA and the defaults should work just fine. You can modify the /etc/asound.conf file to define a different default device. List your devices, then choose one and edit it into the file. The ALSA tools use that configuration the next time they are called to action. The ARTIK only contains a single sound card numbered zero (0). If you add more sound cards to implement a more complex audio/music product, they are listed here if ALSA recognizes them.

If you had more devices (and for the purposes of an example), assume the one you want to make the default is device 1. Edit your /etc/asound.conf file to define a system-wide default. Add the lines shown in Listing 22-6 to your configuration file.

***Listing 22-6.*** Adding a Default Selector for Device 1

```
defaults.pcm.card 1
defaults.ctl.card 1
```

# Upgrading ALSA

The current state of the ALSA system inside your ARTIK is stored in the /var/lib/alsa/asound.state file. Type this command to see the details:

```
cat /var/lib/alsa/asound.state | more
```

To reinstall or upgrade the ALSA library, use the dnf command to download and install the complete ALSA developer kit:dnf install alsa-lib-devel

# The Audio Mixer Tool (amixer)

The amixer command has some basic help built in. Use the command in Listing 22-7 to display it. Access more descriptive help with the man amixer command.

***Listing 22-7.*** Audio Mixer Commands

```
amixer -h

Usage: amixer <options> [command]

Available options:
  -h,--help        this help
  -c,--card N      select the card
  -D,--device N    select the device, default 'default'
  -d,--debug       debug mode
  -n,--nocheck     do not perform range checking
  -v,--version     print version of this program
  -q,--quiet       be quiet
  -i,--inactive    show also inactive controls
  -a,--abstract L select abstraction level (none or basic)
  -s,--stdin       read and execute commands from stdin sequentially
  -R,--raw-volume use the raw value (default)
  -M,--mapped-volume use the mapped volume

Available commands:
  scontrols        show all mixer simple controls
  scontents        show contents of all mixer simple controls (default command)
  sset sID P       set contents for one mixer simple control
  sget sID         get contents for one mixer simple control
  controls         show all controls for given card
  contents         show contents of all controls for given card
  cset cID P       set control contents for one control
  cget cID         get control contents for one control
```

The mixer has some initial configuration which was done during the ARTIK OS build. If the anaconda-ks.cfg file is still present, you can see where it created those defaults and stored them in a script. Restore those mixer defaults by running the /usr/bin/audio_setting.sh script if your mixer configuration gets out of control. Listing 22-8 shows the contents of that file to show the default settings. Set them individually by executing each line in the bash shell.

**Listing 22-8.** Audio Mixer Default Settings

```
amixer sset "Digital Output Volume1 L (Manual Mode)" 120
amixer sset "Digital Output Volume1 R (Manual Mode)" 120
amixer sset "Mic Gain Control" 3
amixer sset "Mic Bias MUX" "IN1"
amixer sset "IN1 MUX" "Mic Bias"
amixer sset "Input Select MUX" "LIN1/RIN1"
amixer sset "ADC MUX1" "Mono"
amixer sset "MIC MUX" "AMIC"
amixer sset "ADCPF MUX" "ADC"
amixer sset "DACHP" "ON"
```

# The Audio Recorder Tool (arecord)

Use the arecord application to check out your sound card where it looks for incoming audio. The arecord application has some basic help built-in. Use the command in Listing 22-9 to display it. Access more descriptive help with the man arecord command.

**Listing 22-9.** Help Display for the arecord Tool

```
arecord -h

Usage: arecord [OPTION]... [FILE]...

-h, --help              help
    --version           print current version
-l, --list-devices      list all soundcards and digital audio devices
-L, --list-pcms         list device names
-D, --device=NAME       select PCM by name
-q, --quiet             quiet mode
-t, --file-type TYPE    file type (voc, wav, raw or au)
-c, --channels=#        channels
-f, --format=FORMAT     sample format (case insensitive)
-r, --rate=#            sample rate
-d, --duration=#        interrupt after # seconds
-M, --mmap              mmap stream
-N, --nonblock          nonblocking mode
-F, --period-time=#     distance between interrupts is # microseconds
-B, --buffer-time=#     buffer duration is # microseconds
    --period-size=#     distance between interrupts is # frames
    --buffer-size=#     buffer duration is # frames
-A, --avail-min=#       min available space for wakeup is # microseconds
-R, --start-delay=#     delay for automatic PCM start is # microseconds
                        (relative to buffer size if <= 0)
-T, --stop-delay=#      delay for automatic PCM stop is # microseconds from xrun
-v, --verbose           show PCM structure and setup (accumulative)
-V, --vumeter=TYPE      enable VU meter (TYPE: mono or stereo)
-I, --separate-channels one file for each channel
-i, --interactive       allow interactive operation from stdin
-m, --chmap=ch1,ch2,..  give the channel map to override or follow
    --disable-resample  disable automatic rate resample
```

```
    --disable-channels  disable automatic channel conversions
    --disable-format    disable automatic format conversions
    --disable-softvol   disable software volume control (softvol)
    --test-position     test ring buffer position
    --test-coef=#       test coefficient for ring buffer position (default 8)
                        expression for validation is: coef * (buffer_size / 2)
    --test-nowait       do not wait for ring buffer - eats whole CPU
    --max-file-time=#   start another output file when the old file has recorded
                        for this many seconds
    --process-id-file   write the process ID here
    --use-strftime      apply the strftime facility to the output file name
    --dump-hw-params    dump hw_params of the device
    --fatal-errors      treat all errors as fatal
Recognized sample formats are: S8 U8 S16_LE S16_BE U16_LE U16_BE S24_LE S24_BE U24_LE U24_BE
S32_LE S32_BE U32_LE U32_BE FLOAT_LE FLOAT_BE FLOAT64_LE FLOAT64_BE IEC958_SUBFRAME_LE
IEC958_SUBFRAME_BE MU_LAW A_LAW IMA_ADPCM MPEG GSM SPECIAL S24_3LE S24_3BE U24_3LE U24_3BE
S20_3LE S20_3BE U20_3LE U20_3BE S18_3LE S18_3BE U18_3LE U18_3BE G723_24 G723_24_1B G723_40
G723_40_1B DSD_U8
Some of these may not be available on selected hardware
The available format shortcuts are:
-f cd (16 bit little endian, 44100, stereo)
-f cdr (16 bit big endian, 44100, stereo)
-f dat (16 bit little endian, 48000, stereo)
```

## The Audio Player Tool (aplay)

Use the aplay application to check out your sound card where it looks for incoming audio. The aplay tool has some basic built-in help. Use the command in Listing 22-10 to display it. Access more descriptive help with the man aplay command.

***Listing 22-10.*** Help Display for the aplay Tool

```
aplay -h

Usage: aplay [OPTION]... [FILE]...

-h, --help              help
    --version           print current version
-l, --list-devices      list all soundcards and digital audio devices
-L, --list-pcms         list device names
-D, --device=NAME       select PCM by name
-q, --quiet             quiet mode
-t, --file-type TYPE    file type (voc, wav, raw or au)
-c, --channels=#        channels
-f, --format=FORMAT     sample format (case insensitive)
-r, --rate=#            sample rate
-d, --duration=#        interrupt after # seconds
-M, --mmap              mmap stream
-N, --nonblock          nonblocking mode
-F, --period-time=#     distance between interrupts is # microseconds
-B, --buffer-time=#     buffer duration is # microseconds
```

```
        --period-size=#      distance between interrupts is # frames
        --buffer-size=#      buffer duration is # frames
-A, --avail-min=#            min available space for wakeup is # microseconds
-R, --start-delay=#          delay for automatic PCM start is # microseconds
                             (relative to buffer size if <= 0)
-T, --stop-delay=#           delay for automatic PCM stop is # microseconds from xrun
-v, --verbose                show PCM structure and setup (accumulative)
-V, --vumeter=TYPE           enable VU meter (TYPE: mono or stereo)
-I, --separate-channels      one file for each channel
-i, --interactive            allow interactive operation from stdin
-m, --chmap=ch1,ch2,..       give the channel map to override or follow
        --disable-resample   disable automatic rate resample
        --disable-channels   disable automatic channel conversions
        --disable-format     disable automatic format conversions
        --disable-softvol    disable software volume control (softvol)
        --test-position      test ring buffer position
        --test-coef=#        test coefficient for ring buffer position (default 8)
                             expression for validation is: coef * (buffer_size / 2)
        --test-nowait        do not wait for ring buffer - eats whole CPU
        --max-file-time=#    start another output file when the old file has recorded
                             for this many seconds
        --process-id-file    write the process ID here
        --use-strftime       apply the strftime facility to the output file name
        --dump-hw-params     dump hw_params of the device
        --fatal-errors       treat all errors as fatal
Recognized sample formats are: S8 U8 S16_LE S16_BE U16_LE U16_BE S24_LE S24_BE U24_LE U24_BE
S32_LE S32_BE U32_LE U32_BE FLOAT_LE FLOAT_BE FLOAT64_LE FLOAT64_BE IEC958_SUBFRAME_LE
IEC958_SUBFRAME_BE MU_LAW A_LAW IMA_ADPCM MPEG GSM SPECIAL S24_3LE S24_3BE U24_3LE U24_3BE
S20_3LE S20_3BE U20_3LE U20_3BE S18_3LE S18_3BE U18_3LE U18_3BE G723_24 G723_24_1B G723_40
G723_40_1B DSD_U8
Some of these may not be available on selected hardware
The available format shortcuts are:
-f cd (16 bit little endian, 44100, stereo)
-f cdr (16 bit big endian, 44100, stereo)
-f dat (16 bit little endian, 48000, stereo)
```

# The Audio/Visual Player Tool (mPlayer)

Use the mPlayer tool on your ARTIK to play audio or video files. Refer to the mPlayer and Wikipedia web sites for details. Go to

```
https://mplayerhq.hu/
https://en.wikipedia.org/wiki/MPlayer
```

Type the mplayer command with no options to see the onscreen help display. Listing 22-11 shows the available command options and more information is available on the manual page.

*Listing 22-11.* Help Display for the mPlayer Tool

```
mplayer

MPlayer 1.2-5.1.1 (C) 2000-2015 MPlayer Team
```

```
Usage:   mplayer [options] [url|path/]filename
```

Basic options: (complete list in the man page)
```
 -vo <drv>       select video output driver ('-vo help' for a list)
 -ao <drv>       select audio output driver ('-ao help' for a list)
 vcd://<trackno> play (S)VCD (Super Video CD) track (raw device, no mount)
 dvd://<titleno> play DVD title from device instead of plain file
 -alang/-slang   select DVD audio/subtitle language (by 2-char country code)
 -ss <position>  seek to given (seconds or hh:mm:ss) position
 -nosound        do not play sound
 -fs             fullscreen playback (or -vm, -zoom, details in the man page)
 -x <x> -y <y>   set display resolution (for use with -vm or -zoom)
 -sub <file>     specify subtitle file to use (also see -subfps, -subdelay)
 -playlist <file> specify playlist file
 -vid x -aid y   select video (x) and audio (y) stream to play
 -fps x -srate y change video (x fps) and audio (y Hz) rate
 -pp <quality>   enable postprocessing filter (details in the man page)
 -framedrop      enable frame dropping (for slow machines)
```

Basic keys: (complete list in the man page, also check input.conf)
```
 <- or ->       seek backward/forward 10 seconds
 down or up     seek backward/forward  1 minute
 pgdown or pgup seek backward/forward 10 minutes
 < or >         step backward/forward in playlist
 p or SPACE     pause movie (press any key to continue)
 q or ESC       stop playing and quit program
 + or -         adjust audio delay by +/- 0.1 second
 o              cycle OSD mode:  none / seekbar / seekbar + timer
 * or /         increase or decrease PCM volume
 x or z         adjust subtitle delay by +/- 0.1 second
 r or t         adjust subtitle position up/down, also see -vf expand
```

```
* * * SEE THE MAN PAGE FOR DETAILS, FURTHER (ADVANCED) OPTIONS AND KEYS * * *
```

## Finding the Sound Card

The ALSA tools tell you about the audio capabilities of your ARTIK. Type the command in Listing 22-12 to see your available sound cards. The report may change with upgrades to the OS or underlying hardware. This report describes the AK4953 audio codec chip as your sound card.

***Listing 22-12.*** Playback Hardware Devices on an ARTIK 5

```
aplay -l

**** List of PLAYBACK Hardware Devices ****
card 0: artikak4953 [artik-ak4953], device 0: Playback ak4953-AIF1-0 []
  Subdevices: 1/1
  Subdevice #0: subdevice #0
```

Check for available sound cards with the aplay -l or arecord -l command. They will both display the same result.

## Testing the Audio Outputs

Test your audio output with the speaker-test tool, as shown in Listing 22-13. Press [**Control**]-[**C**] when you are done to stop the pink noise being played through the audio outputs.

***Listing 22-13.*** Running a Speaker Test

```
speaker-test

speaker-test 1.0.29

Playback device is default
Stream parameters are 48000Hz, S16_LE, 1 channels
Using 16 octaves of pink noise
Rate set to 48000Hz (requested 48000Hz)
Buffer size range from 64 to 65536
Period size range from 32 to 8192
Using max buffer size 65536
Periods = 4
was set period_size = 8192
was set buffer_size = 65536
 0 - Front Left
```

## Recording Audio

To record audio, first you need connect your audio source to the ARTIK inputs. The developer reference boards all have a built-in solid-state microphone connected directly to the audio input of the AK4953 codec chip. The Type 5 and 10 developer kits can use the Arduino-compatible analog inputs for multi-channel recording or just one of them for mono and two of them for stereo. The ARTIK 5 supports only two inputs and the ARTIK 10 supports all six. Configure the input mixer to route the incoming audio to the right place and set the recording levels. Run a software audio recorder to capture the incoming steams of audio samples.

Before starting to record, plug your audio source into analog input 0. Then apply the settings in Listing 22-14 to the mixer with the amixer command.

***Listing 22-14.*** Audio Mixer Settings for Recording

```
amixer sset "Digital Output Volume1 L (Manual Mode)" 120
amixer sset "Digital Output Volume1 R (Manual Mode)" 120
amixer sset "Mic Gain Control" 3
amixer sset "Mic Bias MUX" "IN1"
amixer sset "IN1 MUX" "Mic Bias"
amixer sset "Input Select MUX" "LIN1/RIN1"
amixer sset "ADC MUX1" "Mono"
amixer sset "MIC MUX" "AMIC"
amixer sset "ADCPF MUX" "ADC"
amixer sset "DACHP" "ON"
amixer sset "MIC MUX" "AMIC"
amixer sset "ADCPF MUX" "ADC"
amixer sset "DACHP" "ON"
```

Now you are ready to set the software recorder running with this command:

```
arecord -f dat test.wav
```

Once the recorder has started, start the playback on your audio source if you are dubbing from another medium. When you are done recording, press [**Control**]-[**C**] to stop the recorder. Your finished recording is stored in the test.wav file. Now play the recorded audio with the aplay or mplayer tools.

The -vv option tells the recording tool to display much more information about the recording. The example in Listing 22-15 shows how the file is recorded and stored in the /tmp directory. While the recording is running, the ALSA recording tool shows audio levels at the bottom of the screen. Press [**Control**]-[**C**] to stop the recording.

***Listing 22-15.*** Verbose Recording Command Output

```
arecord -vv -fdat /tmp/foo.wav

Recording WAVE '/tmp/foo.wav' : Signed 16 bit Little Endian, Rate 48000 Hz, Stereo
Plug PCM: Hardware PCM card 0 'artik-ak4953' device 0 subdevice 0
Its setup is:
  stream             : CAPTURE
  access             : RW_INTERLEAVED
  format             : S16_LE
  subformat          : STD
  channels           : 2
  rate               : 48000
  exact rate         : 48000 (48000/1)
  msbits             : 16
  buffer_size        : 24000
  period_size        : 6000
  period_time        : 125000
  tstamp_mode        : NONE
  tstamp_type        : MONOTONIC
  period_step        : 1
  avail_min          : 6000
  period_event       : 0
  start_threshold    : 1
  stop_threshold     : 24000
  silence_threshold: 0
  silence_size       : 0
  boundary           : 1572864000
  appl_ptr           : 0
  hw_ptr             : 0
```

# Playing Audio Files

Use the aplay tool, which is part of the ALSA project built into the ARTIK. Prepare an audio file (foo.wav) and transfer it to the /tmp directory in your ARTIK or record one into the /tmp/foo.wav file with the arecord tool. Then connect an earphone or speaker to the 3.5mm audio jack socket on the developer board. Prepare the ARTIK and set the volume by adjusting the mixer settings as shown in Listing 22-16.

***Listing 22-16.*** Mixer Settings for Playback

```
amixer sset "PFDAC MUX" "SDTI"
amixer sset "DACHP" "ON"
amixer sset "Digital Output Volume1 L (Manual Mode)" 240
amixer sset "Digital Output Volume1 R (Manual Mode)" 240
```

Now you are ready to play the wav file with the aplay tool:

```
aplay /tmp/foo.wav

Playing WAVE '/tmp/foo.wav' : Signed 16 bit Little Endian, Rate 48000 Hz, Stereo
```

Add the -vv options so the aplay tool displays verbose debugging information about the PCM interface as it plays the sound file. Listing 22-17 shows an example of verbose playback reporting.

***Listing 22-17.*** Verbose Audio Playback Command Output

```
aplay -vv /tmp/foo.wav

Playing WAVE '/tmp/foo.wav' : Signed 16 bit Little Endian, Rate 48000 Hz, Stereo
Plug PCM: Hardware PCM card 0 'artik-ak4953' device 0 subdevice 0
Its setup is:
  stream             : PLAYBACK
  access             : RW_INTERLEAVED
  format             : S16_LE
  subformat          : STD
  channels           : 2
  rate               : 48000
  exact rate         : 48000 (48000/1)
  msbits             : 16
  buffer_size        : 24000
  period_size        : 6000
  period_time        : 125000
  tstamp_mode        : NONE
  tstamp_type        : MONOTONIC
  period_step        : 1
  avail_min          : 6000
  period_event       : 0
  start_threshold    : 24000
  stop_threshold     : 24000
  silence_threshold: 0
  silence_size       : 0
  boundary           : 1572864000
  appl_ptr           : 0
  hw_ptr             : 0
```

# Developing Audio Applications

The Samsung developer support team has published some useful help in the developer guide. It shows how to record and play back audio directly with the Python and C language applications. If you want to move on from using the bash command line and do more complex things with audio, refer to the developer page at https://developer.artik.io/documentation/developer-guide/multimedia/audio-guide.html#using-c.

Download the source code for the ALSA libraries and dismantle them to understand how to interact with the I2S bus if you want to directly control your audio input/output from a C language application. You can find more interesting advice and tutorials on audio programming on the Web. Some of the information is very ancient because ALSA has been around for quite a while. Check out these links for more help:

http://equalarea.com/paul/alsa-audio.html
http://tldp.org/HOWTO/Alsa-sound-1.html
http://voices.canonical.com/david.henningsson/2012/07/13/top-five-wrong-ways-to-fix-your-audio/

## Pulse Audio Support

The ALSA toolkit is an important subsystem but there are other alternatives for audio work (OSS, ESD, aRts, JACK, and GStreamer, to name a few). The built-in PulseAudio tools are also well worth investigating to see what they can add to your audio capabilities.

PulseAudio is a useful proxy for your sound applications. It allows you to do advanced operations on your sound data as it passes between your application and hardware. Things like transferring the audio to a different machine, changing the sample format or channel count, and mixing several sounds into one are easily achieved using a PulseAudio sound server.

www.freedesktop.org/wiki/Software/PulseAudio/
https://en.wikipedia.org/wiki/PulseAudio
https://wiki.archlinux.org/index.php/PulseAudio

Type the following command to list your pulse audio device configuration. It produces a very long listing. Pass the output through the more command to display it one page at a time.

```
pactl list | more
```

## How Does I2S Work?

Inter-IC Sound (I2S) is a bus system for transferring digital audio data from one device to another. Like some of the other technology in this category, it was also developed by Phillips (now known as NXP) although it is unrelated to the I2C project that they also sponsored. The design was developed in the 1980s as the CD industry emerged. It stabilized in 1996 and has not needed any major revisions since then. Software for driving this interface is mature and reliable, as is the supporting hardware for implementing it. The audio data is transferred as pulse code modulation (PCM) samples as you would find on a CD. These samples, taken at regular intervals, are converted back into analog audio signals by passing them through a digital-to-analog converter (DAC). The data and clock lines are separated so the data streams can be delivered without any jitter in the recovered waveform. This is important because the samples are driven by the transmitter and must arrive in time to be played out when the timing of the sample conversion demands it to avoid clicks and pauses in the outgoing analog audio. The bus design is very simple and is organized as the three-wire system shown in Figure 22-2.

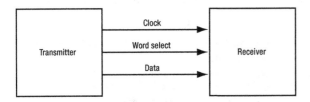

*Figure 22-2.* *Simple I2S connections*

The master clock line pulses once for each bit being transferred from the transmitter to the receiver device via the data line. All bits for all channels are transmitted as a single stream. Lower resolution data with only 8 bits per sample takes fewer clock pulses than 24-bit high-resolution sample data.

The word select line is toggled to route the sample data to the left or right side registers when stereo data is being delivered. This is often called the left-right clock. This is the main differentiator between the I2S and SPI architectural designs. Chip selection is another difference and it has to be done outside of the I2S bus, most likely using GPIO or I2C controls. The word select clock switches once for each sample to marshal the bits left or right. The frequency is the same as the sample rate. Because the samples are the same size for both channels, it has a duty cycle of 50%.

The I2S interface is designed to handle just two channels. To implement a multi-channel solution, your design must incorporate multiple I2S buses, each with their own dedicated decoder. The complexity comes from scaling things up but fundamentally the operation is the same. Your CPU will have to work harder to load the sample data into the transmit ends of the I2S pipelines to maintain the throughput in a multi-channel scenario.

## The ARTIK Implementation

The ARTIK adds a little sophistication to this so it can support a separate playback and record data line, which allows for bidirectional data transfer between the ARTIK and the Audio codec chip. The architecture also adds some I2C and GPIO logic so the ARTIK can control the stereo codec chip. Figure 22-3 shows the main parts of the I2S-related implementation.

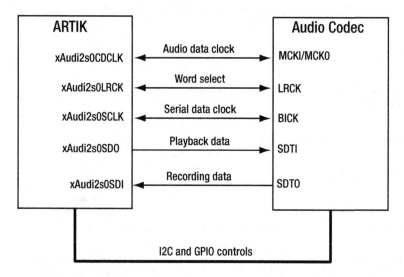

***Figure 22-3.*** *ARTIK I2S implementation*

This implementation allows the ARTIK or the codec chip to assume the role of master in the I2S data transfer process. Consequently, some of the connections are bidirectional. In the case of the MCKI and MCK0 pins on the codec chip, they are unidirectional pins but they are mapped to a bidirectional connection on the ARTIK by a small piece of **glue** logic that switches the connection one way or the other according to which end is the master. The switching is controlled by the **CODEC_PDN** GPIO output from the ARTIK. The Left-Right Clock and the Serial Data Clock lines are genuinely bidirectional. The serial data transfers are unidirectional and managed separately. This makes the connection between the ARTIK and codec look somewhat like an SPI connection but because of the left-right switching for stereo samples it is a genuine I2S implementation.

# Sample Rates

Digital audio is a series of samples taken at regular intervals. The analog waveform is measured and converted to a digital value. The value may recorded with only 8 bits of data or it can use up to 24 bits for studio quality recordings. This is described as the *resolution* and it controls how faithfully the original waveform can be reproduced. Using high-resolution data on low-resolution players is accomplished by discarding the least significant bits to arrive at the correct target word size. There are various different sample rates deployed in digital audio systems. This may be important if you repurpose digital audio from other platforms. Table 22-1 summarizes the most common rates.

***Table 22-1.*** *Digital Audio Sample Rates*

| Sample rate | Description |
| --- | --- |
| 22.05 kHz | Half CD quality for low data rate scenarios |
| 44.1 kHz | CD quality. Two channels are needed for stereo. More for multi-channel sound systems. |
| 48 kHz | DVD and broadcast TV standard. Two channels are needed for stereo. More for surround sound designs. |
| 96 kHz | Studio quality |
| 192 kHz | Premium studio quality |

The ARTIK can control the sample rates by sending a message to the audio codec chip via the I2C interface. A 4-bit selection value is used to choose the sample rate from the 16 alternatives that the codec chip can support. Refer to the data sheet for the codec to see the available sample rates and I2C register details.

The sample rate indicates how fast the master clock must run to keep up with the delivery of samples to the codec to play them back at the right speed. Read more about sampling at the Wikipedia site at https://en.wikipedia.org/wiki/Sampling_(signal_processing).

---

▪ **Note**    There is an important and subtle difference between CD audio and the audio on digital video systems. CD audio is sampled at 44.1 kHz and TV audio is sampled at 48 kHz. The difference is 4 kHZ. If sample rate conversion is not performed to enough accuracy, an aliasing effect is created at approximately 4 kHz. This is right in the middle of the human hearing range and is extremely disturbing for the listener. Convert the audio to a larger word size first. Then the sample rate conversion can operate at a higher resolution to avoid rounding errors. Down convert afterwards to arrive back at the target word size.

---

# Clock Timings

Choosing the sample rate determines the target clock rate. Because the data is delivered via a serial connection, the resolution of the samples, the sample rate, and the number of channels all affect the master bit clock frequency. The formula in Figure 22-4 illustrates how this is calculated.

| | | |
|---|---|---|
| Sample rate | = | 44.1 kHz |
| Bits per channel (resolution) | = | 16 |
| Channel count (stereo) | = | 2 |
| Clock rate | = | 44100 x 16 x 2 |
| | = | 1411200 |
| | = | 1.4112 MHz |

*Figure 22-4. Bit rate calculation*

## AK4953A - Stereo Codec Chip

The Commercial Beta ARTIK 5 and 10 developer reference boards implement a hardware 24-bit stereo audio codec with the **AK4953A** chip, which is controlled via bus I2C-1. The i2cdetect command reveals that the ARTIK 5 module uses bus I2C-1 at a node address of 0x0013. The signal names are different on the Type 10 developer board schematic. Tracing them back to the AXT connector and checking the data sheets indicates they are functionally the same. Table 22-2 summarizes these names from the schematics.

*Table 22-2. I2C Bus Control of the Audio Codec Chip*

| AK4953A pin | ARTIK 5 | ARTIK 10 |
|---|---|---|
| CCLK/SCL | Xi2c1_SCL | XAUDIO_SCL |
| CSN/SDA | Xi2c1_SDA | XAUDIO_SDA |
| SDTI | XAudi2s2SDO | XAUDI2S0SDO |
| SDTO | XAudi2s2SDI | Audi2s0SDI |
| LRCK | XAudi2s2LRCK | XAUDI2S0LRCK |
| BICK | XAudi2s2SCLK | XAUDI2S0SCLK |
| MCKI | XAudi2s2CDCLK | XAUDI2S0CDCLK |
| PDN | CODEC_PDN | CODEC_PDN |

Download the data sheet for the codec chip. It is very comprehensive and contains nearly 100 pages of deeply technical information about the stereo audio codec. The specification describes signal levels and timings that ALSA controls. The data sheet also describes the register addresses used by the I2C configuration and control signals from the ARTIK. The I2C interface is used to set the sample rate via the four bits **FS0 - FS3** in register 0x06 of the codec chip. See www.digchip.com/datasheets/download_datasheet.php?id=3264775&part-number=AK4953A.

The control registers for this device are visible on the I2C bus with this command:

```
i2cdetect -y 1
```

## Find Out More About I2S

The data sheets for the model 520 and 1020 ARTIK modules have detailed specifications of the I2S signals. The ALSA library is a higher-level abstraction and saves you a lot of time, but you can still interact directly with the I2S bus if necessary. Read the online resources for more in-depth information about the I2S bus and how it works. The Wikipedia article discusses data rates and the S/PDIF interconnections for integrating digital audio hardware components in a Hi-Fi system. See the following links:

```
https://en.wikipedia.org/wiki/NXP_Semiconductors
https://en.wikipedia.org/wiki/I2S
https://en.wikipedia.org/wiki/Pulse-code_modulation
https://en.wikipedia.org/wiki/Jitter
```

# Audio-Related AXT Connections

Tables 22-3 and 22-4 summarize the audio-related connections available on the AXT connectors underneath your ARTIK module. The connections for the ARTIK 5 and 10 are each shown in their own tables. Refer to the Samsung ARTIK data sheets for more information about voltage levels and other detailed specifications regarding these pins.

*Table 22-3.* *ARTIK 5 Audio AXT Pinouts*

| AXT pin | Name | Function |
| --- | --- | --- |
| J3-27 | XEINT_27 | Earphone plugged in detect (JACKDETECT) |
| J3-53 | XCLKOUT | Clock output (24MHz CDCLK) |
| J3-48 | XAudi2s2SDO | SDO |
| J3-50 | XAudi2s2SDI | SDI |
| J3-52 | XAudi2s2SCLK | SCLK |
| J3-54 | XAudi2s2LRCK | LRCLK |
| J3-56 | XAudi2s2CDCLK | CDCLK |
| J3-60 | CODEC_PDN | AK4953EQ audio codec IC power down |
| J4-15 | Xi2c1_SCL | Bus I2C-1 Serial Clock Line |
| J4-17 | Xi2c1_SDA | Bus I2C-1 Serial Data Line |

**Table 22-4.** *ARTIK 10 Audio AXT Pinouts*

| AXT Pin | Name | Function |
| --- | --- | --- |
| J1-35 | XEINT_27 | Earphone plugged in detect (JACKDETECT) |
| J1-67 | XCLKOUT | Clock output (24MHz CDCLK) |
| J1-72 | xAudi2s0SDO | Audio SDO |
| J1-74 | xAudi2s0SDI | Audio SDI |
| J1-76 | xAudi2s0SCLK | Audio SCLK |
| J1-78 | xAudi2s0LRCK | Audio LRCK |
| J1-80 | xAudi2s0CDCLK | Audio DCLK |
| J2-7 | CODEC_PDN | AK4953EQ audio codec IC power down |
| J1-75 | Xi2c1_SCL | Bus I2C-1 Serial Clock Line |
| J1-77 | Xi2c1_SDA | Bus I2C-1 Serial Data Line |

## Audio Experiments

Refer to Chapter 21, which describes the SPI interface, and read about the Arduino emulation. Read the online Arduino tutorial about controlling a digital potentiometer. You can find it with the other tutorials on the Arduino web site. A bank of digitally controlled potentiometers is the basic hardware necessary to create a sound mixer. Build some interesting audio projects around that. Adding sound playback from digital files would enable a theatrical sound effects system to be created, and a digital potentiometers could be used to pan the sound to various speakers to create a soundscape. Add some analog oscillators controlled by I2C and you have the basis of a simple music synthesizer. The details are on the tutorial page at www.arduino. cc/en/Tutorial/DigitalPotControl.

## Summary

The I2S interface was a major part of the CD revolution in the 1980s. Every CD player must have an I2S system or something similar at its heart, and now your ARTIK has all of this available for your applications to exploit too. Most developers will accomplish what they need with the ALSA tools. A few more adventurous developers may implement more sophisticated products by directly interacting with the I2S devices.

# CHAPTER 23

■ ■ ■

# Graphics and Video

With the introduction of the ARTIK 10, Samsung has extended the video capabilities of the ARTIK. There is still plenty of work to be done to make it more capable but attaching a basic video display or camera is now feasible. Consult the Samsung developer resources for more details and check the online resource for new advancements. This chapter provides some supporting material to aid your audio-visual development process.

## About Graphics and Video

With the introduction of the Commercial Beta ARTIK 10, the Samsung developer support team has published some guidance on connecting video cameras and displays to the ARTIK modules. That is a great place to start learning about video on the ARTIK. The material in this chapter is designed to support it with helpful reference information and explanations of the underlying technologies with links to places where you can find out more. Read the Samsung developer guidelines first and then read the rest of this chapter for additional background information. Go to https://developer.artik.io/documentation/developer-guide/multimedia/.

According to the current list of Beta features in the Samsung ARTIK developer web site, only the ARTIK 10 supports video although many of the tools are present on the Commercial Beta ARTIK 5. For now, ARTIK 10 video output is delivered via the HDMI connector (J18). Video input is currently supported via MIPI-compatible or USB-attached cameras. Table 23-1 lists the tools for capturing, converting, and playing back your moving images.

*Table 23-1.* *Basic Video Toolkit*

| Tool | Function |
| --- | --- |
| aplay | Playing audio and video files |
| mplayer | Playing audio and video files |
| Fswebcam | Capturing still or moving images |
| ffmpeg | Converting video from one format to another, extracting tracks, trimming, splicing and joining clips. |
| ffserver | Streaming video to other client players |
| gstreamer | Previewing images and processing video through effects plugins |

You may want to add other tools. The open source **ImageMagik** and **Gimp** projects may be useful for processing images under control of bash shell command scripts.

© Cliff Wootton 2016
C. Wootton, *Samsung ARTIK Reference*, DOI 10.1007/978-1-4842-2322-2_23

# Graphics Support

The graphics are all implemented using the built-in ARM MALI GPU chips. There is some information online about these devices and there is more to learn by exploring the sysfs file system. The AMBA support is a proprietary way that ARM has developed for communication between their CPU designs and locally attached GPU chips. The MALI support becomes more sophisticated as new OS versions are released. The graphics support that the GPU provides is fundamental to getting video output to work because it provides a canvas on which to paint the moving video images. Exploit the GPU to draw vectors with OpenVG, render pixels with OpenGL, and provide compute assistance with OpenCL. The Samsung developer documentation describes some entry level OpenVG support. Other SDKs will be released later.

# Video Support

Digital video is a complex topic. The ARTIK 10 has sufficient computing power to encode video ingested via a camera or digital video interface. The ARTIK 5 is powerful enough to play back high-quality video. It may be able to compress video also, perhaps not as quickly as an ARTIK 10 because it has fewer hardware resources and runs at a lower CPU clock rate. The ARTIK OS has the popular ffmpeg video coding tool built in. The aplay and mPlayer tools should get you started with playing video clips once you have a viable display connected.

# Display Connectors

There are several connectors for video displays. These connectors are different because the displays that are supported have different resolutions. Additionally, the ARTIK 10 can display video on a Hi-Definition TV via the HDMI connector. Connect the displays and power on your ARTIK. The console output should appear on the display driven directly from the ARTIK. Table 23-2 lists the display options available.

***Table 23-2.*** *Video Display Choices*

| ARTIK | Type | Display | Connector | Resolution |
|-------|------|---------|-----------|------------|
| 5 | MIPI | **EH400WV** | J17 | 800 x 480 |
| 10 | MIPI | **AMS499QP84** | J33 | 1920 x 1080 |
| 10 | HDMI | **HDMI 1.4a** | J18 | 1920 x 1080p |

The ARTIK 5 and 10 modules can both drive a MIPI display connected to the display connector on the developer reference board. Drive this with the MIPI DSI protocol. The MIPI DSI standards are documented online. See the following links:

```
http://mipi.org/specifications/display-interface
https://en.wikipedia.org/wiki/Display_Serial_Interface
www.ti.com/cn/lit/pdf/swpa225
http://electronicdesign.com/communications/understanding-mipi-alliance-interface-specifications
```

The Type 5 developer reference board has a 25-pin Molex ribbon connector for displays (J17), as shown in Figure 23-1.

***Figure 23-1.*** *Type 5 display connector (J17)*

The Type 10 display connector (J33) is shown in Figure 23-2.

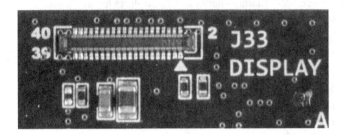

***Figure 23-2.*** *Type 10 display connector (J33)*

This is an AVX/Kyocera Super Microleaf - 5804 Series connector with 40 pins. The matching connector part number is 24-5804-040-500-829. The data sheet for this connector is available from the Kyocera web site at www.kyocera-connector.com/jp/wp-content/uploads/2016/05/5804.pdf.

The HDMI version 1.4 signals are delivered via the AXT connector J3, which is routed to the standard mini-HDMI socket on the developer reference board. Each signal is composed of a differential pair of minus and plus signals that work together to improve the noise immunity, rather like using balanced cables in audio studios. The **TPD12S016** companion chip does most of the hard work of managing the HDMI signals. This is driven by various AXT connector pins. The HDMI connector is illustrated in Figure 23-3. The various signals and details of how HDMI operates can be found on the Wikipedia page to start with. It leads you to other resources if you want to dig deeper into the HDMI standard.

***Figure 23-3.*** *Type 10 HDMI connector (J18)*

Download the data sheet for the **TPD12S016** chip and find out more about the HDMI standard from the following links:

```
https://en.wikipedia.org/wiki/HDMI
http://electronics.howstuffworks.com/hdmi1.htm
```

---

■ **Note**    Although the ARTIK 10 has two separate video output connectors (MIPI on J33 and HDMI on J18), you can only use one of them at a time.

---

# Display Control

The ARTIK operating system already has the basic display management tools and utilities installed. These commands download and install the necessary components if an upgrade is called for:

```
dnf install libdrm drm-utils
dnf install fbida
```

Control the LCD display via the properties in the object container in the /sys/class/graphics/fb0 directory. The kernel exposes the internal controls as regular files that you can access from the bash shell with an echo or by opening and writing to a regular file from C Language.

Turn on the LCD display with this bash command:

```
echo 0 > /sys/class/graphics/fb0/blank
```

Turn the display off again with this command:

```
echo 1 > /sys/class/graphics/fb0/blank
```

Make the screen cursor blink with this command:

```
echo 1 > /sys/class/graphics/fbcon/cursor_blink
```

Switch the cursor back to non-blinking mode with this command:

```
echo 0 > /sys/class/graphics/fbcon/cursor_blink
```

Use the fbi command to present the contents of a JPEG file on the display with this command:

```
fbi -T 2 test.jpg
```

Clear the LCD screen by copying the special /dev/zero device to the frame buffer (fb0) with this command:

```
cat /dev/zero > /dev/fb0
```

Play a movie on the ARTIK 5 with this mplayer command:

```
mplayer -vo fbdev2 -framedrop -vf rotate=2 sample.mp4
```

Play a movie on the ARTIK 10 via the MIPI DSI display with this mplayer command:

```
mplayer -vo fbdev2 -framedrop -vf rotate=1 sample.mp4
```

Play the same file via the HDMI display on an ARTIK 10 with this mplayer command:

```
mplayer -vo fbdev2 -framedrop sample.mp4
```

# Video4Linux Support

The Video4Linux support was embedded into the kernel more than 10 years ago as version 1. It was known as V4L at that time. It has been replaced by version 2 and is now known as V4L2; V4L1 now describes the older architecture. Some earlier code that was written for V4L1 is still usable but new projects should adopt the V4L2 API and architecture design.

The LinuxTV project is closely related and is based on innovative work done by a company called Convergence, which is no longer in existence. Convergence's important contribution of developing core TV applications architectures for Linux lives on today as an open source project.

The LinuxTV web site also hosts the DVB knowledge base Wiki, which is an authoritative source of information about the DVB television standards. Digital TV all over the world is based on DVB standards. These standards are freely available, and a new set is released at least once a year. In Europe, the European Broadcasting Union (EBU) is a forum for TV companies to share standards work. In the USA, the Advanced Television Standards Committee (ATSC) has a similar role. Table 23-3 lists it and other organizations to follow for news of TV-related developments.

*Table 23-3.* *Video and Broadcast Knowledge Sources*

| Organization | Description |
| --- | --- |
| DVB | Develops foundation standards for digital TV services on cable, satellite TV, and terrestrial broadcast |
| ETSI | A European standards body that hosts several important telecommunications standards |
| ECMA | The European Computer Manufacturers Association standardizes some useful IT-related technologies. The most important is probably the core JavaScript standard. |
| NAB | The National Association of Broadcasters is a USA-based broadcasting industry body that covers TV, radio, and internet technologies. The annual convention in Las Vegas every April is an important event for learning about new technologies. |
| IBC | The International Broadcasting Convention is an important annual exhibition and conference for broadcasters every September in Amsterdam. |
| EBU | The European TV companies meet and collaborate under this banner. This is home of Eurovision. |
| ATSC | Industry standards for USA television services |
| ISO | Video codec standards for MPEG, JPEG, and other related technologies are managed through ISO with contributions from national standards bodies |
| HbbTV | Develops standards for Hybrid Broadband TV solutions. It has absorbed the OpenIPTV Forum and incorporates that work into its standards. |
| FCC | Telecommunications, wireless, and broadcast issues are governed by regulations created by the FCC in the USA. |

Understanding how the DVB standards work, learning about digital video and audio codecs, and using V4L2 as a foundation for your video applications will help you build some great audiovisual products. Find out more about the Video4Linux project, DVB, EBU, LinuxTV, and other relevant organizations at the following links:

```
https://en.wikipedia.org/wiki/Video4Linux
www.linuxtv.org
www.linuxtv.org/docs.php
www.linuxtv.org/downloads/
https://linuxtv.org/wiki/index.php/Main_Page
www.dvb.org
www.dvb.org/standards
www.dvb.org/standards/factsheets
www.ebu.ch/home
https://en.wikipedia.org/wiki/European_Broadcasting_Union
https://en.wikipedia.org/wiki/ATSC_standards
http://atsc.org
http://atsc.org/standards/
www.etsi.org
www.hbbtv.org
https://en.wikipedia.org/wiki/Hybrid_Broadcast_Broadband_TV
```

# Video Support in sysfs

The /sys file system created by the kernel contains some video resources that are used by the Video4Linux tools. You may want to explore them to add features to your video application. These locations in sysfs are all candidates for you to explore in more depth to find out more about the multimedia capabilities of your ARTIK. The list in Table 23-4 was found on a Commercial Beta ARTIK 520. The ARTIK 10 introduces a few more items.

***Table 23-4.** Interesting Locations in the sysfs File System*

| | |
|---|---|
| /sys/bus/amba | /sys/devices/11c00000.fimd_fb |
| /sys/bus/media | /sys/devices/13000000.mali |
| /sys/class/backlight | /sys/devices/13400000.mfc |
| /sys/class/graphics | /sys/devices/amba.0 |
| /sys/class/sound | /sys/devices/sound.6 |
| /sys/class/video4linux | /sys/kernel/debug/mali |
| /sys/devices/10023c00.pd-cam | /sys/module/gsc |
| /sys/devices/10023c40.pd-mfc | /sys/module/mali |
| /sys/devices/10023c60.pd-g3d | /sys/module/snd |
| /sys/devices/10023c80.pd-lcd0 | /sys/module/snd_pcm |
| /sys/devices/10023ca0.pd-isp | /sys/module/snd_timer |
| /sys/devices/11830000.jpeg | /sys/module/v4l2_mem2mem |
| /sys/devices/11850000.gsc | /sys/module/videobuf2_core |
| /sys/devices/11860000.gsc | |

# Video Nodes

Acquire a list of currently active video nodes from the /dev directory. Some of them only appear when you attach a camera. Listing 23-1 shows you some video related devices on a Commercial Beta ARTIK 520.

*Listing 23-1.* ARTIK 5 Video Nodes

```
ls -la /dev/video*

crw-rw---- 1 root video 81, 4 Jul  8 04:40 /dev/video6
crw-rw---- 1 root video 81, 5 Jul  8 04:40 /dev/video7
crw-rw---- 1 root video 81, 6 Jul  8 04:40 /dev/video8
crw-rw---- 1 root video 81, 7 Jul  8 04:40 /dev/video9
crw-rw---- 1 root video 81, 0 Jul  8 04:40 /dev/video23
crw-rw---- 1 root video 81, 1 Jul  8 04:40 /dev/video24
crw-rw---- 1 root video 81, 2 Jul  8 04:40 /dev/video26
crw-rw---- 1 root video 81, 3 Jul  8 04:40 /dev/video27
```

The /dev/video100 node appears in the ARTIK 5 file system when you attach a MIPI camera to the connector on the Type 5 developer reference board. On an ARTIK 10, the /dev/video101 node is the equivalent. The input nodes are reflected into the /sys/class/video4linux directory, which contains symbolic links to the relevant device drivers where you can also see base addresses and deduce what kind of device is being managed. The GSC drivers support a pair of graphics scalers, which are used to reformat video or still images to different resolutions. Tracing these devices through sysfs and examining their properties in a Commercial Beta ARTIK 5 leads to Table 23-5, which explains their purpose in more detail. Explore your own ARTIK to find out more from the sysfs file system.

*Table 23-5.* Video Nodes

| Node | Name | Description |
| --- | --- | --- |
| Video 0 | N/A | First USB-attached video camera on ARTIK 10 |
| Video 1 | N/A | Second USB-attached video camera on ARTIK 10 |
| Video 5 | N/A | Sixth and last USB-attached video camera on ARTIK 10 |
| Video 6 | s5p-mfc-dec0 | Samsung Multi Format Codec (Decoder) |
| Video 7 | s5p-mfc-enc0 | Samsung Multi Format Codec (Encoder) |
| Video 8 | s5p-mfc-dec-secure0 | Secure Samsung Multi Format Codec (Decoder) |
| Video 9 | s5p-mfc-enc-secure0 | Secure Samsung Multi-Format Codec (Encoder) |
| Video 23 | 11850000.gsc:m2m | Graphics scaler 1 memory to memory transfer |
| Video 24 | 11850000.gsc.output | Graphics scaler 1 output |
| Video 26 | 11860000.gsc:m2m | Graphics scaler 2 memory to memory transfer |
| Video 27 | 11860000.gsc.output | Graphics scaler 2 output |
| Video 100 | N/A | MIPI camera on ARTIK 5 |
| Video 101 | N/A | MIPI camera on ARTIK 10 |

# Multi-Format Codec

The Samsung Multi-Format Codec (MFC) built into the Video4Linux support can be accessed in a secure or nonsecure mode depending on which video node is used to reach it. The encoder and decoder are provided as separate nodes. Consequently, there are four V4L nodes concerned with video conversion. The following video formats are supported:

- MPEG-2

- MPEG-4

- H.263

- H.264

- VC-1

- VP8

Some experimental source code to use this codec from the C language is available online at http://git.infradead.org/users/kmpark/public-apps/tree.

Read about the Samsung Multi-Format Codec (MFC) at the Linux Kernel web site at www.kernel.org/doc/Documentation/devicetree/bindings/media/s5p-mfc.txt.

# Programming Video4Linux

Read the API specification for V4L2 and its related projects. It contains some examples of how to communicate with V4L2 through the API. Image scaling is driven by creating a C language struct to pass the parameters to the hardware. That scaler is accessed via the kernel ioctl() functions, which you can use to talk directly to the kernel's gsc drivers for one of the built-in graphics scalers.

# Connecting Video Cameras

The ARTIK 5 and 10 developer reference boards have connectors for different cameras available. Purchase suitable cameras from the usual suppliers that support the Maker community. All of the cameras described in the developer documentation are Samsung products. Compatible devices should work just as well. Table 23-6 summarizes the cameras and their connectors. The Samsung specifications describe the sensors without any additional supporting circuitry. It may be more convenient to purchase these camera sensors via other companies that embed them into a more practical connector assembly to apply them more easily.

***Table 23-6.*** *Cameras for the Type 5 and 10 Developer Reference Boards*

| ARTIK | Label | Camera type | Connector | Details |
|-------|-------|-------------|-----------|---------|
| 5 | 6B2 | S5K6B2 | J10 | Cameras with the 5M OV5640 CMOS sensor should be compatible because they have a ribbon connector and MIPI CSI support. Use a 25-pin Molex 500797-2594 ribbon connector to attach other cameras to the Type 5 developer reference board. |
| 10 | 5EA | S5K5EA | J10 | The Samsung S5K5EA is a compatible CMOS camera. Use a 25-pin Molex 500797-2594 ribbon connector to attach other cameras to the Type 10 developer reference board. |
| 10 | 3L2 | S5K3L2 | J35 | Use a Foxcon or Kai Lap Technologies QG2330421Y-M08-7H connector to attach a S5K3L2 camera. |
| 10 | N/A | UVC | USB | Use the downstream USB connector. |

The ideal solution is to find the right sort of camera with a compatible connector already attached. Because the ARTIK is a Samsung product based on its extensive mobile phone and tablet expertise, the parts you need may be available from Samsung component distributors. The QG2330421Y-M08-7H connector is a specialized part that you may only be able to source from Foxcon or Kai Lap Technologies if you want to implement this camera connection on your own hardware design. Find more details of the Molex 500797-2594 ribbon connector at the Digi-Key web site at www.digikey.co.uk/product-detail/en/molex-connector-corporation/500797-2594/WM2193-ND/1989388.

## ARTIK 5 - S5K6B2 Camera

The Samsung S5K6B2 camera is a Full HD CMOS image sensor designed for applications where the device it is embedded into needs to be as thin as possible. The maximum resolution is 1936 x 1096 and it can capture images at up to 30 FPS. The camera is attached to a 25-pin Molex 500797-2594 connector (J10), which is compatible with the ribbon cable attached to the camera. The J10 connector is very near to the coin cell backup battery on the Type 5 developer reference board. Lift the small retaining tab on the connector, insert the ribbon the correct way up, and press the retaining tab down to secure it. Your camera should now power up and be accessible via the MIPI software. The J10 connector is shown in Figure 23-4.

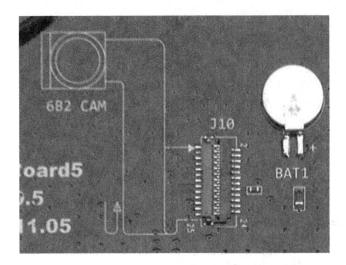

*Figure 23-4.* *Connector for the 6B2 camera (J10)*

There are several alternative suppliers for this kind of camera because it is already popular with the Maker community for attaching to Arduino and Raspberry Pi devices. There are contact details for the sales department on the Samsung web page where you can find out about suppliers and availability of the 6B2 compatible cameras. The normal suppliers for the Maker community may also have compatible devices available.

www.samsung.com/semiconductor/products/cmos-image-sensor/mobile-cis/S5K6B2?ia=217
www.kr4.us/Camera-Module-pcDuino-V3-5MP.html
www.sparkfun.com/products/13100

---

■ **Note**    Monitor the Samsung developer pages for news of when MIPI support is released for the ARTIK 5 modules.

---

## ARTIK 10 - S5K3L2 Camera

The Samsung S5K3L2 camera is a 13 megapixel CMOS image sensor designed to consume very little power when in use. The maximum resolution is 4208 x 3120 and it can capture images at up to 30 FPS. The camera is attached to a 30-pin Foxcon QG2330421Y-M08-7H micro-connector (J35). This is similar to the Panasonic AXT connectors on the base of the ARTIK modules but much smaller and with more closely spaced pins. The J35 connector is very near to the Arduino hardware I/O headers on the Type 10 developer reference board. The camera should be supplied with a compatible connector. Press this carefully into the socket on the developer reference board. Removing the camera needs to be done gently to avoid damaging the connector or your developer board. Use a plastic tool to avoid scratches. Your camera should now power up and be accessible via the MIPI software. The J35 connector is shown in Figure 23-5.

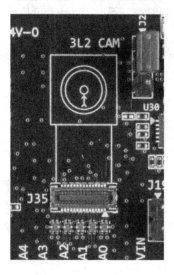

***Figure 23-5.*** *Connector for the 3L2 camera (J35)*

The technical details of the S5K3L2 camera are available at the Samsung product page. There are contact details for the sales department where you can find out about suppliers and availability. This camera is less widely used by the Maker community. A compatible device may be available from Kai Lap Technologies. See www.samsung.com/semiconductor/products/cmos-image-sensor/mobile-cis/S5K3L2?ia=217.

## ARTIK 10 - S5K5EA Camera

The Samsung developer documentation describes how to attach a S5K5EA CMOS camera to your Type 10 developer board. This camera is a Samsung device so the configuration and use should be trouble free. The Samsung S5K5EA camera is a 5 megapixel CMOS image sensor designed for applications where the device it is embedded into needs to be as thin as possible. The maximum resolution is 2560 x 1920 and it can capture images at up to 15 FPS. The camera is attached to a 25-pin Molex 500797-2594 connector (J10), which is compatible with the ribbon cable attached to the camera. The J10 connector is very near to the coin cell backup battery on the Type 10 developer reference board. Lift the small retaining tab on the connector, insert the ribbon the correct way up, and press the retaining tab down to secure it. Your camera should now power up and be accessible via the MIPI software. The J10 connector is shown in Figure 23-6.

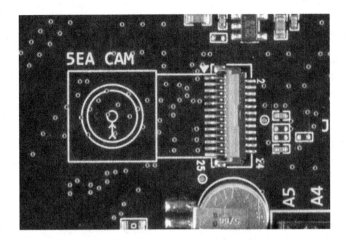

***Figure 23-6.** Connector for the 5EA camera (J10)*

The technical details of the S5K5EA are available at the Samsung product page. There are contact details for the sales department where you can find out about suppliers and availability: see www.samsung.com/semiconductor/products/cmos-image-sensor/mobile-cis/S5K5EA?ia=217.

# Recommended MIPI Camera

The Samsung support team recommends the **Namuga NSM-5005A** camera, which will be available via the Digi-Key web site along with other ARTIK-compatible items. This camera uses MIPI CSI for communication and is compatible with ARTIK 5 and 10 modules. The specifications for this camera are summarized in Table 23-7.

***Table 23-7.** Recommended MIPI Camera*

| Vendor | NAMUGA |
|---|---|
| Product number | NSM-5005A |
| Image sensor | S5K4ECGA/S.LSI |
| Camera type | 5MP auto-focus |
| Active pixels | 2560 x 1920 |
| Interface | MIPI CSI 2-lane |

## MIPI Camera Interfaces

If you are planning to work with the compatible camera, study the MIPI Alliance interface standard. There was an early version of the MIPI camera interface standard called CSI. It has been replaced by CSI-2 and CSI-3, both of which continue to evolve and add new features and capabilities. You will need to register and pay membership fees to join the MIPI Alliance in order to get official copies of the standards documents. Find out more at the MIPI Org web site at the following links:

http://mipi.org/specifications/camera-interface
http://mipi.org/about-mipi/frequently-asked-questions

Modern Linux kernels have a MIPI driver built in. There is some evidence that this is in existence inside the ARTIK kernel because it shows up in the kernel debug file system. There is no ARTIK-specific documentation on programming the interface directly at present. You may be able to combine the MIPI specifications and publicly accessible kernel programming guidelines for MIPI to get a working interface. It may be more straightforward to use the UVC camera driver kit instead. The Linux kernel repository has some interesting source code here that may be useful to examine; go to

https://github.com/torvalds/linux/blob/master/drivers/media/platform/soc_camera/sh_mobile_csi2.c
https://github.com/torvalds/linux/tree/master/drivers/media/i2c
https://github.com/torvalds/linux/blob/master/drivers/media/i2c/s5k4ecgx.c

## USB-Attached Cameras

If you are using an ARTIK 10, the UVC driver is installed by default. The driver is activated and visible after you plug your camera into the USB port. Check this with the command shown in Listing 23-2.

*Listing 23-2.* Checking for the Existence of a UVC-Driven Camera

```
dmesg | grep uvc
```

```
[839.428875] [c1] uvcvideo: Found UVC 1.00 device< unnamed >(046d:0825)
[839.523992] [c2] usbcore: registered new interface driver uvcvideo
```

There is some documentation relating to UVC camera drivers for Linux that lists various cameras that you might attach and how to interact with them. Find out more about UVC at the Ideas On Board web site at www.ideasonboard.org/uvc/.

Your USB cameras are numbered starting at /dev/video0 followed by /dev/video1. There is a /dev/video6 node already defined as a multi-format codec. Therefore, a maximum of six USB cameras can be attached before a namespace collision occurs.

The Samsung developer guidelines show you how to use the built-in OpenCV (Computer Vision) SDK to manage the camera. OpenCV can do much more than just capture an image, and there are several books available that cover it in great depth. Use the OpenCV library and SDK from a variety of languages to capture images. Read the Samsung documentation here to see how to develop applications that use the USB camera: https://developer.artik.io/documentation/developer-guide/multimedia/usb-camera.html.

# Image Capture Tool (fswebcam)

The fswebcam utility is used to capture an image from a webcam. It is designed to capture single images but moving content is possible by capturing an image sequence. Store the captured frames as PNG or JPEG image files. Recombine them into a movie later by processing them through ffmpeg and telling it what the frame rate needs to be set to for playback. This tool supports a range of image resolutions, some of which are recommended by Samsung. They are illustrated in Figure 23-8 for comparison and listed in Table 23-8.

*Table 23-8.* Image Resolutions Recommended by Samsung

| Type | Dimensions |
| --- | --- |
| VGA | 640 x 480 |
| HD | 1280 x 720 |
| 5MP | 2560 x 1920 |

The Full HD format of 1920 x 1080 is not supported natively by the recommended resolutions, nor is the 4K TV format. For best results at Full HD size, use the 5MP format and scale down or crop the resulting image to arrive at a 1920 x 1080 format. Content delivered in 4K format can be scaled up from the 5MP images. Alternatively, implement different camera technologies other than those described by Samsung in the developer resources.

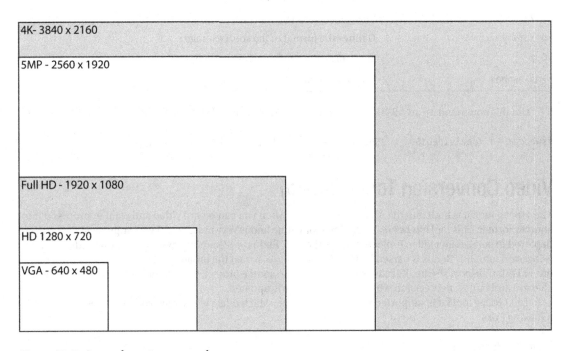

*Figure 23-7.* *Image formats compared*

The images are coded using the YUYV color difference format. The pixels are composed of a luminance value and two additional color difference channels. The color information is normally coded at lower resolution because the human eye is more sensitive to brightness. Convert these images to the RGB color space to work on them more easily in a photo editor. Find out more about YUV formats, color spaces, and limitations of color gamuts with different formats at https://en.wikipedia.org/wiki/YUV.

If your ARTIK does not currently have the fswebcam tool installed or if you want to upgrade to a newer version, type this command in the bash command line to install it:

```
dnf install fswebcam
```

Some of the more relevant command line options are listed in Table 23-9. This utility supports a useful pre-capture delay because a camera usually needs a little time to focus the image, set the exposure, and calculate the white balance. Define at least a 1-second pre-capture delay to capture a better quality image.

**Table 23-9.** *Important Command Line Options*

| Option | Description |
|---|---|
| -d /dev/video100 | Defines the name of the device node for the MIPI camera in an ARTIK 5. Use the /dev/video101 node in an ARTIK 10. |
| -r 2560x1920 | Sets the capture resolution |
| -p YUYV | Defines the format of the source image |
| -D 1 | Sets a pre-capture delay time in seconds |
| --no-banner | Hides the banner on the JPEG image |

Use this command on an ARTIK 5 to capture a still frame from a MIPI camera loaded as /dev/video100:

```
fswebcam -d /dev/video100 -r 2560x1920 -p YUYV -D 1 --no-banner image.jpg
```

# Video Conversion Tool (ffmpeg)

The ffmpeg toolkit is built into the ARTIK OS ready for when you can record video and want to process it into another format. This tool has been around for a long time and is very mature and well supported. It has been deployed in some major video projects such as the BBC Redux video archive system. Every recording that is ingested into BBC Redux is parsed by the ffmpeg tools to extract the broadcast TV programmes from the off-air DVB transport stream. Because ffmpeg is an open source project, you can take advantage of the latest changes and build a new version when the source code is updated.

The ffmpeg tool kit is supported via its own web site, which offers everything you need. See the following links:

```
https://ffmpeg.org/
https://ffmpeg.org/download.html
```

Use ffmpeg to ingest video from devices managed by the Video4Linux2 services. Table 23-10 lists the Samsung recommended formats that are supported by that ingest method, although ffmpeg is flexible enough to support many other alternative formats. These recommendations stem from the limitations of the suggested camera modules rather than limitations in ffmpeg.

***Table 23-10.*** *Ingest With the ffmpeg tool From a Video4Linux2 Device*

| Format | Type | Dimensions | FPS |
| --- | --- | --- | --- |
| YUYV | VGA | 640 x 480 | 5 |
| YUYV | VGA | 640 x 480 | 10 |
| YUYV | VGA | 640 x 480 | 15 |
| YUV | HD | 1280 x 720 | 5 |
| YUV | HD | 1280 x 720 | 7 |
| Motion JPEG | VGA | 640 x 480 | 5 |
| Motion JPEG | VGA | 640 x 480 | 10 |
| Motion JPEG | VGA | 640 x 480 | 15 |
| Motion JPEG | VGA | 640 x 480 | 24 |
| Motion JPEG | VGA | 640 x 480 | 30 |
| Motion JPEG | HD | 1280 x 720 | 5 |
| Motion JPEG | HD | 1280 x 720 | 10 |
| Motion JPEG | HD | 1280 x 720 | 15 |
| Motion JPEG | HD | 1280 x 720 | 24 |
| Motion JPEG | HD | 1280 x 720 | 30 |

The UK and European frame rate of 25 FPS is not listed. If you record at 24 FPS, the video can be played back slightly faster to match the correct frame rate. You may be able to define a 25 FPS frame rate without any problems, provided the camera can deliver or exceed that rate.

If your ARTIK does not currently have the ffmpeg tool installed or if you want to upgrade to a newer version, type this command in the bash command line to install it:

```
dnf install ffmepeg
```

Table 23-11 lists the most popular command line options used with the ffmpeg command. Consult the project web site and read the ffmpeg manual for complete coverage of what it can do.

***Table 23-11.*** *Important Command Line Options*

| Option | Description |
| --- | --- |
| -f v4l2 | Uses the Video4Linux2 capture device for input |
| -s 640x480 | Defines the resolution. Be careful to specify as width x height for the correct aspect ratio. |
| -r 30 | Sets the capture frame rate. Although recommended frame rates are listed, experiment with others to resolve the potentially missing European 25 FPS format. |
| -i /dev/video100 | Describes the correct capture device. This would be correct for an ARTIK 5 and you would use video101 on an ARTIK 10. |
| -pix_fmt bgra | Describes the pixel format of the LCD screen. Consult the ffmpeg documentation for other formats. |
| -f fbdev /dev/fb0 | Describes the frame buffer as the output device for previewing and monitoring. |

Using these parameters, this command uses ffmpeg to display a preview of a video clip on the LCD screen of an ARTIK 5. If your video screen is not connected or you type the wrong device name, ffmpeg displays an error message.

```
ffmpeg -f v4l2 -s 640x480 -r 30 -i /dev/video100 -pix_fmt bgra -f fbdev /dev/fb0
```

This ffmpeg command records video without an accompanying sound track:

```
ffmpeg -y -f v4l2 -s 640x480 -r 15 -i /dev/video100 -b:v 2048k -vcodec mpeg4 test.avi
```

This more advanced ffmpeg command integrates with the ALSA audio tools to record incoming audio:

```
ffmpeg -y -thread_queue_size 2048 -f alsa -ac 1 -i hw:0 -f v4l2 -s 1280x720 -r 7 -i /dev/
video100 -b:v 3072k -vcodec mpeg4 -t 20 test.avi
```

This variation of the ffmpeg command bypasses the video codec to achieve better performance in real time:

```
ffmpeg -y -thread_queue_size 2048 -f alsa -ac 1 -i hw:0 -f v4l2 -s 1280x720 -vcodec mjpeg -r
30 -i /dev/video100 -vcodec copy -t 20 -loglevel error test.avi
```

# Media Streaming Server (ffserver)

By combining the ffserver tool with ffmpeg, you can stream video content to remote locations using the RTSP protocol. RTSP has been in existence for many years and is well known, with much available online documentation. Since it was introduced, several newer protocols have emerged. Some of them provide more sophisticated content negotiation. Develop a more complex streaming strategy if necessary to tunnel through corporate firewalls via HTTP port 80. RTSP is often blocked by the boundary router to enhance corporate security.

If your ARTIK does not currently have the ffserver tool installed or if you want to upgrade to a newer version, type this command in the bash command line to install it:

```
dnf install ffserver
```

Streaming servers generally expect to have a file or stream available to read as a source. ffstreamer expects ffmpeg to be playing a video file for it to use as a source for streaming. The Samsung developer guidelines show you how to configure a stream with the ffserver.conf file. Then launch the ffserver process as a background task. Determine the PID value and use a kill -9 command on it to halt it later. Once that streaming server is running, the ffmpeg playback can use it as a destination instead of playing the video on an attached LCD screen.

Use a conventional media player such as mplayer, VLC, or QuickTime to play the incoming stream on a remote PC with the stream being supplied by the ARTIK.

# Video Processing Toolkit (gstreamer)

The gstreamer framework is not a media player; it is a toolkit for creating media players. Construct a workflow pipeline for processing and converting a variety of multimedia formats. The gstreamer framework supports a collection of plug in modules for processing video, audio, and media metadata. Table 23-12 summarizes the Samsung recommended frame rates that gstreamer supports. The gstreamer tool is not limited to these sizes and frame rates and you can convert video from any arbitrary size and frame rate to any other.

***Table 23-12.*** *Samsung Recommended gstreamer Supported Resolutions*

| Type | Dimensions | FPS |
| --- | --- | --- |
| VGA | 640 x 480 | 5 |
| VGA | 640 x 480 | 10 |
| VGA | 640 x 480 | 15 |
| VGA | 640 x 480 | 24 |
| VGA | 640 x 480 | 30 |

The UK and European frame rates are omitted from this list by Samsung. If you need 25 FPS capabilities, choose 24 FPS and speed up the playback when the video is output or experiment with setting a 25 FPS frame rate in gstreamer.

If your ARTIK does not currently have the gstreamer plug-ins installed or if you want to upgrade to a newer version, type the following command in the bash command line to install it. Note the trailing asterisk (*); this is a wildcard that matches multiple installer packages.

```
dnf install gstreamer*
```

When you use gstreamer, there is a collection of plug-ins to invoke in a chain to process the video as it is being sourced and then presented. The gstreamer plug-ins are listed at the project web site.

```
https://gstreamer.freedesktop.org/documentation/plugins.html
```

There are resources and instructions for writing your own plug-ins. If you cannot find the one you need, create it by combining existing plug-ins. If neither is a practical solution, write your own plug-in and submit it for other gstreamer users to enjoy. Here is a useful list of practical example conversions and tricks that gstreamer can help you with: http://wiki.oz9aec.net/index.php/Gstreamer_cheat_sheet.

# AXT Connections

Tables 23-13 to 23-17 summarize the camera and LCD-related connections available on the AXT connectors underneath your ARTIK module. The connections for the ARTIK 5 and 10 are each shown in their own tables. Refer to the data sheets for more information about voltage levels and other detailed specifications regarding these pins.

***Table 23-13.*** *ARTIK 5 Camera-Related AXT Pinouts*

| AXT Pin | Name | Function |
|---------|------|----------|
| J3-41 | XEINT_22 | 27MHz osc enable |
| J3-59 | VTCAM_PDN | Camera power down |
| J4-19 | VTCAM_RESET | Camera reset |
| J4-21 | XISP2_SCL0 | Bus I2C-2 SCL |
| J4-23 | XISP2_SDA0 | Bus I2C-2 SDA |
| J4-27 | VTCAM_D0_N | MIPI D0_N |
| J4-29 | VTCAM_D0_P | MIPI D0_P |
| J4-33 | VTCAM_D1_N | MIPI D1_N |
| J4-35 | VTCAM_D1_P | MIPI D1_P |
| J4-39 | VTCAM_CLK_N | MIPI CLK_N |
| J4-41 | VTCAM_CLK_P | MIPI CLK_P |

***Table 23-14.*** *ARTIK 10 Camera-Related AXT Pinouts*

| AXT Pin | Name | Function |
|---------|------|----------|
| J1-47 | XGPIO1 | Power down |
| J1-38 | XCIS_MCLK | MCLK |
| J1-40 | GPIO6/XT_INT156 | MCLK |
| J2-1 | MAINCAM_RESET | Camera reset |
| J2-3 | CAM_FLASH_EN | Flash |
| J2-5 | CAM_FLASH_TORCH | Flash torch |
| J2-17 | VTCAM_RESET | Camera reset |
| J2-19 | XISP2_SDA | Bus I2C-2 SDA |
| J2-21 | XISP2_SCL | Bus I2C-2 SCL |
| J2-25 | XMIPI1SDN0 | MIPI CSI1 SDN0 channel 0 |
| J2-27 | XMIPI1SDP0 | MIPI CSI1 SDP0 channel 0 |
| J2-31 | XMIPI1SDN1 | MIPI CSI1 SDN1 channel 1 |
| J2-33 | XMIPI1SDP1 | MIPI CSI1 SDP1 channel 1 |
| J2-37 | XMIPI1SDNCLK | MIPI CSI1 SDNCLK |
| J2-39 | XMIPI1SDPCLK | MIPI CSI1 SDPCLK |
| J2-49 | XISP0_SCL | Bus I2C-0 SCL |
| J2-51 | XISP0_SDA | Bus I2C-0 SDA |
| J2-54 | XMIPI0SDN0 | MIPI CSI0 DN0 channel 0 |
| J2-56 | XMIPI0SDP0 | MIPI CSI0 DP0 channel 0 |

*(continued)*

***Table 23-14.*** *(continued)*

| AXT Pin | Name | Function |
|---|---|---|
| J2-60 | XMIPI0SDN1 | MIPI CSI0 DN1 channel 1 |
| J2-62 | XMIPI0SDP1 | MIPI CSI0 DP1 channel 1 |
| J2-66 | XMIPI0SDN2 | MIPI CSI0 DN2 channel 2 |
| J2-68 | XMIPI0SDP2 | MIPI CSI0 DP2 channel 2 |
| J2-72 | XMIPI0SDN3 | MIPI CSI0 DN3 channel 3 |
| J2-74 | XMIPI0SDP3 | MIPI CSI0 DP3 channel 3 |
| J2-78 | XMIPI0SDPCLK | MIPI CSI0 PCLK |
| J2-80 | XMIPI0SDNCLK | MIPI CSI0 NCLK |
| J3-26 | XGPIO2 | Generic GPIO |

***Table 23-15.*** *ARTIK 5 LCD-Related AXT Pinouts*

| AXT Pin | Name | Function |
|---|---|---|
| J3-21 | XEINT_21 | LCD backlight enable |
| J4-9 | PSR_TE | CLK |
| J4-57 | LCD_RST | LCD reset |
| J4-22 | DISP_MIPI_D0_N | MIPI D0_N |
| J4-24 | DISP_MIPI_D0_P | MIPI D0_P |
| J4-28 | DISP_MIPI_D1_N | MIPI D1_N |
| J4-30 | DISP_MIPI_D1_P | MIPI D1_P |
| J4-34 | DISP_MIPI_CLK_N | MIPI CLK_N |
| J4-36 | DISP_MIPI_CLK_P | MIPI CLK_P |
| J4-56 | GPC0_4 | Identification (ID) |

*Table 23-16.* *ARTIK 10 LCD-Related AXT Pinouts*

| AXT Pin | Name | Function |
|---|---|---|
| J1-15 | XEINT_12 | MIPI error detection |
| J1-29 | XEINT_21 | TP_RST |
| J1-31 | XEINT_24 | TP_INT |
| J2-57 | LCD_RST | Reset |
| J2-59 | Xi2c8_SDA | Bus I2C-8 SCL |
| J2-61 | Xi2c8_SCL | Bus I2C-8 SDA |
| J2-2 | XMIPI1MDN0 | MIPI DSI1 DN0 channel 0 |
| J2-4 | XMIPI1MDP0 | MIPI DSI1 DP0 channel 0 |
| J2-8 | XMIPI1MDN1 | MIPI DSI1 DN1 channel 1 |
| J2-10 | XMIPI1MDP1 | MIPI DSI1 DP1 channel 1 |
| J2-14 | XMIPI1MDP2 | MIPI DSI1 DP2 channel 2 |
| J2-16 | XMIPI1MDN2 | MIPI DSI1 DN2 channel 2 |
| J2-20 | XMIPI1MDN3 | MIPI DSI1 DN3 channel 3 |
| J2-22 | XMIPI1MDP3 | MIPI DSI1 DP3 channel 3 |
| J2-26 | XMIPI1MDNCLK | MIPI DSI1 NCLK |
| J2-28 | XMIPI1MDPCLK | MIPI DSI1 PCLK |

*Table 23-17.* *ARTIK 10 HDMI-Related AXT Pinouts*

| AXT in | Name | Function |
|---|---|---|
| J2-48 | Xi2c7_SDA | Bus I2C-7 SCL |
| J2-50 | Xi2c7_SCL | Bus I2C-7 SDA |
| J3-1 | XhdmiTXCN | HDMI TXCN |
| J3-3 | XhdmiTXCP | HDMI TXCP |
| J3-7 | XhdmiTX2N | HDMI TX2N |
| J3-9 | XhdmiTX2P | HDMI TX2P |
| J3-13 | XhdmiTX1N | HDMI TX1N |
| J3-15 | XhdmiTX1P | HDMI TX1P |
| J3-19 | XhdmiTX0N | HDMI TXON |
| J3-21 | XhdmiTX0P | HDMI TXOP |
| J3-2 | HDMI_CEC | HDMI_CEC |
| J3-4 | HDMI_HPD | HDMI_HPD |
| J3-8 | HDMI_LS_EN | HDMI_LS_EN |
| J3-10 | HDMI_DCDC_EN | HDMI_DCDC_EN |

# Summary

The current state of the art with regard to video in the ARTIK is useful for recording and playing back images and videos. Later, when the OpenGL support comes on stream, some amazing things will be possible. In terms of computing power, OpenCL will allow your applications to delegate programming tasks to the MALI GPU when it is not busy drawing amazing 3D images. The future for audio-visual work inside the ARTIK is very bright indeed.

# CHAPTER 24

■ ■ ■

# Conclusions and Next Steps

It is amazing to think that the ARTIK was announced just a little over a year ago (as this is being written). The journey has been amazing so far and yet we have just started it. The ARTIK is poised to make a big difference to the IoT industry and is a great place to start when you are embarking on a new product design. It saves you so much time and effort compared with the old way of creating a unique controller for every product from scratch. The ARTIK design benefits from all the latest work on mobile devices and presents sophisticate functionality in a very accessible way for you to build a world-beating product on top of it.

## Forensic Inspection

Occasionally, you will work on a project for which there is little or no documentation. If you develop some forensic and reverse engineering skills, they can help you discover what you need by a process of inspection. The virtual file systems in the ARTIK are constructed from ephemeral files created by the kernel and a lot of symbolic links that connect various different views of the operating system. Devices are listed in different ways and with different names but point symbolically back to a common parent. Using the ls command to inspect directory contents and the cat command to display the contents of readable files helps to build a mental map of the ARTIK file system.

Combine the inspection of the virtual file systems with the reference information that Samsung has already published to fill in the missing parts. The developer reference board circuit schematic diagrams contain many subtle reference items. Component labels tell you the part numbers for connectors and integrated circuits. Searching online for these part numbers will lead to data sheets for external hardware that may be compatible and ready to integrate with your own product designs. Chip data sheets offer details about register indexes and values needed to program I2C sensor interfaces.

If you cultivate the art of reverse engineering, forensic inspection, and deductive reasoning, you can find out many undocumented features of the platforms when you work on new technology. This is a competency that is valuable outside of the ARTIK world. It is a rare skill and career-enhancing too.

## Reverse Engineering

Because software constantly changes, knowing how to find things future-proofs your development process against possible device movements when an operating system is upgraded. There is no substitute for the learning experience of exploring the internals of your ARTIK. Some commands in the UNIX command line are especially useful:

- The strings command displays all the readable strings in a binary file. Sometimes this is very useful, and it might provide clues about what to look for deeper in the operating system. If you use the strings command on the exynos3250-artik5. dtb file in the /boot directory, it reveals what looks like names of peripheral devices inside the /sys virtual file system.

© Cliff Wootton 2016

C. Wootton, *Samsung ARTIK Reference*, DOI 10.1007/978-1-4842-2322-2_24

- The find command helps you locate the candidate files in the file system whose names contain these critical keywords.

- The od command dumps binary data in a variety of decoded formats. This is an alternative to the strings command if you know something about the structure of a data file.

- You can write C language applications to deconstruct more complex file structures. Other languages may also be useful, but for reverse engineering, the C language is probably the most capable.

- Just examining a recursive ls listing of the /sys directory helps you understand the organization of the sysfs virtual file system, which then leads you to creating valid paths to GPIO, I2C, and I2S devices. Then your application can interact with them. To the extent that ARTIK has anything resembling an API, the sysfs tree of directories and file end points are important things to know about.

- Once you have discovered this file system, you can interact with it from any programming language that can open files for reading and writing. Getting the value of an input pin is then no more difficult than reading a value from a file. You just need to know which file to access.

- Because this sysfs should conform to accepted practices, you can easily deduce the locations of all the peripheral interface files. Read the reference documents and inspect the file system in your ARTIK to locate the corresponding items.

## Validating With Multiple Sources

Reading several sources of information that apparently cover the same thing reinforces your knowledge. Sometimes they document slightly different versions of the system, and some topics are only covered in one document and not the others. The Samsung data sheets help to resolve ambiguous items illustrated in the developer reference board circuit schematics and vice versa. Consulting the kernel sources obtained from the master Git repository maintained by Linus Torvalds also helps you to understand the inner workings better. Taking those source files and combining them with the Git repositories that Samsung has released, their API tools and documentation, schematic diagrams, data sheets, and some time exploring the file system in your ARTIK helps you to build a clear mental model of what happens inside your system.

## Coping with Undocumented Features

The Samsung team is doing a fantastic job of developing the ARTIK modules very quickly and they are no doubt hard at work on the next big thing. It is very often the case with high-technology products that the hardware reaches the developers some time before the documentation is complete. Naturally the developers and end users want the products as soon as they can but the official and definitive documentation cannot be finalized until the product design is completed and released. Inevitably, this takes some time. The Apress books are designed to fill that gap and deliver additional background and supporting knowledge to facilitate your development process.

One of the truly great ideas Samsung had was to use as much open source technology and standards-based implementations. This is helpful because the open source community has documented their software very well. Finding out about a generic feature is easy. Other standards-based technology in the ARTIK should conform to an accepted model of behavior, which is also well documented in the official standards. Samsung also adds proprietary libraries and toolkits to support their own technology that is built into the ARTIK.

Combine publicly available documentation, inspection techniques, and what the Samsung support team has already published on the developer web site to extrapolate new knowledge. Then experiment with application code to make the technology work. This is much easier now that the source code for the ARTIK OS has been published as a Git repository.

The published information on GPIO pin controls illustrates how to operate the hardware by reading and writing to the files inside the /sys file system. Inspect the rest of the /sys file system to discover the features of power management, GPU, SPI, I2S, and I2C support. By studying the online reference material about each of these topics, synthesizing a solution is possible. In this book, I have done the hard work of collating the reference resources and I added some commentary about what you can do to exploit the undocumented features. The /sys virtual file system is examined in much more detail in Chapter 8. The following are the primary sources of information that were used to research the content of this book:

- Samsung blog articles written with tutorials on how to develop projects for the ARTIK modules

- Example projects on the Hackster•IO blog

- Example projects on the Instructables blog

- Example projects and generated code in the Temboo development system. This is particularly useful for understanding the GPIO structures. The ARTIK support is being developed for later release following the prototype Beta trials.

- Linux kernel org technical notes

- Linux kernel, Fedora, and Red Hat project web sites, which may also cover slightly newer OS versions than the current ARTIK OS

- Wikipedia articles about specific topics, which are weighed for relevance to generic features that are described for all UNIX/Linux systems and relevance to the ARTIK internals

- Reverse engineering the kernel with the strings command to get a (long) list of device references

- Reading the source code for the device tree that the boot loader passes to the kernel

- Recursively listing the virtual file systems under /sys to create a candidate list of hardware devices. This reveals where the I2S, I2C, SPI, and PCI control files are located. This list is different between the ARTIK 5 and 10 and may change with different releases of the ARTIK hardware. The sysfs file system is described in this book but your ARTIK may vary somewhat.

- Examining the contents of the other virtual filesystems (/dev, /proc, and /run).

- The ALSA project is the basis for the audio subsystem in the ARTIK OS. It interacts with the hardware. Look for references to the I2S hardware in the ALSA source code.

- The Video4Linux project documentation points to where the video support is headed.

---

■ **Note** Be version aware in your research. When you are gathering research input in preparation for a reverse engineering job, be aware that a lot of information on the Internet may describe obsolete or prototype versions of the software. Check the version numbers imprinted in the OS and use the corresponding reference resources that are correct for the version you are using. Coverage of later OS versions will describe features you do not yet have available.

---

# Defensive Coding Strategies

One of the major headaches for developers is when the underlying infrastructure changes; it's unfortunate when your application ceases to work because the resources it was accessing have moved. Or perhaps features are present in one revision of the OS and not in others. The same issues crop up when you are trying to write code that is portable across the range of ARTIK modules you are working with.

UNIX (and hence Linux) is designed to be flexible and dynamic. The kernel can be configured to switch features on and off at boot time or it may be compiled with or without features. After the computer has booted, additional devices can be turned on by loading extra modules. Each of these devices is located in the main memory and has a base address that your application must discover to interact with the device. If that base address changes, then the application will break if it is hard-coded.

Avoid that problem entirely by dynamically configuring your application and inspecting the file system to find the devices and determine their base addresses. Now your application is no longer tied to a specific implementation. It should now be resilient to most changes that OS deployment imposes. Provided devices are not withdrawn altogether, your application should be able to find them. It can now cope with an OS upgrade or write code that runs on different ARTIK models because it automatically detects the differences between an ARTIK 5 and 10 at runtime.

# Looking Over the Horizon

Samsung has plans to introduce new API support libraries to interact with the hardware from within your own applications. As these are released they will be documented in the developer online resources. They are not yet available to be covered here. This book is intended to support those libraries and API kits and equip you with knowledge of the underlying technologies. This helps to exploit the libraries more effectively when they are released. Knowing about the low-level interfaces is key to making the best use of the ARTIK modules. In addition to covering those hardware interfaces, the forensic and diagnostic techniques that helped uncover them are explained so you can stay up-to-date with the inevitable changes that happen as new versions of the operating system are released.

Even after writing two books about the ARTIK family, there still is not enough space to cover everything. Some technology is still being developed and it will unfold in due course—no doubt with more books covering the continuous evolution of the platform.

The developer resources contain a table of Beta features that are supported by each revision of the ARTIK modules. This table will be updated as features are added to the ARTIK OS; see `https://developer.artik.io/documentation/beta-features/`.

Video is a very complex topic, and requires audio and graphics support to be fully working first. The ARTIK OS internals reveal some clues to the strategy for future video support, which helps prepare for later when the video support is completed. Some support is already present and working, but there is more to come.

The Commercial Beta versions of the ARTIK 5 and 10 are the current baseline for documenting the internals. They are both now shipping and viable for developing a lot of useful applications. A few topics remain to be implemented when the final versions of these ARTIK modules are released. The anticipated technologies are summarized in Table 24-1.

*Table 24-1. Future Feature Support*

| Topic | Notes |
|-------|-------|
| Video | The video support is different in the ARTIK 5 and 10 modules. The ARTIK OS uses the popular Video4Linux tools. Support for MIPI cameras, USB cameras, and HDMI displays are working in the ARTIK 10, with more support expected soon for both ARTIK modules. The OpenCV library is also in a usable state. |
| Audio | The audio support is a little more advanced and uses the ALSA toolkit. There are already built-in audio players and more will come later. This is also a well-known technology and more details are available online at the project home pages. |
| SPI | This is clearly intended to be an important interfacing technology inside the ARTIK. The modules have several SPI bus connections. There is no published Samsung developer documentation about this as yet. Some SPI support is already working internally because it is needed for the Ethernet controller in the ARTIK 5, although SPI is not yet viable for user space applications. |

Some preliminary material on these topics is documented here after inspecting the Commercial Beta ARTIK modules and their developer reference board circuit schematics.

# Porting Projects from Other Architectures

Almost every example and library from the Arduino resources is usable, apart from anything that is tagged as architecture or Arduino board-specific. Modify anything that uses the SPI/I2C/PWM interfaces to make the pin mapping and values you use in your code compatible with their virtual filesystem locations in your target ARTIK module.

# Hardware and Tools

If you plan to integrate any external hardware devices, sensors, or other peripherals with your ARTIK, setting up a place to work with good quality tools is important. In *Beginning Samsung ARTIK*, I suggested you get at least a multimeter and possibly an oscilloscope. The Tektronix company makes high-quality test instrumentation. They also provide a lot of support materials for educational purposes.

One PDF document in particular is a very useful guide to inspecting and diagnosing the peripheral interconnect buses such as I2C, I2S, and SPI with an oscilloscope. This guide explains what you might see when you probe these interfaces. View the download page for a helpful PDF file covering the low-speed serial data interfaces found in an ARTIK: http://www.tek.com/document/primer/low-speed-serial-data-fundamentals.

# Creating a Bare-Bones Breakout Board

You may want to create a very simple board to run your ARTIK on. For some tasks, the developer reference board is much more than you need but the ARTIK cannot be wired into a product design without creating the equivalent of this reference board.

The data sheets describe the minimum power supply requirements and the circuit schematics for the developer reference boards show you how to implement various subsystems. Build a simple board and start by adding the AXT connectors for your ARTIK. Then add the minimum power supply requirements to your design. Then incorporate only those subsystems you need from the developer reference schematics. Manufacture circuit boards that allow for surface mounted components. To achieve the necessary density, these boards must be multi-layer composites. Once you have a design worked out, you may be able to find a specialist company that can make the boards for you.

## Servo-Controlled Camera

In common with the Maker community, the most intriguing IoT technology solutions should be inexpensive and based on lateral thinking. A steerable video camera can be attached with a ribbon cable to the connector on the developer reference board. This will provide a flexible-enough connection that the camera can be moved to point in different directions.

Adding a pan and tilt mechanism to the camera is possible by using radio-control servos from model boating projects. These servos are controlled by a pulse width modulated signal. The length of the duty cycle of the pulse controls the position of the servo. Two servos are mounted so that one rotates vertically up and down and the other rotates horizontally. This is a very cheap and usable two-axis camera positioning system.

Since the servos are controlled by pulse width modulation, you may be able to use the two PWM channels on an ARTIK to control their position.

## Sample Source Code and Illustrations

The Apress web site contains the sample source code for the examples in this book for you to download. Additionally, I have provided some Adobe Illustrator PDF files that you can use to create your own diagrams. These diagrams will help you design breakout boards or document the wiring of your breadboard, sensor, and control electronics when you connect them to the hardware I/O header pins. The diagrams are listed in Table 24-2.

***Table 24-2.*** *Useful Illustration Artwork Files*

| | |
|---|---|
| ARTIK_5_co_ax_connectors.ai | AXT_40_pins.ai |
| ARTIK_5_connectors.ai | AXT_60_pins.ai |
| ARTIK_5_general_arrangement.ai | AXT_80_pins.ai |
| ARTIK_5_J3_connector_pinouts.ai | Hardware_input_output_headers.ai |
| ARTIK_5_J4_connector_pinouts.ai | J12_JTAG_connector_pinouts.pdf |
| ARTIK_5_J7_connector_pinouts.ai | J24_header_pinout.ai |
| ARTIK_10_co_ax_connectors.ai | J25_header_pinout.ai |
| ARTIK_10_connectors.ai | J26_J27_header_pinout.ai |
| ARTIK_10_general_arrangement.ai | J510_header_pinout.ai |
| ARTIK_10_J1_connector_pinouts.ai | J511_header_pinout.ai |
| ARTIK_10_J2_connector_pinouts.ai | J512_header_pinout.ai |
| ARTIK_10_J3_connector_pinouts.ai | J513_header_pinout.ai |
| ARTIK_10_J4_connector_pinouts.ai | Miniature_coax_connector.ai |
| | SMA_antenna_connectors.ai |

The source code package contains the larger C language listings. Small, single-line code examples are not packaged; they can be typed in easily enough. The command line shell commands are also not packaged as listings because it will encourage you to type them into the bash command line, where you will see them working as you progress line by line through the example. They tend to be very compact and short in any case, usually no more than three or four lines.

## How to Get More Help and Support

While I was writing this book, a few readers of my first ARTIK book, *Beginning Samsung ARTIK*, contacted me to share what they were doing with the ARTIK modules and to ask for help. I am always happy to hear from readers, especially if they are developing something really interesting based on the ARTIK. However, if you need in-depth help and support from the experts, the best place to look for it is on the developer forum. The forum is monitored by the ARTIK support team at Samsung and they have answered many questions. Other developers may also have solved the same issue. Many topics in my two ARTIK books are prompted by questions asked on the forum, but it is impossible to answer every question in advance. I always study the online forum and use the questions there to help me plan new books, so it really is the best place to start when you need help.

I have distilled everything I have learned about the ARTIK modules into these two books. I was continually discovering new things about the ARTIK modules as I composed each chapter. I learned a great deal by experimenting and inspecting the files inside my ARTIK and then researching online to discover what they were for. The fruits of that process yielded the many web links I have included for your benefit. It is important that you also develop and enhance your investigative skills because this facilitates the learning-by-doing approach to education. Become familiar with the operation of the kernel by studying the publicly available source code. Try interacting with the I2C bus to add a new sensor. Without doubt, there is sufficient material to fill many more books. I would encourage you to study the internals of your ARTIK to get to know it better and discover new secrets; then you can tell the rest of the community what you find.

## My Challenge to You

I put this challenge to the readers at the end of *Beginning Samsung ARTIK* and I think it is still valid. Writing this second book about the ARTIK has been a profound learning experience for me. There are technologies I have studied that have intrigued me for many years. Learning about them in the context of the ARTIK will significantly alter how I view some ideas for project designs in the future. As you complete your first ARTIK-based project, you should have significantly expanded what you know. This will make you a much better engineer in the process.

Your journey will be different than mine, and you will discover things that I missed. Your challenge is to find topics that interest you within the context of ARTIK development and become an expert on them. When you discover new things about the ARTIK, get in touch with Apress and talk to them about writing a book based on your newfound area of expertise.

When your ARTIK-based product is ready for the public to see it, contact the ARTIK support people to discuss the possibility of writing a blog article for them to describe your development experience and any useful insights you learned along the way.

There is so much still to be covered in the ARTIK world and the developer community is only just beginning to discover what it can do. The Internet of Things is going to bring a disruptive change to everyone's lifestyles. The ARTIK community is at the vanguard of this, and it is going to be an exciting ride.

# Bibliography

Following is a list of helpful books on useful related topics related to IoT and the various operating system and programming topics in this book.

| Title | Author | ISBN |
| --- | --- | --- |
| *AMBA: Enabling Reusable On-Chip Designs* | David Flynn | July 1997 edition of *IEEE Micro* magazine |
| *Arduino Internals* | Dale Wheat | 978-1430238829 |
| *ARM Assembly Language: Fundamentals and Techniques* | William Hohl and Christopher Hinds | 978-1482229851 |
| *The Designer's Guide to the Cortex-M Processor Family* | Trevor Martin | 978-0081006290 |
| *Practical Micro-controller Engineering with ARM Technology* | Ying Bai | 978-1119052371 |
| *Embedded Systems with ARM Cortex-M Micro-controllers in Assembly Language and C* | Yifeng Zhu | 978-0982692639 |
| *ARM System Developer's Guide* | Andrew Sloss, Dominic Symes, and Chris Wright | 978-1493303748 |
| *Embedded Linux Primer* | Christopher Hallinan | 978-0137017836 |
| *Linux Device Drivers* | Alessandro Rubini and Jonathan Corbet | 978-0596000080 |
| *Linux Kernel Architecture* | Wolfgang Mauerer | 978-1118079911 |
| *Learning OpenCV* | Gary Bradski and Adrian Kaehler | 978-1449314651 |
| *OpenStack Swift* | Joe Arnold | 978-1491900826 |
| *Advanced Programming in the UNIX Environment* | W. Richard Stevens | 978-0321637734 |
| *The Linux Programmer's Toolbox* | John Fusco | 978-0132198578 |
| *Power and Performance: Software Analysis and Optimization* | Jim Kukunas | 978-0128007266 |
| *Mastering the Shell* | Ray Swartz | 978-0672227158 |

(*continued*)

© Cliff Wootton 2016
C. Wootton, *Samsung ARTIK Reference*, DOI 10.1007/978-1-4842-2322-2

BIBLIOGRAPHY

| Title | Author | ISBN |
|-------|--------|------|
| *Classic Shell Scripting* | Arnold Robbins and Nelson H. F. Beebe | 978-0596005955 |
| *Wicked Cool Shell Scripts: 101 Scripts for Linux, OS X, and UNIX Systems* | Dave Taylor and Brandon Perry | 978-1593276027 |
| *The Linux Command Line* | William E Schotts Jr | 978-1593273897 |
| *Correct-by-Construction Approaches for SoC Design* | Roopak Sinha and Parthasarathi Roop | 978-1461478638 |
| *Learning the VI Editor* | Arnold Robbins, Elbert Elbert, and Linda Lamb | 978-0596529833 |

As well, Juan-Mariano de Goyeneche provides a list of recommend books as valuable sources of reference for anyone interested in understanding kernel internals. Find Juan-Mariano's list at the following URL:

`https://github.com/torvalds/linux/blob/master/Documentation/kernel-docs.txt.`

# Index

# Get the eBook for only $5!

Why limit yourself?

Now you can take the weightless companion with you wherever you go and access your content on your PC, phone, tablet, or reader.

Since you've purchased this print book, we're happy to offer you the eBook in all 3 formats for just $5.

Convenient and fully searchable, the PDF version enables you to easily find and copy code—or perform examples by quickly toggling between instructions and applications. The MOBI format is ideal for your Kindle, while the ePUB can be utilized on a variety of mobile devices.

To learn more, go to www.apress.com/companion or contact support@apress.com.

Printed in the United States
By Bookmasters